Yellowstone National Park
Its Exploration and Establishment

by

Aubrey L. Haines

U.S. Department of the Interior

National Park Service

Washington 1974

As the Nation's principal conservation agency, the Department of the Interior has basic responsibilities for water, fish, wildlife, mineral, land, park, and recreational resources. Indian and Territorial affairs are other major concerns of America's "Department of Natural Resources." The Department works to assure the wisest choice in managing all our resources so each will make its full contribution to a better United States—now and in the future.

This publication is one of a series of studies made in connection with the various areas in the National Park System or areas in which the National Park Service has had responsibilities.

Library of Congress Cataloging in Publication Data
Haines, Aubrey L
Yellowstone National Park: its exploration and establishment.
Bibliography: p.
Supt. of Docs. no.: I 29.2: Y3/3
1. Yellowstone National Park. 2. The West—
Discovery and exploration. I. Title.
F722.H16   917.87'52   73-600121

For sale by the Superintendent of Documents, U. S. Government Printing Office
Washington, D. C. 20402–Price $2.70

Stock No. 2405–00499

Yellowstone National Park
Its Exploration and Establishment

CALIFORNIA · WESTERN AMERICANA

The Castle Geyser by Thomas Moran

Presidential Statement

Against the vast span of geologic time out of which its scenic grandeur was born, Yellowstone's first century as a national park came and went in a moment. Today, just as in 1872, Yellowstone's capacity to whet man's sense of wonder and refresh his spirit remains ageless and undiminished.

Equally compelling for us today, one hundred years and more after they first unfolded, are the human lessons in the story of the discovery and exploration of Yellowstone Park and its establishment as a preserve for coming generations of Americans to enjoy unspoiled—the story this book tells so authoritatively.

Parklands and wilderness become more precious to us with each passing year, and the forces that militate against them intensify. This account thus commends itself not only to the general reader as an absorbing narrative of men, the land, and the laws, and to the historian as a long-needed documentary resource, but also to every citizen who wishes to help apply more widely in our own time the kind of environmental wisdom and foresight that created our first national park a century ago.

Richard Nixon
President of the United States

Foreword

The steady growth of the literature on Yellowstone, our nation's first National Park, is a reflection of the continuing fascination American and foreign visitors have both for the Park itself and the concept of National Parks as developed in our country. In view of this continuing interest, it is little wonder that many other nations have drawn upon the experience of Yellowstone in their search for means of preserving land for the benefit and enjoyment of their people. Until now, however, a solidly documented definitive study of the exploration and establishment of Yellowstone has not been available. In this book, Aubrey L. Haines draws on his extensive personal and professional knowledge of Yellowstone, "The Mother of National Parks," to tell us just how this reserve came to be one of our most priceless heritages.

Rogers C. B. Morton
Secretary of the Interior

Preface

This book is a joint undertaking of the National Historical Publications Commission and the National Park Service. It was conceived as a feature of the centennial of Yellowstone National Park by Professor Joe B. Frantz of the University of Texas, a member of both the National Historical Publications Commission and the Secretary of the Interior's Advisory Board on National Parks, Historic Sites, Buildings, and Monuments. At its meeting on September 15, 1969, the Commission gave unanimous consent to a resolution endorsing the project, and an agreement was drawn up between the Commission and the National Park Service for the writing and publication of the book.

The author of this volume, Aubrey L. Haines, retired from the National Park Service in 1968 after a distinguished career as a ranger, engineer, and historian. For more than 15 years he was on the staff of Yellowstone National Park. He has contributed numerous articles to newspapers and historical journals, and is the author of *Mountain Fever: Historic Conquests of Rainier* (1962). He has also edited two other books: *Osborne Russell's Journal of a Trapper* (1955) and *Valley of the Upper Yellowstone* (1963). Mr. Haines and his wife make their home in Bozeman, Montana.

Ronald H. Walker
Director, National Park Service

Table of Contents

Presidential Statement   *iii*

Foreword   *v*

Preface   *vii*

List of Illustrations   *x*

Author's Preface   *xiii*

Introduction   *xvii*

Part I   Early Knowledge   *1*
    The Lewis and Clark Era (1805–14)   *3*
    The Fur Trade Era (1818–42)   *6*
    The Exploring Era (1851–63)   *21*
    The Prospecting Era (1863–71)   *26*

Part II   Definitive Knowledge   *43*
    Background for Exploration   *45*
    The Folsom Party (1869)   *47*
    Peripheral Events (1869–70)   *56*
    The Washburn Party (1870)   *59*
    The Hayden and Barlow Parties (1871)   *99*

Part III   The Park Movement   *107*

Biographical Appendix   *133*

Notes   *153*

Bibliography   *199*

Index   *211*

List of Illustrations

Frontispiece

The Castle Geyser in the Upper Geyser Basin, from an original water color by Thomas Moran, guest artist with the Hayden Survey expedition into the Yellowstone region in 1871. Courtesy of Yellowstone National Park.

Portraits of Yellowstone Explorers (beginning on page 129).

1. Charles W. Cook, c. 1870. Courtesy Mrs. Oscar O. Mueller (*nee* Josephine Cook).

2. Walter W. deLacy. From *Contributions to the Historical Society of Montana*, (1896).

3. Gustavus C. Doane. From Strong, *A Trip to the Yellowstone. . .*, (1876).

4. Truman C. Everts. From Langford, *Diary of the Washburn Expedition. . .*, (1905).

5. David E. Folsom. From Langford, *Diary of the Washburn Expedition. . .*, (1905).

6. Warren C. Gillette. From Langford, *Diary of the Washburn Expedition. . .*, (1905).

7. Samuel T. Hauser. From Langford, *Diary of the Washburn Expedition. . .*, (1905).

8. Ferdinand V. Hayden. Courtesy U.S. Geological Survey.

9. Cornelius Hedges. From Langford, *Diary of the Washburn Expedition. . .*, (1905).

10. Nathaniel P. Langford. Courtesy Minnesota Historical Society.

11. William Peterson. Courtesy Yellowstone National Park.

12. Benjamin F. Stickney. From Langford, *Diary of the Washburn Expedition. . .*, (1905).

13. Jacob W. Smith. Courtesy Herbert F. Seversmith, Chevy Chase, Md. (a grandson).

14. Henry D. Washburn. From an original Brady photograph loaned by Mr. R. H. Washburn, Phoenix, Ariz. (a grandson).

Maps of the Yellowstone Region (beginning on page 185).

1. The manuscript map compiled by William Clark from informants during the period 1806–11. Original in the William Robertson Coe Collection. Beinecke Library, Yale University, New Haven, Conn.

2. The engraving made by Samuel Lewis from Clark's manuscript map, to accompany the *History of the Expedition under the Command of Captains Lewis and Clark*. Philadelphia, 1814.

3. The manuscript map compiled by Capt. Washington Hood, of the Topographical Engineers, in 1839, from information supplied by William Sublette and other leaders of the fur trade in the northern Rocky Mountains.

4. The manuscript map drawn by James Bridger and captioned by Father Pierre-Jean DeSmet in 1851. Original in the Missouri Province Archives (Jesuits), St. Louis University, Mo.

5. The manuscript map compiled by Father Pierre-Jean DeSmet at the Horse Creek Indian Council, near Fort Laramie, in 1851. Original in the Missouri Province Archives (Jesuits), St. Louis University, Mo.

6. The manuscript map compiled by Capt. William Raynolds, of the Topographical Engineers, in 1860. It is the basis for the map published with *The Report of Brevet Brigadier General W. F. Raynolds on the Exploration of the Yellowstone and the Country Drained by that River*, Washington, D.C., 1868.

7. The manuscript map compiled by Walter W. deLacy in 1865 incorporating the geographical information obtained in 1863, and subsequently, by himself and others. This is probably the draft of the published *Map of the Territory of Montana with Portions of the Adjoining Territories. . ., 1865*. Original in the Montana Historical Society collection.

8. The manuscript map probably compiled by Surveyor General Meredith of Montana Territory in 1869 on the basis of prior geographical knowledge.

9. The manuscript map compiled by Surveyor General Washburn of Montana Territory November 1, 1869, showing geographical information obtained from members of the Folsom party of explorers, just returned from the Yellowstone region.

10. The deLacy map as published by G. W. & G. B. Colton & Co. early in 1870, representing a revision of the original deLacy map to accord with the discoveries of the Folsom party in 1869. A copy of this map was carried by the Washburn Expedition of 1870.

11. The manuscript map compiled by Lt. Gustavus C. Doane, commander of the military escort for the Washburn party of explorers in 1870.

12. The manuscript map compiled by Surveyor General Blaine of Montana Territory in 1871, incorporating information obtained by the Washburn party of explorers.

13. The map published by the Geological Survey of the territories (Hayden Survey) as a part of its first report on the Yellowstone region (1872). Separate copies of this map were available late in 1871, and were used by the proponents of the movement which led to the creation of Yellowstone National Park.

14. The manuscript map compiled by Capt. John W. Barlow and Capt. David P. Heap following their field work in the Yellowstone region in 1871. Publication of this map with the Barlow-Heap *Report of a Reconnaissance of the Basin of the Upper Yellowstone in 1871*, Washington, D.C. 1872, concluded the pioneering period of Yellowstone cartography.

Author's Preface

An architectural proposal is generally best comprehended through a preliminary sketch, which, hopefully, will bare the soul of the construction, passing easily over a welter of blueprint details to that one thing that is important to the man who is about to commission a work—its suitability to his purpose. Admittedly, the craft of writing does not have an exact counterpart to the architect's beautifully embowered presentation of his dream; and yet, the author or editor can accomplish a somewhat similar purpose by giving his readers a preliminary glimpse of the organization and scope of his subject, or, put in plainer terms, something of the dreaming behind the scheming.

In this case, the subject at hand—a history, based on documents, of the exploration and establishment of Yellowstone National Park—appeared to lend itself to division into three major parts, presenting, in turn, the accretion of early knowledge, the accumulation of a definitive knowledge, and the progression of the park movement.

Those principal divisions have been subdivided in a manner to show the contributing influences: that is, Part I has subsections setting apart the fragmentary knowledge gained by Lewis and Clark, the fur trappers, the military and religious explorers, and the Montana prospectors—a comprehensive, yet largely ineffectual cognizance; Part II covers the definitive knowledge resulting from three determined explorations—those of the Folsom party (1869), the Washburn party (1870), and the Hayden and Barlow parties (1871), while Part III covers the publicity and legislative aspects of the park movement to its successful conclusion in the establishment of Yellowstone National Park.

Ideally, such a compilation should include the complete text of all important source documents; however, the bulk of the available materials, particularly within Part II, precludes such thoroughness. Faced with the necessity of either presenting selected source documents in their entirety or of relying mainly upon excerpting from a much wider range of materials, the latter was adopted in the belief that it would prove more useful to readers. This will introduce them to both the standard sources and a variety of lesser items which, taken together, are very important to any serious consideration of the establishment of our first national park.

Of course, such a procedure required a connective text to give relevance to the excerpts. However, the added text is not intended as compiled history, for it is seldom complete enough to serve more than its admitted purpose—an aid to a review of what is available. Footnotes have been added both to document and to clarify the materials used.

The author wishes here to acknowledge, in general terms, the all-important assistance of many persons—friends, colleagues, typists, research assistants, archivists, and librarians—though he is aware that this places him somewhat in the position of the man who was asked why he did not say grace at table. His reply was, "*He* knows I am grateful." I only hope *they* know it!

Something does have to be said in more specific terms concerning libraries and repositories used. The source documents and related materials consulted, except for a few rare items, were found in the following places: The Yellowstone Park Reference Library, Yellowstone Park, Wyo., holds the original of the Daniel T. Potts letter (which provided the earliest published description of Yellowstone features), and the original notes of Nathaniel P. Langford's eastern lectures, in its park-oriented collection of publications, manuscripts, photographs and archives—a unique special collection; the Montana Historical Society, Helena, holds the Cornelius Hedges diaries and papers, the Warren C. Gillette diary and the Samuel T. Hauser papers, which, with its excellent files of early Montana newspapers, formed an invaluable resource; the Montana State University Library, Bozeman, holds the manuscript copy of Lt. Gustavus C. Doane's report, and also has a Leggatt collection containing many rare published items; the Minnesota Historical Society, St. Paul, holds the Nathaniel P. Langford papers (diaries, letters, and scrapbooks), and is custodian of the old files of the Northern Pacific Railroad; the Beinecke Rare Book and Manuscript Library, at Yale University, New Haven, Conn., holds William Clark's manuscript map (on which he recorded the visit of John Colter to the Yellowstone region), the manuscript for Osborne Russell's *Journal of a Trapper*, the diary of Samuel T. Hauser and a copy of the journal of A. Bart Henderson; the Pennsylvania Historical Society, Philadelphia, holds the Jay Cooke papers, which throw much light on Nathaniel P. Langford's connection with the Northern Pacific Railroad and its promotional schemes; the Library of Congress, Washington, D.C., holds Gen. James Wilkinson's letters relative to the Yellowstone region—the earliest intimation of its unusual character—in the Jefferson papers, while the vast collection of newspapers found there was particularly helpful in checking eastern coverage of park events; the National Archives, Washington, D.C., holds important maps, and also the several collections of papers relating to the Geological Survey of the territories (Hayden Survey), the office of the Surveyor General of Montana Territory, and to the Yellowstone legislation; the Pius XII Memorial Library, St. Louis University, Mo., holds Father Pierre-Jean DeSmet's manuscript maps covering the Yellowstone region; the Gilcrease Museum, Tulsa, Oklahoma, holds the papers of Thomas Moran; the Henry E. Huntington Library, Pasadena, Calif., holds the papers of Philetus W. Norris, including nearly all that remains of his letters which appeared serially in the *Norris Suburban* under the heading "The Great West"; and the Bancroft Library, University of California, Berkeley, holds the only considerable file of that unusual newspaper, *The Frontier Index*, as well as an incomparable collection of other western newspapers. Other collections used less extensively were those of the Denver Public Library, Colorado; the Church of Jesus Christ of Latter-Day Saints, Salt Lake City, Utah, the Philadelphia Free Library, Pennsylvania; the St. Louis Mercantile Library, Missouri; the Bozeman Public Library, Montana; and the Missouri Historical Society at St. Louis.

The research phase of this project also led the author into friendship with some delightful people, among them, Truman C. Everts, Jr., son of the explorer lost in the Yellowstone wilderness, Miss Beatrice deLacy, niece of that stalwart engineer-explorer who led his "40 thieves" across the southwestern corner of what is now Yellowstone Park away back in 1863, and Mrs. Oscar O. Mueller, *nee* Josephine Cook, daughter of explorer Charles W. Cook. It was her fondest wish to be present at the Yellowstone centennial observance, as her father was present—the last survivor of all the early explorers—at the celebration of the semicentennial in 1922. Fortunately, it was so.

Aubrey L. Haines

Introduction

The one-hundredth anniversary of the establishment of Yellowstone National Park brought renewed interest in the origin of our first and largest national park. It was an interest which went beyond the primacy and uniqueness of the area, for there the Federal Government entered the business of managing wild lands for recreational use, thus bringing into focus a new concept that had been maturing on the American scene. This "national park idea," as it has come to be known,[1] has burgeoned wonderfully, here and abroad, into park systems that are among the better expressions of man's relationship to his environment.

The particular purpose of this history is to make readily available that body of information which led to establishment of Yellowstone National Park. Since a collection of documentary sources could easily point to false conclusions unless accompanied by some knowledge of the park's place in the development of the whole concept, it should be helpful, before undertaking a presentation of source materials, to trace the growth of Western ideas concerning such nonutilitarian use of land.

Emerson perceived the importance of parks to man when he wrote: "Only as far as the masters of the world have called in nature to their aid, can they reach the height of magnificence. This is the meaning of their hanging-gardens, villas, garden-houses, islands, parks and preserves, to back their faulty personality with these strong accessories."[2] Such artifices are at least as ancient as the hanging gardens built by Nebuchadnezzar at Babylon for the pleasure of his Midian wife. That "chief glory of the great palace" was a tiered structure of brick arches covering 4 acres and rising to the height of 75 feet; an artificial mountain planted with trees, vines, and flowering plants (ingeniously watered from the nearby Euphrates River), and containing cool apartments where the queen could take her ease surrounded by verdure and interesting animals and birds.[3] The hanging gardens were royal and private.

Nor was there any place for common people in the royal gardens of the Persians. Those "vast enclosures that included fruit and ornamental trees, flowers, birds and mammals," were called *paradeisos* by the Greek soldier-adventurer Xenophon, and knowledge of their magnificence soon passed from the Greek to the Roman world. There, gaudy replicas appeared to grace the estates of the wealthy and the homes of the humble. The poor man's version—generally consisting of little more than courtyard walls painted to resemble the lush gardens of great villas[4]—was pregnant with possibilities. And yet nothing came of it beyond the feeling that has come down to us through the Latin *paradisus* of the Vulgate Bible to that unsullied English word "paradise." Quite apart from its theological connotation, it evokes visions of a place of ideal beauty and perfect delight. The time was too early for democratization of the park idea.

Instead, the influence of the royal tradition reappeared in the Norman *parcs* of France—those "unruffled hunting estates" of the feudal nobility.[5] From that source, with its emphasis upon wild property, we have taken our word "park." After the Norman Conquest, such hunting parks appeared in England, where the new masters established them in the forests that had belonged to the Saxon kings and, later, upon adjacent common lands.

The way of life that had become established in Saxon England was based upon a village community system where the commonality of lands—group use—had developed under folk-law. With the passage of time, most of the arable lands passed out of the "commons," leaving only the less desirable portions of the townships in that category. But on these remaining lands villagers retained formalized "rights of common," such as pasturage, and access to fuel and building materials.

It would be logical to expect the British to merge their two concepts of game preserves and common holding of land into a form providing the basis for a true park development capable of serving all classes. But they did not. By the Statute of Merton, in 1235 A.D., Norman lawyers established the principle that the common was "the Lord's waste," to do with as he pleased, and the Second Statute of Westminster, a half-century later, enabled the lord to enclose common lands.[6] Thus, many commons were converted to deer parks, a trend that established the pattern of park development so firmly that neither romanticism nor industrialism changed it. The English model remained the game preserve nearly to the end of the 19th century—in fact, until the influence of American experience with wilderness parks was felt.

Although the concept of common holding of lands had little influence on park development in Britain, it was very important on these shores. Enough of the commons survived in the mother country that Englishmen were not strangers to the idea of group holding of lands, and the colonists who settled New England also established that form of land holding in their new home. Boston Common was established in 1634, and similar tracts were features of most New England towns. But they came to serve a different purpose than in England. Here, they were needed less for grazing and, in a land well endowed with natural resources, not at all for fuel and building materials. Thus the commons became the drill grounds of the militia on training day, and the fair grounds at harvest time. They were also the haunts of itinerants and traveling shows, trysting places, and occasionally even focal points for civil disorders. In brief, they emerged from the colonial period as informal village parks, giving the old English concept of commonality a new direction—toward a public park type of use. The only similar progress elsewhere in the American colonies was in Pennsylvania, where the original plan for Philadelphia allocated a number of squares to public use, with the intention of leaving them as tree-shaded islands within the city.[7]

Game preserves, at least in the European sense, did not appear in colonial America because there was no leisure class to champion such use of the land. Even the Great Ponds Act of 1641, like all colonial conservation, whether concerned with fish, wildlife or timber resources, was defensive. The intention of this measure, by which Massachusetts Bay Colony reserved 2,000 bodies of water, with a total area of about 90,000 acres, for "fishing and fowling," was to protect the colony against needs generated by waste and theft.[8]

Further progress of the park idea in colonial New England was impeded by Puritan attitudes toward work, nature, and recreation. Idleness was equated with wickedness, and this work ethic led inexorably to an avoidance of all gay and frivolous things. As for nature, it continued to be viewed very much as William Bradford had written of it in 1620—a "hideous and desolate wilderness, full of wild beasts and wild men,"[9] a wilderness to be struggled with and vanquished in accordance with the Biblical injunction to "Be fruitful and multiply, and replenish the earth, and subdue it; and have dominion over the fish of the sea, and over the fowl of the air, and over every living thing that moveth upon the earth" (Genesis 1:28). As a consequence, there was no place for recreation, as we know it, in those solemn Puritan communities. Even hunting and fishing were proscribed except as they were a means of procuring food.

The 18th century spawned a philosophy that ultimately changed the New England outlook. From Jean Jacques Rousseau's concept of the "natural man"—that noble savage in his wilderness setting, living a happy and contented life—came a great upsurge of admiration for nature and a sentimental attachment to all things primitive. The basis of this romantic movement was a belief in the "oneness of nature—the great nature, embracing God and man, stars out in space, rocks and crystals here on earth." And so, "nature invaded the consciousness of the world."[10]

What is important here is that romanticism had many voices, crying a love of nature—not alone in the French of Rousseau or the German of Goethe, but also in the English of Wordsworth, Coleridge, Scott, Byron, Shelley, Keats, and Blake. And these voices were heard across the sea, transforming the American view of nature. Hans Huth has traced with meticulous care the development of this appreciative outlook.[11] More, however, was required than a romantic viewpoint to get the stalled park idea moving again.

The missing ingredient was a sense of purpose, and this quality was supplied very early in the 19th century by those men best called the New England philosophers. They were intellectuals whose transcendentalist leanings made them particularly perceptive of their surroundings.[12] What they perceived was the change industrialism was then making in familiar New England localities. The spinning mills and foundries of that "inventive age," seen by the poet Wordsworth developing "to most strange issues," turned pastoral villages into squalid factory towns. Gone was the old, slow moving, and secure rustic life, replaced by urban poverty and its attendant misery and crime. To such thinkers as Henry Wadsworth Longfellow, John Greenleaf Whittier, James Russell Lowell, William Cullen Bryant, Henry David Thoreau, and Ralph Waldo Emerson, the degradation was a concomitant of civilization, and for it they saw but one antidote: a return to nature.

Thoreau eloquently presents the thesis of these New England philosophers in this passage from his essay on "Walking":

> I wish to speak a word for Nature, for absolute freedom and wildness, as contrasted with a freedom and culture merely civil, —to regard man as an inhabitant, or a part and parcel of Nature, rather than a member of society. . . . for there are enough champions of civilization: the minister and the school-committee and every one of you will take care of that.[13]

Both Thoreau and Emerson wrote of wondrous nature—this "mother of ours . . . lying all around with such beauty," likened by Emerson to "the music and pictures of the ancient religion." And yet they were realists enough to know there was no returning to the natural state of man. They did not advocate primitivism, but rather a limitation of the unwholesome influences of civilization by keeping closely in touch with nature. Through such a compromise Thoreau could say, "A town is saved, not more by the righteous men in it than by the woods and swamps that surround it," for "in wildness is the preservation of the world." And Emerson thought that "every man is so far a poet as to be susceptible of these enchantments of nature," which are "medicinal, they sober and heal us."[14]

This new conception of nature—as beautiful, kindly, helpful, and restorative, rather than hideous, harsh, obstructive, and degrading— changed the outlook of the American. As one biographer has pointed out, "Imperceptibly Emerson's ideas passed into general currency . . . . Today his influence has spread so wide that, like atmospheric pressure, we are unaware of it. But it has played a vast part in shaping the American way of life."[15] The same may as surely be said of the other New England philosophers. Together they softened the Puritanical outlook of the New England mind, so that it was at last prepared to contribute to the development of the park idea.

The acceptance of this new viewpoint by Americans was manifested in a number of ways, notably in the appearance of a popular literature with outdoor themes, and in the Hudson River school of painting which portrayed landscapes. Such innovations brought nature to the fireside. Equally important, they stimulated a desire to visit scenic places. With improvements in public transportation, first through establishment of comfortable passenger service on river packets and canal boats, and later on the expanding railways, vacation travel to such resorts as Saratoga, White Sulphur Springs, the Adirondacks, Madison-on-Lakes, Appledore, Nahant, Newport, Mount Desert, and Mount Holyoke became feasible. Increasing numbers of the privileged traveled for pleasure.

This acquaintance with the outdoors led naturally to participation in such recreational activities as walking tours, mountain climbing, camping, fishing and hunting, and even to adult games—croquet, in the 1860's, then tennis and golf.[16] Outdoor recreation was not widely indulged in for some time—many people regarded it as a somewhat snobbish activity at first—but at least it soon became respectable.

The park idea flourished in the climate created by that uniquely American type of romanticism generated in New England. The next step beyond the town common (really a town park) was initiated in 1825, when Dr. Jacob Bigelow of Boston called a meeting to consider establishing a town cemetery outside the city. He was convinced of the "impolicy of burials under churches or in church yards approximating closely to the abodes of the living," and was outraged by the "sad, neglected state" of such resting places. His proposal gained the support of influential people, and suitable grounds were found at Mount Auburn, 4 miles from Boston. Here the Nation's first scenic cemetery was dedicated on September 24, 1831.[17]

An area of great beauty, this prototype of the modern cemetery soon drew numerous "parties of pleasure" and couples seeking a trysting place. Such use prompted suggestions that cemeteries ought to be planned "with reference to the living as well as the dead, and therefore should be convenient and pleasant to visitors." In effect, Mount Auburn was serving as a city park, and it was destined to have a far-reaching influence.

Nearly coincident with the establishment of Mount Auburn scenic cemetery came a proposal for another type of park. George Catlin, the artist who ascended the Missouri River in 1832, returned with Indian portraits and a grandiose idea. He would set aside the western high plains from Mexico to Lake Winnepeg as a huge reserve. Here the buffalo and the Indian

> *might* in future be seen, (by some great protecting policy of government) preserved in their pristine beauty and wildness, in a *magnificent park*, where the world could see for ages to come, the native Indian in his classic attire, galloping his wild horse, with sinewy bow, and shield and lance, amid the fleeting herds of elks and buffaloes. What a beautiful and thrilling specimen for America to preserve and hold up to the view of her refined citizens and the world, in future ages! A *nation's park*, containing man and beast, in all the wild and freshness of their nature's beauty!
> I would ask no other monument to my memory, nor any other enrolment of my name amongst the famous dead, than the reputation of having been the founder of such an institution.

Such scenes might easily have been preserved, and still could be cherished on the great plains of the West, without detriment to the country or its border; for the tracts of country on which the buffaloes have assembled, are uniformly sterile, and of no available use to cultivating man.[18]

Catlin's suggestion was as sterile as it was impractical, and deserves no comment beyond a mention that it probably stimulated Henry Thoreau to pose a surprisingly similar question:

The Kings of England formerly had their forests "to hold the King's game," for sport or food, sometimes destroying villages to create or extend them; and I think that they were impelled by a true instinct. Why should not we, who have renounced the King's authority, have our national preserves, where no villages need be destroyed, in which the bear and panther, and some of the hunter race, may still exist, and not be "civilized off the face of the earth," —our forest, not to hold the King's game merely, but to hold and preserve the King himself also, the lord of creation,—not for idle sport or food, but for inspiration and our own true recreation?[19]

If nothing else, the foregoing quotations are evidence that at least two thinkers had pursued the park idea to its ultimate possibility prior to the middle of the 19th century. Catlin exceeded the practical limits of his outdoor museum by including man among its exhibits, but Thoreau appears to have recognized what a wilderness park could do *for* man. Together, these suggestions indicate how well the American mind had been prepared for a further progression of the park idea.

A less flamboyant but sounder suggestion came from William Cullen Bryant, who was sufficiently impressed with the burgeoning scenic cemeteries to advocate a city park for New York. It is said that he discussed this idea with friends as early as 1836, but the public proposal was made in the *New York Evening Post* on July 3, 1844.[20] In 1851 the project for a Central Park got underway with the purchase of necessary lands and the appointment of Frederick Law Olmsted to supervise construction.

Olmsted was a fortunate choice. A student of Andrew Jackson Downing, he benefited from that eminent landscape architect's experience in the development of scenic cemeteries and from his concepts of the Central Park project, which he had ardently promoted. In addition, Olmsted had traveled in Europe and thus was familiar with formal European parks and gardens. From this background he created the prototype of all our great city parks. While not founded on the beauty of wild land, Central Park did simulate it through a judicious blending of formal and informal elements on a large scale. The park idea thereby reached the third stage of its growth on American soil—the city park.

By the same hand the park idea was next elevated to the State level. Olmsted did not always agree with the park commissioners and finally, in May 1863, gave up the superintendency of Central Park, leaving its completion to others.[21] He then undertook the management of the Mariposa estate of Gen. John Charles Frémont in California. Removal to that State brought Olmsted into a fortunate association with the Yosemite Valley and the Big Trees.

These remarkable features of California's central Sierra were well known. A decade earlier an incident involving one of the Calaveras Big Trees—the "Mother of the Forest"—had brought both James Russell Lowell and Oliver Wendell Holmes to condemn commercialization, gaining public support for the conservation of similar wonders. Thus, what was needed in California in the 1860's was a catalytic personality—one capable of directing the existing favorable sentiment toward the protection of the scenic Yosemite Valley as well as the unique Big Trees. Olmsted, fresh from his work on the Nation's first urban park, was just the person to channel the thoughts of influential Californians, and in the year following his arrival, the Congress was persuaded to pass an act whereby the Federal Government made a "grant to the State of California of the 'Yo-Semite Valley,' and of the land embracing the 'Mariposa Big Tree Grove'." As signed into law by President Abraham Lincoln on June 30, 1864, this legislation required that the "said State shall accept this grant upon the express conditions that the premises shall be held for public use, resort, and recreation; shall be inalienable for all time."[22]

The significance of the Yosemite grant has been summarized by H. D. Hampton:

The passage of the Act of 1864, granting to California the two tracts of land, did not establish a "national park" nor did it provide for one. No national laws were legislated by which the areas were to be administered and after passage of the act Congress seems to have dismissed the areas from its collective mind. The novelty of the legislation lies in the fact that it provided for land to be reserved for strictly non-utilitarian purposes, thus establishing a precedent or parallel for the later reservation of the Yellowstone region.[23]

The park idea reached its culmination in the establishment of Yellowstone National Park. This was not only the first area of wild land devoted to recreational use under Federal management, but also the pilot model for perfecting that management. It was the Yellowstone experience over nearly two decades which led to establishment of other national parks, and to the growth of a system of national parks dedicated to the protection and wise use of an irreplaceable national heritage.

The great influence of Yellowstone National Park on the park movement generally is not a concern in this history. The following documentation is related only to the historical factors that combined to produce a national park—the first of its kind. Briefly, these were a slow buildup of vague but enticing knowledge, a short period of definitive explorations which established the true nature of wonderland, and the fortunate "park movement" whereby the Federal Government was committed to the management of wild lands for park purposes.

PART I

Early Knowledge

A fragmentary knowledge of the Yellowstone
region was recorded by the explorers, trappers,
missionaries, and prospectors of the period
from 1805 to 1869. Such information was
often discredited, yet provided the enticement
for more fruitful exploration.

The Lewis and Clark Era

(1805–1814)

The records presently available indicate it was during this period that white men first became aware of the thermal features of the Yellowstone region. With our purchase of Louisiana from France on April 11, 1803, the way was open for official, semiofficial, and private exploration of the western reaches of that vast territory, and such ventures were immediately organized. Chief among these was the party led across the almost unknown West, from St. Louis to the mouth of the Columbia River and back, by Captains Lewis and Clark in 1804–06; and yet, despite the great interest of those explorers in the geography, geology, anthropology, and natural history of the country they traversed, the first notice of something unusual on the headwaters of the Yellowstone River did not come from them.

Instead, it appeared in a letter addressed to the Secretary of War on September 8, 1805, by Gov. James Wilkinson of Louisiana Territory, who included the following:

> I have equipt a Perogue out of my Small private means, not with any view to Self interest, to ascend the missouri and enter the River Piere jaune, or yellow Stone, called by the natives, Unicorn River, the same by which Capt. Lewis I since find expects to return and which my informants tell me is filled with wonders, this Party will not get back before the Summer of 1807—they are natives of this Town, and are just able to give us course and distance, with the names and population of the Indian nations and bring back with them Specimens of the natural products . . . .[1]

Nothing further is known of the expedition Governor Wilkinson claims to have sent out; however, he soon obtained additional information from Indian sources in the form of a map drawn on a buffalo pelt. This delineation of the Missouri River and its southwestern headwaters was forwarded to President Thomas Jefferson on October 22, 1805, with a letter stating:

> The Bearer hereof Capt. Amos Stoddard, who conducts the Indian deputation on their visit to you, has charge of a few natural productions of this Territory, to amuse a liesure Moment, and also a Savage delineation on a Buffaloe Pelt, of the Missouri & its South Western

3

Branches, including the Rivers plate and lycorne or Pierre jaune; This Rude Sketch without Scale or Compass "et remplie de Fantaisies ridicules" is not destitute of Interests, as it exposes the location of several important Objects, & may point the way to useful enquiry—among other things a little incredible, a Volcano is distinctly described on Yellow Stone River . . . .[2]

At some time following its arrival at Washington on December 26, the buffalo-pelt map was placed in the entrance hall of President Jefferson's Virginia home, Monticello.[3] George Ticknor, who visited Monticello in February 1815, mentions this map in his description of the Hall, noting: "On the fourth side, in odd union with a fine painting of the Repentance of Saint Peter, is an Indian map on leather, of the southern waters of the Missouri, and an Indian representation of a bloody battle, handed down in their tradition."[4] It is the opinion of the leading Jeffersonian scholar that the map was transferred to the University of Virginia where it was probably burned when the Rotunda was destroyed by fire.[5]

The Lewis and Clark Expedition passed close to the Yellowstone region with no evident awareness of the thermal features hidden there. Indeed, the description of the Yellowstone River which was subsequently published is geographically vague;[6] however, some information concerning the thermal features of the region was obtained later. In Codex N, of the original journals of the expedition, there are entries which Thwaites believes were added on blank pages by William Clark after his return to St. Louis (probably after 1809). Under the heading, "Notes of Information I believe Correct," he makes this statement about the country south of the "Rochejone":

> At the head of this river the nativs give an account that there is frequently herd a loud noise, like Thunder, which makes the earth Tremble, they State that they seldom go there because their children Cannot sleep—and Conceive it possessed of spirits, who were averse that men Should be near them.[7]

Additional information which came to Clark after the return of the expedition was entered upon a manuscript map he continued to amend for a half-dozen years as reports were received from fur traders who had pushed into the wilderness.[8] One of these was John Colter, a former member of the Lewis and Clark Expedition who remained in the mountains, and, later, while an employee of Manuel Lisa, made an epic winter journey which took him through the Yellowstone region. Something of what Colter saw was passed on to William Clark, who was thus enabled to chart several features of that *terra incognita*.

Lake Biddle (Jackson), Eustis Lake (Yellowstone), and the "Hot Spring Brimstone" shown near the crossing of "Colters rout" over the Yellowstone River are landmarks which confirm John Colter's passage, in 1807–08, through what is now Yellowstone National Park, and his discovery of at least one of its thermal areas. The identification of the latter can be made with reasonable assurance because of the proximity of Clark's notation to the crossing. The ford opposite Tower Fall, where the Bannock Indian trail (an aboriginal thoroughfare connecting the plains of central Idaho with the Yellowstone Valley and the Wyoming Basin) crossed the river, is the only place for many miles in either direction where a man traveling afoot could cross that stream—and then only during the low water of late fall and winter. This crossing is made at the "Sulphur Beds," which, together with the Calcite Springs a short distance downstream, make the locality sufficiently noisome to warrant the use of the term brimstone in its description.

Clark's manuscript map (map 1.) of the Yellowstone features deserves some notice. The relative sizes of the two lakes are reasonably correct, as portrayed, and the outline of Eustis will pass for that of Lake Yellowstone with its prominent indentations rounded-off; also, the distances—from Biddle to the southern shore of Eustis, and from the outlet of the latter to Colter's crossing of Yellowstone River—are acceptable.[9] However, the reasonableness of Clark's cartography was lost in the engraving Samuel Lewis made from the manuscript map. His map,[10] which was the one published in 1814 with the *History* cited in note 6, showed Lakes Biddle and Eustis as nearly equal in size, changing the outlet of the latter to its southern extremity and giving it the elongated shape which was characteristic of most map presentations for a half-century thereafter (map 2).

This is the place to mention what appears to be an unwarranted attempt to substantiate the presence of John Colter in the Yellowstone region. In regard to this supposed discovery, Phillip A. Rollins is quoted as follows:

> In September of 1889, Tazewell Woody (Theodore Roosevelt's hunting guide), John H. Dewing (also a hunting guide), and I, found on the left side of Coulter Creek, some fifty feet from the water and about three quarters of a mile above the creek's mouth, a large pine tree on which was a deeply indented blaze, which after being cleared of sap and loose bark was found to consist of a cross thus 'X' (some five inches in height), and, under it, the initials 'JC' (each some four inches in height).
> The blaze appeared to these training hunting guides, so they stated to me, to be approximately eighty years old.
> They refused to fell the tree and so obtain the exact age of the blaze because they said they guessed the blaze had been made by Colter himself.
> The find was reported to the Government authorities, and the tree was cut down by them in 1889 or 1890, in order that the blazed section might be installed in a museum, but as I was told in the autumn of of 1890 by the then superintendent of the Yellowstone Park, the blazed section had been lost in transit.[11]

It seems more likely that the blaze Rollins found was related to the naming of the nearby stream. Coulter Creek, which flows into Snake River near the south boundary of the park, was named for John Merle Coulter, a botanist with the Hayden Survey, because of an amusing incident which occurred there. One of Dr. Coulter's students at the University of Chicago, where he taught botany in later years, kindly furnished the park with the eminent botanist's own version of the event, as recorded in a classroom notebook in 1922. The student says:

> Dr. Coulter was fishing one day on the bank of a stream when he felt a slap on the shoulder and turned expecting to see one of his companions, but there was a large, black bear. Coulter plunged in and swam across the stream, then looking around saw that the bear had not followed, but was back there grinning at him. The party called this stream Coulter Creek, a name it still bears.[12]

The Fur-trade Era

(1818–1842)

The onset of the War of 1812 put an end to the activity of American fur traders in the West before they were able to ransack such remote areas as the Yellowstone region, and, following that conflict, the better-organized British concerns monopolized the trade in the northern Rocky Mountains for a few years. Their advantage lay in the adoption of a method of trapping based upon the use of roving brigades of *engagees*—mainly Iroquois and French Canadians—who did not have to wait at established trading posts for Indians to bring in the furs, as the Americans did. After 1821, the latter began to use similar tactics and soon took over the fur trade of the far West entirely.

A brigade of North West Co. men operating under Donald McKenzie came within sight of the Teton Range in 1818, and Alexander Ross, who was their scribe, mentions that "Boiling fountains having different degrees of temperature were very numerous; one or two were so very hot as to boil meat."[13] They may have been in the Yellowstone region, but the failure to mention landmarks makes that uncertain.

There was a visitor the following year who is known only by the initials "J. O. R." carved into the base of a pine tree, over the date "AUG. 29. 1819."[14] Superintendent Philetus W. Norris, who found this evidence of white penetration of the Yellowstone wilderness, has described it thus:

> The next earliest evidence of white men in the Park [Colter's primacy had just been discussed], of which I have any knowledge, was discovered by myself at our camp in the little glen, where our bridle-path from the lake makes its last approach to the rapids, one-fourth of a mile above the upper falls. About breast-high upon the west side of a smooth pine tree, about 20 inches in diameter, were found, legibly carved through the bark, and not materially obliterated by overgrowth or decay, in Roman capitals and Arabic numerals, the following record:
>
>
>
> J. O. R.
>
> AUG. 29, 1819
>
>
>
> The camp was soon in excitement, the members of our party developing a marked diversity of opinion as to the real age of the record, the most

experienced favoring the theory that it was really made at the date as represented. Upon the other side of this tree were several small wooden pins, such as were formerly often used in fastening wolverine and other skins while drying (of the actual age of which there was no clew further than they that were very old), but there were certain hatchet hacks near the record, which all agreed were of the same age, and that by cutting them out and counting the layers or annual growths the question should be decided. This was done, and although the layers were unusually thin, they were mainly distinct, and, in the minds of all present, decisive; and as this was upon the 29th day of July [1881], it was only one month short of sixty-two years since some unknown white man had there stood and recorded his visit to the roaring rapids of the "Mystic River," before the birth of any of the band of stalwart but bronzed and grizzled mountaineers who were then grouped around it. This is all which was then or subsequently learned, or perhaps ever will be, of the maker of the record, unless a search which is now in progress results in proving these initials to be those of some early rover of these regions. Prominent among these was a famous Hudson Bay trapper, named Ross. . . . The "R" in the record suggests, rather than proves, identity, which, if established, would be important, as confirming the reality of the legendary visits of the Hudson Bay trappers to the Park at that early day. Thorough search of the grove in which this tree is situated only proved that it was a long abandoned camping ground. Our intelligent, observant mountaineer comrade, Phelps, upon this, as upon previous and subsequent occasions, favored the oldest date claimed by any one, of the traces of men, and, as usual, proved to be correct.[15]

Superintendent Norris never did find out who J. O. R. was, though it now appears they may have lived in the same State. About the turn of the century, a writer who was assisting Olin D. Wheeler with the preparation of Northern Pacific Railroad publicity had an opportunity to interview an aged Frenchman by the name of Roch who lived at Luddington, Mich. In recalling that interview after a lapse of more than 30 years, Mr. Decker wrote:

> He claimed to be over a hundred years old. I met his son at the same time, who was then seventy-five years old. He said his father was between a hundred and a hundred and nine years of age. In my interview with him, he said he went to the Park when a young man as hunter for a fur company, and he spoke of a tree that was marked and dated, and he said it would probably be found by somebody. . . . As near as I can get it, Mr. Roch was in the Park in 1818.[16]

Alexander Ross, the man Norris thought might have been J. O. R. (an unlikely presumption considering the dissimilarity of the first initials), returned to the Missouri headwaters in 1824 as the leader of a brigade of Hudson Bay Co. trappers. Agnes Laut examined the foolscap folios which made up his official report to the company, and she summarizes the activity of the brigade thus:

> One week, the men were spread out in different parties on the Three Forks of the Missouri. Another week they were on the headwaters of the Yellowstone in the National Park of Wyoming. They did not go

eastward beyond sight of the mountains but swung back and forward between Montana and Wyoming.[17]

Mrs. Laut copied a passage from that as-yet-unpublished report which
hints that Ross' brigade was among the great geysers of the Yellowstone:
"Saturday 24th [April, 1824]—we crossed beyond the Boiling Fountains.
The snow is knee-deep half the people are snowblind from sun glare."

The record of British trapping activity in the Yellowstone region is
admittedly sketchy, and all that can be added to it is the surmise of Superintendent Norris that the cache of iron traps found near Obsidian Cliff
by his workmen, during the construction of the Norris road, was made by
Hudson's Bay Co. men more than 50 years earlier.[18]

Just when American trappers began taking fur on the Yellowstone
Plateau is uncertain. An exploration by Jedediah S. Smith and six unidentified trappers, northward from Green River in 1824, seems to have
gotten no closer than Jackson's Hole and Conant Pass;[19] however, they
definitely were there in 1826. A letter written to a brother in Philadelphia
by one of the young men who went to the Rocky Mountains with General
Ashley's expedition in 1822 contains the first clear description of Yellowstone features, and that portion is presented here just as written by Daniel
T. Potts:

> At or near this place heads the Luchkadee or Californ [Green River]
> Stinking fork [Shoshone River] Yellow-Stone South fork of Masuri
> and Henrys fork all those head at an angular point   that of the Yellow-
> Stone has a large fresh water Lake near its head on the very top of the
> Mountain which is about one hundred by fourty Miles in diameter
> and as clear as Crystal   on the South borders of this Lake is a number
> of hot and boiling springs some of water and others of most beautiful
> fine clay and resembles that of a mush pot and throws its particles to
> the immense height of from twenty to thirty feet in height The Clay
> is white and of a pink and water appears fathomless as it appears to
> be entirely hollow under neath. There is also a number of places
> where the pure suphor is sent forth in abundance   one of our men
> Visited one of those wilst taking his recreation there at an instan the
> earth began a tremendious trembling and he with dificulty made his
> escape when an explosion took place resembling that of thunder.
> During our stay in that quarter I heard it every day. From this place
> by a circutous rout to the Nourth west we returned.[20]

Daniel T. Potts continued in the fur trade until the fall of 1828, when
he went to Texas and began buying cattle for shipment to the New Orleans
market. It has been presumed that he died soon afterward in the foundering
of a cattle boat in the Gulf of Mexico. The Potts Hot Spring Basin on the
shore of West Thumb Bay has been named for this trapper whose rude but
very recognizable description of Yellowstone features was the first to
appear in print.

During the period 1827 to 1833 American trappers are reported as
having visited the Yellowstone region every year;[21] however, only the visit
of Joseph L. Meek in 1829 can be documented. According to the reminiscence Mrs. Frances F. Victor obtained from the aged trapper about 1868,

Joe was a novice of only 7 months experience with the firm of Smith, Jackson & Sublette when he approached the Yellowstone region from the north with a party led by William Sublette. They had crossed the mountains which lie between the West Fork of Gallatin River and the Yellowstone Valley and were resting their horses in the latter, near the Devils Slide, when they were suddenly attacked by a Blackfoot war party. Two men were killed and the trappers were scattered with the loss of most of their horses and equipment.

The 19-year-old recruit escaped across the Yellowstone River with only his mule, blanket, and gun, making his way southward into what is now Yellowstone National Park where, 5 days later, he

> . . . ascended a low mountain in the neighborhood of his camp— and behold! the whole country beyond was smoking with the vapor from boiling springs, and burning with gasses, issuing from small craters, each of which was emitting a sharp whistling sound. When the first surprise of this astonishing scene had passed, Joe began to admire its effect in an artistic point of view. The morning being clear, with a sharp frost, he thought himself reminded of the city of Pittsburg, as he had beheld it on a winter morning a couple of years before. This, however, related only to the rising smoke and vapor; for the extent of the volcanic region was immense, reaching far out of sight. The general face of the country was smooth and rolling, being a level plain, dotted with cone-shaped mounds. On the summits of these mounds were small craters from four to eight feet in diameter. Interspersed among these, on the level plain, were larger craters, some of them from four to six miles across. Out of these craters issued blue flames and molten brimstone.
>
> For some minutes Joe gazed and wondered. Curious thoughts came into his head, about hell and the day of doom. With that natural tendency to reckless gayety and humorous absurdities which some temperaments are sensible of in times of great excitement, he began to soliloquize. Said he, to himself, "I have been told the sun would be blown out, and the earth burnt up. If this infernal wind keeps up, I shouldn't be surprized if the sun war blown out. If the earth is *not* burning up over thar, then it is that place the old Methodist preacher used to threaten me with. Any way it suits me to go and see what it's like."
>
> On descending to the plain described, the earth was found to have a hollow sound, and seemed threatening to break through. But Joe found the warmth of the place most delightful, after the freezing cold of the mountains, and remarked to himself again, that "if it war hell, it war a more agreeable climate than he had been in for some time."[22]

Of course, there is no Yellowstone thermal area even remotely resembling Meek's description—a fact which caused historian Chittenden to admit the necessity for "making some allowance for the trapper's tendency to exaggeration;" and yet, he probably did blunder into the Norris Geyser Basin. Such a traumatic experience as he had undergone (a wild flight from a scene of butchery, into a wilderness where he even lost his mule), is liable to leave larger-than-life impressions upon a stripling mind. Fortunately for

Joe, he was found by two experienced trappers sent out by Captain Sublette to track down the fugitives.

Two of the shadowy forays into the Yellowstone region during this period deserve a mention because of their consequences. One is the venture through which Johnson Gardner's name became attached to a beautiful mountain valley at the head of the river in Yellowstone National Park which now immortalizes him. Records kept at Fort Union, a fur post at the mouth of the Yellowstone River, indicate that it was probably in the fall of 1831 or the spring of 1832 when that illiterate, often brutal, trapper discovered the valley known thereafter among his peers as "Gardner's Hole,"[24] and the place-name which now identifies the river flowing from that vale is the second oldest in Yellowstone Park—only the name Yellowstone having an earlier origin.

The other barely known visit which is of great importance through discovery of the great geysers of the Firehole River basins was that of a party of trappers led there by Manuel Alvarez in 1833.[25] The stories told by these men at the annual rendezvous determined a clerk of the American Fur Co.—Warren Angus Ferris—to make an excursion to the geysers at the opening of the next summer season. Of this visit, which made him the first Yellowstone "tourist" (because his motive was curiosity, rather than business), he says:

I had heard in the summer of 1833, while at rendezvous, that remarkable boiling springs had been discovered on the sources of the Madison, by a party of trappers, in their spring hunt; of which the accounts they gave, were so very astonishing, that I determined to examine them myself, before recording their description, though I had the united testimony of more than twenty men on the subject, all declared they saw them, and that they really *were* as extensive and remarkable as they had been described. Having now an opportunity of paying them a visit, and as another or better might not soon occur, I parted with the company after supper, and taking with me two Pen-d'orielles, (who were induced to make the excursion with me, by the promise of an extra present,) set out at a round pace, the night being clear and comfortable. We proceeded over the plain about twenty miles, and halted until day-light, on a fine spring, flowing into Cammas Creek. Refreshed by a few hour's sleep, we started again after a hasty breakfast, and entered a very extensive forest, called the Piny Woods; (a continuous succession of low mountains or hills, entirely covered by a dense growth of this species of timber;) which we passed through, and reached the vicinity of the springs about dark, having seen several small lakes or ponds on the sources of the Madison,[26] and rode about forty miles; which was a hard day's ride, taking into consideration the rough irregularity of the country through which we had travelled.

We regaled ourselves with a cup of coffee, the materials for making which, we had brought with us, and immediately after supper, lay down to rest, sleepy and much fatigued. The continual roaring of the springs, however, (which was distinctly heard,) for some time prevented my going to sleep, and excited an impatient curiosity to examine them, which I was obliged to defer the gratification of, until morning, and filled my slumbers with visions of waterspouts, cataracts, fountains, jets d'eau of immense dimensions, etc. etc.

When I arose in the morning, clouds of vapour seemed like a dense fog to overhang the springs, from which frequent reports or explosions of different loudness, constantly assailed our ears. I immediately proceeded to inspect them, and might have exclaimed with the Queen of Sheba, when their full reality of dimensions and novelty burst upon my view, "the half was not told me."

From the surface of a rocky plain or table, burst forth columns of water of various dimensions, projected high in the air, accompanied by loud explosions, and sulphurous vapors, which were highly disagreeable to the smell. The rock from which these springs burst forth, was calcareous,[27] and probably extends some distance from them, beneath the soil. The largest of these wonderful fountains, projects a column of boiling water several feet in diameter, to the height of more than one hundred and fifty feet, in my opinion; but the party of Alvarez, who discovered it, persist in declaring that it could not be less than four times that distance in height—accompanied with a tremendous noise. These explosions and discharges occur at intervals of about two hours.[28] After having witnessed three of them, I ventured near enough to put my hand into the water of its basin, but withdrew it instantly, for the heat of the water in this immense chauldron [sic], was altogether too great for my comfort; and the agitation of the water, the disagreeable effluvium continually exuding, and the hollow unearthly rumbling under the rock on which I stood, so ill accorded with my notions of personal safety, that I retreated back precipitately, to a respectful distance. The Indians, who were with me, were quite appalled, and could not by any means be induced to approach them. They seemed astonished at my presumption, in advancing up to the large one, and when I safely returned, congratulated me on my "narrow escape." They believed them to be supernatural, and supposed them to be the production of the Evil Spirit. One of them remarked that hell, of which he had heard from the whites, must be in that vicinity.[29] The diameter of the basin into which the waters of the largest jet principally fall, and from the centre of which, through a hole in the rock of about nine or ten feet in diameter, the water spouts up as above related, may be about thirty feet. There are many other smaller fountains, that did not throw their water up so high, but occurred at shorter intervals. In some instances, the volumes were projected obliquely upwards, and fell into the neighbouring fountains, or on the rock or prairie. But their ascent was generally perpendicular, falling in and about their own basins or apertures. These wonderful productions of nature, are situated near the centre of a small valley, surrounded by pine-crowned hills, through which a small fork of the Madison flows.

From several trappers who had recently returned from the Yellow Stone, I received an account of boiling springs, that differ from those seen on Salt river only in magnitude, being on a vastly larger scale; some of their cones are from twenty to thirty feet high, and forty to fifty paces in circumference. Those which have ceased to emit boiling, vapour, Etc., of which there were several, are full of shelving cavities, even some fathoms in extent, which give them, inside, an appearance of honey-comb. The ground for several acres extent in vicinity of the springs is evidently hollow, and constantly exhales a hot steam or vapour of disagreeable odour, and a character entirely to prevent vegetation. They are situated in the valley at the head of that river, near the lake, which constitutes its source.[31]

A short distance from these springs, near the margin of the lake, there is one quite different from any yet described. It is of a circular form, several feet in diameter, clear, *cold* and pure; the bottom appears visible to the eye and *seems* seven or eight feet below the surface of the earth or water, yet it has been sounded with a lodge pole fifteen feet in length, without meeting any resistance. What is most singular with respect to this fountain, is the fact that at regular intervals of about two minutes, a body or column of water bursts up to the height of eight feet, with an explosion as loud as the report of [a] musket, and then falls back into it; for a few seconds the water is roiley, but it speedily settles, and becomes transparent as before the effluxion. A slight tremulous motion of the water and a low rumbling sound from the caverns beneath, precede each explosion. This spring was believed to be connected with the lake by some subterranean passage, but the cause of its periodical eruptions or discharges, is entirely unknown. I have never before heard of a *cold* spring, whose waters exhibit the phenomena of periodical explosive propulsion, in form of a jet.[31] The geysers of Iceland, and the various other European springs, the waters of which are projected upwards, with violence and uniformity, as well as those seen on the head waters of the Madison, are invariably hot.[32]

A point worthy of notice, and one which gives the observations of Warren Angus Ferris a particular value, is the fact that he had been trained as a surveyor, and it was that occupation to which he devoted his life upon abandoning the fur trade in 1835.

The year Ferris left the mountains, the Yellowstone region was visited for the first time by a trapper who came to know the area well during the 9 years he spent in the northern Rocky Mountains; even more important, he left a reliable record of what he saw during those years, for he, too, was a competent journalist.[33] He was Osborne Russell, a Maine farm boy who joined Nathaniel J. Wyeth's Columbia River Fishing & Trading Co. in 1834, becoming a member of the garrison left at Fort Hall, on Snake River, that summer. It was from that isolated post that he went out the following March with a "spring hunt" intended to tap the fur-wealth of the Yellowstone region.

Because of their leader's poor knowledge of the country, the party Russell was with entered the confines of the present Yellowstone National Park by a difficult route which brought them onto the headwaters of Lamar River[34] from the North Fork of the Shoshone. Here is Russell's introduction to the Yellowstone country, as recorded in his manuscript:

[p. 33] 28th [July, 1835] We crossed the mountain in a West direction thro. the thick pines and fallen timber about 12 mls and encamped in a small prairie about a mile in circumference Thro. this valley ran a small stream in a north direction which all agreed in believing to be a branch of the Yellow Stone. 29th We descended the stream about 15 mls thro. the dense forest and at length came to a beautiful valley about 8 Mls. long and 3 or 4 wide[35] surrounded by dark and lofty mountains. The stream after running thro. the center in a NW direction rushed down a tremendous canyon of basaltic rock apparently just wide enough to admit its waters. The banks of the stream in the valley were low and skirted in many places with beautiful Cotton wood groves.

Here we found a few Snake Indians[36] comprising 6 men 7 women and 8 or 10 children who were the only Inhabitants of this lonely and secluded spot. They were all neatly clothed in dressed deer and Sheep skins of the best quality and seemed to be perfectly contented and happy. They were rather surprised at our approach and retreated to the heights where they might have a view of us without apprehending any danger, but having persuaded them of our pacific intentions we then succeeded in getting them to encamp with us. Their personal property consisted of one old butcher Knife nearly worn to the back two old shattered fusees which had long since become useless for want of ammunition a Small Stone pot and about 30 dogs on which they carried their skins, clothing, provisions etc on their hunting excursions. They were well armed with bows and arrows pointed with obsidian. The bows were beautifully wrought from Sheep, Buffaloe and Elk horns secured with Deer and Elk sinews and ornamented with porcupine quills and generally about 3 feet long. We obtained a large number [p. 34] of Elk Deer and Sheep skins from them of the finest quality and three large neatly dressed Panther Skins in return for awls axes kettles tobacco ammunition etc. They would throw the skins at our feet and say "give us whatever you please for them and we are satisfied. We can get plenty of Skins but we do not often see the Tibuboes" (or People of the Sun). They said there had been a great many beaver on the branches of this stream but they had killed nearly all of them and being ignorant of the value of fur had singed it off with fire in order to drip the meat more conveniently. They had seen some whites some years previous who had passed thro, the valley and left a horse behind but he had died during the first winter. They are never at a loss for fire which they produce by the friction of two pieces of wood which are rubbed together with a quick and steady motion. One of them drew a map of the country around us on a white Elk Skin with a piece of Charcoal after which he explained the direction of the different passes, streams etc. From them we discovered that it was about one days travel in a SW direction to the outlet or northern extremity of the Yellow Stone Lake, but the route from his description being difficult and Beaver comparatively scarce our leader gave out the idea of going to it this season as our horses were much jaded and their feet badly worn. Our Geographer also told us that this stream united with the Yellow Stone after leaving this Valley half a days travel in a west direction. The river then ran a long distance thro. a tremendous cut in the mountain in the same direction and emerged into a large plain the extent of which was beyond his geographical knowledge or conception.

Two days later this party continued down the Lamar River to the crossing of the Yellowstone,[37] where they laid over a day while a search was made for a hunter who failed to come into camp. Efforts to locate the lost man failing, the trappers continued westward over the Blacktail Deer Plateau to "Gardner's Hole,"[38] where they stopped again. After trapping for more than 2 weeks in that beautiful mountain valley, the party crossed the Gallatin Range, onto the river which drains its western flank, and were soon out of present Yellowstone Park.

Osborne Russell entered the Yellowstone region the following summer with some of Jim Bridger's trappers, with whom he had joined after quitting the Columbia River Fishing & Trading Co. The route followed was the conventional one from Jackson's Hole to the upper Yellowstone River via Two Ocean Pass. Continuing from Russell's manuscript, he says:

[p. 53] 9th [August, 1836] . . . we came to a smooth prarie about 2 Mls long and half a Ml. wide lying east and west surrounded by pines. On the South side about midway of the prarie stands a high snowy peak from whence issues a [p. 54]. Stream of water which after entering the plain it divides equally one half running West and the other East thus bidding adieu to each other one bound for the Pacific and the other for the Atlantic ocean.[39] Here a trout of 12 inches in length may cross the mountains in safety. Poets have sung of the "meeting of the waters" and fish climbing cataracts but the "parting of the waters and fish crossing mountains" I believe remains unsung as yet by all except the solitary Trapper who sits under the shade of a spreading pine whistling blank-verse and beating time to the tune with a whip on his trap sack whilst musing on the parting advise of these waters.

From Two Ocean Pass, the trappers traveled down Atlantic Creek to the valley of the upper Yellowstone River,[40] which was followed to Yellowstone Lake. The trail then passed along the east shore of the lake to a pleasant camping place near the outlet.[41] While encamped there, Russell wrote this description of Lake Yellowstone and the hot springs at Steamboat Point:

[p. 55] The Lake is about 100 Mls. in circumference bordered on the East by high ranges of Mountains whose spurs terminate at the shore and on the west by a low bed of piney mountains its greatest width is about 15 Mls lying in an oblong form south to north or rather in the shape of a crescent.[42] Near where we encamped were several hot springs which boil perpetually. Near these was an opening in the ground about 8 inches in diameter from which steam issues continually with a noise similar to that made by the steam issuing from a safety valve of an engine and can be heard 5 or 6 Mls. distant. I should think the steam issued with sufficient force to work an engine of 30 horse power.

Osborne Russell and six other trappers separated from the main party and proceeded to the Lamar Valley by way of Pelican Creek. Enroute they camped in a grassy glen where elk ribs were broiled before a blazing fire, and afterward the evening hours were whiled away in storytelling. That this was only the preferred entertainment of men isolated for long periods from civilization, and no reflection on their veracity, is made clear by Russell, who says:

[p. 56] The repast being over the jovial tale goes round the circle the peals of loud laughter break upon the stillness of the night which after being mimicked in the echo from rock to rock it dies away in the solitary glens. Every tale puts an auditor in mind of something similar to it but under different circumstances which being told the "laughing part" gives rise to increasing merriment and furnishes more subjects for good jokes and witty sayings such as Swift never dreamed of. Thus the evening passed with eating drinking and stories enlivened with witty humor until near Midnight all being wrapped in their blankets lying around the fire gradually falling to sleep one by one until the last tale is "encored" by the snoring of the drowsy audience.

After trapping 4 days in that "secluded valley" described by Russell the previous year, this small party continued to Gardners Hole where they rejoined Jim Bridger's camp and soon passed out of the Yellowstone mountains.

Osborne Russell came back to the Yellowstone region in 1837, entering it again by way of Two Ocean Pass—called the "Yellowstone Pass" by some trappers. This third visit followed the same general route as that of 1836 until the Lamar River was reached at a point somewhat south of the "secluded valley"; from there, they turned eastward, to the Hoodoo Basin, and then climbed over the Absaroka Range and out of the park area. After trapping for some time on the North Fork of the Shoshone River (the Stinkingwater River of an earlier day), Russell and his comrades crossed over to the Clark Fork above its great canyon and worked up that stream back into what is now Yellowstone Park. However, they did not tarry on the tributaries of the Lamar River but continued northward over the divide into the Boulder River drainage on September 13.

Osborne Russell went into the Yellowstone region for the last time in the summer of 1839—a visit which provided new sights and experiences. This time he entered the Yellowstone region directly up Snake River from Jackson Lake, very much as the South Entrance Road now does; however, his party passed around the west side of Lewis Lake, continuing up its inlet stream to Shoshone Lake.[43] At the west end of the lake they came upon "about 50 springs of boiling hot water," including at least one active geyser.[44] This "hour spring" was described thus by Russell:

[p. 120] the first thing that attracts the attention is a hole about 15 inches in diameter in which the water is boiling slowly about 4 inches below the surface at length it begins to boil and bubble violently and the water commences raising and shooting upwards until the column arises to the hight of sixty feet from whence it falls to the ground in drops on a circle of about 30 feet in diameter being perfetly cold when it strikes the ground. It continues shooting up in this manner five or six minutes [p. 121] and then sinks back to its former state of Slowly boiling for an hour and then shoots forth as before My Comrade Said he had watched the motions of this Spring for one whole day and part of the night the year previous and found no irregularity whatever in its movements.[45]

From the Shoshone Geyser Basin, Russell's party crossed the divide into the drainage of the Firehole River. They appear to have passed through the geyser basins without seeing a major geyser in action. The peculiarly sculptured cone of Lone Star Geyser was mentioned by Russell, and he was impressed with the convenience of cookery in the geyser basins, where the "kettle is always ready and boiling"; but only one feature of the wonder-filled area was described in detail. Of it he wrote:

[p. 122] At length we came to a boiling Lake about 300 ft in diameter forming nearly a complete circle as we approached on the South side. The steam which arose from it was of three distinct Colors from the west side for one third of the diameter it was white, in the middle it was pale red, and the remaining third on the east light sky blue[46]. Whether it was something peculiar in the state of the atmosphere the day being cloudy or whether it was some Chemical properties contained in the water which produced this phenomenon. I am unable to say and shall leave the explanation to some scientific tourist who may have the Curiosity to visit this place at some future period— The water was of deep indigo blue boiling like an imense cauldron running over the white rock which had formed [round] the edges to the height of 4 or 5 feet from the surface of the earth sloping gradually for 60 or 70 feet. What a field of speculation this presents for chemist and geologist.

From the Lower Geyser Basin, the trappers followed the Firehole River to its junction with the Gibbon—from which he identifies the "Burnt Hole" of the trappers as the present Madison Valley[47]—and then turned eastward into Hayden Valley. After nearly 6 weeks of trapping in familiar country northeast of Yellowstone Lake, the party was encamped on its northern shore when surprised by Blackfoot Indians, who despoiled them.[48] Left destitute, and with himself and another wounded, Russell and his two remaining comrades managed to make their way out of the present park area by passing around the west shore of Lake Yellowstone, crossing over to Heart Lake and down its outlet stream and Snake River. They then made their way across the Teton Range by the Conant Pass and onto the Snake River Plain, where they ultimately found succor at Fort Hall. Though Russell never went back to the Yellowstone region, he had seen enough of it to write the most comprehensive account of that wilderness extant prior to definitive exploration.

Another party of trappers met Blackfoot Indians near Pelican Creek that fall and the resulting battle appears to have been a particularly sanguinary affair. All that is known of this collision comes from "Wild Cat Bill" Hamilton, a trapper who was not a participant but had this story from men he knew well:

In the year 1839 a party of forty men started on an expedition up the Snake River. In the party were Ducharme, [49]Louis Anderson, Jim and John Baker, Joe Power, L'Humphrie, and others. They passed Jackson's Lake, catching many beaver, and crossed the Continental Divide, following down the Upper Yellowstone—Elk[50]—River to the Yellowstone Lake. They described accurately the Lake, the hot springs at the upper end of the lake; Steamboat Springs on the south side; the lower end of the lake, Vinegar Creek, and Pelican Creek, where they caught large quantities of beaver and otter. They also told about the sulphur mountains, and the Yellowstone Falls, and the mud geysers . . . .
They also described a fight that they had with a large party of Piegan Indians at the lower end of the lake on the north side, and

on a prairie of about half a mile in length. The trappers built a corral at the upper end of the prairie and fought desperately for two days, losing five men besides having many wounded. The trappers finally compelled the Piegans to leave, with the loss of many of their bravest warriors. After the wounded were able to travel, they took up an Indian trail and struck a warm-spring creek. This they followed to the Madison River, which at that time was not known to the trappers.[51]

The trappers of the fur trade days were not entirely oblivious to the value of their geographical discoveries. Ferris prepared a manuscript map in 1836 which showed his extensive, and essentially correct, knowledge of the physiography of the northern Rocky Mountains—of interest here because of its notations, "Boiling water volcanoes" southwest of Yellowstone Lake and "Spouting Fountains" on the headwaters of the Madison River (the latter vaguely included within the dashed line enclosing a "Burnt Hole"). However, this map did not influence the cartography of the fur trade era because it remained in the hands of its author and his heirs.[52]

The information attributed to "William Sublette and others,"[53] which appears on a map prepared by Capt. Washington Hood, of the Corps of Topographical Engineers, in 1839, was more useful. In addition to "Yellowstone L." and "Burnt Hole," this excellently drawn map showed a "Yellowstone Pass" (Two Ocean Pass) south of the lake, and a "Gardner's Fork" emptying into Yellowstone River north of the lake. But, most interestingly, the drainage of Gardner River bears the notations "Boiling Spring" and "White Sulphur Banks," the latter being an obvious allusion to the Mammoth Hot Springs.[54] (See map 3.)

William Sublette, the fur trader who provided much of the information for Captain Hood's map, is said to have guided the Scottish sportsman, Sir William Drummond Stewart, through the Yellowstone region in 1843—a visit recalled in the words of a young gentleman of St. Louis, who was a member of that party. He says:

> ...we reached a country that seemed, indeed, to be Nature's wonderworld. The rugged grandeur of the landscape was most impressive, and the beauty of the crystal-clear water falling over huge rocks was a picture to carry forever in one's mind. Here was an ideal spot to camp; so we broke ranks and settled down to our first night's rest in the region now known as Yellowstone National Park.
>
> On approaching, we had noticed at regular intervals of about five or ten minutes what seemed to be a tall column of smoke or steam, such as would arise from a steamboat. On nearer approach, however, we discovered it to be a geyser, which we christened "Steam Boat Geyser." Several other geysers were found near by, some of them so hot that we boiled our bacon in them, as well as the fine speckled trout which we caught in the surrounding streams. One geyser, a soda spring, was so effervescent that I believe the syrup to be the only thing lacking to make it equal a giant ice cream soda of the kind now popular at a drugstore. We tried some experiments with our first discovery by packing it down with armfuls of grass; then we placed a flat stone on top of that, on which four of us, joining hands, stood in a vain attempt to hold it down. In spite of our efforts to curb Nature's most

potent force, when the moment of necessity came, Old Steam Boat would literally rise to the occasion and throw us all high into the air, like so many feathers. It inspired one with great awe for the wonderful works of the Creator to think that this had been going on with the regularity of clockwork for thousands of years, and the thought of our being almost the first white men to see it did not lessen its effect.[55]

The improbability that four men could come away unscathed from such an attempt to throttle a major geyser, combined with the generally vague nature of the foregoing account, justifies a suspicion that it was created to entertain home folks, and only entered the realm of the historical through a daughter's desire to record her father's reminiscences. Thus, until such time as the Sublette-Stewart party's presence so far north of the Oregon Trail route as the Yellowstone region shall be confirmed, Kennerly's experiences there should be viewed with skepticism.

Three years later, James Gemmell—an old trapper known as "Uncle Jimmy" in Montana—passed through the Yellowstone region with Jim Bridger. Olin D. Wheeler, the eminent historian of the Northern Pacific Railway Co. and a dedicated Yellowstone buff, has recorded the visit thus:

Mr. Gemmell said: "In 1846 I started from Fort Bridger in company with old Jim Bridger on a trading expedition to the Crows and Sioux. We left in August with a large and complete outfit, went up Green River and camped for a time near the Three Tetons, and then followed the trail over the divide between Snake River and the streams which flow north into Yellowstone Lake. We camped for a time near the west arm of the lake and here Bridger proposed to show me the wonderful spouting springs on the head of Madison. Leaving our main camp, with a small and select party we took the trail by Snake Lake (now called Shoshone Lake) and visited what have of late years become so famous as the Upper and Lower Geyser Basins. There we spent a week and then returned to our camp, whence we resumed our journey, skirted the Yellowstone Lake along its west side, visited the Upper and Lower Falls, and the Mammoth Hot Springs, which appeared as wonderful to us as had the geysers. Here we camped several days to enjoy the baths and to recuperate our animals, for we had had hard work in getting around the lake and down the river, because of so much fallen timber which had to be removed. We then worked our way down the Yellowstone and camped again for a few days' rest on what is now the [Crow Indian] reservation, opposite to where Benson's landing now is.[56]

Yet another of these belated forays of trappers into the Yellowstone region has been recorded by Captain Topping in *Chronicles of the Yellowstone*. He says:

Kit Carson, Jim Bridger, Lou Anderson, Soos, and about twenty others on a prospecting trip, came from St. Louis, overland, to the Bannock Indian camp on Green River, late in the fall of 1849. They fixed up winter quarters and stayed with these Indians till spring. Then they went up the river and as soon as the snow permitted crossed the mountains to the Yellowstone and down it to the lake and falls; then across the divide to the Madison river. They saw the geysers of the lower basin and named the river that drains them the Fire Hole. Vague reports of this wonderful country had been made before. They had not been credited, but had been considered trapper's tales (more imagination than fact). The report of this party made quite a stir in St. Louis, and a party organized there the next winter to explore this country, but from some, now unknown, cause did not start. . . . The explorers went down the Madison till out of the mountains and then across the country to the Yellowstone.[57]

Whatever stir was created by the information brought back to St. Louis by this party, it left no lasting trace. However, those "trapper's tales," which were discredited in their own day, have proven very durable, and a few words about them are in order.

As Osborne Russell has clearly shown, storytelling was the principal form of entertainment among the illiterate and semiliterate men of the fur trade,[58] a proclivity which those who knew them understood and considered no reflection upon their veracity when speaking of serious matters. Capt. W. F. Raynolds, who was willing enough to have Jim Bridger for his guide in unexplored country, thought it was not at all surprising that such men "should beguile the monotony of camp life by 'spinning yarns' in which each tried to excell all others, and which were repeated so often and insisted upon so strenuously that the narrators came to believe them most religiously."[59]

The storytelling of Jim Bridger has been described by Capt. Eugene F. Ware, an artillerist stationed at Fort Laramie in 1864, whose statements have been combined as follows:

> Major Bridger was a regular old Roman in actions and appearances, and he told stories in such a solemn and firm, convincing way that a person would be likely to believe him . . . One of the difficulties with him was that he would occasionally tell some wonderful story to a pilgrim, and would try to interest a new-comer with a lot of statements which were ludicrous, sometimes greatly exaggerated, and sometimes imaginary. . . . He wasn't the egotistic liar that we so often find. He never in my presence vaunted himself about his own personal actions. He never told about how brave he was, nor how many Indians he had killed. His stories always had reference to some outdoor matter or circumstances . . . He had told each story so often that he had got it into language form, and told it literally alike. He had probably told them so often that he got to believing them himself.[60]

James Stevenson, who knew Jim Bridger well during the period 1859–60, thought Bridger's stories, as told by him, were uncouth.[61]

Of the seven stories about the Yellowstone region attributed to Jim Bridger, there is evidence indicating that four—or tales similar to them—were a part of his repertoire, while the others appear to be relatively recent literary accretions of the type Elbert Hubbard called "kabojolisms" (stories attributed to a person who did *not* tell them, in order to gain popular acceptance for them)—a process best typified as plagiarism in reverse.

The petrified forest story is one of the Yellowstone tales attributed to Jim Bridger. However, it is but a re-phrasing of a story Moses "Black"

Harris put into circulation in 1823. A fellow trapper, James Clyman, noted in his diary that autumn:

> A mountaineer named Harris being in St. Louis some years after [seeing the petrified trees] undertook to describe some of the strange things seen in the mountains, [and] spoke of this petrified grove, in a restaurant, where a caterer for one of the dailies was present; and the next morning his exaggerated statement came out saying a petrified forest was lately discovered where the tree branches, leaves and all, were perfect, and the small birds sitting on them, with their mouths open, singing at the time of their transformation to stone.[62]

A quarter-century later, this story was still being told, in an amplified form—and still attributed to trapper Harris; but the petrifactions were now located in the Black Hills and the year had been advanced to 1833.[63] Undoubtedly, Jim Bridger was aware of that persistent tale almost from its origin, but he is not identified with it—as a narrator—until 1859. In that and the following year he served as a guide for the Raynolds expedition to the headwaters of the Yellowstone River, and, while in that service, he told some of those "Munchausen tales," which Captain Raynolds thought "altogether too good to be lost." That officer recorded a petrified prairie story (presumably Jim's) which goes thus:

> In many parts of the country petrifactions and fossils are very numerous; and, as a consequence, it was claimed that in some locality (I was not able to fix it definitely) a large tract of sage is perfectly petrified, with all the leaves and branches in perfect condition, the general appearance of the plain being [not] unlike that of the rest of the country, but *all is stone*, while the rabbits, sage hens, and other animals usually found in such localites are still there, perfectly petrified and as natural as when they were living; and more wonderful still, these petrified bushes bear the most wonderful fruit—diamonds, rubies, sapphires, emeralds, etc., etc., as large as black walnuts, are found in abundance. "I tell you, sir", said one narrator, "it is true, for I gathered a quart myself, and sent them down the country."[64]

Thus, the petrified forest story had, toward the end of its fourth decade, been generalized and divested of its specifics of time and place and was very likely a part of Bridger's repertoire. That he finally did turn that into a stock petrified forest story based on a Yellowstone feature seems probable from a second-hand tale told by General Nelson A. Miles in 1897. According to him,

> . . . one night after supper, a comrade who in his travels had gone as far south as the Zuni Village, New Mexico, and had discovered the famous petrified forest of Arizona, inquired of Bridger:
> "Jim, were you ever down to Zuni?"
> "No, thar ain't no beaver down thar."
> "But Jim, there are some things in this world besides beaver. I was down there last winter and saw great trees with limbs and bark all turned to stone."
> "O," returned Jim, "that's peetrifaction. Come with me to the Yellowstone next summer, and I'll show you peetrified trees a-growing, with peetrified birds on 'em a-singing peetrified songs."[65]

Such a remark hardly justifies the additions Historian Chittenden made to this vague oral tradition of the trapping fraternity, where he poetically states: "Even flowers are blooming in colors of crystal, and birds soar with wings spread in motionless flight, while the air floats with music and perfume silicious, and the sun and the moon shine with petrified light!"[66]

In a similar manner, the glass mountain story which Bridger is credited with telling to tenderfeet along the emigrant road was altered to fit Obsidian Cliff in present Yellowstone Park. This we have on the authority of Superintendent Norris, who says:

> So with his famous legend of a lake with millions of beaver nearly impossible to kill because of their superior cuteness; with haunts and houses in inaccessible grottoes in the base of a glistening mountain of glass, which every mountaineer of our party at once recognized as an exaggeration of the artificial lake [Beaver Lake] and obsidian mountain [Obsidian Cliff] which I this year discovered . . . .[68]

The other two authentic Bridger stories referring to the Yellowstone region are those concerning the stream-heated-by-friction and Hell-close-below. The former was recorded by Raynolds,[69] while we are indebted to Ware for the latter.[70] Several other tall tales concerned with the use of an echo as an alarm clock, the convenient suspension of gravity, and the shrinking ability of certain waters, have no traceable antecedents in fur trade days, and probably are of more recent origin.

The Exploring Era
(1851–1863)

Between the fur trade and prospecting eras is a brief period of missionary and military exploration which advanced the general knowledge of the Yellowstone region without any actual penetration of its fastnesses. Through their maps and writings these explorers became the means of preserving an important residual from that store of accurate geographical information amassed by the men of the fur trade. The fact that Jim Bridger provided most of the information set on paper by intelligent, perceptive men testifies to the good repute in which his serious utterances were held.

Bridger was present in 1851 at the great treaty council held at Fort Laramie to secure the emigrant road from Indian molestation, and, while there, he made a map for the Jesuit priest, Father Pierre-Jean DeSmet, which showed the streams heading in and around the Yellowstone region.[71] Bridger's remarkable map set the missionary-explorer straight on the rumors he had heard in 1839 concerning manifestations of volcanism on the headwaters of the Missouri River,[72] allowing him to add important details to his manuscript map.[73]

The Bridger map is essentially a hydrographic sketch of amazing accuracy when one accepts its lack of scale. Two Ocean Pass is indicated by the meeting of Atlantic and Pacific Creeks (both named), and the ultimate sources of the upper Yellowstone River are shown as originating on the flank of the Absaroka Range opposite Wind River. An oval Yellowstone Lake—unnamed but containing the notation "60 by 7"—has "Hot Springs" noted on its eastern shore (Steamboat Point) and "Volcano" near its outlet (Mud Geyser Area). The Grand Canyon of the Yellowstone is indicated by a crinkled outline, with "Falls 250 Feet" at its upper end and a ford below—shown by a heavy pen stroke across the river. The Lamar River, marked "Meadow", is shown with its feeder streams nestled against the Absaroka Range, and north of it a short stream marked "Beaver" (Slough Creek) terminates in a lake (Abundance). The prominant leftward trend of the Yellowstone River from its junction with the Lamar is shown, and farther down the rightward swing, as the river turns back toward a north course, is indicated. "Gardener's Cr." is shown entering at the latter point, and on its west bank is a "Sulphur Mtn." (Mammoth Hot Springs).

The presentation of the "Madison" and "Gallatin" headwaters of the Missouri River suffers from being cramped. A mass of pen curls on both the southern and northern branches of the Madison appear to represent the Firehole and Norris thermal areas, with the notation "volcanic country" between them. Centered in the triangle formed by Yellowstone Lake, the mouth of Lamar River, and the head of Gibbon River is a circled notation "Great Volcanic Country 100 miles in extent." Of particular importance beyond the Yellowstone Plateau is the notation at the forks of the "Stinking River" (Shoshone): "Sulphur Springs Colter's Hell."

Such was Bridger's own delineation of the Yellowstone region, with names added by DeSmet (see map 4). Most of that information was transferred to DeSmet's manuscript map, but there are some changes and additions worthy of mention. At Two Ocean Pass, he added a short "Two Ocean Rv." (recognizable as Two Ocean Creek, the stream which flows from the mountains into the pass to split into Atlantic and Pacific creeks), and, on the upper Yellowstone River, he added a "Bridger's Lake & Riv." (both misplaced). The DeSmet manuscript map names Yellowstone Lake, retaining the notation concerning its size, but omits both the outline of the Grand Canyon and the reference to the falls at its upper end; however, a name—"Little Falls"—appears at just the right place to represent Tower Fall. Lamar River is mislabeled "Beaver Creek" (it was "Meadow" on Bridger's map), and the Slough Creek and Hellroaring drainages were omitted.

But it was in presenting the headwaters of the Madison River that DeSmet deviated most from Bridger's information. The eastward-trending branch is named "Fire Hole Riv.," while a southern branch, passing through two small lakes, is shown as "DeSmet's L. and Riv." This latter addition appears to portray the Lewis-Shoshone system, but with its river flowing to the Madison rather than Snake River (see map 5).

22

The changes which appear on DeSmet's manuscript map may represent additional information received in oral form from Bridger, or they may have come from an entirely different source, but the result was so much better than the best maps available to the Indian commissioners that he was asked to prepare a general map suitable for their purpose—an outcome which he explains thus:

When I was at the council ground in 1851, on the Platte River, at the mouth of Horse creek, I was requested by Colonel Mitchell to make a map of the whole Indian country, relating particularly to the Upper Missouri, the waters of the upper Platte, east of the Rocky mountains and of the headwaters of the Columbia and its tributaries west of these mountains. In compliance with this request I drew up the map from scraps then in my possession. The map, so prepared, was seemingly approved and made use of by the gentlemen assembled in council, and subsequently sent on to Washington together with the treaty then made with the Indians.[74]

In a letter written from the council grounds to his superiors, DeSmet describes the Yellowstone thermal features as follows:[75]

Near the source of the river Puante [Stinking Water, now called Shoshone] which empties into the Big Horn, and the sulphurous waters of which have probably the same medicinal qualities as the celebrated Blue Lick Springs of Kentucky, is a place called Colter's Hell—from a beaver hunter of that name. This locality is often agitated with subterranean fires. The sulphurous gases which escape in great volumes from the burning soil infect the atmosphere for several miles, and render the earth so barren that even the wild worm wood cannot grow on it. The beaver hunters have assured me that the frequent underground noises and explosions are frightful.

However, I think that the most extraordinary spot in this respect, and perhaps the most marvelous of all the northern half of this continent, is in the very heart of the Rocky Mountains, between the forty-third and forty-fifth degrees of latitude and 109th and 11th degrees of longitude, that is, between the sources of the Madison and Yellowstone. It reaches more than a hundred miles. Bituminous, sulphurous and boiling springs are very numerous in it. The hot springs contain a large quantity of calcareous matter [silicious], and form hills more or less elevated, which resemble in their nature, perhaps, if not in their extent, the famous springs of Pambuk Kalessi, in Asia Minor, so well described by Chandler [Richard Chandler, English Archaeologist, 1738–1810]. The earth is thrown up very high, and the influence of the elements causes it to take the most varied and the most fantastic shapes. Gas, vapor and smoke are continually escaping by a thousand openings, from the base to the summit of the volcanic pile; the noise at times resembles the steam let off by a boat. Strong subterranean explosions occur, like those in 'Colter's Hell'. The hunters and Indians speak of it with a superstitious fear, and consider it the abode of evil spirits, that is to say, a kind of hell. Indians seldom approach it without offering some sacrifice, or at least without presenting the calumet of peace to the turbulent spirits, that they may be propitious. They declare that the subterranean noises proceed from the forging of warlike weapons: each eruption of earth is, in their eyes, the result of a

23

combat between the infernal spirits, and becomes a monument of a new victory or calamity.[76]

Near Gardiner river, a tributary of the Yellowstone, and in the vicinity of the region I have just been describing, there is a mountain of sulphur [Mammoth Hot Springs]. I have this report from Captain Bridger, who is familiar with every one of these mountains, having passed thirty years of his life near them.

Lt. J. W. Gunnison, an army officer attached to the Stansbury exploring party which Jim Bridger guided to the Great Salt Lake in 1849, was sufficiently impressed with Jim's geographical knowledge to comment as follows:

He has been very active, and traversed the region from the head-waters of the Missouri to the Del Norte—and along the Gila to the Gulf, and thence throughout Oregon and the interior of California. His graphic sketches are delightful romances. With a buffalo-skin and a piece of charcoal, he will map out any portion of this immense region, and delineate mountains, streams, and the circular valleys called 'holes', with wonderful accuracy; at least we may so speak of that portion we traversed after his descriptions were given. He gives a picture, most romantic and enticing of the head-waters of the Yellow Stone. A lake sixty miles long, cold and pellucid, lies embosomed amid high precipitous mountains. On the west side is a sloping plain several miles wide, with clumps of trees and groves of pine. The ground resounds to the tread of horses. Geysers spout up seventy feet high, with a terrific hissing noise, at regular intervals. Waterfalls are sparkling, leaping, and thundering down the precipices, and collect in the pool below. The river issues from this lake, and for fifteen miles roars through the perpendicular canyon at the outlet. In this section are the Great Springs, so hot that meat is readily cooked in them, and as they descend on the successive terraces, afford at length delightful baths. On the other side is an acid spring, which gushes out in a river torrent; and below is a cave which supplies "vermillion" for the savages in abundance. Bear, elk, deer, wolf, and fox are among the game, and the feathered tribe yields its share for variety, on the sportsman's table of rock or turf.[77]

The figure Gunnison gave for the length of Yellowstone Lake—60 miles—is the same as that shown on DeSmet's manuscript map. Such consistency, and an innate conservatism, were both characteristics of Bridger's recital when passing on serious geographical information.

Jim Bridger was not the only purveyor of information about the Yellowstone region; other ex-trappers who had located along the emigrant road to trade in horses and oxen, provide supplies and do a little guiding, occasionally told wayfarers of the things they had seen on the headwaters of the Yellowstone River. Joaquin Miller was one of those who heard such tales, of which he says:

...when with my father on Bear River between Fort Hall and Salt Lake at a place then known as Steamboat Spring, in 1852, a trapper told us that there were thousands of such springs at the head of the Yellowstone, and that the Indians there used stone knives and axes. We had Lewis and Clarke's as well as some of Fremont's journals,

24

and not finding any of these hot springs and geysers mentioned in their pages, we paid little attention to the old man's tale.[78]

Indians sometimes served as informants, as Capt. John Mullan noted:

As early as the winter of 1853, which I spent in these mountains, my attention was called to the mild open region lying between the Deer Lodge Valley and Fort Laramie . . . . Upon investigating the peculiarities of the country, I learned from the Indians, and afterwards confirmed by my own explorations, the fact of the existence of an infinite number of hot springs at the headwaters of the Missouri, Columbia, and Yellowstone rivers, and that hot geysers, similar to those of California, existed at the head of the Yellowstone; that this line of hot springs was traced to the Big Horn, where a coal-oil spring, similar in all respects to those worked in west Pennsylvania and Ohio, exists.[79]

Yet another army officer who gained some knowledge of the Yellowstone region during this period was Capt. William F. Raynolds of the Corps of Topographical Engineers. The expedition he commanded was charged particularly with determining the most direct and feasible route "From the Yellowstone to the South Pass, and to ascertaining the practicability of a route from the sources of Wind river to those of the Missouri." Thus, his exploration of the headwaters of the Yellowstone River had to be subordinated to those objectives. The first was accomplished by Lt. H. E. Maynadier, who took a party from Wind River northward through the Wyoming Basin to the Yellowstone River and thence to the Three Forks of the Missouri, where he was to meet Captain Raynolds, who hoped to cross directly to the upper Yellowstone and follow that stream down to the meeting place. However, this second part of the plan went awry.

Of his desire to pass from the head of Wind River to the head of the Yellowstone, Raynolds admits:

Bridger had said at the outset that this would be impossible . . . [and] remarked triumphantly and forcibly to me upon reaching this spot, "I told you you could not go through. A bird can't fly over that without taking a supply of grub along." I had no reply to offer, and mentally conceded the accuracy of the information of "the old man of the mountains."[80]

Being thus prevented from reaching the Yellowstone region from the Atlantic slope, Raynolds crossed the Continental Divide by way of Union Pass and made another attempt from the Gros Ventre fork of Snake River. But late-lying snow banks baffled him there, and, having used as much time as his close schedule allowed, he decided to pass around the western flank of the Yellowstone Plateau and down the Madison River to the rendezvous at the Three Forks. Some idea of the disappointment that decision brought is evident in Captain Raynolds' statement:

We were compelled to content ourselves with listening to marvellous tales of burning plains, immense lakes, and boiling springs, without being able to verify these wonders. I know of but two white men who claim to have visited this part of the Yellowstone valley—James Bridger and Robert Meldrum. The narratives of both of these men are very remarkable, and Bridger in one of his recitals, describes an immense boiling spring that is the very counterpart of the geysers of Iceland. . . . I have little doubt that he spoke of what he had actually seen. The burning plains described by these men may be volcanic, or more probably beds of lignite, similar to those on Powder river, which are known to be in a state of ignition. Bridger also insisted that immediately west [north] of the point at which we made our final effort to penetrate this singular valley, there is a stream of considerable size, which divides and flows down either side of the water-shed, thus discharging its waters into both the Atlantic and Pacific oceans. Having seen this phenomenon on a small scale in the highlands of Maine, where a rivulet discharges a portion of its waters into the Atlantic and the remainder into the St. Lawrence, I am prepared to concede that Bridger's "Two Ocean river" *may* be a verity.[81]

To that the captain added that he could not doubt "that at no very distant day the mysteries of this region will be fully revealed, and though small in extent, I regard the valley of the upper Yellowstone as the most interesting unexplored district in our widely expanded country."

The map which accompanied Captain Raynolds' belated report (publication was delayed by the Civil War), though generally less informative than either the Hood or the Bridger-DeSmet maps, does add something to the body of knowledge concerning the Yellowstone region.[82] Northwest of the outlet of a spindle-shaped "Yellowstone Lake"—but south of "Falls of the Yellowstone"—is "Elephants Back Mt." Below the falls, and in the proper location to represent Mammoth Hot Springs, is "Sulpher Mt.," while a "Mt. Gallatin" makes its appearance in the position of present Mount Holmes. Raynolds' map also confirms the location of the "Burnt Hole" of the trappers, showing it to lie between Henry's Lake and Mount Holmes (see map 6).

Of that valley, which would later be confused with the geyser basins on Firehole River, Raynolds says:

After crossing Lake fork [below Henrys Lake], Mr. Hutton, Dr. Hayden, and two attendants turned to the east and visited the pass [Targhee] over the mountains, leading into the Burnt Hole valley [Madison Basin]. They found the summit distant only about five miles from our route, and report the pass as in all respects equal to that through which the train had gone [Raynolds Pass]. From it they could see a second pass upon the other side of the valley, which Bridger states to lead to the Gallatin. He also says that between that point and the Yellowstone there are no mountains to be crossed."[83]

The Prospecting Era

(1863–1871)

Gold strikes on the Clearwater, Salmon, Owyhee, and Boise tributaries of Snake River in the opening years of the 1860's led to establishment of the "Idaho mines," from which prospectors moved eastward, across the Continental Divide, to yet another goldfield. But the placers on Grasshopper Creek, where the town of Bannack sprang up in 1862–63, were disappointing to many and they continued to search for gold east of the Rocky Mountains.

Among the latter were 40 prospectors who banded together under "Colonel" Walter Washington deLacy to explore the headwaters of Snake River in the late summer of 1863. By the time they reached the forks of Snake River and were within the south boundary of the present park, the party had splintered several times, and another division near that place resulted in Charles Ream leading a group up Lewis River to Shoshone Lake, over the divide to the Firehole River and down that stream to the Madison, while deLacy conducted his party across the Pitchstone Plateau to Shoshone Lake, then over the divide by way of DeLacy and White Creeks into the Lower Geyser Basin, from which they, too, continued down Firehole River to the Madison and out of the Yellowstone region proper.

Two years later deLacy, who was a well-trained civil engineer, prepared a map of the Territory of Montana which was used by the First Legislative Assembly for laying out the original counties,[84] and the discoveries made by the 1863 parties were thus made public knowledge. The principal contribution of deLacy's map to the geographical knowledge of the Yellowstone region was its essentially correct delineation of the Lewis River headwaters of the Snake. He was the first to show that branch as heading in what is now Shoshone Lake (he did not name the Lake,[85] though he noted its hot spring basin; see map 7). Thus, he avoided the mistake made by DeSmet in 1851, and later by the Hayden Survey, in assigning Lewis and Shoshone Lakes to the Madison drainage. This map also indicated the geyser basins of the Firehole River in its label, "Hot Spring Valley."

It is sometimes claimed that deLacy forfeited his right to consideration as the discoverer of Yellowstone's thermal features because he did not adequately publish his findings, a line of reasoning which assumes he was too much concerned with prospecting to appreciate the wonderful region he passed through. However, an excerpt from one of his letters which found its way into print in 1869 shows that he understood both the extent and the nature of the thermal areas he saw, for he wrote: "At the head of the South Snake, and also on the south fork of the Madison, there are hundreds of hot springs, many of which are 'Geysers'."[86]

The extent of deLacy's familiarity with the southwestern quarter of what is now Yellowstone National Park is evident in the account he later published from notes made in 1863 (cited in Note 85):

[p. 128] We had not traveled more than three miles next day (September 5th), when we came to the forks of the stream that we had been ascending. One branch came from the northeast [Snake River] and the other from the north [Lewis River], and there were hot springs with cones four or five feet high near the junction. Neither of the streams were large, and it was thought that we would soon reach the divide. It being impracticable to go up either branch, on account of fallen timber, we commenced climbing up the mountain side to the west, where the timber was more open, and after ascending about one thousand feet with much difficulty, reached a large open prairie, apparently on the summit, [p. 129] where there were two small lakes, of a beautiful blue, and small streams flowing in opposite directions.[87] I judged that one of them ran into the North Snake [Henrys Fork]. Here we stopped for dinner.

Here another split of the party took place. Some of the men had noticed veins of quartz, as they supposed, down below, and resolved to return and examine them. This left me about thirteen men to go forward with.

Our friend Brown had been completely disgusted, during the last few days, with his whip-saw, owing to the number of times every day that he had to stop to adjust the pack in going through the woods, and now left that useful implement leaning against a tree, with the remark that "he had packed the damned thing far enough."

On starting, we kept a northerly course and passed over low undulating ridges, covered with open pine timber [Pitchstone Plateau]. The rocks, where exposed, seem to be vitrified sandstone. We killed two deer this evening which was the first large game shot on the trip. After traveling several miles, we saw an opening beneath us which looked like a valley, and descending the mountain, which was very steep and high, reached a small stream flowing northeasterly [Moose Creek], just about dark, and camped where there was plenty of grass, wood, and water.

In the morning (6th), we descended the stream for about five miles, and to the great surprise of us all, came to the bank of a large lake [Shoshone]. We were all lost in conjectures as to what it could be. Some thought that it must be the Yellowstone Lake, and others that it must flow into the Madison or Gallatin. We finally resolved to go around the southern end,[88] which was not very far from us apparently, and then go around the other side. We then traveled along the lake shore for some three or four miles, when we came to [p. 130] the outlet of the lake, a large stream flowing *south* into Snake river. Instead of going around the *head*, as we had thought to do, we had been going around the foot.

One thing puzzled me. The outflowing stream was much larger than either of the forks of the South Snake that we had left before. I afterward found out, however, that it flowed into another lake, now called Lewis Lake, from one of the men who went back at our noon halt.

This party which left us, had returned to the forks, and not finding the quartz, as they expected, ascended the stream coming from the north. They encountered a fire in the woods which gave them some trouble, and found some very high falls in the stream. They passed Lake Lewis, and came to the foot of the large lake, where they found our old camp. Here they went up the west side of the lake to its head, and there found a large number of hot springs [Shoshone Geyser Basin], some of which were geysers, which they saw in action, spouting up the water to a great height, and thence went over to the South Fork of the Fire Hole river, where they again saw our camps, and thence down the Madison river to Virginia City. These facts I obtained afterward at Bannack City, from Mr. Charles Ream, one of the party, and it was thus established conclusively that the large lake was the head of the South Snake, and I was enabled to correct the course of the Madison river, and connect my surveys with it. . . .

To return to our own party. We camped at the mouth of the lake and prospected and hunted for the rest of the [p. 131] day, but without any success. The lake seemed to be about ten or twelve miles long, running northwest and southeast, and to be surrounded by low and thickly wooded hills which came down to the water's edge. There was a point projecting into the lake on the west side, which hid a large part of the lake from us, although we did not know it them.

On the next day (7th), we went up the eastern side, near the water, passing through scrubby pines, without underbrush. There were many game trails made by the wood buffalo, whose tracks appeared numerous and fresh. We did not see any, and finally, at noon, stopped on a small prairie, for dinner. In the evening we left the lake altogether, and took a northerly course, hoping to cross the divide to some other stream. Our course lay through timber, and over and around fallen logs, but the ground, though undulating, was not rocky, and we found many game trails leading in our direction.

Whenever we could obtain a glimpse of the outside world, we could see high ranges of mountains on every side. We kept on till late, without finding any place to camp, but just at dark arrived at a small dry prairie, where we camped [DeLacy Park].[89] There was a damp place in the center, where, by digging about three feet, we soon obtained water for both ourselves and animals . . . [p. 132] It rained heavily during the night and also during the next day, and we remained here, as we now had plenty of water and grass.

On the 9th, we continued our journey, and after traveling three miles, descended the mountain side into an open country. In another mile we reached the head of a small stream [White Creek], the water of which was hot, and soon entered a valley or basin, through which the stream meandered, and which was occupied on every side by hot springs. They were so thick and close that we had to dismount and lead our horses, winding in and out between them as we best could. The ground sounded hollow beneath our feet, and we were in great fear of breaking through, and proceeded with great caution. The water of these springs was intensely hot, of a beautiful utramarine blue, some boiling up in the middle, and many of them of very large size, being at least twenty feet in diameter and as deep. There were hundreds of these springs, and in the distance we could see and hear others, which would eject a column of steam with a loud noise. These were probably geysers, and the boys called them "steamboat springs." No one in the company had ever seen or heard of anything like this region, and we were all delighted with what we saw. This was what was afterward called the "Lower Geyser Basin" of the Madison, by Prof. Hayden.

We thus went on for several miles, stopping occasionally [p. 133] to admire the beauty, variety, and grandeur of the sight, and at length came to a large stream flowing northerly [Firehole River], near the banks of which were scattering hot springs, and some of which had been hot once, but had now cooled apparently, the water being tepid and muddy, with a strong smell of sulphur.

We "nooned" on the left bank of this stream, and then continued our way north, crossing the river again, by a deep ford, in about three miles, and camped for the evening on the edge of a small prairie, near where a large fork came in the southeast [Gibbon River]. On the left bank of the south fork was a high, perpendicular wall of rock,[90] and we could see the smoke of hot springs up the east fork [Terrace Spring].

We had great discussions in the evening as to where we were, some thinking we were on the North Snake river, and others that we were on the Madison. The map which I had, represented the North Snake river as running around and leading to the northeast of the South Snake, and these streams seemed to run that way. In reality, we were at the forks of the Fire Hole river, a branch of the Madison.

In the morning (September 10th), we continued our journey down the main river, crossing the east fork just above the junction. The weather looked stormy and threatening. The main river was about fifty yards wide, its valley very narrow, with high, rocky hills on either side covered with pine, and the general course westerly. After traveling about five miles, rain came down heavily, and we were forced to go into camp on the river, and at the head of what appeared to be a cañon.

In the evening, during an interval of calm, I went forward on the trail across the mountain to explore. In about one and half miles I came to the foot of the cañon, [p. 134] when I perceived that the country opened out into a large basin [Madison Valley], through which the main river ran.

Unlike the Ream party, which passed down the Madison River after leaving the Yellowstone region, deLacy turned north, crossing the Madison Basin to the pass leading to the West Gallatin River, which he followed down to Spanish Creek.

One of the men who accompanied deLacy in 1863 returned to the Yellowstone region the following year. He was John C. Davis, a member of James Stuart's 1864 expedition down the Yellowstone River to prospect the Bighorn and Stinkingwater (Shoshone) Rivers. Upon the breakup of that venture, a remnant of the party worked southward under the leadership of Adam "Horn" Miller. Six of these men eventually reached Jackson's Hole, from which Davis and two others left for the Yellowstone region. He says,[91] according to the Louisville, Ky., *Courier-Journal*:

We came into the park just above the lake, and immediately found ourselves in the midst of the wonders of this enchanted land. The boiling springs and geysers were all around us, and, accustomed as we were to the marvels of Western scenery, we hardly knew what to think of the phenomena. Having visited this place the preceding year I was, however, less surprized than the others. We wandered along the shore for a while, and leaving the lake we went into camp about a mile and a half above the falls. The roaring of the great cataract reached us, but was barely discernible at this distance, and we were among so many wonders that we paid it little attention. After camping I took my gun and started out in the hope of finding an elk for dinner. I went down the bank, and in short time came to the Upper Falls. The full grandeur of the scene did not burst on me at once. Men who have engaged in a hand-to-hand struggle for a frontier existence lose sentiment after a few years; but when I realized the stupendous leap of water, I could not help being impressed. I stood gazing at it for a long time, and I remember estimating the height of the falls at only about 200 feet.[92]

30

I did not then think that I was the first white man to behold one of the greatest wonders of the Western world.

In the afternoon we crossed the river on our ponies. Going below we reached the Grand Canyon, along which we wandered for a short distance. I remember that we crept to the edge and looked over to where the river, a mere silvery thread, was winding its way in silence and darkness 1,200 feet below where we stood. After we crossed we remain in the valley awhile, and then there was again a division of the party.[93] William Armstead and Johnston Shelton, both Scotchmen, returned with me to Virginia City, or Alder Gulch, as it was then called.

We saw plenty of Indian signs, but we fortunately eluded any of these gentry. Shortly afterwards one section of our party were attacked by a hostile gang of Crows, and a man named Harris was killed. The interpreter of the original party was with this company, and he was also captured, but he afterwards made his escape by ingratiating himself with the chief.

When we first reached the volcanic region of the geysers we were much alarmed at the yielding of the ground. Finally we struck a buffalo track, and followed this with some feeling of safety. None of our party thought to give names to anything in the valley. I remember one little incident connected with Pelican Creek, however, which may have suggested its name. We camped on this creek, and noticed several large birds which appeared to be wild geese. I shot one, which managed to fly out some distance in the lake before it fell. I swam out after it, and became very much exhausted before I reached it. It looked as if it might be good to eat so I skinned it, and then the boys concluded it would hardly do. I hung the pelican—for that was what it was—on a tree, and it was found afterward by Miller, who came by with his party.[94]

The editor of the *Courier-Journal* appended this comment to the Davis account: "It would be remembered that the first public announcement of the valley's discovery was made after the visit of an exploring party in 1869 (Folsom party). Before this it had been visited by hunters, but there is no account of any visit prior to that of Mr. Davis, and it seems that he and his party are entitled to the honor of its discovery, though they failed to make use of the lucky accident. His story can be vouched for."

Other prospectors were in the Yellowstone region that summer. Thomas Curry's discovery of gold at "Curry's Gulch" (later known as Emigrant Gulch) in the late fall of 1863 brought a well-equipped party under George A. Huston the following spring. But most of the reinforcement thought they could do better and continued up the Yellowstone River and its "East Fork" (now Lamar River). The scanty information available on their adventure comes from two writers who knew many of the participants personally. E. S. Topping says:

> . . . Prospecting parties were going out in every direction. One of these consisting of thirty men under the leadership of Austin [George A. Hustin], went to and up the Yellowstone. When they arrived at the east fork of the Yellowstone, they went up that stream to the first creek coming in from the left above Soda Butte creek, up which they

went. They made a camp at its head and, as they had seen no signs of Indians, let their horses run loose. The next morning at daylight a band of Arrapahoes swooped in and drove away all their stock but one jackass. It was useless to chase them without horses, and the boys, not being ready to go back, cached their things and, packing the jackass heavily and themselves lightly, went over the divide to Clarke's Fork and down it to below the mouth of the canyon. Here they found some prospects, but no pay; so turned back to their cache, and taking from this the most valuable articles, struck out on their back trail for Virginia City.[95]

Superintendent Norris elaborates somewhat on that in his annual report for 1881:

In the spring of 1864, H. W. Wayant, now a leading citizen of Silver city, Idaho, William Hamilton, and other prospectors, to the number of forty men, with saddle horses, pack train, and outfit, ascended the east side of the Yellowstone from the Gate of the Mountains to Emigrant, Bear and Crevice Gulches, forks of the Yellowstone, East Fork, and Soda Butte; thence over the western foothills of Mount Norris to the bluffs upon the south side of Cache Creek, where their horses were all stolen by some unknown Indians, but their only two donkeys would not stampede, and remained with them. Here the party broke up; Wyant, Harrison, and ten others, with one jack, and what he could carry, ascended Cache Creek to Crandall Creek, Clarke's Fork, Heart Mountain, thence by way of Index Peak and the Soda Butte returned to the cache made by the other party of what they could not carry, aided by their donkey, from where set afoot, and hence called Cache Creek.

Norris adds that "Later in the same season George Huston and party ascended the main Fire Hole River, and from the marvelous eruption of the Giantess and other geysers, and the suffocating fumes of brimstone, fearing they were nearing the infernal regions, hastily decamped."[96]

The Yellowstone region was visited a number of times in 1865. A Montana prospector and mountaineer named George Harvey Bacon is said to have reached the Upper Geyser Basin with a party of Indians,[97] and Jim Bridger passed entirely through the area with three ex-trappers—John Dunn and two others.[98] Another former trapper, James Gemmel, is said to have passed through the Yellowstone region with his daughter, Jeanette (who may have been the first white woman to enter the area),[99] but the most interesting visitor that year was Father Francis Xavier Kuppens, a Belgian priest of the Jesuit Order, who had this recollection to offer 32 years later:

[p. 400] About the years 1865–66 I was stationed at the old Mission of St. Peter's on the Missouri River near the mouth of Sun River. A great part of that winter [1864–65, according to other records] and spring I spent with the Pigeon [Piegan] Indians roaming from place to place south of Fort Benton, and on the Judith River. It was while leading this nomad life that I first heard of the Yellowstone. Many an evening in the tent of Baptiste Champagne or Chief Big Lake the conversation, what little there was of it, turned on the beauties of that wonderful spot. I do not know that the narrator always adhered strictly to facts, but making allowance for fervid imagination there was sufficient in the tale to excite my curiosity and awaken in me a strong desire to see for myself this enchanted if not enchanting land. In the spring with a small party of Indians hunting buffalo, I persuaded a few young men to show me [p. 401] the wonderland of which they had talked so much. Thus I got my first sight of the Yellowstone. I shall not attempt to describe it, that has been done by many abler pens than mine; but you may be sure that before leaving I saw the chief attraction,—the Grand Cañon, hot and cold geysers, variegated layers of rock, the Fire Hole, etc. I was very much impressed with the wild grandeur of the scenery, and on my return gave an account of it to Fathers Ravalli and Imoda, then stationed at the old Mission of St. Peter's.[100]

The effect of Father Kuppens' visit on the definitive exploration of the Yellowstone region will be considered in Part II.

The hostility of the Sioux Indians, who were determined to prevent a reopening of Bozeman's emigrant road into Montana Territory, hampered the activity of prospectors in the Yellowstone region during 1866. Only one incursion into the area has been recorded, and that small party, led by George Huston, entered from the west, up the Madison River, passing from the geyser basins to the Mud Volcano by way of the "east fork" (Nez Perce Creek), around the west side of Yellowstone Lake to Heart Lake, then across rough country to the Yellowstone River above its lake. From there they followed the eastern shore to the outlet, descended the river to the great falls and across the Mirror Plateau to the east fork of the Yellowstone (Lamar River), after which they passed down that stream and the Yellowstone to Emigrant Gulch.[101]

How much factual information Huston's far-ranging party brought back is unknown, for contemporary reportage is lacking; but enough was known of the Yellowstone region and its superlative nature to allow the editor of Montana's first newspaper to compare it with the Yosemite Valley, in these words:

> The scenery of the Yosemite Valley, as described by Bowles in his new book, "Across the Continent," though very grand and peculiar, is not more remarkable than the scenery at the passage of the Yellowstone through the Snowy Range, one hundred miles northeast of this city. The rocks on either side, for a great distance, are equal in height to those of the Yosemite, and the river steals through them with the swiftness and stillness of an immense serpent, leaping into joyous rapids at the point of its release. We should like to have Brierstadt [sic] visit this portion of our Territory. He could make a picture from this piece of scenery surpassing either of his other views of the Rocky Mountains.[102]

The death of John Bozeman at the hands of Indians early in 1867 led Acting Governor Thomas Francis Meagher to raise and arm "territorial volunteers" who built and occupied two posts intended to serve as barriers against incursions of hostile Indians into the settlements of southwestern Montana. These outposts—Fort Elizabeth Meagher, east of the town of Bozeman, and Camp Ida Thoroughman, at the mouth of Shield's River—

effectively screened the northern approach to the Yellowstone region, allowing a resumption of prospecting in that wilderness.

Interest had been sparked anew by the luck of "Uncle" Joe Brown and three others, who worked a river bar at the mouth of Bear Creek during the fall and winter of 1866–67, taking out $8,000 in gold dust and nuggets. "A. Patron," writing from that place as spring came, publicized their good fortune in a Helena newspaper through his mention that "the bright scales of 22 ounce gold peculiar to this locality have been washing down the Yellowstone in liberal, unmeasured quantities of late, showing that there must be a heavy deposit above."[103]

Among those attracted to the Bear Creek strike was Lou Anderson, who soon moved on up the Yellowstone with a small party. This search for the lode is of interest because of its legacy of three place-names. According to E. S. Topping, the circumstances which generated the names were these:

> Early in the summer of 1867, Lou Anderson . . . with [A. H.] Hubble [George W.] Reese, Caldwell and another man, went up the river on the east side. They found gold in a crevice at the mouth of the first stream above Bear, and named it in consequence, Crevice gulch. Hubble went ahead the next day for a hunt and upon his return he was asked what kind of a stream the next creek was. "It's a hell roarer," was his reply, and Hell Roaring is its name to this day.
>
> The second day after this he [Hubble] was again ahead, and the same question being asked him, he said. "Twas but a slough." When the party came to it they found a rushing torrent, and in crossing, a pack horse and his load were swept away, but the name of Slough Creek remains.[104]

Early that summer a notice appeared in the Virginia City newspaper, announcing:

> Organized. The expedition to the Yellowstone country mentioned a short time since, is now organized, and it is the purpose of the party to start from the camp on Shield's river in about two weeks. The expedition will be gone some three weeks and will go up the river as far as Yellowstone Lake. As a number of gentlemen have expressed a desire to join the party, we refer those in Helena to Gen. Thoroughman who will be at that city on Monday, and will give all desired information. Parties here, who have the leisure to make this fascinating jaunt can ascertain particulars from Judge Hosmer or T. C. Everts.[105]

But that proposal, which appears to have originated in Acting Governor Meagher's interest in the Yellowstone region (of which more will be said in Part II), was vitiated by his death in the Missouri River at Fort Benton on the eve of departure.

However, the mounting interest in the diggings developing along the Yellowstone River was not lost on the unpaid citizen-soldiers lounging around Camp Thoroughman (renamed Camp Green Clay Smith after Meagher's death),[106] and, though their morale was low with regard to all things military, they were willing enough to accompany Capt. Charley Curtis on a scout up the river.[107]

This expedition was reported in the Virginia City newspaper from information supplied by Dr. James Dunlevy, surgeon for the volunteers, and, though egocentric and couched in hyperbole (possibly an editorial fault), it is yet a very interesting impression, of value for its glimpse of the Mammoth Hot Springs. Here is Dunlevy's account as rendered by an unidentified "B.G."[108]

Dr. Dunlevy left Camp Green Clay Smith, near the mouth of the Yellowstone Canyon, about the 12th ult., with a small party, following up the western side of the river for about ninety or one hundred miles,[109] and within a few miles of the lake near the head of this great river; traveling through a valley of great extent, richness and beauty, interspersed with scenery of most impressive grandeur and magnitude, unsurpassed in the world. Tall spires of colossal grandeur which in beauty and symmetry are superior to any works of art; beetling cliffs of rock, rising from the waters edge thousands of feet in height; while wood-crowned mountains, with delightful slopes and vista like parks coursed with purling streams and mountains covered with snows, capped and rising to cone shaped peaks and knife-like edges, or turretted like castles, and rolling away off in beautiful white pyramidal forms, were to be seen on every side. Language is not adequate to convey an idea of the marvelous beauty of the scenery, which is beyond the power of description, and begets a wonderful fascination in the mind of the beholder who reverently gazes at the snow-crowned summits, that seem as if "They were to show How earth may pierce to Heaven and leave vain man below." In addition to this, Dr. Dunlevy informs us that he discovered several large streams coming in from the western side, that are yet unnamed. When near the end of his journey his attention was called to something resembling steam or smoke, near the crest of a mountain, and observing springs of hot water gushing out of its side, he was induced to attempt to reach it, which he succeeded in accomplishing with very little trouble, there to find something that proved to be the key-stone to the arch of wonders— a boiling hot lake, covering an area of about forty acres![110] A herd of antelope were quietly licking the salt along the edge, when a shot from his rifle brought one of them down, a sheath-knife soon severed off a ham which was fastened to a lariat and thrown into the lake, and in less than forty minutes it was taken out completely boiled and salted![111] The party ate of it and represented it as having a peculiar but pleasant flavor. The Doctor supposed the water to contain a large percentage of tincal, the crude property from which borax is manufactured, and has already taken the necessary steps to have it preempted and a company organized to have it thoroughly tested. . . . We have not the space to give an elaborate report of Dr. Dunlevy's trip, but can only say that it abounded in the rarest scenes and incidents, equalling almost the experience of Captains Speke and Grant, in their effort to discover the source of the Nile; and we trust ere long that some select party, well prepared and equipped, will be able to penetrate these wilds and reveal to the world its manifest beauties, existing as they do in all their pristine grandeur. The Doctor deserves credit for the daring, invincible spirit displayed by him in thus far exploring this remote region, which example we trust will be emulated by many others. He was compelled to return to camp as his time was limited, and what matches he had with him became dampened and spoiled. He reports the country filled with game of all kinds, including mountain bison, and reports mining in three different gulches on the eastern side of the river, including Bear and Emigrant gulches."

Prospectors returning to Yellowstone City (at the mouth of Emigrant Gulch) late in August had some information on the country between Mammoth Hot Springs and Lake Yellowstone, and some of it was forwarded to a Virginia City newspaper by David Weaver, a miner who was laboring in the shafts and drains then being constructed to get at the gold below Emigrant Gulch. He says:[112]

A portion of the Bear Gulch stampeders have returned. They have been to the Lake at the head of Yellowstone and report the greatest wonder of the age. For eight days they traveled thro' a volcanic country emitting blue flames, living streams of molten brimstone, and almost every variety of minerals known to chemists. The appearance of the country was smooth and rolling, with long level plains intervening. On the summits of these rolling mounds [Crater Hills] were craters from four to eight feet in diameter; and everywhere upon the level plains, dotting it like prairie dog holes, were smaller ones, from four to six inches and upwards. The steam and blaze was constantly discharging from these subterranean channels in regular evolutions or exhaustions, like the boilers of our steamboats, and gave the same roaring, whistling sound. As far as the eye could trace, this motion was observed. They were fearful to ascend to the craters lest the thin crust should give way and swallow them. Mr. Hubbel, (one of the party,) who has visited this region before, ventured to approach one of the smaller ones. As he neared its mouth his feet broke through and the blue flame and smoke gushed forth, enveloping him. Dropping upon his body, he crawled to within a couple of feet of the crater and saw that the crust around its edge was like a thin wafer. Lighting a match he extended it to the mouth and instantly it was on fire.[113] The hollow ground resounded beneath their feet as they travelled on, and every moment it seemed liable to break through and bury them in its fiery vaults. The atmosphere was intensely suffocating, and they report that life could not long be sustained there. Not a living thing, bird or beast, was seen in the vicinity. The prospectors have given it the significant name—"Hell!" They declare they have been to that "bad place," and even seen the "Devil's horns"; but through the interposition of Providence (not to speak profanely) their "souls have been delivered", and they emphatically aver, if a "straight and narrow" course during their sojourn on the Yellowstone will save them, they will never go there again. On their return, between the Lake and the falls, they encountered four men on four splendid American horses, driving thirty-six large mules, in fine condition, all branded "U.S." Said individuals wore linen dusters and heavy gold rings on their fingers—travelled southward—understood the country—acted suspiciously, and that's all that's known.[114]

Another party of prospectors passed through the Yellowstone region in the fall of 1867, and, though their venturing did not come to the attention of the local newspapers, the diary kept by one of them, A. Bart Henderson, contains the best account of the area to come out of the era of the prospectors.[115] This party entered what is now Yellowstone Park at its southeast corner after coming up Snake River and over Two Ocean Pass, as the trappers had earlier.

> [p. 76] Aug. 30th 1867. It was from this camp [near Bridger Lake] that we first looked upon the far-famed Yellowstone Lake, about 15 miles northwest.
>
> We were at a very great loss to know what it was. Capt. Bracey said he would soon settle that question & let us know the facts. He soon had Capt DeLacys map spread on the grass, tracing out the different rivers that he found marked on the map.[116]
>
> The Yellowstone Lake he soon found to be 15 miles long & 5 miles wide. This was all contrary to what we could see with our own eyes . . .
>
> However we all concluded that we was on the Yellow Stone, & in sight of the famous lake.

Henderson's party moved northward to Yellowstone Lake, where they came upon a lone Englishman—Jack Jones, called by them "John Bull"— who was traveling afoot through the wilderness. He was taken with them as they moved down the eastern shore of the lake. While camped at Sedge Creek, the party made two interesting discoveries: the parasitic worms (*Bulbodacnitis scotti*) which they found infesting many of the lake trout, and the wave-formed stones they thought to be relics of the Aztec Indians. The Washburn party gave the name "Curiosity Point" to the beach where the latter were found.

A less agreeable discovery, on the following day, of "about 80 barefooted tracks, fresh made" (presumably by Blackfoot Indians), caused the Henderson party to change course abruptly by swimming Yellowstone River a short distance above its Upper Fall. While their supplies and equipage were drying in the sun, Henderson went to view the falls, an experience he described in these words:

> I was very much surprised to see the water disappear from sight. [p. 80] I walked out on a rock & made two steps at the same time, one forward, the other backward, for I had unawares as it were, looked down into the depths or bowels of the earth, into which the Yellow plunged as if to cool the infernal region that lay under all this wonderful country of lava & boiling springs. The water fell several feet, struck a reef of rock that projected further than the main rock above. This reef caused the water to fall the remainder of the way in spray. We judged the falls to be 80 or 90 feet high, perhaps higher [Upper Fall is 109 feet].

From the falls of the Yellowstone, Henderson's party crossed the Washburn Range on a dim Indian trail to Tower Fall,[117] which was recognized by Henderson as "the most beautiful falls I ever saw." Henderson commented on other important features as his party continued down the river to Emigrant Gulch.

The Yellowstone region was well enough known by the close of 1867 that at least one frontier journalist was led to prophesy its future. Called "a correspondent of the *Frontier Index*," but probably editor Legh Freeman himself,[118] an informant writes as follows concerning the country at the headwaters of the Yellowstone:

> Two main forks of the Yellowstone—one heading opposite Wind and Green rivers, and the other opposite Henry's Fork of Snake river, in the same vicinity that the Madison and Gallatin rise—empty into the big lake which has for its outlet the Yellowstone river, and just below the lake the whole river falls over the face of a mountain thousands of feet, the spray rising several hundred. A pebble was timed by a watch in dropping from an overhanging crag of one perpendicular fall, and is said to have required eleven and a half seconds to strike the river below. That beat Niagara Falls all "hollow". The river at these greatest falls is represented to be half as large as the Missouri at Omaha, and as clear as crystal. The great lake, like all others in these mountains, is thick with salmon trout of from five to forty pounds weight, and where the milky boiling mineral waters from the star bolt geysers intermingle with the pure, clear water from the running streams, elegant fish can be forked up by the boat load. A few years more and the U.P. Railroad will bring thousands of pleasure-seekers, sight-seers, and invalids from every part of the globe, to see this land of surpassing wonders.[119]

While the foregoing account contains some blatant exaggerations, it was at least founded upon truth, and that could not be said of another news item which appeared at nearly the same time. According to this story, which was reprinted from an eastern paper,

> Mr. Edward Parsons, just returned from Montana, tells the editor of the *Leavenworth Commercial* a marvelous story. Last July, himself and four companions, while exploring the headwaters of the Yellowstone, came upon an Indian mound, surmounted by a huge stone. Dislodging this stone and several others, they found themselves in an Indian catacomb, containing the skeletons of thirty warriors. Lying beside the bones were numerous ornaments, among them many twisted circlets of gold. Some of these were of unusual size, weighing one and a half to two pounds. What chiefly attracted attention was a massive basin or kettle that occupied the centre of the apartment. This massive article proved to be pure gold, and was so heavy that the party had great difficulty in removing it from its resting place and bringing it into the upper air. The adventurers were enabled, by means of their axes, to sever the mass into portable pieces, laden with which, the party turned their steps homeward, having themselves to walk the greater part of the way, to give relief to their burdened animals. The whole amount of gold was brought to Helena, and Mr. Edward Parsons calculated that his share of the treasure amounted to about $21,000, the whole bulk being at least $100,000 in value.[120]

In 1868, Legh Freeman continued to publish stories and items about the Yellowstone region. However, his verities were so often obscured by Munchausen details that the effect was to discredit the area's wonders rather than to expose them. The wildest of these tales was his "Greatest Bear Story Yet"—an outrageous distortion of known facts and current tall tales, of which the following are examples:[121]

> I looked up the petrified tree, and out on a petrified limb saw a petrified bird singing; a petrified song sticking out his mouth about ten

petrified feet. Looking down, I saw that the ground was covered with petrified balls like sycamore balls, and from these a considerable forest was growing up and stretching away to the east.

This is the largest and strangest mountain lake in the world. It being sixty by twenty-five miles in size and surrounded by all manner of large game, including an occasional white buffalo, that is seen to rush down the perpetual snowy peaks that tower above, and plunge up to its sides into the water. It is filled with fish half as large as a man, some of which have a mouth and horns and skin like a catfish and legs like a lizzard. This cross range backs up the waters from the head tributaries of the Yellowstone, and thus the lake is formed; and where the water of the lake breaks over the northern face of this cross ridge, there is a perpendicular fall of fifteen hundred feet over one cliff, which is by far the highest fall of any large river, and considering the surrounding scenery, is the most sublime spot on earth.

The foregoing, with the remainder of Freeman's article, could be consigned to oblivion except that it was so widely read and so influential in creating that reputation for "indulging in flights of fancy when recounting their adventures" with which the prospectors were generally branded. Freeman was almost factual in a later issue, where he compared certain areas of the Sierra Nevada Range with the "Yellowstone Hell,"[122] and less-so, still later, when describing Yellowstone Lake as "so clear and so deep, that by looking into it you can see them making tea in China."[123] Just before an enraged mob put The *Frontier Index* out of business by burning its boxcar-office during a riot at Green River City, Wyo., Freeman published a last comment on the Yellowstone region, repeating his prophesy of a year earlier. This followed a reprint of a description of the American Falls, on Snake River, published earlier in the *Idaho Statesman*, concerning which he remarked:

Ha! Mr. *Statesman*, you should pass over the divide from the head of Snake river and go through the great volcanic region about the Yellowstone lake, on down to the great Yellowstone Falls, fifteen miles below the lower neck of the lake and view a crystal stream as large as Snake river, as it falls over one perpendicular precipice, where we threw down a pine log, which was 11½ seconds striking the river below. Make your own calculations for rates of velocity of falling bodies and see if the Yellowstone Falls are not about six times as great as Niagara. How are your Shoshone Falls? We will show you a summer resort on the Yellowstone in a few years, at which the gentry of all nations will be recreating.[124]

The era of the prospector extends through 1870, when gold was discovered at the head of the Clark Fork of the Yellowstone (the area around present Cooke City, Mont.). The party which made that strike included A. Bart Henderson, whose diary records the appearance of several place names, and a brief fight with Indians, during their wanderings in the northern and eastern reaches of the present park. Descending Hell Roaring Creek, they turned eastward across the Buffalo Plateau, which received its name from them.

Wyoming Territory, June 21, 1870. Clear & warm. Raised camp early. Followed down the stream east. Here the hills come down on both sides forming a very rough cañon. We turned to the left, crossed a low divide or gap, & came to a beautiful flat, which we gave the name of Buffalo Flat [Buffalo Plateau], as we found thousands of buffalo quietly grazing. This flat is something like 10 miles by 6, with numerous lakes scattered over it, & the finest range in the world. Here we found all manner of wild game—buffalo, elk, blacktail deer, bear & moose. Camped here.[125]

From Buffalo Plateau this party moved north and east, investigating the headwaters of Buffalo and Slough Creeks (discovering both gold and grizzly bears at Lake Abundance) before descending to Clark Fork River. There they made the strike which developed into the New World Mining District, though they did no more than prospect at that time. Instead of settling down, those restless men crossed the mountains south of Pilot and Index Peaks, hoping to do even better. Their odyssey is recorded thus by Henderson:

[p. 92] 22nd [July, 1870] Clear & cold. Raised camp early. Traveled south, came down on a very rough stream [Cache Creek], high lava peaks on both sides. The country soon changes to open rolling hills [with] fine grass [and] game trails running in all directions. Here we camped at the forks for the purpose of prospecting.[126] Found no gold. This days travel was south, thro buffalo, elk & bear—all very tame.
23rd Cloudy & cold. Raised camp early [and] followed down [p. 93] creek in south direction. 8 miles below came to open country on the East Fork [Lamar River] of the Yellowstone.
   Here we found thousands of hot or boiling springs.[127] Camped on East Fork, south side. Just opposite camp a small creek empties into river. One mile up this creek is a very singular butte, some 40 feet high, which has been formed by soda water. We gave the cone the name of Soda butte, & the creek the name of Soda Butte Creek.

The prospectors then descended Lamar River to its mouth, doubled back along the Specimen Ridge-Amethyst Mountain divide to Flint Creek, where they descended to Lamar River again. They then moved up that stream to the Little Lamar River, which was ascended to the high country between the drainages of Lamar River, Sunlight Creek, and the North Fork of Shoshone River. It was there, just as they had reached what they recognized as mining country (later the Sunlight Mining District), that they were attacked by Indians who made off with their animals.[128] The result was the abandonment of most of their outfit and a retreat across the northeast corner of the present park toward succor at the Crow Agency (Fort Parker, near present Livingston, Mont.). Their escape was a harrowing experience made worse by dissension, an attack by wolves at the mouth of Miller Creek,[129] and another brush with Indians wherein they followed the rule of "shoot first and ask questions later."[130]

   A story which appeared in the *Helena Daily Herald* that summer, though a complete phony both in its description of Yellowstone geography and in the central event—the supposed death of 18 Indians at the Falls of the

Yellowstone[131]—does expose an attitude which was, by then, common among the prospectors. Despite the fact that Crows killed Crandall and Daugherty, and Arapahos were behind the attack on the Henderson party (this according to James Gourley), the inoffensive "sheep-eater" residents of the Yellowstone region tended to get the blame, and nowhere is this more obvious than in Sunderlee's statement:

> We felt no great uneasiness however, knowing full well that with our improved firearms, we would be enabled to overcome fifty of the sneaking red devils. It is proper here to add, that the "Sheep Eaters" are those of the Snake and Bannack tribes, who would not live with their brethren in peace with the whites; but who prefer living remote from all Indians, and civilized beings: foes of their former tribes and of the whites. A body of savages who would gladly welcome death in preference to capture, either by the white man or red man; hated and hunted by their former associates, they are compelled to seek asylum in the mountains, where it is so sterile that no game but the wild sheep abound. Here they exist as best they can, which is but little removed from starvation.

That was not true in any respect, but it was so generally believed as to constitute a very real danger for the Shoshoni-Bannock "sheep-eaters" who were living in the Yellowstone region in the old way of pre-horse days. Thus, they willingly accepted Chief Washakie's invitation to join his Shoshonis on the Wind River Reservation in 1871, and abandoned their Yellowstone home forever.

The body of knowledge concerning the Yellowstone region made available by the explorers, trappers, and prospectors of this period, though extensive, was yet fragmentary and often contradictory, and it did not constitute a comprehensive view of the Yellowstone region and its wonders. Such a picture of the area only materialized out of definitive exploration.

41

PART II

Definitive Knowledge

A systematic knowledge of the Yellowstone region resulted from the explorations of the Folsom party (1869), the Washburn party (1870), and the Hayden party (1871). Their combined efforts provided a basis for the reservation of the Yellowstone wonders in the public interest.

Background for Exploration

The exploring parties of 1869, 1870, and 1871, whose cumulative accomplishment was a definitive knowledge of the Yellowstone region, were a direct outgrowth of an earlier interest in the area's wonders. Thus, it is necessary to go back a few years for the genesis of those efforts through which the true nature of "wonderland" became generally recognized.

An incidental outcome of the visit of Father Francis Xavier Kuppens to the Yellowstone region in the company of Blackfoot Indians in the spring of 1865 (see Part I) was his relation of that experience to a party of gentlemen who were stormbound for several days at the old St. Peter's Mission near the mouth of Sun River the following October. These men, among whom were acting Territorial Governor Thomas Francis Meagher, Territorial Judges H. L. Hosmer and Lyman E. Munson, two deputy U.S. Marshals—X. Beidler and Neil Homie—and a young lawyer named Cornelius Hedges, were traveling from Helena to Fort Benton to assist in negotiating a treaty with the Piegan Indians when overwhelmed by a sudden, savage blizzard and forced to seek shelter at the mission.

Hedges says: ". . . We were received with a warm welcome and all our wants were abundantly supplied and we were in condition to appreciate our royal entertainment."[1] Concerning the story-telling with which the time was passed during that stay at the mission, Father Kuppens adds:[2]

> On that occasion I spoke to him [Meagher] about the wonders of the Yellowstone. His interest was greatly aroused by my recital and perhaps even more so, by that of a certain Mr. Viell[3]—an old Canadian married to a Blackfoot squaw—who during a lull in the storm had come over to see the distinguished visitors. When he was questioned about the Yellowstone he described everything in a most graphic manner. None of the visitors had ever heard of the wonderful place. Gen. Meagher said if things were as described the government ought to reserve the territory for a national park. All the visitors agreed that efforts should be made to explore the region and that a report of it should be sent to the government.

As previously mentioned, the Indian unrest occasioned by the opening of the Bozeman Trail route prevented an implementation of Meagher's suggestion during 1866, and, when conditions were at last satisfactory for

45

an expedition into the Yellowstone region—through establishment of Fort Elizabeth Meagher and Camp Ida Thoroughman by the Montana volunteers early in 1867—the tragic death of Acting Governor Meagher cooled the enthusiasm of most of the gentlemen who had made plans to explore the headwaters of the Yellowstone River. While a party did go as far as Mammoth Hot Springs (the Curtis-Dunlevy expedition mentioned in Part I), their visit was essentially a prospecting junket.

No effort was made during 1868 to organize a general exploration of the Yellowstone region, at least so far as the public records show; but there was individual interest in such a project. Of this, Charles W. Cook says:

> The first attempt made by me to make an exploration trip to the headwaters of the Yellowstone and Madison rivers was in 1868. At that time I had charge of the "Boulder Ditch Company" at Diamond City. A Mr. Clark, who as I remember, was connected with some mining operations was at Diamond City, and since there was no hotel, was staying at the "Ditch Office." I found he had traveled extensively and had, at times contributed articles to magazines. I told him about the region at the headwaters of the Yellowstone and Madison rivers, which had not been explored, and he became very much interested. We went to Helena to see H. H. McGuire, who published a paper called the *Pick and Plow* at Bozeman, Montana, but who was at that time visiting Helena. Mr. McGuire advised us that since it was getting late, being then about the middle of September, it was not best to attempt the trip that year.[4]

The following summer, 1869, there was a renewed interest in implementing Meagher's suggestion that the Yellowstone region should be explored. This was publicized in the *Helena Herald*, in an item announcing:

> A letter from Fort Ellis, dated the 19th, says that an expedition is organizing, composed of soldiers and citizens, and will start for the upper waters of the Yellowstone the latter part of August, and will hunt and explore a month or so. Among the places of note which they will visit, are the Falls, Coulter's Hell and Lake, and the Mysterious Mounds. The expedition is regarded as a very important one, and the result of their explorations will be looked forward to with unusual interest.[5]

That notice is undoubtedly the "rumor" which Cook notes as inducing himself and his friend, David E. Folsom, to hold themselves "in readiness to make the trip," to which he adds:

> . . . but sometime in the month of August, not having heard from the party, I made a trip to Helena to find out if anyone intended going, and was unable to find anyone who had any intention of making the trip that year. After I returned to Diamond City, David E. Folsom and William Peterson volunteered to make the trip with me.[6]

The manner in which that decision—certainly no trivial one—was arrived at is indicated in the reminiscences of William Peterson:

> Myself and two friends—Charley Cook and D. E. Folsom who worked

for the same company at Diamond that I did—after having made a trip to Helena to join the big party and finding out that they were not going to go, decided to go ourselves. It happened this way: When we got back from Helena, Cook says, "If I could get one man to go with me, I'd go anyway." I spoke up and said, "Well, Charley, I guess I can go as far as you can," and Folsom says, "Well, I can go as far as both of ye's," and the next thing it was, "Shall we go?" and then, "When shall we start?" We decided to go and started next day . . . .[7]

The Folsom Party

(1869)

Fifty-three years later Cook recalled that start, and the attitude with which friends viewed their venture, quoting thus from his diary:

The long-talked-of expedition to the Yellowstone is off at last but shorn of the prestige attached to the names of a score of the brightest luminaries in the social firmament of Montana, as it was first announced. It has assumed proportions of utter insignificance, and of no importance to anybody in the world except the three actors themselves. Our leave-taking from friends who had assembled to see us start this morning was impressive, in the highest degree and rather cheering withal. "Good-bye, boys, look out for your hair." "If you get into a scrap, remember I warned you." "If you get back at all you will come on foot." "It is the next thing to suicide," etc. etc., were the parting salutations that greeted our ears as we put spurs to our horses and left home and friends behind.[8]

Following their return from the Yellowstone region these explorers were reluctant to prepare an account of what they had seen, for, as Folsom later commented, "I doubted if any magazine editor would look upon a truthful description in any other light than the production of the too-vivid imagination of a typical Rocky Mountain liar."[9] However, they soon received an encouragement which was irresistible. According to Cook, it happened this way:

Soon after my return from the trip of 1869, I received a letter from Mr. Clark, a friend whom I had met the previous year, stating that he had read that an expedition to the source of the Yellowstone and Madison rivers had been contemplated, and, supposing of course that I was with it, wanted to know what we had discovered. I at once answered this letter, giving him some idea of our trip and discoveries. He at once replied and asked for a writeup of all details. I then took the matter up with Mr. Folsom and, as we had not much to do that winter at the "Ditch Company," we prepared an amplified diary by working over both the diaries made on the trip, and combining them into one. . . . Mr. Folsom then added to this diary a preliminary statement, and I forwarded the same to Mr. Clark. He wrote back at once asking my permission to have it published to which request we gave our consent. Later I received a letter from Mr. Clark stating that he

47

had made an effort to have our amplified diary published in the *New York Tribune*, and also in *Scribner's* or *Harper's* magazines, but both refused to consider it for the reason that "they had a reputation that they could not risk with such unreliable material." Finally, he secured its publication in the *Western Monthly Magazine*, published at Chicago, Illinois, and received, as a compensation, the sum of $18.00. The condition in which this amplified diary appeared in the June number of the *Western Monthly Magazine* was neither the fault of Mr. Folsom nor myself, as the editor cut out portions of the diary which destroyed its continuity, so far as giving a reliable description of our trip and the regions explored.

In the original article, I alone, was credited with writing the article, but later, when a reprint was made of it by N. P. Langford, he credited it to D. E. Folsom, neither of which are correct. We did not sign the diary sent to Mr. Clark, and, as he did not know Mr. Folsom but had carried on the correspondence with me, he had it credited to me; but the actual facts are as above outlined.[10]

David E. Folsom, Charles W. Cook, and William Peterson left Diamond City, Mont., on September 6, 1869, traveling with saddle and pack animals to the Gallatin Valley. At the town of Bozeman, where they obtained provisions, an attempt was made to recruit some of the townsmen into their enterprise, but without success; however, they did receive some valuable information from George Phelps, one of the prospectors who had returned through the Yellowstone region following the breakup of James Stuart's expedition down the Yellowstone River and into the Wyoming Basin in 1864. From Bozeman the three explorers took the miner's route, by way of Meadow and Trail Creeks, to the Yellowstone River nearly opposite Emigrant Gulch. The account is continued from that point mainly with excerpts from the Cook-Folsom article as it appeared in 1870.[11]

We pushed on up the valley, following the general course of the river as well as we could, but frequently making short *detours* through the foot-hills, to avoid the deep ravines and places where the hills terminated abruptly at the water's edge. On the eighth day out, we encountered a band of Indians—who, however, proved to be Tonkeys, or Sheepeaters, and friendly; the discovery of their character relieved our minds of apprehension, and we conversed with them as well as their limited knowledge of English and ours of pantomine would permit.[12] For several hours after leaving them, we travelled over a high rolling table-land, diversified by sparkling lakes, picturesque rocks, and beautiful groves of timber. Two or three miles to our left, we could see the deep gorge which the river, flowing westward, had cut through the mountains.[13] The river soon after resumed its northern course; and from this point to the falls, a distance of twenty-five or thirty miles, it is believed to flow through one continuous *cañon*, through which no one has ever been able to pass.[14]

At this point we left the main river, intending to follow up the east branch for one day, then to turn in a southwest course and endeavor to strike the river again near the falls. After going a short distance, we encountered a *cañon* about three miles in length, and while passing around it we caught a glimpse of scenery so grand and striking that we decided to stop for a day or two and give it a more extended examination.[15] We picked our way to a timbered point about mid-way of the *cañon*, and found ourselves upon the verge of an overhanging cliff at least seven hundred feet in height. The opposite bluff was about on a level with the place where we were standing; and it maintained this height for a mile up the river, but gradually sloped away toward the foot of the *cañon*. The upper half presented an unbroken face, with here and there a re-entering angle, but everywhere maintained its perpendicularity; the lower half was composed of the *debris* that had fallen from the wall. But the most singular feature was the formation of the perpendicular wall. At the top, there was a stratum of basalt, from thirty to forty feet thick, standing in hexagonal columns; beneath that, a bed of conglomerate eighty feet thick, composed of washed gravel and boulders; then another stratum of columnar basalt of about half the thickness of the first; and lastly what appeared to be a bed of coarse sandstone. A short distance above us, rising from the bed of the river, stood a monument or pyramid of conglomerate, circular in form, which we estimated to be forty feet in diameter at the base, and three hundred feet high, diminishing in size in a true taper to its top, which was not more than three feet across. It was so slender that it looked as if one man could topple it over. How it was formed I leave others to conjecture.[16] We could see the river for nearly the whole distance through the *cañon*—now dashing over some miniature cataract, now fretting against huge boulders that seemed to have been hurled by some giant hand to stay its progress, and anon circling in quiet eddies beneath the dark shadows of some projecting rock. The water was so transparent that we could see the bottom from where we were standing, and it had that peculiar liquid emerald tinge so characteristic of our mountain streams.

Half a mile down the river, and near the foot of the bluff, was a chalky-looking bank, from which steam and smoke were rising; and on repairing to the spot, we found a vast number of hot sulphur springs.[17] The steam was issuing from every crevice and hole in the rocks; and, being highly impregnated with sulphur, it threw off sulphuretted hydrogen, making a stench that was very unpleasant. All the crevices were lined with beautiful crystals of sulphur, as delicate as frost-work. At some former period, not far distant, there must have been a volcanic eruption here. Much of the *scoria* and ashes which were then thrown out has been carried off by the river, but enough still remains to form a bar, seventy-five or a hundred feet in depth. Smoke was still issuing from the rocks in one place, from which a considerable amount of lava had been discharged within a few days or weeks at farthest. While we were standing by, several gallons of a black liquid ran down and hardened upon the rocks; we broke some of this off and brought it away, and it proved to be sulphur, pure enough to burn readily when ignited.[18]

Reference to the reconstructed account (1965, pp. 26–29) shows that the editor of the *Western Monthly* cut out that portion of the original manuscript covering the crossing of Yellowstone River, the journey up Lamar River to the mouth of Calfee Creek, and the ascent of Flint Creek to a storm-bound encampment below the rim of Mirror Plateau. The magazine account resumes at that point:

September 18th—the twelfth day out—we found that ice had formed one-fourth of an inch thick during the night, and six inches of snow had fallen. The situation began to look a little disagreeable; but the next day was bright and clear, with promise of warm weather again in a few days. Resuming our journey, we soon saw the serrated peaks of the Big Horn Range glistening like burnished silver in the sunlight, and, over-towering them in the dim distance, the Wind River Mountains seemed to blend with the few fleecy clouds that skirted their tops;[19] while in the opposite direction, in contrast to the barren snow-capped peaks behind us, as far as the eye could reach, mountain and valley were covered with timber, whose dark green foliage deepened in hue as it receded, till it terminated at the horizon in a boundless black forest. Taking our bearings as well as we could, we shaped our course in the direction in which we supposed the falls to be.

The next day (September 20th), we came to a gentle declivity at the head of a shallow ravine, from which steam rose in a hundred columns and united in a cloud so dense as to obscure the sun. In some places it spurted from the rocks in jets not larger than a pipe-stem; in others it curled gracefully up from the surface of boiling pools from five to fifteen feet in diameter. In some springs the water was clear and transparent; others contained so much sulphur that they looked like pots of boiling yellow paint. One of the largest was as black as ink. Near this was a fissure in the rocks, several rods long and two feet across in the widest place at the surface, but enlarging as it descended. We could not see down to any great depth, on account of the steam; but the ground echoed beneath our tread with a hollow sound, and we could hear the waters surging below, sending up a dull, resonant roar like the break of the ocean surf into a cave. At these springs but little water was discharged at the surface, it seeming to pass off by some subterranean passage. About half a mile down the ravine, the springs broke out again. Here they were in groups, spreading out over several acres of ground. One of these groups—a collection of mud springs of various colors, situated one above the other on the left slope of the ravine—we christened "The Chemical Works."[20] The mud, as it was discharged from the lower side, gave each spring the form of a basin or pool. At the bottom of the slope was a vat, ten by thirty feet, where all the ingredients from the springs above were united in a greenish-yellow compound of the consistency of white lead. Three miles further on we found more hot springs along the sides of a deep ravine, at the bottom of which flowed a creek twenty feet wide.[21] Near the bank of the creek, through an aperture four inches in diameter, a column of steam rushed with a deafening roar, with such force that it maintained its size for forty feet in the air, then spread out and rolled away in a great cloud toward the heavens. We found here inexhaustible beds of sulphur and saltpetre. Alum was also abundant; a small pond in the vicinity, some three hundred yards long and half as wide, contained as much alum as it could hold in solution, and the mud along the shore was white with the same substance, crystallized by evaporation.

On September 21st, a pleasant ride of eighteen miles over an undulating country brought us to the great *cañon*, two miles below the falls;[22] but there being no grass convenient, we passed on up the river to a point half a mile above the upper falls, and camped on a narrow flat, close to the river bank.[23] We spent the next day at the falls—a day that was a succession of surprises; and we returned to camp realizing as we had never done before how utterly insignificant are man's mightiest efforts when compared with the fulfillment of Omnipotent will. Language is entirely inadequate to convey a just conception of the awful grandeur and sublimity of this masterpiece of nature's handiwork; and in my brief description I shall confine myself to bare facts. Above our camp the river is about one hundred and fifty yards wide, and glides smoothly along between gently-sloping banks; but just below, the hills crowd in on either side, forcing the water into a narrow channel, through which it hurries with increasing speed, until, rushing through a *chute* sixty feet wide, it falls in an unbroken sheet over a precipice one hundred and fifteen feet in height.[24] It widens out again, flows with steady course for half a mile between steep timbered bluffs four hundred feet high, and again narrowing in till it is not more than seventy-five feet wide, it makes the final fearful leap of three hundred and fifty feet.[25] The ragged edges of the precipice tear the water into a thousand streams—all united together, and yet apparently separate,—changing it to the appearance of molten silver; the outer ones decrease in size as they increase in velocity, curl outward, and break into mist long before they reach the bottom. This cloud of mist conceals the river for two hundred yards, but it dashes out from beneath the rainbow-arch that spans the chasm, and thence, rushing over a succession of rapids and cascades, it vanishes at last, where a sudden turn of the river seems to bring the two walls of the *cañon* together. Below the falls, the hills gradually increase in height for two miles, where they assume the proportions of mountains. Here the *cañon* is at least fifteen hundred feet deep, with an average width of twice that distance at the top. For one-third of the distance downwards the sides are perpendicular,—from thence running down to the river in steep ridges crowned by rocks of the most grotesque form and color; and it required no stretch of the imagination to picture fortresses, castles, watch-towers, and other ancient structures, of every conceivable shape. In several places near the bottom, steam issued from the rocks; and, judging from the indications, there were at some former period hot springs or steam-jets of immense size all along the wall.

The next day we resumed our journey, traversing the northern slope of a high plateau between the Yellowstone and Snake Rivers.[26] Unlike the dashing mountain-stream we had thus far followed, the Yellowstone was in this part of its course wide and deep, flowing with a gentle current along the foot of low hills, or meandering in graceful curves through broad and grassy meadows. Some twelve miles from the falls we came to a collection of hot springs that deserve more than a passing notice. These, like the most we saw, were situated upon a hillside; and as we approached them we could see the steam rising in puffs at regular intervals of fifteen or twenty seconds, accompanied by dull explosions which could be heard half a mile away, sounding like the discharge of a blast underground. These explosions came from a large cave that ran back under the hill,[27] from which mud had been discharged in such quantities as to form a heavy embankment twenty feet higher than the floor of the cave, which prevented the mud from flowing off; but the escaping steam had kept a hole, some twenty feet in diameter, open up through the mud in front of the entrance to the cave. The cave seemed nearly filled with mud, and the steam rushed out with such volume and force as to lift the whole mass up against the roof and dash it out into the open space in front; and then, as the cloud of steam lifted, we could see the mud settling back in turbid waves into the cavern again. Three hundred yards from the mud-cave was another that discharged pure water; the entrance to it was in the form of a perfect arch, seven feet in height and five in width.[28] A short distance below these caves were several large sulphur springs, the most remarkable of which was a shallow pool seventy-five feet in diameter, in which clear water on one side and yellow mud on the other were gently boiling without mingling.

September 24th we arrived at Yellowstone Lake,[29] about twenty miles from the falls. The main body of this beautiful sheet of water is ten miles wide from east to west, and sixteen miles long from north to south; but at the south end it puts out two arms, one to the southeast and the other to the southwest, making the entire length of the lake about thirty miles. Its shores—whether gently sloping mountains, bold promontories, low necks, or level prairies—are everywhere covered with timber. The lake has three small islands, which are also heavily timbered. The outlet is at the northwest extremity. The lake abounds with trout, and the shallow water in its coves affords feeding ground for thousands of wild ducks, geese, pelicans, and swans.

We ascended to the head of the lake,[30] and remained in its vicinity for several days, resting ourselves and our horses, and viewing the many objects of interest and wonder. Among these were springs differing from any we had previously seen. They were situated along the shore for a distance of two miles, extending back from it about five hundred yards and into the lake perhaps as many feet. The ground in many places gradually sloped down to the water's edge, while in others the white chalky cliffs rose fifteen feet high—the waves having worn the rock away at the base, leaving the upper portion projecting over in some places twenty feet. There were several hundred springs here, varying in size from miniature fountains to pools or wells seventy-five feet in diameter and of great depth; the water had a pale violet tinge, and was very clear, enabling us to discern small objects fifty or sixty feet below the surface. In some of these, vast openings led off at the side; and as the slanting rays of the sun lit up these deep caverns, we could see the rocks hanging from their roofs, their water-worn sides and rocky floors, almost as plainly as if we had been traversing their silent chambers. These springs were intermittent, flowing or boiling at irregular intervals. The greater portion of them were perfectly quiet while we were there, although nearly all gave unmistakable evidence of frequent activity. Some of them would quietly settle for ten feet, while another would as quietly rise until it overflowed its banks, and send a torrent of hot water sweeping down to the lake. At the same time, one near at hand would send up a sparkling jet of water ten or twelve feet high, which would fall back into its basin, and then perhaps instantly stop boiling and quietly settle into the earth, or suddenly rise and discharge its waters in every direction over the rim; while another, as if wishing to attract our wondering gaze, would throw up a cone six feet in diameter and eight feet high, with a loud roar. These changes, each one of which would possess some new feature, were constantly going on; sometimes they would occur within the space of a few minutes, and again hours would elapse before any change could be noted. At the water's edge, along the lake shore, there were several mounds of solid stone, on the top of each of which was a small basin with a perforated bottom; these also overflowed at times, and the hot water trickled down on every side. Thus, by the slow process of precipitation, through the countless lapse of ages, these stone monuments have been formed. A small cluster of mud springs near by claimed our attention.[31] They were like hollow truncated cones and oblong mounds, three or four feet in height. These were filled with mud, resembling thick paint of the finest quality—differing in color, from pure white to the various shades of yellow, pink, red, and violet. Some of these boiling pots were less than a foot in diameter. The mud in them would slowly rise and fall as the bubbles of escaping steam, following one after the other, would burst upon the surface. During the afternoon, they threw mud to the height of fifteen feet for a few minutes, and then settled back to their former quietude.

As we were about departing on our homeward trip, we ascended the summit of a neighboring hill, and took a final look at Yellowstone Lake. Nestled among the forest-crowned hills which bounded our vision, lay this inland sea, its crystal waves dancing and sparkling in the sunlight, as if laughing with joy for their wild freedom. It is a scene of transcendent beauty, which has been viewed by but few white men; and we felt glad to have looked upon it before its primeval solitude should be broken by the crowds of pleasure-seekers which at no distant day will throng its shores.[32]

September 29th, we took up our march for home. Our plan was to cross the range in a northwesterly direction, find the Madison River, and follow it down to civilization. Twelve miles brought us to a small triangular-shaped lake, about eight miles long, deeply set among the hills.[33] We kept on in a northwesterly direction, as near as the rugged nature of the country would permit; and on the third day (October 1st) came to a small irregularly shaped valley, some six miles across in the widest place, from every part of which great clouds of steam arose. From descriptions which we had had of this valley, from persons who had previously visited it, we recognized it as the place known as "Burnt Hole," or "Death Valley." The Madison River flows through it, and from the general contour of the country we knew that it headed in the lake which we passed two days ago,[34] only twelve miles from the Yellowstone. We descended into the valley, and found that the springs had the same general characteristics as those I have already described, although some of them were much larger and discharged a vast amount of water. One of them, at a little distance, attracted our attention by the immense amount of steam it threw off; and upon approaching it we found it to be an intermittent geyser in active operation.[35] The hole through which the water was discharged was ten feet in diameter, and was situated in the centre of a large circular shallow basin, into which the water fell. There was a stiff breeze blowing at the time, and by going to the windward side and carefully picking our way over convenient stones, we were enabled to reach the edge of the hole. At that moment the escaping steam was causing the water to boil up in a fountain five or six feet high. It stopped in an instant, and commenced settling down—twenty, thirty, forty feet—until we concluded that the bottom had fallen out; but the next instant, without any warning, it came rushing up and shot into the air at least eighty feet, causing us to stampede for higher ground. It continued to spout at intervals of a few minutes, for some time; but finally subsided, and was quiet during the remainder of the time we stayed in the vicinity. We followed up the Madison five miles, and there found the most gigantic hot springs we had seen. They were situated along the river bank, and discharged so much hot water that the river was blood-warm a quarter of a mile below. One of the springs was two hundred and fifty feet in diameter, and had every indication of spouting powerfully at times.[36] The waters from the hot springs in this valley, if united, would form a

53

large stream; and they increase the size of the river nearly one-half. Although we experienced no bad effects from passing through the "Valley of Death," yet we were not disposed to dispute the propriety of giving it that name.[37] It seemed to be shunned by all animated nature. There were no fish in the river, no birds in the trees, no animals—not even a track—anywhere to be seen; although in one spring we saw the entire skeleton of a buffalo that had probably fallen in accidentally and been boiled down to soup.

Leaving this remarkable valley, we followed the course of the Madison—sometimes through level valleys, and sometimes through deep cuts in mountain ranges,—and on the fourth of October emerged from a *cañon*, ten miles long and with high and precipitous mountain sides, to find the broad valley of the Lower Madison spread out before us. Here we could recognize familiar landmarks in some of the mountain peaks around Virginia City. From this point we completed our journey by easy stages, and arrived at home on the evening of the eleventh. We had been absent thirty-six days—a much longer time than our friends had anticipated;—and we found that they were seriously contemplating organizing a party to go in search of us.

Nathaniel P. Langford deprecated the importance of the foregoing Cook-Folsom article, stating:

The office of the *Western Monthly*, of Chicago, was destroyed by fire soon after the publication of Mr. Folsom's account of his discoveries, and the only copy of that magazine which he possessed, and which he presented to the Historical Society of Montana, met a like fate in the great Helena fire. The copy which I possess is perhaps the only one to be found.[38]

However, the office of the *Western Monthly*, or the *Lakeside Monthly* as it was called after 1870, was destroyed in the Chicago fire of October 3–9, 1871, so that subscribers had the July 1870 issue for well over a year prior to that holocaust, and it is not as rare as Langford supposed.

There is no way to judge the impact of the Cook-Folsom article, but there is evidence that the information brought back by the Folsom party of 1869 was influential in launching the Washburn party of 1870. N. P. Langford has testified to the inspirational value of this exploration in the following words:

On his return to Helena he [Folsom] related to a few of his intimate friends many of the incidents of his journey, and Mr. Samuel T. Hauser and I invited him to meet a number of the citizens of Helena at the director's room of the First National Bank in Helena; but on assembling there were so many present who were unknown to Mr. Folsom that he was unwilling to risk his reputation for veracity, by a full recital, in the presence of strangers, of the wonders he had seen. He said that he did not wish to be regarded as a liar by those who were unacquainted with his reputation. But the accounts which he gave to Hauser, Gillette and myself renewed in us our determination to visit that region during the following year.[39]

But encouragement was not the whole of Folsom's assistance to the Washburn party; he also provided geographical information. Soon after his return from the Yellowstone wilderness, Folsom took employment in the Helena office of the new Surveyor-General of Montana Territory, Henry D. Washburn. There, he worked with that other civil engineer and Yellowstone explorer, Walter W. deLacy, and together they turned out a noteworthy map.

This map,[40] which is endorsed over the signature of Commissioner Joseph S. Wilson of the General Land Office as "accompanying Commissioner's Annual Report for 1869," was dated at Helena, Mont., November 1, 1869—a mere 21 days after the return of the Folsom party to Diamond City. On it, the Yellowstone region was revealed in greater detail than ever before, and its portrayal was, at last, reasonably accurate (see map 9.). The "Route of Messrs Cook & Folsom 1869" was shown, and along that track, such prominent features as "Gardner's River," with its "Hot Spgs" (Mammoth Hot Springs); the "East Fork," now Lamar River, with "Burning Spring" (Calcite Springs) near its mouth; "Alum Creek" and some thermal features on Broad Creek; the falls of the Yellowstone (the upper noted as "115 ft." and the lower as "350 ft."); "Hot Spgs." noted at the Crater Hills and on Trout Creek, and a "Mud Spring" nearer the outlet of Yellowstone Lake (the Mud Volcano area). The lake was shown as a two-armed body of water, with a "Main Fork" (Upper Yellowstone River) discharging into the large, southern arm, and "Hot Spgs" on the west shore of the bulbous western arm. Interestingly, three islands were clearly shown in the lake (Stevenson, Dot, and Frank), and "Hot Springs" were noted on a point on the northeastern shore (Steamboat Point), and near Pelican Creek.

A new feature added by these explorers was a triangular "Madison Lake," placed west of Yellowstone Lake in accordance with their experience of coming down on the east shore of a large lake after traveling westward from the hot springs at West Thumb. This lake was not recognized for what it was—"Delacy's" or Shoshone Lake—because of an accumulation of mapping errors. Most Yellowstone features are positioned 15 or more miles too far to the west on this General Land Office map, and 11 to 20 miles too far to the north, when compared with present-day maps. However, "DeLacy's Lake," although similarly misplaced in its longitude, is shown only 2 miles north of the correct latitude for its outlet.[41] Thus, when the Folsom party found a large lake nearly 20 miles north of the map position of deLacy's, they failed to relate the two and added a lake which they presumed to be the head of the Madison River, hence its name.

On the Madison River, "Hot Springs" were shown at the head of its southern branch (Firehole River), and both "Hot Springs" and "Geysers" where the eastern branch—presumed to drain "Madison Lake"—joined the former stream. Except for the inconsistencies caused by the introduction of the fictitious "Madison Lake," and omission of Heart Lake and the headwaters of Snake River, the Cook-Folsom information had produced a reasonably good map. How much better it was than the map it superseded[42] is evident at a glance (see map 8).

The information brought back by the Folsom party soon appeared in another form of greater importance than the General Land Office map because of its wider distribution and the fact that a copy was carried through the Yellowstone region by the Washburn party of 1870. A comparison (see map 10), shows that this map had profited from the same improvements apparent on the 1869 General Land Office map, and the usefulness of this 1870 edition of the deLacy map to the Yellowstone explorers of that year is mentioned by Oscar O. Mueller, who says:

> Naturally after their return from the exploration trip, they [Cook and Folsom] gave the Surveyor General's Office every possible information they could regarding the region explored and what they had found. W. W. deLacy was employed by the Territory to prepare maps and, therefore, with the assistance of Mr. Folsom, prepared a new map of the Territory of Montana, showing also the north half of the Wyoming Territory. These maps were printed . . . [and] General Washburn took with him, on his exploration trip to the Yellowstone region in 1870, one of these maps and also a copy of the diary of Mr. Cook and Folsom. It can be readily seen, from the inspection of the map covering the Yellowstone region, how valuable an assistance it was to the 1870 expedition. Washburn and Langford were advised to seek a short cut from Tower Falls to the Yellowstone Canyon and Falls. It was this that made General Washburn leave the party at Tower Falls on a Sunday afternoon, and ride up to the top of what is now known as Mount Washburn, from which he could see that the short cut was feasible, and thus they deviated at that point from the route followed by Cook and Folsom in 1869.[44]

While yet employed in the surveyor-general's office—Langford says it was "on the eve of the departure of our expedition from Helena"[45]—Folsom suggested to General Washburn that at least a part of the Yellowstone region should be made into a park.[46]

The contributions of the Folsom party of 1869 to the definitive exploration of the Yellowstone region are these: a descriptive magazine article, a greatly improved map, a suggestion for reservation in the public interest, and the encouragement of the Washburn party of explorers.

Peripheral Events
(1869-70)

The motivation that sent the Washburn party into the Yellowstone region in 1870 was largely an outgrowth of two unrelated events of the previous year—the effort to activate the Northern Pacific Railway project, and the struggle over the governorship of the Territory of Montana. Thus, it is necessary to consider these peripheral events before continuing with the definitive exploration of the Yellowstone wilderness.

An act of Congress chartering the Northern Pacific Railway was signed into law by President Abraham Lincoln on July 2, 1864, but the enterprise remained a paper venture (in which the resources provided by the stockholders were consumed without apparent benefit) through 1869. In that year, the board of directors, made desperate by the knowledge, that they would lose both the charter and the munificent land-grant which accompanied it if the prescribed amount of line was not in operation by the end of 1870, turned to the investment house of Jay Cooke & Co., for help.[47]

This marriage of convenience was not consummated at once, for neither group trusted the other. The "old NP faction," headed by J. Gregory Smith—generally addressed as "Governor"—talked of "keeping things in our hands," because "Jay knows nothing of RR Building,"[48] and they moved their secretary, the astute and crafty Samuel Wilkeson, into an office in New York City, from whence he could advise the Cooke people and divine something of their maneuverings from the city's financial gossip.

The Cooke group, which also included Henry D. Cooke, Pitt Cooke, William G. Moorhead, H. C. Fahnstock, Edward Dodge, John W. Sexton, and George C. Thomas, was not as poorly informed as their distrustful confederates presumed, for they had the excellent counsel of A. B. Nettleton (Cooke's office manager) who, as a general officer in the Civil War, had built and operated many of the railroads which gave the North its logistical superiority in that struggle. These financiers were fearful that the railroaders would waste construction funds in contractual arrangements with cronies, and that the lands available under the railroad's grant—the real security for its bond issues—would be wasted.

The two groups sparred over terms during the remainder of 1869, but finally reached an agreement which gave the banking house representation on the Northern Pacific board and a controlling interest in the railroad's stock in return for an immediate advance of $5 million.[49] That funding allowed construction to begin on the Minnesota shore of Lake Superior, February 15, 1870, on ground thawed with bonfires.[50]

The enterprise thus launched had supporters in and out of the Government, from House Speaker James G. Blaine to Henry Ward Beecher, most of whom had such compelling reasons for their interest as the ownership of Northern Pacific stock or acceptance of gratuities and "fees"; and there were would-be-friends in the West who sought to ingratiate themselves with the enterprise for various opportunistic reasons. Some of the latter found a measure of acceptance with the Cooke faction, but to the railroaders they were nearly all anathema—a viewpoint which is explained by the following excerpt:

> . . . Governor Ashley and a rich man from Toledo, Ohio have put squatters on our pet, *our choice*, location at Thompson Falls. The choisest and best land on our line of reconnaissance within a year *will be gone.*[51]

One westerner—a term intended only to designate those men whose sphere of activity was Minnesota and Montana, rather than the financial centers of the East—who nearly made the grade with the old Northern Pacific group was the editor of the *Helena Herald*. He was introduced to

President Smith in these glowing terms penned by Samuel Wilkeson:

> Robert E. Fiske—the bearer—is *the* Republican Editor of Montana—
> and *the* Republican brains & heart of that future mighty State.
> He loves our Road—Our Road should love & cherish him.
> Every syllable of his advice is worth heeding.[52]

But he was not heeded; rather, he was soon considered a "wicked or mean" man, on the advice of one whose contacts were Montana Democrats.[53] The railroaders thus turned their backs on a group which could have been formed into a powerful ally.

The Cooke people were not so disdainful of westerners. They made use of Governor Ashley, even after his true character was all too clear, and they leaned heavily on William R. Marshall, the Governor of Minnesota (1866–70).[54] Quite probably, the latter arrangement included Marshall's brother-in-law, James W. Taylor,[55] that enthusiastic apostle of American economic penetration of the Canadian prairies (which he presumed would eventuate as a "Northern Texas," wrested from British rule by American citizens), but what is important here is the influence of these men— particularly Taylor—on a younger brother-in-law, Nathaniel Pitt Langford. Of this influence, one biographer says:

> Langford's story in Montana's early history is well known. That he was an "agent of an agent" there seems little doubt. Indirectly he was an observer and a protagonist for the northern railroad routes. During his time in Montana he seems always to be acting as he would expect Taylor to act and speak if he were there on the scene. His interest in getting Virginia City's gold safely to Washington, and in securing the resources of the area for the Union seem honestly to have been his conscious effort. . . . That N. P. Langford was *not* James Wicks Taylor is just as obvious, but he did his best.[56]

Taylor, of course, was the source of Langford's political leverage. As a former law partner of Salmon P. Chase (with whom he enjoyed a close ideological rapport), Taylor was able to obtain the position of Collector of Internal Revenue for Montana Territory for his protégé, and he nearly managed the governorship of the territory for him in 1869.[57] Following that defeat Langford gradually became involved in the familial interest— the Northern Pacific Railroad.

Langford, whose diary indicates that he left Montana on October 26, 1869,[58] showed up at the New York office of the Northern Pacific on March 18, 1870. Secretary Wilkeson reported this visit to President Smith in a confidential letter, as follows:

> A smart fellow, anciently a bookkeeper—during the war detailed as quartermaster to an expedition from Minnesota overland to Fort Benton and thence through Cadottes, the Deer Lodge & other passes, came in yesterday to get employment. Before he left he asked me if Vibbard & Co. were to have the contract of supplying the Northern Road—and said that *he was told by that house the day preceding that they expected to have the contract.* Canfield probably told you of my conversation with Vibbard six months ago on the subject of that contract. I was told then that I was to have an interest in it.[59]

An item which appeared in the Philadelphia *Press* the day following this visit is so patent a re-statement of James W. Taylor's views that Langford may be suspected of supplying the material to enhance the sale-value of his knowledge of Montana and the northern railroad route.[60] But he was displaying his wares in a poor market, for the railroad could not afford a salary for its secretary at that time.

From April 4 to May 11, Langford accompanied brother-in-law Marshall on a trip to Fort Garry, in British territory. By the middle of the month, Marshall was advocating the construction of a White Cloud-Pembina line to tap the rich Red River Valley (He made several attempts to communicate his enthusiasm for that route to President Smith[61]). As June opened, Langford was in Washington, D.C., in a further attempt to contact Smith.[62]

Though unable to reach the autocrat of the Northern Pacific Railroad, Langford did manage a meeting with Jay Cooke 2 days later. This is noted in Langford's diary as follows:

> June 4, 1870, Sat. Met Jay Cooke [illegible] and went to Ogontz[63] with Mr. Cook.
> June 5, 1870, Sun. Spent day with Mr. Cook.

What their common interest was remains a matter for speculation, but the directness with which Langford returned to Montana Territory and began organizing the 1870 exploring party hints that the Yellowstone region figured in the conversations. Regardless, Langford had found a place as one of the corps of lecturers who were to expedite the sale of Northern Pacific Railway bonds by popularizing the region through which the line was to be built.

The Washburn Party
(1870)

From Philadelphia, Langford proceeded to the family home at Utica, N.Y., where he visited briefly before going on to St. Paul, Minn., and a series of pleasant visits with his many relatives in that area. While there, he called upon Maj. Gen. Winfield S. Hancock, who commanded the Military Department of Dakota (of which Montana was then a part), and that officer

> ... showed great interest in the plan of exploration which I outlined to him, and expressed a desire to obtain additional information concerning the Yellowstone country ... and he assured me that, unless some unforeseen exigency prevented, he would, when the time arrived, give a favorable response to our application for a military escort, if one were needed.[64]

Even as Langford was making his plans for a late summer expedition into the Yellowstone region, another interested explorer made an attempt to enter that area. While his venture contributed nothing to the knowledge of Yellowstone's unusual features, it may have influenced the Washburn party in their selection of the Yellowstone River route as the proper approach to the wilderness, and it does expose the vagueness of whatever plan existed locally, prior to Langford's return early in August 1870.

As spring turned to summer, Philetus W. Norris returned to Montana to further his various land schemes along the projected route of the Northern Pacific Railway. Of this visit he says:[65]

At Helena I learned from Gen. Washburn and T. C. Everts that there were rumors of Capt. deLacy, Messrs. Cook and Folsom, and some gold hunters having at various times reached some portions of the Geyser regions, but so far I have failed to find any published or other reliable description of them, or their location or route of reaching them.

Gov. Ashley, Washburn and Everts were talking of a party up the Madison in the following autumn.

Firm in the opinion that the Yellowstone route was the true one, I obtained all possible information here and at Bozeman, and near the latter place found an old used up mountaineer named Dunn, who claimed to have gone with James Bridger and another trapper, who was soon after killed by the Indians in Arizona, *via* Yellowstone Lake to Green River, in 1865, and, from his statements I made a rough map of their route.[66]

Leaving Everts at Fort Ellis [where he had business with the post sutler], with horse and Winchester rifle, I alone followed the Indian trail through the famous Spring Cañon, and left the main pass and trail near the lignite coal bed. I thence crossed the beautiful grassy divide, still full of buffalo wallows, and following a continuous line of rough stone heaps from 2 to 5 feet high, to, and beyond Trail creek an estimated distance of 40 miles from here without seeing a human habitation, to the only one of white men upon the north bank of the Yellowstone.

Norris stopped there for several days with the Bottler brothers—Frederick, Philip, and Henry,[67] enjoying their wild solitude. However,

The main object of my visit being to ascertain the possibility of an exploring party going through the upper cañon and the Lava, or ancient volcanic country beyond, so as to reach the wonders said to be around Yellowstone Lake, several days were spent, with Frederick Bottler as guide, in climbing the Basaltic mountains and dark defiles, the mountain horses of Cayuse characteristics, climbing, like goats or mountain sheep, much of the way. Assured that with the fall of waters a party might in August reach at least the great falls of Yellowstone, we ought to have returned, but believing the Indians were across the next range of mountains upon a buffalo hunt, elated with the wonders found, and hoping to reach greater, and if possible be the first men to reach the Sulphur Mountains and Mud Volcanoes, and possibly the great falls and Yellowstone Lake, we rashly pushed on.

Although the snow-capped cliffs and yawning chasms in the basaltic or ancient lava beds, fringed with snow-crushed, tangled timber and impetuous torrents of mingled hot-spring and melted-snow water, made our progress—mainly on foot, leading our horses—slow, tedious and dangerous, we perservered until near a large river[68] that came dashing down from the Southwestern Madison range. There while crossing a mountain torrent, though the water was not over 20 feet wide and less than knee deep, such was its velocity that Bottler, who first entered, was carried from his feet and swept away much faster than I could follow, and though in great danger of being dashed amongst the rocks, he fortunately caught an overhanging cottonwood and by our united efforts was saved, but his valuable needle-gun, hat, ammunition-belt and equipments went dashing down toward the Yellowstone and were lost.

With my only companion sadly bruised by the rocks, benumbed, the remnants of his dressed elk-skin garments saturated by the snow-water, without gun or pistol, in a snow-bound mountain defile in an Indian country, even a June night was far from pleasant for us.

A morning view with an eight-mile field-glass, though disclosing distant clouds of smoke or spray [Mammoth Hot Springs], yet convinced us both of the utter folly of further effort until melting snows reduced the velocity and number of these mountain torrents, and we should be prepared with more than one gun for procuring food and defence from animals and Indians. As Bottler was unable to climb the mountains,[69] we returned through the unknown second cañon, camping in it while I explored the route.

In a note added at the time he edited these earlier writings for publication (which was never accomplished), he says:

> ... We really visited comparatively little of the Park, yet from a spur of what is now called Electric Peak, we had a fine view of much of it and in returning on the west side of the Yellowstone through its second cañon we explored the route which has been followed by nearly all others, and which is now the main route to the Headquarters of the Park.

In closing the letter in which he forwarded an account of the foregoing exploration to the *Norris Suburban*,[70] Norris mentioned the choice which he had to make with regard to his activities that summer:

> Shall soon decide whether General Washburn, Surveyor General of this Territory, friend Everts and Judge Hosmer, once of Toledo, Major Squier, the Bottlers and our humble self join in another expedition to the unexplored region of the Yellowstone Lake. If so, shall go no farther west this season; if not, shall try to cross the mountains to Oregon, down to Columbia, then to California, and return in autumn.

A footnote to the published letter completes the story. In it Norris adds:

> I returned from Missoula to Helena August 1st, 1870, finding Gov. Ashley (who had been active for the Yellowstone expedition), removed, the new Governor (Potts), not arrived, Hauser, Langford and other prominent friends of the enterprise absent,[71] and very little prospect of exploration that year, while the N. P. R. R., and other surveying parties down the Columbia promised various benefits in that direction. With no time to waste in deliberation, I chose the latter, returned to Missoula, assisted in surveying my own and other interests there, and then down the Columbia.

After a month's isolation from news of the outside world, I was intensely mortified to learn that Messrs. Langford, Hauser, and others had returned and gone up the Yellowstone, and at San Francisco also learned that friend Everts was lost near the head of Yellowstone Lake, and though after 37 days of such exposure, starvation and suffering as probably few if any other human beings ever survived, he was found by Baronette and Prichette; yet his horse (the one he used on our return from Fort Ellis), his gun, equipments, and entire outfit, including my map, notes, etc., left with him, were totally lost, and no trace of them has ever been, or perhaps ever will be found.

Having thus, by unforeseen accidents and circumstances not especially the fault of myself or of others, failed in my long cherished hope of a prominent record among the first explorers of the Yellowstone Park, [72] and overtasked with business at home, it was not until 1875 that I again reached my Bottler friends. . . .[73]

Nathaniel P. Langford could not have reached Helena, Mont., before the evening of July 28, and, with a stopover at Virginia City, his arrival could have been later; thus, his statement, "About the 1st of August 1870, our plans took definite shape, and some 20 men were enrolled as members of the exploring party,"[74] indicates that he arrived with a matured plan which was embarked upon with little or no delay. He adds:

About this time the Crow Indians again "broke loose," and a raid of the Gallatin and Yellowstone valleys was threatened, and a majority of those who had enrolled their names, experiencing that decline of courage so aptly illustrated by Bob Acres, suddenly found excuse for withdrawal in various emergent occupations.

There was a scare about that time, but it seems to have resulted more from the presence of Sioux and Blackfoot Indians near the settlements than from any disposition of the Crows to be unfriendly. The following letter written by 1st Lt. E. M. Camp, who commanded the small guard of soldiers stationed at the Crow Agency (Fort Parker, east of present Livingston, Mont.), clarifies the situation:

Both Sioux and Blackfeet have often been seen near the agency, and there is danger of an attack from them at any time. Both tribes being hostile to whites and Crows. The agency is located Thirty-five (35) miles from Fort Ellis. Wild Country intervening. The Guard at present Consists of one (1) Sergt two (2) Corpls and ten (10) Privates from Co. A 7th U.S. Infantry.[75]

An unsettling note had been struck earlier by the post commander at Camp Baker, who had reported bands of Piegans and River Crows near that place. Both "are believed to be friendly but it is possible some of their young men may commit depredations."[76] Given such tensions, no more than a rumor was required to alarm the fainthearted.

According to Langford:

After a few days of suspense and doubt, Samuel T. Hauser told me that if he could find two men whom he knew, who would accompany him, he would attempt the journey; and he asked me to join him in a letter to James Stuart, living at Deer Lodge, proposing that he should go with us. Benjamin Stickney, one of the most enthusiastic of our number, also wrote to Mr. Stuart that there were eight persons who would go at all hazards and asked him (Stuart) to be a member of the party. Stuart replied to Hauser and myself as follows:[77]

"Deer Lodge City, M.T. Aug. 9th, 1870.

"Dear Sam and Langford:

"Stickney wrote me that the Yellow Stone party had dwindled down to eight persons. That is not enough to stand guard, and I won't go into that country without having a guard every night. From present news it is probable that the Crows will be scattered on all the head-waters of the Yellow Stone, and if that is the case, they would not want any better fun than to clean up a party of eight (that does not stand guard) and say that the Sioux did it, as they said when they went through us on the Big Horn.[78] It will not be safe to go into that country with less than fifteen men, and not very safe with that number. I would like it better if it was a fight from the start; we would then kill every Crow that we saw, & take the chances of their rubbing us out. As it is, we will have to let them alone until they will get the best of us by stealing our horses or killing some of us; then we will be so crippled that we can't do them any damage.

"At the commencement of this letter I said I would not go unless the party stood guard. I will take that back, for I am just *d- - d* fool enough to go anywhere that anybody else is willing to go,—only I want it understood that very likely some of us will lose our hair. I will be on hand Sunday evening, unless I hear that the trip is postponed. Fraternally Yours,

Jas. Stuart

"Since writing the above, I have received a telegram saying, 'twelve of us going certain.' Glad to hear it,—the more the better. Will bring two Pack horses and one Pack saddle."

Meanwhile, Henry D. Washburn had written Lt. Gustavus C. Doane, an officer of the Second United States Cavalry stationed at Fort Ellis, concerning his interest in the proposed exploration.[79] The answer, which could not have reached Helena before August 14th, advised,

Your kind favor of the 9th ult.—came yesterday—and I reply—at the first opportunity for transmittal. Judge Hosmer was correct as regards my *earnest desire* to go on the trip proposed—but mistaken in relation to my *free agency* in the premises. To obtain permission for an escort will require an order from Genl Hitchcock [*sic*]—authorizing Col Baker—to make the detail.
If Hauser and yourself will telegraph at once on rec't to Genl Hitchcock at Saint Paul, Minn.—stating the object of the expedition &c and requesting that an order be sent to the Comdg officer at Fort Ellis, M. T. to furnish an escort of An Officer five men—it will doubtless be favorably considered—and you can bring the reply from the office when you come down or send it before—if answer comes in time Col Baker has promised me the detail if authority be furnished. And by

your telegraphing instead of him—the circumlocution at Dist Hdqrs will be obviated I will reimburse you the expense of the messages which should be *paid both ways* to insure prompt attention.

I will be able to furnish Tents and camp equipage better than you can get in Helena—and can furnish them without trouble to your whole party.

Hoping that we can make the trip in company. . . .[80]

The wise advice of Lieutenant Doane was taken, for Langford later wrote:

About this time Gen. Henry D. Washburn, the surveyor general of Montana, joined with Mr. Hauser in a telegram to General Hancock, at St. Paul, requesting him to provide the promised escort of a company of cavalry. General Hancock immediately responded, and on August 14th telegraphed an order on the commandant at Fort Ellis, near Bozeman, for such escort as would be deemed necessary to insure the safety of our party.[81]

General Hancock's telegram (sent to Col. John Gibbon at Fort Shaw, on August 15) authorized the expedition in these words:

The Surveyor General of Montana, H. D. Washburn, wishes to determine location of Lake and Falls of Yellowstone and asks for a small escort of an officer and five or ten men. I have no objections to this and would like to have an intelligent officer of cavalry who can make a correct map of the country go along, but the escort should be strong, about a company of cavalry—If there is no obstacle to such an expedition other than is known to me, you can order a company or more from Major Baker's command for this service and suggest to him to go along if he thinks proper and to take charge of the conduct of the expedition unless you desire to go yourself.[82]

The Surveyor General was informed the same day by a telegram stating:

Will send orders to Col. Baker for your escort by Wednesday's mail under cover to you at Helena, so you can take them with you to Ellis. Col. Baker will furnish the escort if he has men to spare. I presume he has them.[83]

The plans of the expeditioners had already appeared in the *Helena Daily Herald*,[84] where it was noted:

Monday morning at eight o'clock, is the time set for the departure of the long talked of Yellowstone Expedition. The roll has been called, thus far the following gentlemen from Helena have answered to their names promptly, and given an affirmative response: Hon. H. D. Washburn, Surveyor General of the Territory, Hon. N. P. Langford, Hon. Truman C. Everts, late Assessor of Internal Revenue,[85] M. F. Truett, Judge of the Probate Court, Sam'l T. Hauser, President of the First National Bank, Warren C. Gillette, Esq., Cornelius Hedges, Esq., Benjamin Stickney and Walter Trumbell [*sic*]. Deer Lodge will be represented in the person of James Stuart, of the well known mercantile firm of Dance, Stuart & Co., who has become quite famous in the mountain country as a daring and successful Indian fighter. Boulder Valley, (we are informed by Mr. Langford) will be represented by J. M. Greene, who will join the expedition at Bozeman City. At Fort Ellis, the party will be strengthened by a military escort, consisting of Lieutenant Doan [sic] and twelve men. At the Yellowstone Agency, the party will probably receive another small reinforcement, as Capt. E. M. Camp has signified his intention of going through with the expedition. As a great portion of the country through which they will traverse is claimed by the hostile Sioux, the expeditionists will likely encounter some of these bands of roving Indians, and while it is proper to exercise all necessary precaution against unforseen dangers, we apprehend no serious troubles from this source. It will be remembered, however, that Stuart and his party, during their trip to these almost unexplored regions, in 1863, had a most desperate fight with a band of Indians, supposed to have been Crows, which outnumbered them five to one, and it was only by good luck and good generalship combined, that they were saved from a terrible fate. One of the party, we believe was killed in the engagement and two others mortally wounded. We merely refer to this event in order that every man who contemplates this long and dangerous trip, may be prepared for any emergency that may rise. General H. D. Washburn, we understand, has been chosen as commander of the expedition.[86] The General will make a safe and trusty leader, and if it becomes necessary to fight the Indians, he will always be found at the post of duty.

P.S. Since the above was in type, we learn the time for departure has been postponed until Wednesday next [17th], one of the party—Mr. Stuart of Deer Lodge, having business that will detain him until then.

On the 16th, the same newspaper noted that Colonel Gibbon's telegram authorizing a military escort had been received, adding: "The *Herald*, which will send a reporter along, will furnish its readers with important letters from various points as opportunity and the limited facilities for transmission will afford."[87]

The departure of the expedition from Helena had been set for 9 a.m. on Wednesday, August 17, but difficulties with the pack stock caused a delay noted thus by the *Herald*:

It was not until two o'clock yesterday afternoon, when the Yellowstone exploring party took their departure from the rendezvous on Rodney street, and even then all did not get off. Several of the party, we are informed, were "under the weather" and tarried in the gay Metropolis until "night drew her sable curtain down," when they started off in search of the expedition. The party expected to make their first camp about twenty miles from the city.[88]

Cornelius Hedges, who was really not an outdoors person, characterized the start as a "dismal day of dust, wind and cold,"[89] while Samuel T. Hauser put it this way in his rudimentary diary: "considerable bother getting off—started 1 p.m.—3 packs off—within 300 yards—sent back for a second pack[er]—Left packers and Darkeys."[90] He also identifies one of the revelers left behind when the main party cantered out of town about 4 in the afternoon; following Ben Stickney's name in his roster of the expedition's personnel, Hauser added, "tight." The other—from his absence from Hedges' list of those who went together to the "half-way house" run by Nick Greenish 4 miles from Helena—could only have been Jake Smith.

After a night during which Hedges "Didn't sleep at all—dogs bothered," the party reached Vantilburg's by noon, and as it "Started in snowing just as we got in, voted to stay." Hedges' diary also contains this confession: "I felt very sore and was glad of rest." Of this layover, Hauser noted: "All playing cards."

An early start the following morning got them to Major Campbell's by 2:30 p.m., where dinner was ordered at once. Gillette says:

> . . . but the shrewd old man kept us waiting till 6 O clock in order to compell [sic] us to stay all night. There was much growling from hungry men but a good supper of chicken & trout, good coffee & cream, with a desert of blanc-mange restored the party to its former good humor.[91]

Langford, who had pushed on alone, reached Bozeman about 7 p.m. on the 19th, which gave him time to arrange with Major Baker for their escort before the other expeditioners arrived the following day.[92] The party put up at the Guy House, and entered upon a lively evening which included a cold supper provided by the proprietors of the firm of Willson & Rich. Gillette thought they were "nine pretty rough looking men to come into the presence of three fine ladies," and Hedges was "much embarrassed" because all had white collars but himself. Afterward, Langford and Hedges called at Gallatin Lodge No. 6 of the Masonic Order, where Langford, as Grand Master, placed the charter in arrest as the best means of ending a grievous dispute. Then everyone went to the Guy House for champagne and musical entertainment at the rooms of Captain and Mrs. Fiske.

Cornelius Hedges described Sunday the 21st as "all commotion, running around, saying goodbye, talking with Masons. Sperling gave box of cigars. Everyone kind, with many good wishes." He also noted:

> Went out to camp near Fort & cook our dinner. Lieut Doane brought us a big tent & helped us put it up. shelter from wind, sun & cold. . . . Unpacked our things to get what we wanted. read papers. Jake Smith opened a game & got busted in a few moments.[93] visted by several prospectors who tell us much about the country.

Hedges' mood had changed for the better as the day of departure from Fort Ellis arrived, perhaps as a consequence of that "fine bed and sleep," and the gaiety of that "merry company." He also recorded a note of dissent that would reappear occasionally: "Smith is disgusted at prospect of standing guard," then penned a last-minute dispatch to the *Herald*,[94] and the Yellowstone Expedition was ready to enter the wilderness.

The official report prepared by Lt. Gustavus C. Doane immediately following the return of the expedition is the best account written by a member.[95] Therefore, the details that follow have been taken from his report unless otherwise noted.

Doane's report, which is prefaced by an extract from Special Order No. 100, issued at Fort Ellis, Montana Territory, August 21, 1870, begins:

> In obedience to the above order, I joined the party of General H. D.

Washburn, in-route for the Yellowstone, and then encamped near Fort Ellis, M.T. with a detachment of F. Co 2d Cavalry, consisting of Sergeant William Baker, Privates Chas. Moore, John Williamson, William Leipler and George W. McConnell.

The detachment was supplied with two extra saddle horses, and five pack mules for the transportation of supplies. A large pavillion tent was carried for the accommodation of the whole party, in case of stormy weather being encountered; also forty days rations and an abundant supply of ammunition.

The party of civilians from Helena consisted of General H. D. Washburn, Surveyor General of Montana, Hon. N. P. Langford, Hon. T. C. Everts, Judge C. Hedges of Helena, Saml T. Hauser, Warren C. Gillette, Benj C. Stickney, Jr., Walter Trumbull, and Jacob Smith, all of Helena, together with two packers, and two cooks.[96]

They were furnished with a saddle horse apiece, and nine pack animals for the whole outfit: They were provided with one Aneroid Barometer, one Thermometer, and several pocket compasses, by means of which observations were to be taken at different points on the route.

The route from Fort Ellis was the same as that followed by the Folsom party the previous year, with the first encampment on Trail Creek, about 15 miles from the Post.[97]

On the second day, August 23, 1870, the party made 20 miles, which brought them to the Bottler Ranch. The only incident the lieutenant found worth noting was the sighting of a few Indians, who were casually dismissed with the entry, "In the afternoon we met several Indians belonging to the Crow Agency 30 miles below."[98]

Rain began in the evening, so that the pavillion tent had to be put up near the Bottler cabin.[99]

The weather cleared the following morning and camp was moved up the river to a pleasant place below what Doane called "the lower cañon"[100] —present Yankee Jim Canyon, which is really the second canyon going upstream, and was so called until the mid-eighties. It was evident they were in Indian country, so guards were posted and the horses were picketed or hobbled.

On the 25th, the party made their way through Yankee Jim Canyon on a difficult Indian trail,[101] then debouched into an arid valley. Continuing on the west bank of the Yellowstone, they past that "Red Streak Mountain" some prospectors had earlier thought to contain cinnabar,[102] to an encampment at the mouth of Gardner River.[103] Doane called this "our first poor camping place, grass being very scarce, and the slopes of the ranges covered entirely with sage brush," and he added, "From this camp was seen the smoke of fires on the mountains in front, while Indian signs became more numerous and distinct."[104]

The route on the 26th followed what would later be known as the "Turkey Pen Road," and Lieutenant Doane, Everts, and Private Williamson went ahead as an advance party. Contact with the main group was soon lost due to the latter's difficulty with pack animals made nervous by smoke from the burned-over area on Mount Everts. Thus, the train was unable to follow Doane through to Tower Fall, but had to camp for the night on what Langford called "Antelope Creek"—present Rescue Creek—but which was designated more accurately by Hauser as "Lost Trail Creek," because they lost Doane's trail near the marshy pond on that stream.

Doane, who was following the trail of two "hunters" (probably miners from nearby Bear Gulch),[105] had turned south in order to get on the Bannock Indian trail which passed directly over the Blacktail Deer Plateau, well back from the nearly impassable "middle cañon."[106] That heavily used trail led the advanced party to the first thermal springs on their route—a tepid, sulphurous outflow near present Roosevelt Lodge—and on to Warm Spring Creek,[107] where they camped with the hunters they had been following.

The next day, August 27, while waiting for the main party to come up, Doane had an opportunity to examine the hot springs scattered along the Yellowstone from the mouth of Tower Creek nearly to the entry of Lamar River, and he had time to contemplate the chief feature of the locality, Tower Fall,[108] which he typified in these words:

Nothing can be more chastely beautiful than this lovely cascade, hidden away in the dim light of overshadowing rocks and woods, its very voice hushed to a low murmur unheard at the distance of a few hundred yards. Thousands might pass by within half a mile and not dream of its existence, but once seen, it passes to the list of most pleasant memories.

The remainder of the party arrived that afternoon, and it was decided there was enough to see in the vicinity to justify a layover; thus, a pleasant camp was established where the party remained during the 28th.[109] It was there that the felon on Lieutenant Doane's right thumb was first opened, "three times to the bone, with a very dull knife," in the hope of providing him with relief from his "infernal agonies," but without success.[110]

On August 29, the party broke camp and proceeded toward the falls of the Yellowstone by the route General Washburn had pioneered the previous day.[111] Those who went to the summit of Mount Washburn took a reading from which Doane computed the elevation as 9,966 feet above sea level.[112]

It was while passing over the Washburn Range that these explorers were at last convinced they were entering a land of wonders. Of the view from Dunraven Pass, Doane wrote:

A column of steam rising from the dense woods to the height of several hundred feet, became distinctly visible. We had all heard fabulous stories of this region and were somewhat skeptical as to appearances. At first, it was pronounced a fire in the woods, but presently some one noticed that the vapor rose in regular puffs, and as if expelled with a great force. Then conviction was forced upon us. It was indeed a great column of steam, puffing away on the lofty mountainside, escaping with a roaring sound, audible at a long distance even through the heavy forest.

A hearty cheer rang out at this discovery and we pressed onward with renewed enthusiasm.

Camp was made that evening on the stream that drains most of the southern side of Mount Washburn,[113] and the evening was spent investigating several prominent thermal features nearby.[114] This exploration took them to the rim of the Grand Canyon, which Doane likened to "a second edition of the bottomless pit."

The move made the following day was short—only 8 miles, to a campsite on the lower edge of the meadows on Cascade Creek. With much of the afternoon left for exploring, the members of the party made their way toward the falls singly and in small groups.[115] The views obtained convinced all that there was enough more to see that they were warranted in again laying over a day. Accordingly, the last day of August was also passed in exploring the locality.

Langford proceeded to measure the drop of both the Upper and Lower Falls of the Yellowstone by the same method the Folsom party had used in 1869, and with an identical result at the Upper Fall.[116] Hauser and Stickney managed to scramble down into the Grand Canyon $2\frac{1}{2}$ miles below the Lower Fall,[117] while Lieutenant Doane and Private McConnell climbed down to some hot springs bordering the river a mile farther down the canyon. Hedges, who was less active, spent several hours viewing the Lower Fall, then wandered along the canyon rim until filled with "too much and too great satisfaction to relate." It was Doane's opinion that:

> Both of these cataracts deserve to be ranked among the great waterfalls of the continent. No adequate standard of comparison between such objects, either in beauty or grandeur can well be obtained . . . [but] In scenic beauty the upper cataract far excels the lower; it has life, animation, while the lower one simply follows its channel; both however are eclipsed as it were by the singular wonders of the mighty cañon below.

The expedition left the camp on Cascade Creek on September 1, moving southward through Hayden Valley. In contrast to the wild flood which foamed powerfully through the Grand Canyon, the Yellowstone River, where it flows through the grasslands created by the shrinkage of Lake Yellowstone, is slow-flowing and sedate—described by Doane in these words:

> The stream here changes its character altogether, running in the center of an open glade, back full, with grassy margins, a slow current, and spread out to a width of from two hundred to four hundred feet. The bottom is pebbly, or quick-sand, the water of crystal clearness, and cold again.

Two miles above the Upper Fall, they came to a swampy stream, west of the river, which Doane mistakenly called Alum Creek,[118] while another, nearly opposite, was similarly mis-identified as "Hellroaring River."[119] In the middle of the valley was a group of hills which Doane wanted to call the "Seven Hills,"[120] where they found an interesting array of sulphurous hot springs and vents. Some time was spent examining the locality, but a lack of drinkable water induced them to move 5 miles farther up the valley before camping.

This camp, where the expedition lay over on the 2d, was a half mile north of the Mud Volcano and quite close to the feature now called the Sulphur Cauldron. The drinking water obtained from the river tasted of chemicals, but the fishing was fabulous. Among the nearby springs was the first true geyser seen on the trip,[121] as well as features identifiable as Dragons Mouth Spring (a green-gabled grotto called "Cave Spring" by Gillette) and the Mud Volcano.[122] The last was described by Doane as follows:

> A few hundred yards from here is an object of the greatest interest. On the slope of a small and steep wooded ravine is the crater of a mud volcano, thirty feet in diameter at the rim, which is elevated a few feet above the surface on the lower side and bounded by the slope of the hill on the upper, converging as it deepens to the diameter of fifteen feet at the lowest visible point, about forty feet down. Heavy volumes of steam escape from this opening, ascending to the height of three hundred feet. From far down in the earth come a jarring sound in regular beats of five seconds with a concussion that shook the ground at two hundred yards distant. After each concussion, came a splash of mud as if thrown to a great height; sometimes it could be seen from the edge of the crater but none was entirely ejected while we were there. Occasionally an explosion was heard like the bursting of heavy guns behind an embankment and causing the earth to tremble for a mile around. These explosions were accompanied by a vast increase of the volumes of steam poured forth from the crater. This volcano has not been long in operation, as young pines crushed flat to the earth under the rim of mud, were still alive at the tops.

On September 3 the main party crossed the Yellowstone River at what would later be known as the "Nez Perce ford," while Washburn and Langford rode back to the hot springs in Hayden Valley and a scary experience there.[123]

The trail on the east side of the river was good as far as the crossing of a marshy stream east of present Fishing Bridge settlement.[124] There the pack train mired and had to make a detour of several miles. A good campsite was found on the shore of Lake Yellowstone, near the Beach Springs and about a half-mile east of the Folsom party's encampment.

The party again delayed a day, a halt made necessary by the condition of Doane's hand. He had been suffering severe pain for a number of days and loss of sleep had taken its toll of his strength. Another operation was performed soon after arrival at the lake.[125] With relief from the inflammation, Doane slept through the night, the following day, and a second night.

Meanwhile, the other members of the party spent the time playing cards, exploring the nearby hot springs and that beach Hedges called the "Curiosity Shop." The presence of islands (Stevenson, Frank, and Dot), which were thought never to have been "trodden by human footsteps," encouraged the building of a raft for the exploration of those shores, but the waves of the lake dashed it to pieces within an hour of the launching. Nor was that the only unproductive effort; the triangulation attempted on the 5th, following the breaking of camp, was equally futile.[126]

The decision to follow the east shore of the lake upon leaving the "Hot Spring Camp" was a result of a reconnaissance made in that direction by General Washburn while the party awaited Doane's recovery. However, that route around the lake eventually proved more difficult than expected.

Fifteen miles were traveled the first day, to an overnight camp at Park Point, but the increasing difficulty with fallen timber reduced their progress on the 6th to 10 miles. Even so, the route was not so onerous but what some members of the party could be spared to make an excursion into a Brimstone Basin lying east of the trail.[127] It was toward the end of the day that they encountered a really formidable obstacle. An attempt to cross the estuary of the Upper Yellowstone River by following the beach fronting on the lake got the pack train into a difficult cul-de-sac, so that they camped that night in considerable anxiety about the route.[128]

On the following morning, General Washburn went ahead to find a way through the estuarial swamps, while Langford and Doane climbed a nearby peak to get a better view of the entire region south of Lake Yellowstone. Doane noted: "We were 4 hours reaching the highest point, climbing for over a mile over shelly feldspathic granite after leaving our horses at the limit of pines." He found the summit to have an elevation of 10,327 feet (by aneroid barometer).[129] Doane's description of the country as seen from the summit is interesting:

The view from this peak commanded completely the lake enabling us to sketch a map,[130] of its inlets and bearings with considerable accuracy. On the southwestern portion of the lake rose a high mountain of a yellow rock [Mount Sheridan], forming a divide or water shed in the centre of the great basin beyond which the waters flowed south and west.

The stream we failed in crossing on the previous day rises in the south east range running east several miles and joining another stream from the south west at Bridgers lake, a sheet of water about two miles in diameter at the foot of a rocky peak about twenty five miles to the south from whence, the stream flows due north in a straight valley to the Yellowstone lake.

This valley has a uniform width of about three miles is level and swampy through its whole extent with numerous lakelets of considerable size scattered at intervals over its surface. South of Bridgers lake and beyond the snake river divide were seen two vast columns of vapor thirty miles away which rose at least five hundred feet above the tops of the hills.[131] They were twenty times as large as any we had previously seen but lay a long distance out of our course and were not visited.

Looking east one mountain succeeds another with precipitous ravines volcanic, rugged, and in many places impassable, as if all the fusible portions of the mountains had melted and run away leaving a vast cinder behind. There were no ranges of peaks it was a great level

71

plain of summits with the softer portions melted out, the elevations all coming up to the same level and capped with horizontal beds of surface lava. This formation extended to the limit of vision. The deep and narrow valleys were grassed and timbered, had sparkling streams and furnished basins for numbers of small lakes; in fact there are lakes here everywhere on the summits of mountains and on their terraced slopes in valleys, and in ravines, of all sizes, shapes and qualities of water.

On descending from the peak, Langford and Doane followed the trail of the main party to their encampment on the lakeshore, southwest of the Molly Islands. The information brought back was so helpful that General Washburn later gave Langford's name to the peak climbed with Doane, while the lieutenant's name was given to a lower summit north of the saddle where the horses were left; but the Hayden Survey did not allow either name to remain as intended.

The following morning, September 8, Hedges and Everts climbed the prominent elevation which rises above the southern extremity of the Southeast Arm (this is not truly a mountain, but only the northern end of Two Ocean Plateau), and the facility with which Everts found his way back to camp created an unwarranted confidence in his woodsmanship.[132]

The difficult terrain encountered beyond the Southeast Arm limited the party's progress on the 8th to about 7 miles, airline, so that they camped on Grouse Creek, east of Channel Mountain. Doane notes: "In the evening a Grizzly Bear with cubs was roused by some of the party, but as they had not lost any bears she got away with her interesting family undisturbed."[133] He adds, in regard to their general lack of success in hunting, "our party kept up such a rackett of yelling and firing as to drive off all game for miles ahead of us."

On September 9 the party crossed Chicken Ridge, north of Channel Mountain, and descended onto Surprise Creek, where they encamped in a meadow near its head. They had been so entangled in "fallen timber of the worst description," and so preoccupied with getting the pack train through, that Everts was not missed until he failed to come into camp. Even then, there was no particular alarm (several men went back along the trail and signal guns were fired), for it was thought Everts could make his way to the agreed rallying point at the hot springs on West Thumb. Hedges reflected the general feeling in his diary: "All in but Everts and we felt well around the fire."

A short move on the 10th took the party over a shoulder of Flat Mountain, to an encampment on Flat Mountain Arm. From there, men went back along the trail and into the country on each side searching for the lost man. Hauser and Langford ascended the height above camp and fired the woods to create a beacon, but all these measures were unavailing.

All were now convinced that Everts had gone to the rendezvous point, so camp was moved again on the 11th—northwesterly, to the shore of West Thumb, near the mouth of Solution Creek. From that camp, searchers went out by pairs on the following day. Trumbull and Smith followed the

72

beach entirely around the promontory that holds Delusion Lake without finding anything more than some human footprints in the sand. Washburn and Langford rode southward toward the "yellow mountain" (Mount Sheridan), turning back just short of Heart Lake when Langford's horse broke through the turf into hot mud which severely scalded his legs.[134] Hauser and Gilette checked the back-track and came near being lost also,[135] while Lieutenant Doane went around to the West Thumb Geyser Basin and searched there.

The party remained encamped on West Thumb the 12th, 13th, 14th, and 15th, searching constantly despite the intermittent snow storms which brought the depth of snow on the ground to 20 inches.

On September 16 camp was moved to the West Thumb Geyser Basin as the first step in extricating the party from a situation which was rapidly becoming hazardous for all. The near exhaustion of their rations, the continuing storminess of the weather, and the fatigue of the entire party all indicated the wisdom of an immediate withdrawal from the Yellowstone region. Such was the wish of all the expeditioners except Gillette, who remained behind with two soldiers when the return to the settlements was begun on the 17th.[136]

The route of the main party was westward, about as the highway now goes between West Thumb and Old Faithful. DeLacy Creek and the large lake seen to the left of their line of travel were assigned to the "Fire Hole branch of the Madison" by Doane, but Langford placed them properly.[137] A night camp was made on the head of Spring Creek.

Continuing the march on the 18th, the Firehole River was reached in about 3 miles, and, soon after, they passed "two fine roaring cascades," of which Doane remarked:

> These pretty little falls if located on an eastern stream would be cele-
> brated in history and song; here amid objects so grand as to strain con-
> ception and stagger belief they were passed without a halt.[138] Shortly
> after, the cañon widened a little and on descending on a level with the
> stream, we found ourselves once more in the dominions of the Fire
> King.

The Upper Geyser Basin came into view suddenly as they were riding along the east bank of Firehole River, and, just at that moment, Old Faithful Geyser began to play. That grand display caused the entire cavalcade to bolt through the river in their haste to reach what was the first major geyser found by the expedition.[139] Lieutenant Doane's journal account indicates some prior knowledge of the wonder-filled area they had entered, for he wrote:

> This valley is known in the wretched nomenclature of this region as the
> Fire Hole,[140] and contains phenomena of thermal springs unparalleled
> upon the surface of the globe. Crossing the river we moved down to a
> central point of the valley and camped in a little grove of pine timber
> near the margin of a small marshy lake around which were to be seen
> numerous fresh signs of Buffalo driven out by the noise of our hasty
> intrusion.

From their camp west of Firehole River and nearly opposite the Lion group of geysers, the expeditioners scattered out through the basin observing and naming geysers.[141] The marked regularity of the geyser seen in action as they arrived led General Washburn to designate it Old Faithful—a spouter which had more than punctuality to recommend it, as Doane noted:

> Those who have seen stage representations of Aladdins Cave and the home of the Dragon Fly, as produced in a first class theatre, can form an idea of the wonderful coloring but not of the intricate frost work of this fairy like yet solid mound of rock growing up amid clouds of steam and showers of boiling water. One instinctively touches the hot ledges with his hands and sounds with a stick the depths of the cavities in the slope, in utter doubt in the evidence of his own eyes. The beauty of the scene takes away ones breath. It is overpowering, transcending the visions of Masoleums Paradise, the earth affords not its equal, it is the most lovely inanimate object in existence.

To the west of their encampment, across the marshy lake (which has since been drained), stood the largest geyser cone in the basin; a "castelated turret 40 feet in height and 200 feet in circumference at the base," which they called "The Castle" from its resemblance to an old feudal tower partially in ruins.

Down the river a few hundred yards beyond Castle Geyser was another with a cone described as "resembling a huge shattered ham," which, considering the size of its aperture (7 feet in diameter) and the length of its play (3 hours), was thought to be the greatest of all the great geysers, and so was named "The Giant."[142] Doane says: "While playing, it doubled the size of the Firehole River."

Two hundred yards farther they found a peculiar cone consisting of pillars and interstices, suggestive of a grotto, and it was named accordingly.[143] Beyond that was a peculiar geyser which alternated steam and fanlike jets in a cycle which continued for hours.[144]

Across the river from their encampment, on an extensive ridge of "formation" (silicious sinter, or geyserite, produced by the action of hot water on igneous rock and redeposited on cooling), was a large well which erupted its contents—a body of water 20 by 25 feet—into the air to the height of 90 feet, with individual jets rocketing to 250 feet. This great fountain, which played for 20 minutes, was considered a fit companion for The Giant and so was called "The Giantess."

Another geyser on the same side of the river took the party quite by surprise, as Doane noted:

> *29th day* This morning we were awakened by a fearful hissing sound accompanied by falling water, and looking out saw on the other side of the stream a small crater three feet in height and with an opening of twenty six inches in diameter which had scarcely been noticed on the previous day, and was now playing a perpendicular jet to the heighth of two hundred and nineteen feet with great clouds of steam escaping, and causing the ground to tremble as the heavy body of water fell with tremendous splashes upon the shelly strata below.

Huge masses of the rocks were torn from their places and borne away into the river channel. it played thus steadily for ten minutes giving us time to obtain an accurate measurement by triangulation which resulted as above stated. . . . Its appearance and size were altogether insignificant compared with others.[145]

Though convinced that further observation would discover other great geysers in that basin, the near exhaustion of their supplies required them to move on. Thus, the pack train moved out on the morning of September 19, the remainder of the party following toward noon. They stopped briefly at the Grand Prismatic Spring and noted a a 50-foot jet playing from a large crater nearby.[146] But they passed through the Lower Geyser Basin with no more than a vague awareness of its thermal riches.

Lieutenant Doane's preconceived idea of the Madison drainage led him to show an entirely fictitious headwater for that stream, including a large "Madison Lake" south of the Upper Geyser Basin.[147] The encampment that evening was at the junction of the Firehole and Gibbon Rivers, the accepted "head" of the Madison River.[148] It was from there that the party had their last view of the Yellowstone's thermal activity, which Doane described as follows:

September 20th. We now thought ourselves clear of the geysers but in the morning were surprised to see a graceful column of steam ascending to the heighth of three hundred feet on the opposite side of the creek and in the elbow of a mountain range.

We did not visit this group [Terrace Spring, on Gibbon River], but forded the Madison twice just below camp and followed down its right bank.

The party soon passed into the Madison Basin—the "Burnt Hole" of the trappers—where they were beyond the boundary of the present Yellowstone National Park. The evening of the 22d they camped within sight of settlers' cabins in the Madison Valley, and Langford rode into Virginia City the following morning with news of the loss of Truman C. Everts.[149] Lieutenant Doane reached Fort Ellis on the 24th,[150] and the Helena contingent—excepting Gillette—were all home by the evening of September 27.

The progress of the small party which remained in the Yellowstone wilderness to search for the lost Everts is detailed by Gillette, who wrote in his diary:

Had no trouble in reaching the snow Camp but after passing that a storm came on and we bore to [sic] far to the south camping on the Lake this side of where we intended. Met a man in the woods, who said he was one of a party of 4 who came up Snake river and were camped near our Snow Camp.[151] from his illy repressed nervous manner took him for a man who was fleeing justice. told him of the loss of Everts. I killed a chicken to day with my pistol. roasted it this evening. was very sweet.—with our Fish it made a good meal Kept a sharp look out for any signs or tracks of Everts or his horse. but could see none. It rained nearly all night & my bed which was in a hollow was partly filled with water

Sept 18 Sunday. The weather this AM looked fair, but after we were well on the way, a drenching rain came on & we camped while it was still raining about 2 miles from our camp of the 10th and 11th. Williamson left Moore & myself to make a shelter (which we did with poles & blankets) while he went out to hunt. in about an hour we heard him halow in the mountain. heard his shots first. Moore took the mule & went to where we heard the shots & returned with a fine fat 2 Year old Heifer Elk we ate the liver, for supper I must not forget that I killed another chicken to day with my pistol., of which I feel quite proud. We are in high spirits. Weather cleared and looks well for tomorrow

Sept 19*th* We left camp early this A.M. passing up the south end of the Lake, going easterly. Found the provision we left for Everts at our camp of the 10th untouched showing that he has not made his way to this part of the lake. About a mile above this camp we turned up the Mountain to the South found our old trail, the snow having almost entirely disappeared.

We passed our camp of the 9th (which has been burned over by the fire we left.) and followed down a stream below where we crossed the same day. (9th) with the train. Camped on this creek [Surprise Creek]. After supper looked for signs of Everts on the creek. Saw none.

Sept 20th This morning got an early start. Took Moore with me, leaving Williamson in camp. (his horse being lame) we went back about a ½ mile found our trail on the east side of the creek, which we followed back to the point when Everts was supposed to have left us,—looked carefully to find in what direction he went.—Saw tracks on a trail which led down over a steep side-hill. here we lost the tracks, but kept on It took us to a small pond [Outlet Lake], the outlet of which ran S W. we followed it to its mouth which was 6 or 7 miles from our camp south. Seeing an opening in the trees on the opposite side of the creek into which it emptied, we went over and discovered a good sized lake, say 2 by 3 miles wide & long.[152] Examined carefully for any signs of a fire or horse tracks, saw none We crossed at the outlet of lake, and kept down the stream, which is here almost a river for a distance of 6 miles, where it opened out into a large basin across which large mountains could be seen. We were satisfied this stream was the head of Snake river, as it was getting late we retraced our steps and arrived in Camp a little after dusk

Sept 21*st* I had determined that night to go over the Mountain on the right bank of the creek on which we were camped, but a storm being imminent this morning and the men anxious to get away before a snow fell so as to obliterate the trail, & the rations being light also, I abandoned the idea, and thought it better to go to the lake at once. I hated to leave for home, while there was a possibility of finding poor Everts but the chance of our finding him being so very small, even if we knew in which direction he went, that I turned our horses northward, hoping, to hear, when we arrived at the settlements, that he had gotten out of the mountains, and would be found at Virginia City or Helena Nothing of note has occurred to day. We found the meat we "cached" all right, and after a hard & long days march (as the soldiers say) have reached our camp of the 16th The wind is blowing strong from the N.E. but with a fine shelter made with poles & blankets, shall sleep soundly. Where is the poor man Everts is he alive? is he dead? in the mountains wandering, he knows not whither? or back home safely. Did he kill his horse? if so I wonder how he likes Horseflesh With dried horse meat he could live 30 or 40 days. How he must have suffered even at the best! The reflection that he may be within 10 or 15 miles of us [*sic*].

Sept 22d [no entry]

Sept *23rd* Camped on the Madison River this noon, in the midst of an innumerable number of Hot Springs, & real Geysers. I write this from the top of a mound at least 30 feet higher than the surroundings formed by a Geyser which at present does not throw water out of its Crater. The water comes near the top & hot steam is issuing continually with heavy roaring irregular sound. This mound is 40 feet in width & circular being cone shaped. it is of a whitish, grey color and composed of soda lime & a little sulphur.

24th Traveled to day down the Madison going over some of the worst fallen timber we have seen. during the fore part of the day. This afternoon the way was better as to timber but many marshy places. Hot springs occur all along our route to day some upon the opposite side of the river that I did not examine. Travelled on the right bank followed the Margin of the river till we came to the Cascades when we took to the timber and camped in the forks of a large river coming from the south East. Traveled to day, say 20 miles Tried fishing my only fly was taken off and could get no bites from meat bait

25th Left camp early this AM Keeping the margin of river The river still to our left after going some 6 or 8 miles we went up on a trail to our right supposing it to lead north but found when we were on the Mountain that the trail was lost. The view amply repaid us for the labor. A broad basin lay like a Map before us white capped mountains in the S.W. & to the north & immense forests of pine covered the whole country we passed down into the basin [Madison Basin] . . .

Gillette and the two soldiers continued in the wake of the main party, and Gillette reached Helena on October 2 with his unhappy confirmation of a fact already too apparent—Everts was certainly lost.

The first information about the Yellowstone expedition which the press was able to provide to the public concerned the loss of Everts, which was reported thus in the *Helena Daily Herald:*[153]

We are in receipt, this afternoon, of a dispatch from Virginia City, dated 23d, announcing the arrival there of N. P. Langford, of the Yellowstone expedition, who brings the sad intelligence of the loss of Truman C. Everts, ex-United States Assessor, who was one of the party. The members of the expedition spent eight days hunting for him in the mountains, but found no trace of him. No particulars have come to hand.

LATER

Just before going to press the following special dispatch to the HERALD was received:

Virginia City, September 23.

General H. D. Washburne, commander of the Yellowstone expedition, with his party, camped on the Madison, opposite Virginia City, last night, and will be in Helena next Monday. Hon. T. C. Everts was lost September 9th, in the dense forests on the south side of the lake. The party searched seven days for him without discovering any traces of him. Warren C. Gillette and two cavalrymen remained to make further search, the others giving them all their provisions, except enough to subsist them until they reached home. The party made accurate maps of the Lake and river.

Nothing more was available on the Yellowstone region and its wonders until the 26th, when the *Helena Daily Herald* devoted two columns of its front page to the "Interesting Data of the Trip, from Notes Furnished by Hon. N. P. Langford."[154] The following is this brief account which introduced the party's discoveries:

The party left Bozeman the 22nd of August, reaching the Yellowstone on the 24th, and traveling up that river until the 27th, when they reached the Lower Fall creek [Tower Creek], where they remained in camp one day. On this creek is the Lower Fall, a beautiful cascade 115 feet high. The Indian trail crosses the Yellowstone at this point to the east side, but the party kept upon the west side of the river, near the base of Mt. Washburn, a peak 10,570 feet in height, passing the Hellbroth Springs on the 29th, and on 30th camping opposite the Great Falls of the Yellowstone, on Cascade creek. Nearly two days were spent in examining the Falls and their surroundings. Mr. Langford suspended a weight perpendicularly from the rock adjoining the Falls, 491 feet to the bottom of the cañon, and deducting from this the distance from the top of the rock to the surface of the water above the Fall, found it to be 350 feet in height. The Upper Fall, half a mile further up the stream, is 115 feet high. A day and a half more brought the party to the Hot Sulphur and Mud Springs, sixty to seventy-five in number, of diameters varying from two to seventy feet. From scores of craters on the side of the mountain adjoining these springs, issue hot vapors, the edges of the craters being incrusted with pure sulphur. Six miles further on is the first geyser, which throws a column of water twenty feet in diameter in the height of thirty to thirty-five feet. Nearby is a volcano, which throws up mud from the bottom of its crater to the height of thirty feet or more, with explosions resembling distant discharges of cannon, the pulsations occurring at intervals of five seconds, and the explosions shaking the ground for a long distance. This volcano has evidently been in existence but a short time—a few months—as the newly grown grass was covered for nearly two hundred feet with the clayey mud that was thrown out at the first outbreak. The crater of this volcano is about thirty feet in diameter at its mouth, and is narrowed down to a diameter of fifteen feet at a depth of twenty feet from the top, and the surface of the mud down in the crater appeared, when for a few seconds it was in a quiescent state, to be about sixty feet below the mouth of the crater.

At this point the party forded the river, and traveled along the east bank twelve miles to the Yellowstone Lake, a beautiful sheet of water of very irregular shape, but of an average length of twenty-two miles, and width of fifteen miles. An accurate map of the lake was made from observations taken by Messrs. Hauser and Langford, from the tops of three mountains on different sides of the lake. One of these mountains was 11,200 feet high, as measured by the barometer.

The journey around the lake was rendered very difficult by the fallen timber, the party sometimes halting at night not more than six or seven miles from their morning camp.

From the lake the party struck off to the Fire Hole River, on which, in the Geyser Basin, they found a most remarkable collection of springs and craters. In the basin, which extends about two miles down the river, and is a mile in width, are between seven and eight hundred springs and craters of all diameters, from two to one hundred feet. The party found here twelve geysers, five of which threw columns of water to heights varying from ninety to one hundred and fifty feet, the columns being from three to twenty feet in diameter. The column of water from the sixth was discharged from the apex of a conical-shaped mound, through a nozzel two feet by three, and rose to the height of two hundred and nineteen feet, Messrs. Hauser and Langford carefully measuring the column by triangulation.

We learn the following concerning the loss of Mr. Everts: He was with the rest of the party at noon on September 9th, all slowly working their way through the fallen timber. In making search for a passage through it, one or another of the members of the party would, for a brief time, become separated from the main body, but would readily find his way back again. At two o'clock p.m., the company camped for the night,—all being present but Mr. Everts. In camp it was found that Mr. Hedges' packhorse, which had that day rolled down a steep hill, thirty or forty feet, with his pack on his back, was missing and Mr. Langford, with the two packers, went in search of him, finding him about two miles from camp and returning about five o'clock, but discovering no sign of Mr. Everts.

The *objective point* of the party at this time was the southwest arm of the lake, and any one lost or separated from the train would have pushed on to that point. On the morning of the 11th Lieutenant Doan [*sic*], Langford and Hauser, leaving the train, pushed on with provisions to this arm of the lake, confidently expecting to find Mr. Everts, but no trace of him could be discovered. The rest of the party reached the lake at night, and all remained at that point five days longer. Messrs. Gillette and Hauser, the following day, returned on the trail, four days march, or near to the camp occupied by the party two days before Mr. Everts was lost, but could discover no trace of him—the trail made by the thirty-seven horses belonging to the party being in many places entirely obliterated. Messrs. Trumbull and Smith followed the shore of the lake, and General Washburne and Mr. Langford traveled south to the head waters of Snake river, but neither party could find any trace of the lost man. While in camp on the lake, snow fell to the depth of two feet. An inventory of provisions was then taken, and on the 17th, eight days after the loss of Mr. Everts, most of the party started for the Madison, with sufficient supplies to carry them home, leaving Mr. Gillette and Messrs. More and Williamson, of the 2nd cavalry, with the balance of the provisions to prosecute the search.

It was the opinion of all the members of the party, when Mr. Langford left them on the Madison, that if Mr. Everts had not then been heard from in Virginia or Helena, he had been shot by Indians. The only route that he could have taken that would not have brought him to Virginia or Helena a week since, is that leading by the 'Three Tetons' to Eagle Rock Bridge, which point he could have reached several days ago; and had he done so, would undoubtedly have telegraphed his friends here.

It is the intention of Mr. Langford to prepare for publication, as soon as practicable, a detailed report of the journey to and from this most interesting portion of our country, where, in a space so circumscribed, are presented at once the wonders of Iceland, Italy, and South America.

General Washburn's account of the trip through Wonderland appeared in two installments,[155] subtitled "Explorations in a New and Wonderful Country." This account was the first written by a member of the Washburn party (the brief account already presented was prepared by the editor from Langford's notes), and it was also the first account of the party's discoveries to go beyond the boundaries of Montana Territory. Thus it is of more than ordinary interest. The text follows:

As your readers are aware, the Yellowstone Expedition left Ft. Ellis on the 22d of August, through the Bozeman Pass,[156] finding it all that the Bozemanites claim for it—easy and practicable—and camped for the first night on Trail creek, having a fine view of the mountains beyond the Yellowstone. The next day they struck the valley, and their journey up the river commenced. They camped for the night at the ranch of Mr. Bottler, the last settler up the river. Crow Indians were quite plenty during the day, and a heavy rain at night gave anything but a pleasing aspect to the commencement of the trip; but a bright sun, about 10 o'clock, made everything right, and we moved to the cañon of the river [Yankee Jim Canyon], about fourteen miles distant, and camped on one of the loveliest spots in Montana. Two small streams put in from the east from an elevation near camp. The river and valley can be seen stretching away far to the north, the river bank plainly defined by the trees skirting its margin. South, the river can be seen pouring through the cañon; while far away to the east and west the mountain peaks were then covered with snow—the setting sun brightening both in its last rays, before night's mantle was thrown over the party.

We passed through the cañon next morning, and found it about six miles long—the trail leading us along the side of the torrent, and sometimes hundreds of feet above it. Night found us at the mouth of Gardiner river, a fine mountain stream coming from the south, and entering the Yellowstone just below the Grand Canon, over thirty miles in length and nearly equally divided by the east fork [Lamar River]. The cañon proving impracticable, we took to the mountains, camping one night in them, and the next night a few miles above. The river runs for sixteen miles in nearly a due west course here. Our camp was on a fine stream coming in from the opposite side of the east fork, and designated by us as Tower Creek. The camp was called Camp Comfort. Game and trout were abundant. We found here our first hot springs, small but attractive, and of five or six different kinds—sulphur, iron, etc. This cañon of the river is grand. Basaltic columns, of enormous size, are quite numerous. But the great attraction here was the falls on the creek, near our camp. The stream is about as large as the Prickly Pear, and for a mile rushes down with fearful velocity. It seems at some time to have been checked by a mountain range, through which it has torn its way, not entirely removing the barrier, but tearing through, leaving portions still standing; and these, by the elements, have been formed into sharp pinnacles. Looking from the canyon below, it appears like some old castle with its turrets dismantled but still standing. From between two of these turrets the stream makes its final leap of 110 measured feet, and then, as if satisfied with itself, flows peacefully into the Yellowstone. We attempted to compare it with the famous Minne-ha-ha, but those who had seen both said there was no comparison. It was not as terrible in its sublimity as Niagara, but beautiful and glorious. You felt none of the shrinking back so common at the Great Fall, but rather, as you stood below and gazed upon its waters broken into white spray, you felt as though you wanted to dash into it and catch it as it fell. By a vote of the majority of the party this fall was called Tower Fall.

The cañon of the main river here runs in a southwest direction. The party crossed over a high range of mountains [Washburn Range], and in two days reached the Great Falls. In crossing the range, from an elevated peak a very fine view was had. The country before us was a vast basin. Far away in the distance, but plainly seen, was the Yellowstone Lake. Around the basin the jagged peaks of the Wind River, Big Horn, and Lower Yellowstone ranges of mountains, while just over the lake could be seen the tops of the Tetons. Our course lay over the mountains and through dense timber. Camping for the night eight or ten miles from the falls, we visited some hot springs that, in any other country, would be a great curiosity; boiling up two or three feet, giving off immense volumes of steam, while their sides were incrusted with sulphur. It needed but a little stretch of imagination on the part of one of the party to christen them, "Hellbroth Springs." Our next camp was near the Great Falls, upon a small stream running into the main river between the Upper and Lower Falls [Cascade Creek]. This stream has torn its way through a mountain range, making a fearful chasm through lava rock, leaving it in every conceivable shape. This gorge was christened the "Devil's Den." Below this is a beautiful cascade, the first fall of which is five feet, the second twenty feet, and the final leap eighty-four feet. From its exceedingly clear and sparkling beauty it was named Crystal Cascade.

Crossing above the Upper Falls of the Yellowstone, you find the river one hundred yards in width, flowing peacefully and quiet. A little lower down it becomes a frightful torrent, pouring through a narrow gorge over loose boulders and fixed rocks, leaping from ledge to ledge, until, narrowed by the mountains and confined to a space of about eight feet, it takes a sudden leap, breaking into white spray in its descent a hundred and fifteen feet. Two hundred yards below the river again resumes its peaceful career. The pool below the falls is a beautiful green capped with white. On the right hand side a clump of pines grew just above the falls, and the grand amphitheatre, worn by the maddened waters on the same side, is covered with a dense growth of the same. The left side is steep and craggy. Towering above the falls, half way down and upon a level with the water, is a projecting crag, from which the falls can be seen in all their glory. No perceptible change can be seen in the volume of water here from what it was where we first struck the river. At the head of the rapids are four apparently enormous boulders standing as sentinels in the middle of the stream. Pines are growing upon two of them. From the Upper Fall to the Lower there is no difficulty in reaching the bottom of the cañon. The Lower Falls are about half a mile below the Upper, where the mountains again, as if striving for the mastery, close in on either side, and are not more than seventy feet apart. And here the waters are thrown over a perpendicular fall of three hundred and fifty feet. The cañon below is steep and rocky, and volcanic in its formation. The water, just before it breaks into spray, has a beautiful green tint, as has also the water in the cañon below. Just below, on the left hand side, is a ledge of rock from which the falls and cañon may be seen. The mingling of green water and white spray with the rainbow tints is beautiful beyond description.

This cañon is a fearful chasm, at the lower falls a thousand feet deep, and growing deeper as it passes on, until nearly double that depth. Jutting over the cañon is a rock two hundred feet high, on the top of which is an eagle's nest which covers the whole top. Messrs. Hauser, Stickney and Lieut. Doan [sic] succeeded in reaching the bottom, but it was a dangerous journey. Two and a half miles below the falls, on the right, a little rivulet [Silver Cord Cascade], as if to show its temerity, dashes from the top of the cañon and is broken into a million fragments in its daring attempt.

After spending one day at the falls we moved up the river. Above the falls there is but little current comparatively for several miles, and the country opens into a wide, open, treeless plain. About eight miles from the falls, and in this plain, we found three hills, or rather mountains, thrown up by volcanic agency, and consisting of scoria and a large admixture of brimstone. These hills are several hundred feet high, and evidently are now resting over what was once the crater of a volcano. A third of the way up on the side of one of these hills is a large sulphuric spring, twenty feet by twelve, filled with boiling water, and this water is thrown up from three to five feet. The basin of this spring is pure solid brimstone, as clear and bright as any brimstone of commerce. Quite a stream flows from the spring, and sulphur is found encrusting nearly everything. Near the base of the hills is a place containing about half an acre, but covered with springs of nearly every description,—yellow, green, blue and pink. Flowing from the base of the hill is a very strong spring of alum water—not only alum in solution, but crystallized. This place we called Crater Hill, and as we passed over, the dull sound coming from our horses feet as they struck, proved to us that it was not far through the crust. All over the hill were small fissures, giving out sulphurous vapors. The amount of brimstone in these hills is beyond belief.

Passing over the plain we camped on the river bank, near a series of mud springs [Mud Volcano area]. Three of the largest were about ten feet over the top and had built up ten or twelve feet high. In the bottom of the crater thus [erected mud was] sputtering and splashing, as we have often seen in a pot of hasty pudding when nearly cooked. Near these we found a cave under the side of the mountain, from which was running a stream of clear but very hot water [Dragon's Mouth Spring]. At regular intervals the steam was puffing out. For some time we had been hearing a noise as of distant artillery, and soon we found the cause. Some distance above the level of the river we found the crater of a mud volcano, forty feet over at its mouth. It grew smaller until at the depth of thirty feet, when it again enlarged. At intervals a volume of mud and steam was thrown up with tremendous power and noise. It was impossible to stand near, and one of the party, Mr. Hedges, paid for his temerity in venturing too close by being thrown backward down the hill. A short time before our visit, mud had been thrown two or three hundred feet high, as shown by the trees in the vicinity. Not far from this we found our first geyser [Mud Geyser]. When discovered it was throwing water thirty or forty feet high. The crater was funnel-shaped, and seventy-five by thirty-five feet at its mouth. We stayed and watched it one day. Without warning it suddenly ceased to spout, and the water commenced sinking until it had gone down thirty feet or more. It then gradually commenced rising again, and three times during the day threw up water thirty or forty feet.

The next day we recrossed the river[157] and succeeded in reaching the lake, and camped on the lower end. The fishing, which had been good all the way up the river, proved remarkably so in the lake. Trout, from 2 to 4 pounds, were to be had for the taking. Flies proved useless, as the fish had not been educated up to that point. Remaining over Sunday, we took up the line of march around the south side of the lake, which took us through a dense growth of pine, filled with fallen timber. The third [fourth] day's march was over a mountain, and but little progress was made, the train going into camp about 2 o'clock. Mr. Everts failed to come into camp,—but this occasioned no uneasiness, as we had all expected to reach the lake, and believed he had pushed on to the lake, as he had once before done, and was awaiting our arrival. Moving on five miles we struck an arm of the lake, but found no trace of him. A party was sent down the shore, and two other parties to climb adjacent mountains to search for him, and to build fires on them to attract his attention. Next morning, no news being heard of him, a council was held and the camp moved to the main lake, and search commenced vigorously, but without avail. The fourth night[158] a snowstorm commenced and continued for two days, rendering the search during that time impossible. The situation of the party was becoming precarious; away from the settlements, no trail, without a guide, and snow covering the ground. Another council was held, and it was determined that it was best to move towards the settlements. Mr. Gillette volunteered to stay and prolong the search, and two soldiers were left with him. Mr. Gillette is one of the best mountain men of the party, and there is hope that he may bring some tidings of the missing man. On the south end of the lake is a very beautiful collection of hot springs and wells— in many the water is so clear that you can see down fifty or a hundred feet. The lake is eight thousand feet [7,733] above the level of the sea, a beautiful sheet of water, with numerous islands and bays, and will in time be a great summer resort, for its various inlets, surrounded by the finest mountain scenery, cannot fail to be very popular to the seeker of pleasure, while its high elevation and numerous medicinal springs will attract the invalid. Its size is about twenty two by fifteen miles.

Leaving the lake we moved nearly west, over several high ranges, and camped in the snow amid the mountains. Next day about noon we struck the Fire Hole river and camped in Burnt Hole valley [Upper Geyser Basin]. This is the most remarkable valley we found. Hot springs are almost innumerable. Geysers were spouting in such size and number as to startle all, and are beyond description. Enormous columns of hot water and steam were thrown into the air with a velocity and noise truly amazing. We classified and named some of them according to size.

No. 1. The Giant, seven by ten feet, throwing a solid column of water from eighty to one hundred and twenty feet high.

No. 2. The Giantess, twenty by thirty, throwing a solid column and jets from one hundred fifty to two hundred feet high.

No. 3. Old Faithful, seven by eight, irregular in shape, a solid column each hour seventy-five feet high.

No..4. Bee Hive, twenty-four by fifteen inches, stream measured two hundred and nineteen feet.

No. 5. Fan Tail, Irregular shape, throwing a double stream sixty feet high.

No. 6. is a beautiful arched spray, called by us the Grotto, with several aperatures [sic], through which, when quiet, one can easily pass, but when in action, each making so many vents for the water and steam.

Upon going into camp we observed a small hot spring that had apparently built itself up about three feet. The water was warm but resting very quietly, and we camped within two hundred yards of it. While we were eating breakfast, this spring, without any warning, threw, as if it were the nozzle of an enormous steam engine, a stream of water into the air two hundred and nineteen feet, and continued doing so for some time, thereby enabling us to measure it, and then suddenly subsided.

Surrounded by these hot springs is a beautiful cold spring of tolerable fair water. Here we found a beautiful spring or well. Raised around it was a border of pure white, carved as if by the hand of a master workman, the water pure. Looking down into it one can see the sides white and clear as alabaster, and carved in every conceivable shape, down, down, until the eye tires impenetrating [sic].

Standing and looking down into the steam and vapor of the crater of the Giantess, with the sun upon your back, the shadow is surrounded by a beautiful rainbow, and by getting the proper angle, the rainbow, surrounding only the head, gives that halo so many painters have vainly tried to give in paintings of the Savior. Standing near the fountain when in motion, and the sun shining, the scene is grandly magnificent; each of the broken atoms of water shining like so many brilliants, while myriads of rainbows are dancing attendance. No wonder then that our usually staid and sober companions threw up their hats and shouted with ecstasy at the sight.

We bid farewell to the Geysers, little dreaming there were more beyond. Five miles beyond Burnt Hole we found the "Lake of Fire and Brimstone." In the valley we found a lake measuring four hundred and fifty yards in diameter, gently overflowing, that had built itself up by deposit of white substrata, at least fifty feet above the plain. This body of water was steaming hot. Below this was a similar spring, but of smaller dimentions [sic], while between the two, and apparently having no connection with either, was a spring of enormous volume flowing into the Madison [Firehole River], and is undoubtedly the spring which Bridger has been laughed at so much about, as heating the Madison for two miles below. For some distance down the river we found hot springs and evidences of volcanic action. Our passage down the river was a little rough but generally very pleasant, and on the evening of the 22nd we reached the first ranche on the Madison, where we found a paper dated September 1st, the latest news from the inside world. Next day we went to Virginia for papers, and soon found that the world had been moving.

Our trip was a grand success, only marred by the loss of one of our number. If he is merely lost there is still hopes of his return, as he had a good horse and plenty of ammunition and matches. The danger is that he has been killed by the Indians for his horse and gun.   H.D.W.

The return of the Washburn party appears to have received little notice outside Montana Territory. The earliest report, evidently based on the scanty information received by telegraph, was published at Salt Lake City and contained nothing of particular interest, being only a brief note to the effect that the "Yellowstone exploring expedition" had returned to Helena after accurately determining the height of "the falls" and the location of lakes. There was no mention of the finding of hot springs and geysers, but the loss of Everts was mistakenly coupled with a sanguinary event in Idaho Territory.[159]

A more adequate presentation of the expedition's findings followed the receipt of the *Helena Herald* articles of the 27th and 28th by newspapers with which an exchange was maintained by mail. The Denver, Colorado, *Rocky Mountain News* reprinted that part of General Washburn's account concerned with the thermal wonders of the Upper Geyser Basin, prefacing it with this statement:

> There are a great many wonderful things in the West, and many wonderful stories are told regarding them. From the Montana Herald's account of the recent Yellowstone expedition, we take the following, which while it may interest and astonish the reader, will also draw somewhat on his powers of credulity.[160]

Such skepticism prompted a Montana editor to vouch for the explorers. He reminded his journalistic brethren:

> As we have not published these accounts, our statement may be taken as that of a disinterested witness. We assure our contemporaries outside of Montana, that the expedition was composed of intelligent and reliable gentlemen, and that their published reports are entitled to and receive the fullest credence in Montana.[161]

That the information provided by Langford and Washburn did not seem incredible to more sophisticated editors is evident from the fact that the St. Paul, Minn., *Pioneer Press* reprinted the Washburn and Langford accounts in full, and without comment,[162] while the *New York Times* had this to say of General Washburn's narrative:[163]

> Accounts of travel are often rather uninteresting, partly because of the lack of interest in the places visited, and partly through the defective way in which they are described. A poetic imagination may, however, invest the dreariest spots with attraction, and the loveliest nooks of earth may seem poor and arid if sketched with a dullard's pencil. But, perhaps, the most graphic and effective descriptions of actual scenery come from those "plain people," as Mr. Lincoln would have called them, who, aiming at no graces of rhetoric, are unconsciously eloquent by the force of simplicity.
>
> A record of the Yellowstone Exploring Expedition, which has just happened to reach us, is distinguished by this graphic directness and unpretending eloquence. It is partial and fragmentary, but it reads like the realization of a child's fairy tale. We mean no disparagement, but the reverse, of the Notes of the Surveyor-General of Montana, in saying this. No unstudied description that we have read of the internal scenery of the American Continent, surpasses his notes in any particular. The country he had to describe certainly offers great advantages. But it is much to his credit that he has performed the task in so unpretending a manner. Where temptation to fall into the besetting sins of tourists is great, the merit of avoiding them is equally great.

A review of Washburn's account was concluded with a statement in which the editor of the *Times* again commented favorably upon it, noting,

We have said that this record reads like a fairy tale, and readers will by this time agree with us. Its official character, however, may be added to the evidence of that simplicity of style already commended as earnest of the trustworthiness of the narrative. Rarely do descriptions of nature come to our hands so unaffectedly expressed, and yet so gilded with true romance.

Despite the foregoing evidences of newspaper reportage varying from undisguised scoffing to excessive enthusiasm, it is probably a fact that the early reports made little impression on the public. Such great and influential papers as the *Philadelphia Public Ledger*, *St. Louis Times*, and *San Francisco Chronicle* were either unaware of, or uninterested in, the Yellowstone region. The Portland *Oregonian*, which was certainly neither, made no mention of the Washburn party, though it devoted nearly a column to a meaningless account of a visit to the Yellowstone Falls obtained from the Bozeman *Montana Pick and Plow*.[164]

Word of what the explorers had found in the Yellowstone wilderness appears to have reached New York City at least 4 days prior to publication of the *Times* article. In a letter to Jay Cooke on October 10, the Northern Pacific's crotchety secretary, Samuel Wilkeson, complained: "The villains in Helena are wholly uncovering the nakedness of our sleeping Yellowstone Beauty. It breaks my heart."[165] That lament was based on the desire of the railroaders to lay claim to the choice lands along their line under the provisions of the grant allowed by the Congress, and advance publicity could only defeat their objective. It also hints that they had some knowledge of the Yellowstone region and were even then thinking of its possible value to their future development plans.

Locally, the interest in the Langford and Washburn articles was so great that the *Helena Daily Herald* announced on September 30: "We to-day reproduce the articles of both these gentlemen, and print a large number extra of the paper to supply the public demand." And before that interest had waned, Warren C. Gillette was back from his vain search for Everts.

Gillette's negative report furnished the material for a lengthy newspaper article of considerable interest because of the dreadful possibility it raised in connection with Everts' disappearance. In this,[166] the public was informed:

While making their way through the forest they suddenly came upon a man mounted on a grey horse. Mr. Gillette asked him if there were any others with him. He replied that there were three others. Mr. Gillette asked him what they were doing up there. With much hesitation and stammering, as if at a loss what reply to make, he finally answered with assured *nonchalance*, that they were fishing and trapping. He also said that the others were in camp near the lake shore at a point which was but a short distance from the five days' camp of the whole Yellowstone party, before leaving the lake. The general appearance of the man was so bad, and his actions so suspicious, that Mr. Gillette's party were all fully convinced that he was an outlaw or fugitive from justice. They soon after, in a more open part of the woods, found the trail of the party, plainly discernable in the snow, and made by eighteen or twenty horses, all or nearly all unshod. Among them were the tracts [sic] of a colt. It was evident, from the appearance of the trail, that there were more than four men, as the evenness and uniformity of the trail through the snow plainly evidenced the fact that it was made by horses under the saddle and not by loose or packed animals; there being but comparatively few tracts outside of the trail, in the snow.

They followed this trail a mile or more, but as it was storming hard at the time they finally left it, and as they had in the meantime lost their own reckoning, they struck off to the right, finding the trail of the party and then leaving it again, when their efforts were diverted to the task of determining their own position in respect to the lake, which was the first thing to be done before any systematic search with any hope of final success could be instituted.

And here we may properly refer to a circumstance to which allusion was made in our issue of September 28th A lot of horses having been stolen near Pleasant valley [on the Montana stage route], a party of men followed the thieves up a branch of Snake river, and on the 10th of September accidentally came to the place where General Washburn's party camped September 9th, the day Mr. Everts was lost. Near this point they lost trace of the thieves, who had evidently succeeded in secreting themselves somewhere in the fallen timber. [If] Mr. Everts, in his wanderings, had accidentally struck the trail of the horse thieves and had followed it (for he would have followed any trail) until he came near where they were concealed; Can it be doubted that they, seeing a man approaching them armed with a needle-gun, revolver, and a belt full of cartridges, would have concluded that he was one of the pursuing party on their trail, and would have shot him at once?

We have conversed with Messrs. Gillette, Hauser and Langford, whose experience here for the past eight years, and knowledge of the desperate character of the horse thieves and road agents that infest Montana, and familiarity with all the circumstances that may be even remotely connected with this most unfortunate affair, entitle their opinions to the fullest weight, and they are of the opinion that there is but little hope that Mr. Everts can be alive Mr. Gillette thinks he probably perished during the storm that prevailed the fourth and fifth days after he was lost, rather than that he met his death at the hands of the road agents or Indians. Messrs. Hauser and Langford, on the other hand, think it more probable that he has been shot by horse thieves or Indians— Mr. Hauser favoring the former idea, and Mr. Langford the latter.

All of the party, however, are fully agreed that any further search for Mr. Everts will be entirely fruitless, as in that dense and almost interminable forest, in which the ground was covered with fallen timber, through which their pack train could move but from six to eight miles a day, a thousand men might search a month and find no trace of a lost man. The pine leaves were lying so thickly upon the surface of the ground, that the tracks of nearly forty horses, (shod) belonging to the expedition, trailing one another, were hardly discernable two hours after they were made.

We feel fully assured that everything has been done for the recovery of Mr. Everts that humanity can suggest, and to Mr. Gillette is due the highest credit and the gratitude of all our citizens for the fidelity with which he has discharged the trust voluntarily assumed in behalf of the members of the Yellowstone expedition.

Fortunately for the lost man, the rescue efforts were not allowed to rest there. Judge Lawrence, the law partner of Cornelius Hedges, offered a reward for the recovery of Everts.[167] Contained in the announcement was word of yet another attempt to find Everts:

A party consisting of two men, George A Pritchett and John Baronet,[168] was organized and outfitted in this city, yesterday, and left this morning for the Yellowstone country, to search for the Hon. T. C. Everts, who was lost in the mountains on the 9th ult. Messrs. Pritchett and Baronet will proceed to the Crow Agency, procure the services of two or three Indians, follow up the trail of the Expedition to the lake, where Mr. Everts was lost, then commence their search. These men are both familiar with the country, having visited it last Summer, a year ago, are well supplied with provisions, blankets, arms, ammunition and everything necessary for such a trip. They also have with them a map of the Yellowstone Lake and adjacent country, drawn by Col. S. T. Hauser. Messrs. Pritchett and Baronet propose to remain until the deep snows of winter drive them back, unless they shall have succeeded in finding the lost man before that time.

Judge Lawrence, of this city, has offered a reward of $600 for the recovery of the lost man.

The *Herald's* own correspondent with the Yellowstone expedition, Cornelius Hedges, produced nothing for that paper until 2 weeks after his return, and that beginning appears to have been prompted by a desire to honor the yet lost Everts. His article, entitled "Mount Everts," is descriptive both of the man and of the eminence overlooking the southeast arm of Yellowstone Lake which they had climbed together. The text follows:[169]

To the Editor of the Herald:

Please allow me, through your columns, to relate an incident connected with the recent trip of the Yellowstone party, to which subsequent events have added melancholy interest. It occurred at our first camp on the south shore of Yellowstone Lake, where we bivouacked on the evening of September 7. On that day, by a long detour through tangled thickets and fallen timber, through swampy flats surrounding the inlet of the Yellowstone River into the lake of the same name, we had reached a point but little farther east than we had made the day before, and been compelled to retrace our steps by reason of impassable sloughs. We no longer had any sort of trail, and the difficulties of traveling were multiplying upon us; besides, the southern lake shore is very irregular—long promontories or points jutting out from the mainland for miles into the lake. It became to all of us a matter of first importance to curtail our route by making cuts across the necks of these points. With that object in view, General Washburn and myself, after pitching camp and disposing of supper, took a ramble to spy out a route for our next day's drive. At about a mile from camp, in nearly a due-east course, we came upon a game trail, passed an old Indian tepee at least a year old, skirted a little lake about 50 feet above the main lake, snugly tucked up about the foot of a high, bold, bluffy point partly open and partly covered with standing and fallen timber. At that time we only ascended a short distance, as the sun had already set and we were not altogether fresh after the scratching and floundering of the day's journey. We were anxious to know what could be seen from

88

the top of that mountain, and Mr. Everts proposed to me that I should go with him as soon as breakfast was over in the morning, September 8. Accordingly we went. He manifested much eagerness to go and seemed in more than usual good spirits. The point reached the night before was soon passed, and we stood upon what appeared as the top seen from the base, but we found it but one step to a much bolder point, whose base was concealed from our view below. Not knowing the persistency of the man, I asked him if we had better go to the top, and his quick response was, "By all means." The sides of this mountain were in places so nearly perpendicular that we made slow and labored progress. Sometimes losing our foothold, we would slide back several feet. In one instance I lost ground about 4 rods and was indebted to a dwarf pine for not losing more distance and perhaps even worse consequences. Thrice we halted on what seemed from below to be the summit, and still we found the top beyond us, which we reached by a final desperate attempt, making the last 50 feet by drawing ourselves up, grasping projecting rocks along the face of an almost perpendicular ledge of dark, coarse, conglomerate rock. Here we stood on a broad, level, rocky rim to a high plateau, pine covered as it receded, which commands a most magnificent view of the whole lake and the dark-green piney basin in which it nestles. In admiration of the pluck and perseverance of my companion, I told him that point should be named Mount Everts. During the half hour we remained on this mountain, probably 12,000 [1,200] feet above the lake's surface, we traced almost its entire outline, as well the part that we proposed to traverse as that over which we had already come. We could even see through a gap in the easternmost of the southern promontories the blue waters of the southeast [West] arm of the lake, near which we expected to take our departure for the headwaters of the Madison. I then noticed, with some surprise, that with his glasses he could see such distant features as I called to his notice. We examined, as minutely as time allowed, the intervening space, tracing out what we thought the most practicable route across the necks of several points reaching miles away into the lake. This was only the day before he got separated from us, and so strong was my faith that he knew our course and would appear at some point in our advance that I scarcely entertained a fear till we finally reached the farthest point where we left the lake.

In descending the mountains Mr. Everts took a shorter line to camp than that by which we came, while I was unwilling to take any chances of missing my way, and returned as I went. I found Mr. Everts in camp when I reached it. It increased greatly my confidence in his good judgment as a woodsman.

The company, of course, assented to my proposed name for the mountain we had visited, and let future tourists respect this monumental record. What more fitting monument can transmit to future generations the name of our lamented companion? As it towers in self-complacent grandeur above the beautiful lake, and serenely marks the passage of storms, and seasons, and centuries, Mount Everts seems a fitting type of that noble, self-reliant spirit, destined, as we fear, so soon after to be quenched by a dismal fate in the wooded wilderness near its base.

The hope of his rescue so long deferred makes the heart sicken with gloom. Baffled in all our hopes, we incline to believe that he became a victim to the gang of desperadoes that, flying from hot pursuit by way of Snake River, found their refuge in the impenetrable forests and swamps of the south shore of Yellowstone Lake. It is some melancholy satisfaction, should the mystery of his fate never be cleared up, that I had some instrumentality in providing for him so fitting a monument as Mount Everts.

Yours truly,

CORNELIUS HEDGES

Helena, October 8, 1870

The slowness of Cornelius Hedges to get into print is explained in a letter written on October 2 to an eastern newspaper.[170] His description of the trip as far as Tower Fall was concluded with the statement: "I would try to write you more but the territorial fair and district court, in addition to arrears of business leave me little prospect of doing more at present." Likewise, he wrote his father at the time, "If I were not overcrowded with business at present I would write you an account of some of the objects of wonder that I saw on my recent trip."[171]

With the "Mount Everts" article, Hedges had begun his series describing Yellowstone features: "The Great Falls of the Yellowstone, A Graphic Picture of Their Grandeur and Beauty" appeared in the *Helena Herald's* issue of October 15; "Hell-Broth Springs," on October 19; "Pictures of the Yellowstone Country—Sulphur Mountain and Mud Volcano," on October 24; and "Yellowstone Lake," on November 9.[172] The last is of more than ordinary interest because it contains the only statement to come from the pen of a member of the Washburn party, prior to inception of the park movement, proposing reservation of Yellowstone features in the public interest. This statement is contained in the following paragraph:

> This beautiful body of water is situated in the extreme northwest corner of Wyoming, and, with its tributaries and sister lakes of smaller dimensions, is entirely cut off from all access from any portion of that Territory by the impassable and eternally snow-clad range of the Wind River Range of mountains. Hence the propriety that the Territorial lines be so readjusted that Montana should embrace all that lake region west of the Wind River Range,[173] a matter in which we hope our citizens will soon move to accomplish, as well as to secure its future appropriation to the public use.

A close examination of this suggestion shows it to have two distinct parts: one, calling for inclusion of what is essentially the present park within the Territory of Montana, and the other calling for a dedication to an undefined "public use." There is no way of divining what public use Cornelius Hedges had in mind, for he never elaborated the idea. But subsequent statements in the Montana press indicate that a grant to the Territory of Montana, similar to the grant made to the State of California of the Yosemite Valley and Big Trees, was desired by some influential persons.[174] Thus it is entirely possible Hedges was thinking in the same terms.

How influential Hedge's published suggestion was is speculative. The only evidence of contemporary publication outside of Montana thus far found is a clipping from the *Independence* (Iowa) *Conservative*.[175]

Publicity during the period immediately following the return of the Washburn party was dominated by the *Helena Herald*. However, the rival *Rocky Mountain Gazette* also had a correspondent with the expedition, Walter Trumbull, and he contributed both a brief sketch of the exploration and two serialized accounts.[176] These were done in the witty style characteristic of Trumbull's writing (he had been a reporter for the New York Sun), but were mere travelogue lacking even a suggestion of prognosis. In an introduction to the weekly series, however, the editor commented: "We are satisfied that this wonderful region only needs to become known to attract as much attention as any other on the face of the globe." To that point, Helena's two newspapers were in agreement concerning the Yellowstone region.

The unlikely recovery of the lost expeditioner, Truman C. Everts, created another flurry of dispatches and accounts. The news that Baronett and Pritchett had found him alive appeared in the *Helena Daily Herald* of October 21, 1870,[177] which printed a letter from Pritchett, addressed at Fort Ellis "To. Messrs. King, Gillette, Langford, Lawrence and other Gentlemen":

> We have found Mr. Everts. He is alive and safe, but very low in flesh. It seems difficult to realize the fact that he lived, but nevertheless it is so. We sent a messenger to this post for a surgeon, and afterwards I started with a fresh horse to meet him, but did not do so, and came on here: the messenger had left about an hour before I arrived with an ambulance by the wagon road,[178] and I missed him. I return tomorrow.
>
> I understand that the messenger who came here in advance of me, sent or went to Helena to apprise the friends of Mr. Everts of his safety, and may exagerate his condition,[174] but I think you need not give yourselves the least uneasiness, as he has all the attention possible under the circumstances, and when the surgeon gets there he will be all right.
>
> We found him on the 16 inst., on the summit of the first big mountain beyond Warm Spring Creek, about seventy-five miles from this fort.[180] He says he subsisted all this time on one snow bird, two small minnows, and the wing of a bird which he found and mashed between two stones, and made some broth in a yeast powder can. This was all, with the exception of thistle roots (of which he had a fair supply) he has subsisted on.
>
> He lost his mare, saddle, gun and cantenas the first day out, and was left without fishing tackle or matches; but after making his bed over warm holes for several nights he thought he might produce fire from his opera glass, and did so. He lost both his knives. During his wanderings he saw no human beings, neither whites nor Indians, until we found him.

A note from Dr. Leander W. Frary, of Bozeman, published the following day buoyed the hope that Everts would live.[181] After the rescued man had been returned to Fort Ellis, Samuel Langhorne provided the *Helena Herald* with a longer account based on details obtained from Jack Baronett and on Everts' own recollections.[182] Another dispatch from the same correspondent appeared on the 28th to fill in gaps in what had already become a marvelous tale. Langhorne found it hard to draw a pen-picture of Everts, who was "very spare, not weighing more than 80 pounds," with a partially paralysed arm and one foot worn to the bone on the outside, yet "converses freely and pleasantly with all who come to see him."[183]

Some of the things he said seem to have led callers to believe Everts was deranged during his 39-day ordeal, an impression he attempted to scotch in the following letter written to Judge Lawrence on the 25th:

> My Dear Old Friends: I am unable, as you see, to write intelligently as yet, but I desire to express my gratitude to you and other good friends, who have taken an interest in my return to life. I am getting along very well, and will try and get to Helena in ten days. Settle with the man who came to my rescue as you agreed. What it is I do not know. I will make it right with you. They took all the care they could of me, and were very kind.
>
> I can give you no particulars now, but please believe no absurd stories of my being deranged. I have been all right in this respect, and only suffer from exhaustion.[184]

The return of Truman C. Everts to Helena was reported on November 5, and he was later feted at a banquet at the Kan-Kan Restaurant—a repast called "one of the most elaborate and elegant ever served in Montana."[185]

The cumulative effect of the publicity generated by the Washburn party is summarized by an unidentified correspondent writing to the *Helena Herald* in "Our Washington Letter." The writer says:

> The Yellowstone Expedition, of which we have been so fully and graphically informed through the columns of the HERALD, has from the first excited a deep interest here and throughout the East; while the news of the final recovery of Mr. Everts, as copied from the HERALD into all the papers of this city yesterday, sent a thrill of sympathetic joy through the entire community. The wonderful discoveries reported by General Washburn (whose report thereof, by the way, is lavishly complimented by the New York Journals) are likely and almost certain to lead to an early and thorough exploration of those mysterious regions under the patronage of the General Government and the Smithsonian Institute [*sic*], and other prominant institutions of the country. I think this will be sure to take place next season; at least, as this and other matters progress, you shall hear occasionally from THE OLD MAN.[186]

A primary purpose of the Washburn party had been to improve the cartographic knowledge of the Yellowstone region. General Washburn had stressed the need to determine the location of Yellowstone Lake and the falls on its outlet river when requesting an escort of soldiers, and General Hancock's approval specified that the detail should go to "an intelligent officer of calvary who can make a correct map of the country."[187] Two manuscript maps were produced, one by Doane and one by Washburn (see maps 11 and 12), but neither improved on the deLacy-Folsom portrayal except in providing a better outline of Lake Yellowstone. In fact, they retained nearly all the distortions and ambiguities of that model.

The foregoing covers the Washburn party and its immediate effect in publicizing the Yellowstone region, but such newspaper reportage was less important than the lectures and magazine articles which soon appeared. The latter, in particular, reached a large and sophisticated segment of the American public, so that the national park movement of the winter of 1871–72 built upon a subject that was not altogether unfamiliar.

Nathaniel P. Langford returned from the Yellowstone region with plans for publishing something more pretentious than the brief newspaper account which was his immediate contribution.[189] However, what he did during the 6 weeks between his return and November 11 was to produce a manuscript which was suited more to lecturing than publication. It consisted of approximately 13,000 words, written with ink in a large, clear hand in a ledger. The text occupied alternate pages, with their opposites unused except for occasional notes. There was no title.[190]

The *Helena Daily Herald* informed its readers of Langford's plans by quoting the *Gazette*, thus:

> Lectures.—Hon. N. P. Langford, we understand, is to lecture in the States this winter, on the wonders of the Yellowstone country. Mr. Langford is a good writer, and the wonderful scenes which he has to describe must insure the delight and attention of any audience—even in the plainest narration. They are eloquent of themselves. We understand that Mr. Langford will deliver his lecture here before his departure, at the request of a number of citizens. The Herald, of this city, announced recently that Hon. James M. Ashley is to lecture to a number of societies this winter on the Resources of Montana. The theme chosen by the lecturer, and the difusion of knowledge in relation to our Territory among his hearers will be very beneficial to our interests—while an orator desirous of making a creditable literary effort could not be inspired by a nobler subject.[191]

The promised lecture was presented on the evening of November 18 at the Methodist Episcopal Church in Helena under the auspices of the Library Association. The Editor of the *Herald* had cajoled the townspeople to "come out in force," because "This lecture has been prepared with great care, and is the same, substantially, that Mr. Langford will deliver (in filling his engagements with the Literary and Scientific Associations of the East) before the most polished and learned audiences of the country."[192]

A second lecture in Montana was presented at Virginia City on November 22,[193] but the press failed to record the response to it, and Langford's personal diary indicates he left "for the States" at 6 p.m. the following day.

The first presentation of Langford's lecture in the East was given in Lincoln Hall in Washington, D.C., where an unexpectedly large audience gathered on the evening of January 19 to enjoy "an entertainment equal in thrilling interest to any of the season." According to the reporter who covered the lecture, "The speaker, being introduced by Speaker [James G.] Blaine [of the House of Representatives], read a written statement of his adventures in exploration of the Yellowstone Valley," and the half-column review indicates a travelogue treatment of the subject which made it "evident that even the wonders of YoSemite are eclipsed by the Yellowstone Valley."[194] The reportage does not mention the idea of reservation of the Yellowstone region in the public interest, and, since it is stated that Langford "read" his discourse, it was probably a word-for-word rendering of the manuscript cited in note 190.

One who listened attentively to Langford's description of the Yellowstone wonders had, himself, narrowly missed seeing them a decade earlier. He was Dr. Ferninand V. Hayden, head of the Geological Survey of the Territories, who has been accused of borrowing the idea for a Yellowstone National Park from Langford's lecture.[195] However, it is more likely that he was merely inspired by Langford to direct the investigative efforts of his Survey toward the Yellowstone region.

The second lecture in the East was presented in New York City's Cooper Union Hall on January 21, 1871, and it was in his conclusion to this particular lecture, as Langford later stated, that he suggested the creation of Yellowstone National Park. In confirmation, he furnished Hiram M. Chittenden, author of *The Yellowstone National Park*, published in 1895, with the following excerpt said to have been taken from the *New York Tribune* of January 23, 1871:

> This is probably the most remarkable region of natural attractions in the world; and, while we already have our Niagara and Yosemite, this new field of wonders should be at once withdrawn from occupancy, and set apart as a public National Park for the enjoyment of the American people for all time.[196]

The scholar who first discovered that this statement was not a part of the review in which it was supposed to have been published corresponded with Langford and Chittenden concerning it,[197] but without resolving the discrepancy. Langford offered this possible explanation (pp. 379–380):

> It is a matter of great surprise to me, that the quotation from my lecture referred to, cannot be found in the *New York Tribune* report of the lecture. I have in my scrap-book a report of the lecture, which I have always supposed was published in the *New York Tribune* of 23 January, 1871, and which contains the words quoted. The caption *New York Daily Tribune, Monday, January 23, 1871*, was cut from the top of the Tribune, and is pasted in my scrap-book at the head of the report of my lecture. It seems almost incredible that I could have placed the *Tribune* caption over a report taken from another paper,— but if I made such a blunder, then what paper was it? I cannot tell. Yet such a blunder might have been possible, considering the amount of matter which the various papers at that time contained in their eagerness to publish something concerning our discoveries, so marvellous and new to them.

Langford held to an avowal that "whatever reports of my lecture have been made,—whether complete or incomplete,—the fact remains that I advocated the park scheme, in those few words, both in Washington and

New York City."[198] For his part, Chittenden says: "I saw the clipping in question and copied it myself from Mr. Langford's scrapbook and on the border it was noted, as is frequently done in such cases, the date and the paper from which it was taken."[199]

As mentioned, the *New York Daily Tribune* article makes no reference to reservation of the Yellowstone region as a "public National Park" or otherwise. The nearest it comes to emphasizing the area's superlative nature is in this statement: "The explorers were much impressed by the beauty and grandeur of the valley of the Yellowstone River, and found cañons rivaling those of the Colorado."[200] The accounts which appeared in two other New York newspapers were also travelogs unconcerned with the future of the Yellowstone region, while the fourth major newspaper did not cover the lecture.[201] The only press coverage outside New York City which has been found to this writing was in Langford's hometown newspaper—the St. Paul, Minn., *Pioneer Press*—which merely reprinted the *New York Tribune* article in its issue of January 28. Montana's *Helena Daily Herald* did not mention either of the eastern lectures, but its issue of January 26 carried an item which indicates that Langford was also engaged in lobbying at the national capital at that time.[202]

Although newspaper research has not discovered the origin of Langford's quotation, the paragraph invites analysis. Most of the opening line, to the semicolon, appears to have been taken directly from the last line of the penultimate paragraph of Langford's lecture notes. The reference to Niagara Falls is intriguing. If Langford intended to relate Niagara to Yosemite as a public reservation, in 1871 we did not "have our Niagara." The approaches to the falls were entirely in private hands and visitors were charged a fee for access to viewing places—after passing through an unsightly hodge-podge of tea rooms, curio shops, and advertising signs. Not until 15 years later, in 1885, did the State of New York establish Niagara Falls Reservation in order to satisfy public clamor for free access.[203] On the other hand, the passage may simply represent an intention to relate Niagara and Yosemite to Yellowstone as spectacular natural wonders.

The thrust of Langford's lecture, as it appears in his untitled notes, was popularization of the Northern Pacific Railroad route, a purpose he summarizes thus in his concluding paragraph:

What, then, is the one thing wanting to render this remarkable region of natural wonders, accessible. I answer, the very improvement now in process of construction, the N.P.R.R. by means of which, the traveller, crossing the rich grasslands of Dakota will strike the Yellowstone a short distance above its mouth, traverse for 500 miles the beautiful lower valley of that river with its strange scenery, and will be enabled to reach this region from the Atlantic seaboard within 3 days, and can see all the wonders I have here described. Besides these marvels of the Upper Yellowstone, he may also see the Great Falls of the Missouri, the grotesque groups of eroded rocks below Fort Benton, the beautiful cañon of the Prickly Pear, with its massive scenery of rock and forest, and the stupendous architecture of the vast chains and spurs of mountains which everywhere lie along the line of the road in its transit of the Rocky Mountains.[204]

Langford remained in New York City for a few days following his lecture there, and during that time he talked with Secretary Samuel Wilkeson, of the Northern Pacific Railroad, which caused him to address the following letter to Jay Cooke:

> Mr. Wilkison [*sic*] desires me to communicate with Mr. Coffin (Carlton) upon matters connected with the interests of the N.P.R.R.—lectures upon the subject of resources of the country etc.—and requested me to write to you, to see if you could put me in communication with him. My address will be St Nicholas Hotel till tomorrow night, and thereafter will be Utica, N.Y.[205]

Jay Cooke attempted to reach Langford at New York City but did not get a reply from him until he had been several days at Utica (where he had been scheduled to deliver another lecture). This three-page missive explains much.[206] Langford had been confined, following his arrival, by a "severe attack of congestion of the lungs," but hoped for a rapid improvement which would allow him to fulfill his speaking engagement there and at other places. He apologized for his inability to come at once to Philadelphia, suggesting:

> As it will not be prudent for me to leave home for some days yet, will you please write me on receipt of this, what you especially desire me to do;—the nature of the lectures to be given,—the principal points to be presented,—where delivered, etc. I ask to be advised of the main points to be presented, that I may assure myself that I can serve the R.R. Co. as well as its officers and friends whom I have met in New York, seem to think I can. And I should be very glad to deliver my lecture on the "Wonders of the Upper Yellowstone," in Philadelphia, that you may the better judge of my fitness for a field so new to me. Can arrangements be made under the auspices of any of your Lecture Associations?

Langford's question concerning sponsorship, as well as his interest in the particular emphasis desired for the new presentation, must be considered in the light of changes then taking place. Cooke & Company's arrangement with lecture groups to create a general interest in the country through which the Northern Pacific line was to be built was being dropped in favor of a railroad-managed publicity campaign to promote emigration to this country. The first approach was a means of creating a market for railroad bonds, while the latter was intended to sell land obtained under the Northern Pacific grant.

The illness Langford had contracted persisted for 5 weeks as a sore throat which kept him under a physician's care in Utica—except for 1 day when he felt better and "imprudently went to New York."[207] Even then he was in no condition to return to the lecture circuit, for a letter written to Jay Cooke from New York in mid-March has this note penciled on the back: "Have telegraphed him to get well as soon as possible and begin lecture course."[208]

Langford was not idle during his long illness. He corresponded with Henry L. Lamb, a New York State Senator (why remains obscure) who then wrote to the President of the Northern Pacific Railroad:

I have a very interesting private letter from *Hon. N. P. Langford* concerning the Yellow Stone Valley and the region on your line from the Red River to the mountains on Upper Yellow Stone. He is not a supporter of my notions, but—I do not feel so pig-headed in regard to my own observations as to suppress Mr. Langford.[209]

In this is a hint that Langford was only tolerated by some of the railroaders.

Langford was also engaged in preparing an article on the Yellowstone region for *Scribner's Monthly*—a project begun at least as early as his arrival in the East in mid-December.[210] His manuscript was evidently in the hands of the editor prior to March 16, 1871, for the letter of that date (see note 208) mentions "the engravings that appear in the May number,"[211] naming "Mr. Moran" as the artist "who drew them on wood." The letter just mentioned indicates that Jay Cooke contemplated some other use of the Moran engravings, but what this was is not clear.

Yet another project which had Langford's attention during his illness was the preparation of a second lecture—this one emphasizing the resources and natural advantages of the Territory of Montana. It was undoubtedly prepared with due regard to those instructions Langford had solicited from Jay Cooke in his letter of January 29, 1871 (cited in note 206). Thus, the thrust of his presentation was diverted from travelog to summation of those factors of climate, geography, agriculture, and mineralization which could provide a basis for "speedy settlement and rapid development" of the region. In this new context, Yellowstone received barely a notice:

A few years only can elapse, before the marvels of the Upper Yellowstone, its geysers, boiling mud springs, and sulphur mountains, and the great falls of the Missouri . . . will attract thousands of visitors and tourists annually to that distant Territory, to view the wonders of nature, and the granduer of natural scenery.[212]

It was probably this second lecture that was presented May 14, 1871, at Philadelphia; of which Robert E. Fiske, an editor of the *Helena Herald*, spoke in a letter to his paper from New York, May 26, 1871:

Mr. Langford, whom I have had the pleasure of meeting several times in the city, lectured last week at the house of Jay Cooke, near Philadelphia, in the interest of the Northern Pacific Railroad Co. Mr. Langford has an engagement for a series of lectures which he will deliver in Pennsylvania the present month should his threatened bronchial trouble permit.[213]

Evidently Langford had already abandoned the lecturing which had brought him to the East, for his sister, Chloe Taylor, writing to her daughter on May 3, 1871, mentioned that "Louise says Eliza wrote to her, that Tan had been there, and that he had given up his lectures—that he had seen a physician, who says if he does not get relief from his throat

97

trouble, he is a *doomed man* in less than 3 years."[214] No evidence has been found that Langford gave any more lectures after his appearance in Philadelphia, and he appears not to have been concerned with the Yellowstone region again until after his return to Montana Territory in October.

Meanwhile, others were publishing readable accounts of the Yellowstone exploration in popular periodicals. Walter Trumbull's article, "The Washburn Yellowstone Expedition" appeared in the May and June issues of *The Overland Monthly*,[215] but he departed no further from a travelog approach than to recommend the area for sheep raising, and as a waterplace or summer resort when "by means of the Northern Pacific Railroad, the falls of the Yellowstone and the geyser basin are rendered easy of access" [p. 496].

But the most influential result of the Washburn party's exploration of the Yellowstone region was the publication of Lieutenant Doane's report as a Government document. General Hancock's authorization of an escort for the 1870 party specifically required that it include "an intelligent officer of cavalry who can make a correct map of the country" (cited in note 82). That this was no idle thought is evidenced by a copy of a telegram forwarded by Col. John Gibbon from his headquarters (District of Montana) to Maj. E. M. Baker at Fort Ellis. It had originated at the St. Paul, Minn., headquarters of the Army's Department of Dakota, and stated:

> No report has yet been received from the officer who went with Surveyor-General Washburn to the falls of the Yellowstone—in command of escort— The commanding General desires his report, accompanied by such maps as he can make, as soon as possible.[216]

Doane's report was put in order for transmittal by December 15, 1870, and it came out of the Committee on the Territories and was ordered to be printed on March 3, 1871 (see note 95). It was available as a Government document prior to June 12, 1871, when U.S. Representative William D. Kelley drew heavily upon it in his address, "The New Northwest," which he presented at the American Academy of Music in Philadelphia. In this dissertation on the "Northern Pacific Railway, in Its Relations to the Development of the Northwestern Section of the United States," the speaker noted:

> Thanks to the admirable scientific training given our army officers at West Point, and the desire of that distinguished soldier and son of Pennsylvania, Gen. Winfield S. Hancock, [applause,] to ascertain and disclose the resources of the district of which he is in command, we have a recent official report on the characteristics of a hitherto unexplored section of Montana, the wonders of which not only exceed those of Niagara and the geysers of California, but rival in magnitude and extraordinary combination those of the Yo Semite, the cañons of Colorado and the geysers of Iceland.[217]

The importance of the foregoing statement lies in the fact that Congressman Kelley, a longtime advocate of transcontinental railroads and an ardent supporter of the Northern Pacific route, soon afterward advanced the suggestion which helped to initiate the movement leading directly to the establishment of Yellowstone National Park. Before considering his suggestion and the manner of its implementation, it is necessary to speak of the Yellowstone explorations of 1871.

The Hayden and Barlow Parties

(1871)

An early result of the 1870 exploration into the Yellowstone wilderness was the interest it developed among scientists. The first evidence of this was the mention, soon after the Washburn party's return, that their discoveries were likely to lead to an early exploration of the Yellowstone region "under the patronage of the general Government and the Smithsonian Institute, [sic] and other prominent institutions of the country."[218]

Just how Ferdinand V. Hayden and his U.S. Geological Survey of the Territories came to be the agency through which that prognosis was fulfilled is unknown, but it would appear to be only a logical result of his success in resisting the adverse and stultifying influence of Commissioner Joseph S. Wilson, of the General Land Office.[219] Through the support given him by those scientists whose spokesman was Spencer Baird of the Smithsonian Institution, and his friends at the national capital (these included James G. Blaine, Speaker of the House after March 1869, and Henry L. Dawes, Chairman of the House Committee on Appropriations), Hayden's position in the Department of the Interior was greatly improved and his organization was favored with increased means—$40,000 provided under the Sundry Civil Act for the fiscal year beginning July 1, 1871.[220]

The conditions under which Hayden was to do his field work in 1871 were spelled out in a letter of instruction from the Secretary of the Interior:

In accordance with the act of the third session of the 41st Congress, making appropriations for the continuation of the Geological Survey of the Territories of the United States, dated March 4, 1871, you are appointed U.S. Geologist, to date from the first day of July, 1871, with a salary of four thousand dollars per annum [an increase of $1,000]. You will be permitted to select your own assistants who will be entirely subject to your orders, and all your expenditures of the public funds are expected to be made with judicious economy and care.

The area of your explorations must be, to some extent, discretionary, but in order that you may continue your labors of preceding years, geographically, your explorations of the present season will be confined mostly to the Territories of Idaho and Montana. It is probable that your most available point of departure will be Salt Lake City, proceeding thence northward along the mail route as a base to Helena, Montana, and completing the season's work about the sources of the Missouri and Yellow Stone rivers. You will be required to make such instrumental observations, astronomical and barometrical, as are necessary for the construction of an accurate geographical map of the district explored, upon which the different geological formations may be represented with suitable colors.

As the object of the expedition is to secure as much information as possible, both scientific and practical, you will give your attention to the geological, mineralogical, zoological, botanical, and agricultural resources of the country. You will collect as ample material as possible for the illustration of your final reports, such as sketches, sections, photographs, etc.

Should your route lead you in the vicinity of any of our Indian tribes, you will secure such information in regard to them as will be useful to this Department, or the Country. It is desirable that your collections in all Departments shall be as complete as possible, and you will forward them to the Smithsonian Institution to be arranged according to law.

You will be expected to prepare a preliminary report of your labors, which will be ready for publication by Jan'y 1, 1872.[221]

Though Hayden was unable to draw upon his appropriation until July 1, the beginning of the fiscal year, he was still able to assemble and equip his expedition with the help of the Army and the railroads.

Immediately upon the passage of the Sundry Civil bill, Hayden applied to the Secretary of War for permission to draw on the equipment, stores, and transportation at frontier army posts. This was authorized, together with a small escort "when deemed necessary and the public service will permit."[222] Likewise, the Union Pacific and Central Pacific Railroads agreed to carry Hayden's men and equipment without cost. Thus, his experienced assistant, James Stevenson, was able to outfit at Fort D. A. Russell (near Cheyenne, Wyo.) and transport the equipment, subsistence, wagons, and animals he needed by rail to Ogden, Utah, where a base camp was established in mid-May on an old lake terrace a mile east of the city. During the following weeks, the scientists, young men, and old frontiersmen who were to make up the party gathered there.

Hayden's party eventually included, in addition to Managing Director Stevenson, Henry W. Elliot, an artist; Professor Cyrus Thomas, agricultural statistician and entomologist; Anton Schönborn, chief topographer, a veteran of the prewar Corps of Topographical Engineers; A. J. Smith, assistant topographer; William H. Jackson, an Omaha photographer attracted to the Hayden Survey the previous year; George B. Dixon, assistant photographer; J. W. Beaman, meteorologist; Professor G. N. Allen, botanist; Robert Adams, Jr., assistant botanist (later United States Minister to Brazil and a member of Congress from 1893 to 1906); Dr. A. C. Peale, mineralogist (also a medical doctor and a grandson of the naturalist, Reubens Peale); Dr. Charles S. Turnbull, physician and general assistant; Campbell Carrington, zoologist; William B. Logan (son of Representative John A. Logan of Illinois), secretary; F. J. Huse, Chester M. Dawes (son of Representative Henry L. Dawes of Massachusetts), D. Dev. Negley, and J. W. Duncan, all general assistants.[223]

While the members of his party were assembling at Ogden, Hayden received a letter from Capt. John W. Barlow, chief engineer of the army's

Division of Missouri, informing him that,

> Genl Sheridan desires me to join your party previous to its entering the "Great Basin" of the Yellow Stone lake—and I am greatly delighted at the prospect of seeing the wonders of that region under such favorable auspices.[224]

In this correspondence, which was intended to arrange a time and place at which he could join Hayden's expedition, Barlow added:

> I had determined some time ago to endeavor to make an excursion into that country this summer taking a small party along, but as you are to make such a thoroughly exhaustive examination there will probably be no occasion for undergoing the expense of a second expedition of like magnitude.

About the time the expedition began its northward trek, Hayden received a letter from Jay Cooke's office manager asking him to take a guest into the Yellowstone region. He was speaking for the artist Thomas Moran, who was introduced thus:

> —my friend, Thos. Moran, an artist of Philadelphia of rare genius, has completed arrangements for spending a month or two in the Yellowstone country, taking sketches for painting. He is very desirous of joining your party at Virginia City or Helena, and accompanying you to the head of the Yellowstone. I have encouraged him to believe that you [would] be glad to have him join your party, & that you would in all probability extend to him every possible facility. Please understand that we do not wish to burden you with more people than you can attend to, but I think that Mr. Moran will be a very desirable addition to your expedition, and that he will be almost no trouble at all, and it will be a great accomodation to both our house [Jay Cooke & Co.] & the road, if you will assist him in his efforts. He, or course, expects to pay his own expenses, and simply wishes to take advantage of your cavalry escort for protection. You may also have six square feet in some tent, which he can occupy nights. Please write on receipt of this saying what you can do in the way of accomodating him, so that he may know what to take with him, & what to leave behind.
> It is possible, also, that Bierstadt may join you in Montana, before you start for the Yellowstone, but this is only a possibility. Mr. Moran will possibly go to Corinne by rail, & then cross over by stage to Helena in time to join you there.[225]

While enroute to the Yellowstone region, Hayden received a letter from his scientific mentor at the Smithsonian Institution, Spencer Baird, confirming the wisdom of the plan under which the field work was being conducted. He wrote: "I think your plan of operations is good, and you will make more capital and accomplish more for science by concentrating effort upon some one region like the Yellow Stone, than by attempting to traverse an immense section of country."[226]

The plan pursued in the prosecution of the field work during the 1871 season was outlined by Hayden in his letter to the Secretary of the Interior, on the eve of the departure from "Camp Stevenson," the base camp near

> Our route will be along the mail route to Virginia City, and Fort Ellis. We have already made the necessary observations in this valley and propose to connect our work Topographical and Geological with the Pacific Rail Road line. We then propose to examine a belt of country, northward fifty to one hundred miles in width to Fort Ellis, which point we hope to reach about the 10th or 15th of July. The remainder of the season we desire to spend about the sources of those rivers—Yellowstone, Missouri, Green, and Columbia,[228] which have their sources near together in this region.

Captain Barlow's plans matured at this time. In his letter thanking Hayden for "your very cordial invitation to suit my own convenience in joining your party," the captain mentioned that Gen. A. A. Humphreys, Chief of Engineers, had provided financial assistance from the appropriation for surveys, and had suggested he take several assistants with him. He planned to bring Capt. David P. Heap, engineer officer of the Department of Dakota, and "two or three others . . . possibly I may take along a photographer for obtaining views."[229] He intended to organize a small pack train at Fort Ellis and regulate his movements beyond that point so as to share the escort allowed Hayden's party (a factor which may have caused the latter group to abandon the proposed exploration of Snake River for that season).

The progress of the expedition was reported to the Secretary of the Interior in four letters. The first, written July 18 from Bottler's ranch, on the Yellowstone River,[230] reported the establishment of a base camp at that point, beyond which the wheeled vehicles could not be taken. There had been no misfortunes, and Captain Barlow was then a day behind with the escort (Troop F, Second Cavalry). Hayden was able to add: "We have explored a most interesting belt of country from Ogden to this point, observations for the Topography, Geology and Natural History have been made. We found all the maps, official and otherwise, utterly inadequate to travel by."

Hayden's second letter from the area he was exploring was written at Yellowstone Lake on August 8, 1871,[231] following his return from a side trip to the geyser basins on Firehole River. Of his progress within the Yellowstone wilderness he wrote;

> . . . made a pretty careful examination of the Geyser region, Map of the whole region, Charts of the Springs and Geysers, with temperatures of each. Sketches, Photographs etc. I have made quite thorough soundings of the Lake,[232] explored the north and west sides and will now move to the south and east sides. We are making a good topographical and geological map of the entire district.

At this point Lieutenant Doane arrived to take over the escort from Captain Taylor.

Hayden's letter of August 28, again from Bottler's ranch, reported that his survey of the Yellowstone region had been completed without misadventure, so that he felt justified in saying, "no portion of the West has been more carefully surveyed than the Yellow Stone basin."[233]

A final letter from the field, written at Fort Hall on September 20, mentioned the mapping of a belt of country along the return route of his party and set October 1 as the date for the termination of work at Fort Bridger, Wyo.

Meanwhile, Captain Barlow (who had arrived at Fort Ellis on July 12 with Captain Heap and three assistants) had managed to outfit his party in 2 days and move out behind Hayden. Though the two groups shared a common escort, they continued that tandem movement, proceeding through the Yellowstone wilderness a day or two apart but not always by the same route.

Captain Barlow's smaller party concentrated on topographical work, its particular contribution being the establishment of the latitude and longitude of a sufficient number of points to provide the "control" for accurate mapping of the area—a groundwork which served as a fitting conclusion to the exploratory period. Barlow's photographer made what would have been a significant pictorial record had the negatives survived the great Chicago fire.

Both parties suffered reverses following their return to civilization. Hayden's stemmed from the death of his topographer, Anton Schönborn, who took his own life at Omaha on the return to Washington, D.C. This was a lesser calamity than at first supposed because personnel of the U.S. Coast Survey were later successful in interpreting the dead man's field notes.[234] While the resulting map was undoubtedly something less than it might have been, it served Hayden's immediate purpose—as an illustration in his report, and as a base on which to delimit the proposed national park (see map 13).[235]

Captain Barlow's calamity was beyond remedy. The fire which leveled most of Chicago on October 8–11, 1871, also destroyed the headquarters of the Military Division of the Missouri, and with it much of the results of the expedition from which Barlow had just returned. In a letter to Hayden, he explained,

> You will sympathize with me I know when I tell you that our great fire swept away all my photographic plates before prints were taken from them. Only 16 prints were made on Saturday previous to the fire, these 16 Mr. Hine had taken to his house & saved. I lost some of my notes also, though my journal was saved from which I can make a report. The map notes were up at St. Paul & Capt. Heap has sent me a sketch of our route. As we only partially surveyed the *Lake* (knowing that you were doing so with great care) I depended upon your work in that particular, & hope to receive a copy of your map very soon . . . I shall have to trust to our old friendship & your generosity, *now*, respecting an exchange of photographic views. I can only offer you 16 copies, instead of near 200, that I expected to have had. Not one single paper or other property was saved from my office. All my instruments, maps, books, & everything brought back from the Yellowstone, including specimens were consumed. I have had to begin all anew.[236]

Hayden was able to send 100 large prints and an equal number of stereoscopic views as samples, from which Captain Barlow was to pick the photographs he needed. It was necessary for the latter to deal directly with William H. Jackson to obtain his prints because the photographer had retained all the negatives as a condition of employment.[237] Captain Barlow desired the photographs for distribution with his report,[238] and for illustrating the several articles General Sheridan urged him to write.

But General Sheridan was not alone in urging an exposé; Thomas Moran's presence with the Hayden contingent was dictated by *Scribner's* need for illustrative material for yet another Yellowstone article by N. P. Langford (who had been expected to accompany the 1871 expedition in the interest of J. Cooke & Co.). However, Langford was either unable or unwilling, so editor R. W. Gildess found it necessary to write Hayden at Fort Hall, admitting they were "at sea for some literary accompaniment" for Moran's sketches (he had returned to the East early). The question put to Hayden was, "Can you do it for us?" The editor wanted something within a month; if that were not possible, "could you do it for us when you get back to Washington?"[239] It had to be the latter, and it was published in time to be very helpful in bringing the effort to establish Yellowstone Park to a successful conclusion.

The 1871 exploration received an immediate and enthusiastic notice in the press. As the *Helena Daily Herald* said, "The results of the observations and examinations of the late scientific expedition, will soon be given to the public by press, and through it excite a curiosity and interest, which the wonders of Vesuvius, Niagara, and the geysers of Iceland, have never yet caused to be felt."[240] Less than a week later the *New York Times*, while anticipating "trustworthy, exact, and comprehensive . . . information of one of the most wonderful tracts of the American continent," stated:

> There is someting romantic in the thought that, in spite of the restless activity of our people, and the almost fabulous rapidity of their increase, vast tracts of the national domain yet remain unexplored. As little is known of these regions as of the topography of the sources of the Nile or the interior of Australia. They are enveloped in a certain mystery, and their attractions to the adventurous are constantly enhanced by remarkable discoveries. . . . Sometimes, as in the case of the Yellowstone Valley, the natural phenomena are so unusual, so startlingly different from any known elsewhere, that the interest and curiosity excited are not less universal and decided.[241]

Something of the persistent skepticism with which information concerning the Yellowstone region was received is evident in an item subsequently published in the same columns. Under the title, "The New Wonderland" (probably the first *published* use of the term "wonderland" to typify what is now the park), the *Times* made the following comment in regard to the information received from the expedition's artist, Henry Elliot:

> The accounts of the Yellowstone country hitherto received, even when brought by authorities so respectable as Lieut. Doane, have been so

extraordinary that confirmatory testimony has been anxiously looked for. Even now, and with every respect for the new witness, part of whose evidence we shall quote, the official narrative of the Hayden Expedition must be deemed needful before we can altogether accept stories of wonder hardly short of fairy tales in the astounding phenomena they describe.[242]

But regardless of the lingering skepticism, the information obtained in 1871 was reaching the reading public from one side of the Nation to the other. Comments and narratives stemming from expedition personnel appeared in the *Boston Advertiser* (Massachusetts), the *Cleveland Herald* (Ohio), the *Omaha Herald* (Nebraska), and the *Sacramento Bee* (California). *Leslie's Illustrated* for September 31, 1871, carried an article by Henry Elliot—spoken of as "our artist."[243]

However not all the publicity generated at this time originated with the Hayden and Barlow parties. Truman C. Everts' article in *Scribner's Monthly* (November, 1871) was a holdover from the expedition of 1870,[244] and a series of articles which appeared in the Deer Lodge *New North-West* (Montana) resulted from a visit by a party that entered the Yellowstone region from the west in August.[245] This group, which included U.S. Mining Commissioner R. W. Raymond; his assistant, a Mr. Eiler; A. F. Thrasher, a Virginia City photographer; J. S. Daugherty, an Indiana business man traveling for his health; C. C. Clawson, a reporter and author of the "Notes," and Gilman Sawtell, settler at Henry's Lake and guide, were the vanguard of that tourism which, a century later, swelled to more than 2 million persons annually.

There were other signs of the end of the period of definitive exploration, among them the appearance of settlers within the Yellowstone region. The Hayden and Barlow parties found intrusions at three points. On Gardner River, near the great outflow of hot water that had caused the prospectors to name it "Warm-Stream Creek," they found a haphazard encampment of invalids who called their rude spa "Chestnutville"—a place Matthew McGuirk claimed that fall and developed into "McGuirk's Medicinal Springs."[246] Upon the hot spring terraces then generally known as "Soda Mountain," two Bozeman men had laid claim to the hot springs and built a cabin.[247] They were Harry Horr, the same who had accompanied the springwagon sent up to Yankee Jim Canyon to convey the rescued Truman C. Everts out of the wilderness, and James C. McCartney. Jack Baronett, whose rescue of Everts had gained him nothing but the inspiration to build a toll bridge over the Yellowstone River on the road to the new mines on Clark Fork (the present Cooke City area), had control of a site at the mouth of Lamar River. His was the first bridge to span the Yellowstone River at any point.[248]

One of the men bathing at "Chestnutville" (Hot River) when Hayden and Barlow arrived was A. Bart Henderson, whose diary entry for July 24, 1871, notes:

Left camp at 9 o'clock & followed down the river. Arrived at Bottlers

Ranch. Here I remained a few days, resting and viewing out a road which I located on the 12 day of Aug. 1871. It is to run from Bozeman to the Yellowstone Lake, by the Mammoth Hot Springs, built for the benefit of the travel to & from Wonderland, & to be a toll road. I soon commenced work on the same . . .[249]

Even before the explorers of 1871 turned homeward with their notes and specimens, the process of subduing the Yellowstone wilderness had been begun in the style of the American frontier—by raising cabins and building roads within its fastnesses, and surely it would have gone the way of many another pristine locality except for a letter that came to Dr. Hayden in the City of Washington.

PART III

The Park Movement

The increased knowledge resulting from definitive exploration of the Yellowstone region spawned a park movement which led directly to establishment of Yellowstone National Park by the Act of Congress signed into law on March 1, 1872. This was the first reservation of wild lands for recreational purposes under the direct management of the Federal government.

The field work of the Geological and Geographical Survey of the Territories was terminated at Fort Bridger, Wyo., on October 2, 1871, and Ferdinand V. Hayden was back in Washington, D.C., before the end of the month. A letter which reached him there on the 28th probably served to acquaint him with an idea of which he seems not to have been aware—the idea that it was desirable to reserve the Yellowstone region and its wonders for public use, rather than allow its superlatives to pass into private ownership and control. The proposition was essentially the same as those earlier suggestions advanced by Thomas F. Meagher (1865), David E. Folsom (1869), and Cornelius Hedges (1870), but, in this case, it helped to shape a course of action which accomplished the objective.

The letter which came to Hayden's hand was written by A. B. Nettleton on the stationery of "Jay Cooke & Co., Bankers, Financial Agents, Northern Pacific Railroad Company,"[1] and it said:

Dear Doctor:

Judge Kelley has made a suggestion which strikes me as being an excellent one, viz.: Let Congress pass a bill reserving the Great Geyser Basin as a public park forever—just as it has reserved that far inferior wonder the Yosemite valley and big trees. If you approve this would such a recommendation be appropriate in your official report?[2]

The Judge Kelley from whom Nettleton received that suggestion was William Darrah Kelley, a Philadelphia jurist who entered Congress on March 4, 1861, as a Republican representative from Pennsylvania, serving in all the Congresses until his death on January 9, 1890. Judge Kelley had come under the influence of Asa Whitney in 1845 and, thereafter, was a constant supporter of the idea of spanning the Nation with iron rails. His familiarity with the Yellowstone region was gained from Lieutenant Doane's published report from which he divined the peculiar importance of that area. Being influential in the affairs of Jay Cooke & Co., and familiar with the firm's advertising campaign, he preferred to advance his suggestion through Nettleton rather than directly in Congress.

Judge Kelley's suggestion was forwarded to an influential man. Though Hayden had not previously evidenced any but a scientific interest in the Yellowstone region, he recognized the propriety of reserving its wonders

109

and acted immediately—which is the more surprising considering the pressure he was then under (an official report to be written before the end of the year, a pile of deferred paper work on his desk, and two important magazine articles to write;[3] all that, when his wedding day was only weeks away!).

Hayden's positive response—an assurance that he would present Kelley's suggestion in his official report—led Jay Cooke to write at once to W. Milner Roberts, the Northern Pacific engineer then locating the main line through Montana, as follows:

> It is proposed by Mr. Hayden in his report to Congress that the Geyser region around Yellowstone Lake shall be set apart by government as a reservation as park, similar to that of the Great Trees & other reservations in California. Would this conflict with our land grant, or interfere with us in any way? Please give me your views on this subject. It is important to do something speedily, or squatters & claimants will go in there, and we can probably deal much better with the government in any improvements we may desire to make for the benefit of our pleasure travel than with individuals.[4]

The engineer's reply, which was telegraphed from Helena, Mont., on November 21, advised: "Yours October thirtieth & November sixth Recd Geysers outside our grant advise Congressional reservation."[5] Jay Cooke's letter of November 6 has not been located, hence its import is unknown; however, the foregoing exchange is sufficient to reveal important origins of the movement to create a Yellowstone Park.

Evidently, Cooke did not wait to hear from Roberts before actively involving the Northern Pacific in the park movement. On November 9, 1871, the Montana press noted:

> Hon. N. P. Langford,—who, by the way, has been back here [Helena] only a few days,—yesterday received a dispatch from Gov. Marshall, of Minnesota to return immediately to Minnesota as important business concerning the Northern Pacific Railroad awaited him. Mr. Langford took the Overland coach this evening for Corinne.[6]

Before Langford's arrival in Washington, D.C., about November 14, the Northern Pacific Land Office in New York City received a telegraphic reply from Jno W. Sexton, a member of the directorate of Jay Cooke & Co., informing that *Scribner's Magazine* had "published nothing of Langford's except article in June *Scribner* Have no copies here."[7] The inquiry was preparatory—undoubtedly the opening move in that publicity campaign which put the Langford article and selected Jackson photographs in the hands of influential congressmen.

There is a dearth of information regarding the course of events in Washington from the time of Langford's arrival until legislation proposing establishment of a national park in the Yellowstone region was introduced on December 18. However, an item which appeared in a local newspaper on the 7th gives some indication of the thinking prior to that date. According to the editor,

> The great falls and wonderful geysers of the Upper Yellowstone, now receiving universal attention, should be forever set apart as a resort for the scientific students and pleasure seekers of the world; and for the convenience of protective local legislation, they should be included within the boundaries of Montana Territory. They are situated beyond our lines and within the jurisdiction of Wyoming; but are practically a barren heritage to our sister Territory, for the reason that rugged, and in winter altogether impassible, mountains separate them from her capital and chief cities. . . . From this side, the Great Falls may be reached and all the surrounding wonders and curiosities explored at any month of the year. . . . As nearly the entire length of the Yellowstone river is in Montana, it is eminently right and proper that its fountains should also be. Congress should donate the extreme Upper Yellowstone, with its mighty cataracts and other marvels to this Territory, to be set apart and protected under appropriate local legislation, as a resort for pleasure and scientific investigation forever. Has not Montana thrown as much gold into the commercial channels of trade and commerce as California had, up to the time that the valley of the Yosemite was thus granted to her by the General Government? And we are satisfied our neighbors of Wyoming would be too reasonable and generous to object to the grant, in the face of the fact that natural circumstances render the prize utterly worthless to them. We understand our wide-awake Delegate will introduce a bill, the present session, asking for appointment of a commission to readjust our boundary, so as to include the Upper Yellowstone, and we suggest to Messrs. Beck and Vivion, our representatives in the Legislature, that a cooperative memorial would be very proper.[8]

It is suggested that the idea presented in the foregoing article—that Montana should be given the Yellowstone region as a grant from the Federal Government, as the State of California had been given the Yosemite Valley—was the original intent of the men who undertook, early in December, the framing of legislation to effect such reservation. However, it was soon evident that the precedent set by the Yosemite grant did not apply because the area Montana wanted lay beyond its boundaries, in Wyoming Territory. It was equally evident that to take from the one for the benefit of the other would not only create trouble between neighbors, but also set a precedent no thinking politician would care to have lurking about lest his own environs somehow fall victim to it. As Hampton has pointed out, "The only way to preserve the area and withhold it from settlement was to place it directly under Federal control."[9]

Regardless of the impropriety of the Yosemite Grant Act as a precedent, its usefulness as a model was not missed. The bill drawn for the consideration of the 42d Congress at its second session has so many points of similarity with the earlier legislation that there can be little doubt from whence it was taken. The parallelism of the two acts is shown in the excerpts

111

arrayed below, which are also in their natural order:

YOSEMITE (1864)	YELLOWSTONE (1872)
. . . the said State shall accept this grant upon the express conditions that the premises shall be held for public use, resort, and recreation; shall be inalienable for all time;	. . . is hereby reserved and withdrawn from settlement, occupancy, or sale. . . and dedicated and set apart as a public park or pleasuring-ground for the benefit and enjoyment of the people. . . .
. . . but leases not exceeding 10 years may be granted for portions of said premises.	The Secretary may, in his discretion, grant leases for building purposes for terms not exceeding 10 years, of small parcels of ground. . . .
. . . all incomes derived from leases of privileges to be expended in the preservation and improvement of the property, or the roads leading thereto. . . .	. . . all of the proceeds of said leases, and all other revenues that may be derived from any source connected with said park, to be expended under his direction in the management of the same, and the construction of roads and bridle paths therein.

Both Hampton and Goetzmann have cast Langford and the Montana group as initiators of the park movement.[10] But in truth several interests came together at this time. Hayden, prompted by Nettleton's transmittal of Representative Kelley's suggestion, was thinking in terms of public reservation, and he had important connections with Representative Henry L. Dawes, a powerful figure in the House and one of the guiding hands of the earlier Yosemite legislation. Langford had been summoned to Washington by his brother-in-law in behalf of Jay Cooke and Northern Pacific interests. Delegate Clagett wanted to advance Montana's interest in the Yellowstone. Cornelius Hedges, although not in Washington at this or any other time in 1871, as his diary reveals, was working in Montana in this cause. All played important roles in forwarding an idea that successive explorations had inspired and popularized and that Jay Cooke and associates had appropriated as useful for their purposes. All these forces united to produce a bill to set aside the Yellowstone country, first on the Yosemite model, and then, as the political perils of that became apparent, as a national park.

Considerable weight has been given to William Horace Clagett's latter-day statement regarding the origin and events of the movement which led to the establishment of Yellowstone National Park.[11] His observations so frequently differ from the facts that they require some mention here as prelude to consideration of the legislative effort on behalf of the Yellowstone region.

Essentially, Clagett exaggerated his own role, picturing himself as the originator of the park idea and the foremost laborer for its attainment. In support of the first, he says:

In the fall of 1870, soon after the return of the Washburn-Langford party, two printers at Deer Lodge City, Mont., went into the Firehole basin and cut a large number of poles, intending to come back the next summer and fence in the tract of land containing the principal geysers, and hold possession for speculative purposes, as the Hutchins family so long held the Yosemite valley. One of these men was named Harry Norton. He subsequently wrote a book on the park.[12] The other one was named Brown. He now lives in Spokane, Wash., and both of them in the summer of 1871 worked in the New Northwest office at Deer Lodge.[13] When I learned from them in the late fall of 1870 or spring of 1871 what they proposed to do, I remonstrated with them and stated that from the description given by them and by members of Mr. Langford's party, the whole region should be made into a National Park and no private proprietorship be allowed.

He goes on to say, on the basis of that remonstrance, that "so far as my personal knowledge goes, the first idea of making it a public park occurred to myself," to which he adds, "but from information received from Langford and others, it has always been my opinion that Hedges, Langford, and myself formed the same idea about the same time."

On the other point, that he took the lead in getting the park established, Clagett says:

I was elected Delegate to Congress from Montana in August, 1871, and after the election, Nathaniel P. Langford, Cornelius Hedges and myself had a consultation in Helena,[14] and agreed that every effort should be made to establish the Park as soon as possible. . . . In December, 1871, Mr. Langford came to Washington and remained there for some time, and we two counseled together about the Park project. I drew the bill to establish the Park,[15] and never knew Professor Hayden in connection with that bill, except that I requested Mr. Langford to get from him a description of the boundaries of the proposed Park. There was some delay in getting the description, and my recollection is that Langford brought me the description after consultation with Professor Hayden. I then filled the blank in the bill with the description, and the bill passed both Houses of Congress just as it was drawn and without any change or amendment whatsoever.[16]

Clagett's account of his connection with the Yellowstone Park legislation ends with the statement, "Langford and I probably did two-thirds, if not three-fourths of all the work connected with its passage." The improbability of that will be evident as the bill is followed through the legislative toils.

Clagett says he "had a clean copy made of the bill and on the first call day in the House, introduced the original there, and then went over to the Senate Chamber and handed the copy to Senator Pomeroy, who immediately introduced it in the Senate." Again, Cramton comments:

The proceedings as reported in the Congressional Globe do not seem to me to conform to Mr. Clagett's recollection as to Pomeroy. Senator Pomeroy was the first one to introduce a bill that day in the Senate and the order of introduction of bills came very early in the day's proceedings. While that order of business likewise came early in the House, Mr. Clagett was not the first one to introduce a bill in the House, but followed quite a number of others. It is evident he could not have introduced the bill first and then gone over to the Senate to give a copy to Senator Pomeroy in time for Senator Pomeroy to take the action he did.[17]

A search was made for the original Senate bill in the hope that it might throw some light upon the question of authorship, but the document appears not to have been saved. Likewise, the file of Senator Pomeroy's Committee on the Public Lands is barren of even a mention of the Yellowstone bill.[18]

Clagett's attempt to have his bill referred to the Committee on Territories (it was sent to the Committee on the Public Lands on the motion of Representative Stevenson) ended his efforts on behalf of the legislation—insofar as the public record is concerned. However, there is no reason for doubting a later statement that, between Hayden, Langford, and Clagett, "there was not a single member of Congress in either House who was not fully posted by one or the other of us in personal interviews."[19]

Another part of the campaign to influence the legislators was carried on by Hayden, who "brought with him a large number of specimens from different parts of the Park, which were on exhibition in one of the rooms of the Capitol or in the Smithsonian Institution (one or the other), while Congress was in session,"[20] and he is also credited with exhibiting the specimens and explaining the geological and other features of the proposed park. Unfortunately, neither Hayden nor Langford left an adequate record of his activities during this period, and, except for the brief statement just quoted, an assessment will have to rest on the statement of historian Chittenden, who says of their work:[21]

> Dr. Hayden occupied a commanding position in this work, as representative of the government in the explorations of 1871. He was thoroughly familiar with the subject, and was equipped with an exhaustive collection of photographs and specimens gathered the previous summer. These were placed on exhibition and were probably seen by all members of Congress. They did a work which no other agency could do, and doubtless convinced every one who saw them that the region where such wonders existed should be carefully preserved to the people forever. Dr. Hayden gave to the cause the energy of a genuine enthusiasm, and his work that winter will always hold a prominent place in the history of the Park.[22]
>
> Mr. Langford, as already stated, had publicly advocated the measure in the previous winter. He had rendered service of the utmost importance, through his publications in *Scribner's Magazine* in the preceding May and June. Four hundred copies of these magazines were brought and placed upon the desks of members of Congress on the days when the the measure was to be brought to vote. During the entire winter, Mr. Langford devoted much of his time to the promotion of this work.[23]

Truman C. Everts, who had just come into prominence through the appearance of his article, "Thirty-seven Days of Peril," in *Scribner's Monthly* (November, 1871), entered the Washington scene early in January, but the only evidence yet found to indicate a connection with the park movement is his letter transmitting a set of Jackson's photographs to J. Gregory Smith, president of the Northern Pacific Railroad.[24]

A latter-day effort to turn Thomas Moran into "The Father of National Parks" hints that he, also, was involved in promoting the park movement;[25] however, there is no factual basis for such an interpretation. His great painting, an 8- by 15-foot oil developed from a sketch of the Grand Canyon of the Yellowstone as he saw it from Grand View in 1871, was yet incomplete at the time the Yellowstone Act was signed into law. In a letter to Hayden shortly thereafter he wrote:

> I have been intending to write to you for some month's past but have been so *very* busy with Yellowstone drawings, & so absorbed in designing & painting my picture of the Great Cañon that I could not find the time to write to anybody. The picture is now more than half finished & I feel confident that it will produce a most decided sensation in Art Circles. . . . I cast all my claims to being an Artist, into this one picture of the Great Cañon & am willing to abide by the judgement upon it.[26]

Whether or not the public came to look fondly upon Hayden's guest as Thomas "Yellowstone" Moran, the fact remains that he was not among those who labored significantly to establish our first national park.

Before considering the progress of the Yellowstone legislation, it is appropriate to note the paucity of editorial comment upon such a novel proposal. Only two Western newspapers appear to have grasped the significance of it—the Deer Lodge *New North-West* (Montana) and the Virginia City *Daily Territorial Enterprise* (Nevada). The former, after calling the Yellowstone region "a very *Arcana Inferne*," suggested that

> . . . to it will come in the coming years thousands from every quarter of the globe, to look with awe upon its amazing phenomena, and with pen, pencil, tongue and camera publish its marvels to the enlightened realms. Let this, too, be set apart by Congress as a domain retained unto all mankind, (Indians not taxed, excepted), and let it be *esto perpetua*.[27]

The *Territorial Enterprise*, with less flamboyance noted:

> The Hon. N. P. Langford of Montana, the leader [*sic*] of the famous Yellowstone Expedition of 1870, and several scientific and literary gentlemen, is engaged in an effort to have the Yellowstone region declared a National Park. The district, of which some features have been described in *Scribner's Monthly*, is said to be unadapted to agriculture, mining or manufacturing purposes, and it is proposed to have its magnificent scenery, hot springs, geysers and cataracts forever dedicated to public uses as a grand national reservation. Congress is to be petitioned to this effect.[28]

Returning to the Yellowstone legislation, it was the Senate version of the bill—Pomeroy's S. 392—which prospered. On January 22, the Senator from Kansas attempted to report his bill from the Committee on Public Lands in a proceeding which is reported thus:

> Mr. POMEROY. I am instructed by the Committee on Public Lands to report back and recommend the passage of the bill (S. No. 392) to set apart a certain tract of land lying near the headwaters of the

115

Yellowstone river as a public park. It will be remembered that an appropriation was made last year of about ten thousand dollars to explore that country. Professor Hayden and party have been there, and this bill is drawn on the recommendation of that gentleman to consecrate for public uses this country as a public park. It contains about forty miles square. It embraces those geysers, those great natural curiosities which have attracted so much attention. It is thought that it ought to be set apart for public uses. I would like to have the bill acted on now. The committee felt that if we were going to set it apart at all, it ought to be done before individual preemptions or homestead claims attach.

The VICE PRESIDENT. The Senator from Massachusetts and the Senator from Kentucky both gave way only for current morning business, but the Senator from Kansas now asks unanimous consent for the consideration of the bill which he has just reported.

Several Senators objected.

Mr. POMEROY. Then I withdraw the report for the present.[29]

The following day Senator Pomeroy presented his bill again:

Mr. POMEROY. The Committee on Public Lands, to whom was referred the bill (S. No. 392) to set apart a tract of land lying near the headwaters of the Yellowstone as a public park, have directed me to report it back without amendment, to recommend its passage, and to ask that it have the present consideration of the Senate.

The VICE PRESIDENT. The Senator from Kansas asks unanimous consent of the Senate for the present consideration of the bill reported by him. It will be reported in full, subject to objection.

The Chief Clerk read the bill.

The Committee on Public Lands reported the bill with an amendment in line nineteen to strike out the words "after the passage of this act," and in line twenty, after the word "upon", to insert the words "or occupying a part of;" so as to make the clause read, "and all persons who shall locate or settle upon or occupy any part of the same, or any part thereof, except as hereinafter provided, shall be considered as trespassers and removed therefrom."

The VICE PRESIDENT. Is there objection to the present consideration of this bill?

Mr. CAMERON. I should like to know from somebody having charge of the bill, in the first place, how many miles square are to be set apart, or how many acres, for this purpose, and what is the necessity for the park belonging to the United States.

Mr. POMEROY. This bill originated as the result of the exploration, made by Professor Hayden, under an appropriation of Congress last year. With a party he explored the headwaters of the Yellowstone and found it to be a great natural curiosity, great geysers, as they are termed, water-spouts, and hot springs, and having platted the ground himself, and having given me the dimensions of it, the bill was drawn up, as it was thought best to consecrate and set apart this great place of national resort, as it may be in the future, for the pusposes of public enjoyment.

Mr. MORTON. How many square miles are there in it?

Mr. POMEROY. It is substantially forty miles square. It is north and south forty-four miles, and east and west forty miles. He was careful to make a survey so as to include all the basin where the Yellowstone has its source.

Mr. CAMERON. That is several times larger than the District of Columbia.

Mr. POMEROY. Yes, Sir. There are no arable lands; no agricultural lands there. It is the highest elevation from which our springs descend, and as it cannot interfere with any settlement for legitimate agricultural purposes, it was thought that it ought to be set apart early for this purpose. We found when we set apart the Yosemite valley that there were one or two persons who had made claims there, and there has been a contest, and it has finally gone to the Supreme Court to decide whether persons who settle on unsurveyed lands before the Government takes possession of them by any special act of Congress have rights as against the Government. The court has held that settlers on unsurveyed lands have no rights as against the Government. The Government can make an appropriation of any unsurveyed lands, notwithstanding settlers may be upon them. As this region would be attractive only on account of preempting a hot spring or some valuable mineral, it was thought such claims had better be excluded from the bill.

There are several Senators whose attention has been called to this matter, and there are photographs of the valley and the curiosities, which Senators can see. The only object of the bill is to take early possession of it by the United States and set it apart, so that it cannot be included in any claim or occupied by any settlers.

Mr. TRUMBULL. Mr. President—

The VICE PRESIDENT. The Chair must state that the Senate have not yet given their consent to the present consideration of the bill. The Senator from Pennsylvania desired some explanation in regard to it. Does he reserve the right to object?

Mr. CAMERON. I make no objection.

Mr. THURMAN. I object.

Mr. SHERMAN. I will not object if it is not going to lead to debate.

Mr. TRUMBULL. It can be disposed of in a minute.

Mr. THURMAN. I object to the consideration of this bill in the morning hour. I am willing to take it up when we can attend to it, but not now.[30]

The Yellowstone bill was again brought up for consideration by the Senate on January 30—in its regular order. This crucial session is recorded in *The Congressional Globe* (p. 697) under the heading "Yellowstone Park" a term not used previously in debate. Continuing from the record:

The VICE PRESIDENT. The bill (S. No. 392) to set apart a certain tract of land lying near the headwaters of the Yellowstone river as a public park, taken up on the motion of the Senator from Kansas, which was reported by the Committee on Public Lands, is now before the Senate as in Committee of the Whole.

The bill was read—[followed by a restatement of the amendments previously reported by the Committee on Public Lands].

The VICE PRESIDENT. These amendments will be regarded as agreed to unless objected to. They are agreed to.

Mr. ANTHONY. I observe that the destruction of game and fish for gain or profit is forbidden. I move to strike out the words "for gain or profit," so that there shall be no destruction of game there for any purpose. We do not want sportsmen going over there with their guns.

Mr. POMEROY. The only object was to prevent the wanton destruction of the fish and game; but we thought parties who encamped there and caught fish for their own use ought not to be restrained from doing so. The bill will allow parties there to shoot game or catch fish for their own subsistence. The provision of the bill is designed to stop the wanton destruction of game or fish for merchandise.

Mr. ANTHONY. I do not know but that that covers it. What I mean is that this park should not be used for sporting. If people are encamped there, and desire to catch fish and kill game for their own sustenance while they remain there, there can be no objection to that; but I do not think it ought to be used as a preserve for sporting.

Mr. POMEROY. I agree with the Senator, but I think the bill as drawn protects the game and fish as well as can be done.

Mr. ANTHONY. Very well; I am satisfied.

The VICE PRESIDENT. The Senator does not insist on his amendment?

Mr. ANTHONY. No, sir.

Mr. TIPTON. I think if this is to become a public park, a place of great national resort, and we allow the shooting of game or the taking of fish without any restriction at all, the game will soon be utterly destroyed. I think, therefore, there should be a prohibition against their destruction for any purpose, for if the door is once opened I fear there will ultimately be an entire destruction of all the game in that park.[31]

Mr. POMEROY. It will be entirely under the control of the Secretary of the Interior. He is to make the rules that shall govern the destruction and capture of game. I think in that respect the Secretary of the Interior, whoever he may be, will be as vigilant as we would be.

The VICE PRESIDENT. Perhaps the Secretary had better report the sentence referred to by Senators as bearing on this question, and then any Senator who desires to amend can move to do so.

The Chief Clerk read as follows:

"He shall provide against the wanton destruction of the fish and game found within said park, and against their capture or destruction for the purposes of merchandise or profit."

Mr. EDMUNDS. I hope this bill will pass. I have taken some pains to make myself acquainted with the history of this most interesting region. It is so far elevated above the sea that it cannot be used for private occupation at all, but it is probably one of the most wonderful regions in that space of territory which the globe exhibits anywhere, and therefore we are doing no harm to the material interests of the people in endeavoring to preserve it. I hope the bill will pass unanimously.

Mr. COLE. I have grave doubts about the propriety of passing this bill. The natural curiosities there cannot be interfered with by anything that man can do. The geysers will remain, no matter where the ownership of the land may be, and I do not know why settlers should be excluded from a tract of land forty miles square, as I understand this to be, in the Rocky mountains or any other place. I cannot see how the natural curiosities can be interfered with if settlers are allowed to approach them. I suppose there is very little timber on this tract of land, certainly no more than is necessary for the use and convenience of persons going upon it. I do not see the reason or propriety of setting apart a large tract of land of that kind in the Territories of the United States for a public park. There is abundance of public park ground in the Rocky mountains that will never be occupied. It is all one great park, and never can be anything else; large portions of it at all events. There are some places, perhaps this is one, where persons can and would go and settle and improve and cultivate the grounds, if there be ground fit for cultivation.

Mr. EDMUNDS. Has my friend forgotten that this ground is north of latitude forty, and is over seven thousand feet above the level of the sea? You cannot cultivate that kind of ground.

Mr. COLE. The Senator is probably mistaken in that. Ground of a greater height than that has been cultivated and occupied.

Mr. EDMUNDS. In that latitude?

Mr. COLE: Yes, sir. But if it cannot be occupied and cultivated, why should we make a public park of it? If it cannot be occupied by man, why protect it from occupation? I see no reason in that. If nature has excluded men from its occupation, why set it apart and exclude persons from it? If there is any sound reason for the passage of the bill, of course I would not oppose it; but really I do not see any myself.[32]

Mr. TRUMBULL. I think our experience with the wonderful natural curiosity, if I may so call it, in the Senator's own State, should admonish us of the propriety of passing such a bill as this. There is the wonderful Yosemite valley, which one or two persons are now claiming by virtue of preemption. Here is a region of country away up in the Rocky mountains, where there are the most wonderful geysers on the face of the earth; a country that is not likely ever to be inhabited for the purposes of agriculture; but it is possible that some person may go there and plant himself right across the only path that leads to these wonders, and charge every man that passes along between the gorges of these mountains a fee of a dollar or five dollars. He may place an obstruction there, and toll may be gathered from every person who goes to see these wonders of creation.

Now this tract of land is uninhabited; nobody lives there; it was never trod by civilized man until within a short period. Perhaps a year or two ago was the first time that this country was ever explored by anybody. It is now proposed, while it is in this condition, to reserve it from sale and occupation in this way. I think it is a very proper bill to pass, and now is the time to enact it. We did set apart the region of country on which the mammoth trees grow in California, and the Yosemite valley also we have undertaken to reserve, but there is a dispute about it. Now, before there is any dispute as to this wonderful country, I hope we shall except it from the general disposition of the public lands, and reserve it to the Government. At some future time, if we desire to do so, we can repeal this law if it is in anybody's way; but now I think it a very appropriate bill to pass.[33]

The bill was reported to the Senate as amended; and the amendments were concurred in. The bill was ordered to be engrossed for a third reading, read a third time, and passed.

The passage of the Senate version of the Yellowstone bill was noted briefly in the Washington *Evening Star*: "Mr. Pomeroy called up the bill setting apart the Yellowstone Valley as a public park forever, which was passed,"[34] but the more discerning coverage appeared in Montana. On receipt of word of the Senate's action, a Helena newspaper remarked:

We have not seen the text of this particular bill, and cannot say if it is identical with that introduced in the House by our Delegate, but presume it to be essentially the same; and judging from the readiness with which the idea has been taken up, put into shape, and passed the Senate, there can be little doubt that very soon it will receive the sanction of the necessary parties and become a law. In fact, since the idea was first conceived by the party of gentlemen from this city, who visited this region of wonders in the summer of 1869 [*sic*], and gave to the world the first reliable reports concerning its marvelous wealth of natural curiosities, the project has gained ground with surprizing rapidity. The letters of Mr. Hedges, first published in the HERALD, the lectures of Mr. Langford, the articles of Mr. Trumbull, and later still, the story of [the] peril and adventure of Mr. Everts, all of the same party, were widely circulated by the press of the country, and not merely excited a passing curiosity, but created a living, general interest that has since received strength and larger proportions by the publication of Lieutenant Doane's official report to the War Department of the same expedition; followed, as it was, by the expedition of Professor Hayden, during the last summer, under the patronage of the Smithsonian Institution, with its fully appointed corps of scientific gentlemen and distinguished artists, whose reports have more than confirmed all descriptions of the Washburn party. Such, in brief, has been the origin and progress of this project now about to receive a definite and permanent shape in the establishment of a National Park. It will be a park worthy of the Great Republic. If it contains the proportions set forth in Clagett's bill, it will embrace about 2,500 square miles, and include the great canyon, the Falls and Lake of the Yellowstone, with a score of other magnificent lakes, the great geyser basin of the Madison, and thousands of mineral and boiling springs. Should the whole surface of the earth be gleaned, another spot of equal dimensions could not be found that contains on such a magnificent scale one-half the attractions here grouped together.[35]

The editor also noted that "Without a doubt the Northern Pacific Railroad will have a branch track penetrating this Plutonian region, and few seasons will pass before excursion trains will daily be sweeping into this great park thousands of the curious from all parts of the world." Thus, citizens of Montana Territory "who would look upon this scene in its wild, primitive beauty, before art has practised any of its tricks upon nature," were advised to visit the area at once.

That there was a strong sentiment, locally, favoring such a park movement is evidenced by the appearance at just this time of the memorial to Congress which had originated in the Montana Legislature as Council Joint Memorial No. 5. This interesting document, authored by Cornelius Hedges and introduced by Councilman Seth Bullock, was addressed "To the Honorable Senate and House of Representatives of the United States in Congress assembled," which were reminded that

> . . . a small portion of the Territory of Wyoming, as now constituted in its extreme northwest corner, is separated from the main portion of that Territory by the almost impassable ranges of mountains that divide the headwaters of the Madison from those of the Snake river on the south, connecting with those dividing the waters of the Yellowstone from those of Big Horn and Wind Rivers on the east; that this portion of Wyoming is only accessible from the side of Montana; con-

tains the heads of streams whose course is wholly through Montana; while through the enterprise of citizens of Montana it has been thoroughly explored, and its innumerable and magnificent array of wonders in geysers, boiling springs, mud volcanoes, burning mountains, lakes, and waterfalls brought to the attention of the world. Your memorialists would, therefore, urge upon your Honorable bodies that the said portion of Wyoming be ceded to Montana by an extension of its southern line from 111 degrees of longitude east and north along the crest of said mountain ranges dividing the headwaters of the Madison and Yellowstone rivers from those of the Snake, Bighorn and Wind Rivers, till it intersects with the present southern line of Montana, on the 45th degree of latitude. Your memorialists would further urge that the above described district of country, with so much more of the present Territory of Montana as may be necessary to include the Lake, Great Falls, and Canyon of the Yellowstone, the great geyser basin of the Madison, with its associate [sic] boiling, mineral and mud springs, as may be determined from the surveys made by Prof. Hayden and party past season, or to be determined by surveys hereafter to be made, be dedicated and devoted to public use, resort and recreation, for all time to come as a great National Park, under such care and restrictions as to your Honorable bodies may seem best calculated to secure the ends proposed.[36]

But, if there was evident support for the park legislation, its success in the Senate also raised misgivings which eventually hardened into a very determined opposition. This antipathy arose out of the effort of Harry R. Horr and James C. McCartney to get their tract of land at Mammoth Hot Springs (where they had located as squatters during the summer of 1871) excepted from the provisions of the bill. As soon as the text of the bill was made available, these settlers began circulating a petition by means of which they hoped to influence Congress in their favor,[37] but in that they were disappointed.

A little more than 2 weeks later the Helena *Rocky Mountain Weekly Gazette* took its stand with the settlers, commenting on the park proposal in these words:

As for ourselves we regard the project with little favor, unless Congress will go still further and make appropriations to open carriage roads through, and hostels in, the reserved district, so that ordinary humanity can get into it without having to ride on the "Hurricane deck" of a mule. . . . Already private enterprise was taking measures to render the country accessible to such tourists as are not strong enough to endure the fatigues of a regular exploring expedition. . . .

If Congress sets off that scope of country as proposed, all these private enterprises will immediately cease, and as it is not at all likely that the Government will make any appropriations to open roads or hostelries, the country will be remanded into a wilderness and rendered inaccessible to the great mass of travelers and tourists for many years to come. . . .

We are opposed to any scheme which will have a tendency to remand it into perpetual solitude, by shutting out private enterprise and by preventing individual energy from opening the country to the general traveling public. . . .[38]

The Gazette continued to champion the Yellowstone settlers and the issue they had raised, and will be heard from again.

Of greater importance, while the Yellowstone legislation was yet under consideration in Congress, was the effect of a number of popular and scientific articles which appeared in various publications. The artist with the Hayden Survey party in 1871, Henry W. Elliott, was also a field correspondent for *Leslie's Illustrated*, and he provided that magazine with a brief description of the Yellowstone region as he had seen it.[39] Captain Barlow, whose small party had accompanied Hayden's through the Yellowstone region in 1871, provided the *Chicago Evening Journal* with a detailed account, and later prepared an official report.[40] But it was geologist Ferdinand V. Hayden who was most influential in both the popular and scientific medium.

Hayden's article in *Scribner's Monthly* (written to accompany Thomas Moran's sketches) reached a large and influential body of readers, to whom he brought this message: "Why will not Congress at once pass a law setting it [the Yellowstone region] apart as a great public park for all time to come, as has been done with that far inferior wonder, the Yosemite Valley?"[41] His scientific article, though written prior to the passage of the Yellowstone legislation, did not appear until later;[42] thus, the closing statement, another powerful call for reservation of the Yellowstone region as a national park, could have influenced only those who had seen Hayden's draft. Regardless, the title, "On the Yellowstone Park," is a measure of his considerable faith in the legislation then awaiting the action of the House of Representatives.

Before following the Yellowstone legislation to its conclusion, it is necessary to note a letter written to F. V. Hayden on February 19. In it, George A. Crofutt, author of a prominent tourist guidebook, expressed his indignation at the failure of a news item in the *New York World* of the previous day to give the geologist proper credit for the maturing park scheme.[43] Evidently, N. P. Langford had been identified as the king-pin of the movement, and not just by the *World*; similar releases have been found in the *St. Joseph Herald* (Missouri), and the *Virginia Daily Territorial Enterprise* (Nevada).[44]

While the Senate bill, S. 392, was making such splendid progress, its counterpart in the House, Delegate Clagett's H.R. 764, remained with the Committee on Public Lands, unreported for more than 2 months. During this time, the only action taken on the measure was a request from the chairman of the subcommittee to the Secretary of the Interior for a copy of Hayden's report. In his letter to Secretary Delano, January 27, 1872, Representative Mark H. Dunnell stated:

> The Committee on Public Lands has under consideration the Bill to set apart some land for a Park in Wyoming T. As Ch. of a subcommittee on the bill, I will be pleased to receive the report made by Prof. Hayden or such report as he may be able to give us on the subject.[45]

Dunnell's request reached the Secretary on the 29th and was answered by him the same day.[46] His reply not only provided the desired information in the form of a brief special report prepared by Hayden, but also included this comment: "I fully concur in his recommendations, and trust that the bill referred to may speedily become a law."

Hayden's full report was in draft at that time, for Capt. John Barlow had mentioned seeing and approving it earlier;[47] however, it was not suited to the purpose at hand and a synopsis was substituted. This document was held by the House Committee on Public Lands for nearly a month without further action; in the vernacular, they "sat upon it."

Meanwhile, the bill which had passed the Senate—Pomeroy's S. 392—went over to the House and was brought up on February 27 in the regular order of business. Immediately upon its introduction, the following exchange took place:[48]

Mr. SCOFIELD. I move that the bill be referred to the Committee on the Public Lands.

Mr. DAWES. I hope that bill will be put upon its passage at once. It seems to be a meritorious measure.

Mr. TAFFE. I move that it be referred to the Committee on the Territories.

Mr. SCOFIELD. At the request of the gentleman from Massachusetts [Rep. Dawes], I withdraw my motion.

Mr. HAWLEY. This question was referred to the Committee on the Public Lands in a House bill exactly similar in all its respects to this bill; it was considered by that committee, and the gentleman having it in charge was instructed to report it favorably to the House,[49] and if the committee were on call it would be reported.

Mr. DUNNELL. I was instructed by the committee to ask the House to pass a bill precisely like the bill passed by the Senate. I have examined the question thoroughly and with a great deal of care, and I am satisfied that the bill ought to pass.[50]

Mr. DAWES. It seems very desirable that the bill should pass as early as possible, in order that the depredations in that country shall be stopped.

Mr. FINKELNBURG. I would like to have the bill read.

The bill was read. [The text of the bill, as amended by the Senate, was given in full.]

Mr. DAWES. This bill follows the analogy of the bill passed by Congress six or eight years ago, setting apart the Yosemite valley and the "big tree country" for the public park, with this difference: that that bill granted to the State of California the jurisdiction over that land beyond the control of the United States. This bill reserves the control over the land, and preserves the control over it to the United States,[51] so that at any time when it shall appear that it will be better to devote it to any other purpose it will be perfectly within the control of the United States to do it.

It is a region of country seven thousand feet above the level of the sea, where there is frost every month of the year, and where nobody can dwell upon it for the purpose of agriculture, containing the most sublime scenery in the United States excepting the Yosemite valley, and the most wonderful geysers ever found in the country.[52]

The purpose of this bill is to preserve that country from depredations, but to put it where if the United States deems it best to appropriate it to some other use it can be used for that purpose. It is rocky, mountainous, full of gorges, and, from the descriptions given by those who visited it during the last summer, is unfit for agricultural purposes; but if upon a more minute survey it shall be found that it can be made useful for settlers, and not depredators, it will be perfectly proper this bill should pass; it will infringe upon no vested rights, the title to it will still remain in the United States, different from the case of the Yosemite valley, where it now requires the coordinate legislative action of Congress and the State of California to interfere with the title.[53] This bill treads upon no rights of the settler, infringes upon no permanent prospect of settlement of that Territory, and it receives the urgent and ardent support of the Legislature of the Territory, and of the Delegate himself, who is unfortunately now absent, and of those who surveyed it and brought the attention of the country to its remarkable and wonderful features. We part with no control; we put no obstacle in the way of any other disposition of it; we but interfere with what is represented as the exposure of that country to those who are attracted by the wonderful descriptions of it by the reports of the geologists, and who are going there to plunder this wonderful manifestation of nature.

Mr. TAFFE. I desire to ask the gentleman a question, and it is whether this measures does not interfere with the Sioux reservation; and in the next place I know that that treaty, if you call it a treaty, which I never thought it was, because the law raising the commission said the treaty should be ratified by Congress and not by the Senate, and under that you abandoned the right to go into the country between the Missouri river and the Big Horn mountain. Now, I ask the gentleman if this bill does not infringe upon the territory set apart for these Indian tribes?

Mr. DAWES. The gentleman has my answer, because he has heard it a great many times here. Both Houses have acted upon the theory that all of the treaties made by this commission are simple matters of legislation.

Mr. TAFFE. That does not answer my question as to the right of settlers to go upon this land. If that is not included in the treaty, then settlers have a right to go upon that land to-day; if that is the treaty, then nobody has a right to go into the country between the Big Horn mountain and the Missouri river except with the consent of these Indian tribes.[54]

Mr. DAWES. That may be; but the Indians can no more live there than they can upon the precipitous sides of the Yosemite valley.

Mr. SCOFIELD. I call the previous question.

The previous question was seconded and the main question ordered, which was upon the third reading of the bill.

Mr. STEVENSON. I ask leave to have printed in the *Globe* some remarks upon this bill.

No objection was made; and leave was accordingly granted. [See Appendix][55]

The question was upon ordering the bill to be read a third time; and upon a division there were—ayes 81, noes 41.

So the bill was ordered to be read a third time; and it was accordingly read the third time.

The question was upon the passage of the bill.

Mr. MORGAN. Upon that question I call for the yeas and nays.

The question was taken upon ordering the yeas and nays; and there were twenty-seven in the affirmative.

So (the affirmative being one fifth of the last vote) the yeas and nays were ordered.

The question was then taken; and it was decided in the affirmative—yeas 115, nays 65, not voting 60; as follows:

YEAS—Messrs. Ames, Archer, Averill, Banks, Barber, Barry, Beatty, Beveridge, Bigby, Biggs, Bingham, Austin Blair, Boles, George M. Brooks, Buckley, Buffiington, Burchard, Burdett, Roderick R. Butler, William T. Clarke, Cobb, Coburn, Conger, Cotton, Cox, Crebs, Crocker, Darrall, Dawes, Dickey, Donnan, Duell, Dunnell, Eames, Farnsworth, Farwell, Wilder D. Foster, Frye, Garfield, Hale, Hambleton, Harmer, George E. Harris, Havens, Hawley, Hays, Gerry W. Hazelton, John W. Hazelton, Hereford, Hill, Hoar, Hooper, Houghton, Kelley, Kellogg, Kendall, Ketcham, Lamport, Leach, Maynard, McCrary, McGrew, McHenry, McJunkin, McNeely, Mercur, Merriam, Mitchell, Monroe, Leonard Myers, Negley, Orr, Packard, Packer, Palmer, Peck, Pendleton, Aaron F. Perry, Peters, Potter, Ellis H. Roberts, Rusk, Sargent, Sawyer, Scofield, Seeley, Sessions, Sheldon, Shellabarger, Sherwood, Shoemaker, Sloss, H. Boardman Smith, John A. Smith, Snapp, Snyder, Sprague, Stevens, Stevenson, Stoughton, Swann, Washington Townsend, Turner, Tuthill, Twichell, Upson, Wakeman, Waldron, Wallace, Wheeler, Willard, Williams of New York, Jeremiah M. Wilson, John T. Wilson, and Wood—115.

NAYS—Messrs. Acker, Arthur, Barnum, Beck, Bird, Braxton, Caldwell, Coghlan, Comingo, Conner, Critcher, Crossland, DuBose, Duke, Eldredge, Finkelnburg, Forker, Henry D. Foster, Garrett, Getz, Golladay, Griffith, Haldeman, Handley, Hanks, John T. Harris, Hay, Herndon, Hibbard, Holman, Kerr, Killinger, Lewis, Lowe, Manson, McClelland, McCormick, McIntyre, Benjamin F. Meyers, Morgan, Niblack, Eli Perry, Price, Prindle, Rainey, Read, Edward Y. Rice, John M. Rice, William R. Roberts, Shanks, Slater, Slocum, R. Milton Speer, Thomas J. Speer, Starkweather, Strong, Taffe, Terry, Tyner, Van Trump, Voorhees, Waddell, Whitthorne, Winchester, and Young—65.

NOT VOTING—Messrs. Adams, Ambler, Bell, James G. Blair, Bright, James Brooks, Benjamin F. Butler, Campbell, Carroll, Freeman Clarke, Creely, Davis, De Large, Dox, Elliott, Ely, Charles Foster, Goodrich, Halsey, Hancock, Harper, King, Kinsetta, Lamison, Lansing, Lynch, Marshall, McKee, McKinney, Merrick, Moore, Morey, Morphis, Hosea W. Parker, Isaac C. Parker, Perce, Platt, Poland, Porter, Randall, Ritchie, Robinson, Rogers, Roosevelt, Shober, Worthington C. Smith, Storm, Stowell, St. John, Sutherland, Sypher, Thomas, Dwight Townsend, Vaughan, Walden, Walls, Warren, Wells, Whiteley, and Williams of Indiana—60.

So the bill was passed.[56]

Mr DAWES moved to reconsider the vote by which the bill was passed; and also moved that the motion to reconsider be laid on the table.

The latter motion was agreed to.

The enrolled bill was signed by the Speaker of the House on the following day, and, though it had yet to be approved by the President, the success of the measure was widely noted. *The St. Louis Times* (Missouri), and the Denver *Daily Rocky Mountain News* (Colorado), provided telegraphic notices that the "Yellowstone Valley" in Wyoming and Montana had been set apart, as a "national park" or a "public park," but only Montana's *Helena Daily Herald* had any serious comment to offer so soon. In its front-page article, this proponent of the park movement stated:[75]

Our dispatches announce the passage in the House of the Senate bill setting apart the Upper Yellowstone Valley for the purposes of a National Park. The importance to Montana of this Congressional enactment cannot be too highly estimated. It will redound to the untold good of this Territory, inasmuch as a measure of this character is well calculated to direct the world's attention to a very important section of country that to the present time has passed largely unnoticed. It will be the means of centering on Montana the attention of thousands heretofore comparatively uninformed of a Territory abounding in such resources of mines and of agriculture and of wonderland as we can boast, spread everywhere about us. The efficacy to this people of having in Congress a Delegate able, active, zealous and untiring in his labors, as well as in political harmony with the General Government, [58] is being amply demonstrated in the success attending the representative stewardship of Mr. Clagett. Our Delegate, surely is performing deeds in the interest of his constituents which none of them can gainsay or overlook, and those deeds are being recorded to his credit in the public's great ledger and in the hearts of us all.

On the following day, the *New York Times* commented in a broader vein, and without the partisan tootling:

It is a satisfaction to know that the Yellowstone Park bill has passed the House. Our readers have been made well acquainted with the beautiful and astonishing features of a region unlike any other in the world; and will approve the policy by which, while the title is still vested in the United States, provision has been made to retain it perpetually for the nation. The Yosemite Valley was similarly appropriated to public use some years back, and that magnificent spot was thus saved from possible defacement or other unseemly treatment that might have attended its remaining in private hands. . . . The new National Park lies in two Territories, Montana and Wyoming, but the jurisdiction of the soil, by the passage of the bill, remains forever with the Federal Government. In this respect the position of the Yellowstone Park differs from that of the Yosemite; since the latter was granted by Government to the State of California on certain conditions, one of which excludes the local control of the United States; while the former will always be within that control.

Perhaps, no scenery in the world surpasses for sublimity that of the Yellowstone Valley; and certainly no region anywhere is so rich, in the same space, in wonderful natural curiosities. In addition to this, from the height of the land, and the salubrity of the atmosphere, physicians are of opinion that the Yellowstone Park will become a valuable resort for certain classes of invalids; and in all probability it will soon appear that the mineral springs, with which the place abounds, possess various curative powers. It is far from unlikely that the park may become in a few years the Baden or Homburg of America, and that strangers may flock thither from all parts of the world to drink the waters, and gaze on picturesque splendors only to be seen in the heart of the American Continent. [59]

The Yellowstone Park Act had the approval of President Ulysses S. Grant, who signed it into law on March 1, 1872.[60] The text of the act follows:

Be it enacted by the Senate and House of Representatives of the United States of America in Congress assembled,

That the tract of land in the Territories of Montana and Wyoming lying near the head-waters of the Yellowstone River, and described as follows, to wit, commencing at the junction of Gardiner's River with the Yellowstone River, and running east to the meridian passing ten miles to the eastward of the most eastern point of—Yellowstone lake; thence south along said meridian to the parallel of latitude passing ten miles south of the most southern point of Yellowstone Lake; thence west along said parallel to the meridian passing fifteen miles west of the most western point of Madison Lake; thence north along said meridian to the latitude of the junction of the Yellowstone and Gardiner's Rivers; thence east to the place of beginning is hereby reserved and with-drawn from settlement, occupancy, or sale under the laws of the United States, and dedicated and set apart as a public park or pleasur-ing-ground for the benefit and enjoyment of the people; and all persons who shall locate or settle upon or occupy the same, or any part thereof, except as hereinafter provided, shall be considered trespassers, and removed therefrom.

SEC. 2. That said public park shall be under the exclusive control of the Secretary of the Interior, whose duty it shall be, as soon as practicable, to make and publish such rules and regulations as he may deem necessary or proper for the care and management of the same. Such regulations shall provide for the preservation, from injury or spoliation, or all timber, mineral deposits, natural curiosities, or wonders within said park, and their retention in their natural condi-tion. The Secretary may, in his discretion, grant leases for building purposes for terms not exceeding ten years, of small parcels of ground, at such places in said park as shall require the erection of buildings for the accommodation of visitors; all of the proceeds of said leases, and all other revenues that may be derived from any source connected with said park, to be expended under his direction in the management of the same, and the construction of roads and bridle-paths therein. He shall provide against the wanton destruction of the fish and game found within said park, and against their capture or destruction for the purposes of merchandise or profit. He shall also cause all persons trespassing upon the same after the passage of this act to be removed therefrom, and generally shall be authorized to take all such measures as shall be necessary or proper to fully carry out the objects and purposes of this act.[61]

The new park was received with mixed emotions in Montana. Helena's *Rocky Mountain Gazette*, which had previously expressed a fear that the park legislation would remand the Yellowstone region into "perpetual solitude," stated:

In our opinion, the effect of this measure will be to keep the country a wilderness, and shut out, for many years, the travel that would seek that curious region if good roads were opened through it and hotels built therein. We regard the passage of the act as a great blow struck at the prosperity of the towns of Bozeman and Virginia City, which might naturally look for considerable travel to this section, if it were thrown open to a curious but comfort-loving public.[62]

The sarcastic reply of the *Herald* turned the controversy into a political mud-slinging contest, with the only sensible comments coming from other newspapers. The Bozeman *Avant Courier* sided with the *Gazette* in the matter of the settler's interests in the new park, stating, in regard to the setting aside of the area, "we were certainly under the impression that, in case such was done, ample provision would be made in the bill for opening up the country by making good roads and establishment of hotels and other accomodations," adding, "unless some such provisions are yet incorporated in the bill by amendment, we agree with the Gazette, that it would have been better to have left its development open to the enterprising pioneers, who had already commenced the work."[63]

The Deer Lodge *New North-West* preferred to remain on neutral ground, reminding the contending editors that, as the settlers upon park lands were really residents of Wyoming Territory, "we are unable to see how it [reservation] will damage citizens of this Territory." Attention was also called to another largely overlooked fact: that regardless of the act setting aside the Yellowstone region, such settlers "are of course trespassers against the General Government, as all persons who reside upon unsurveyed public lands not mineral."[64]

A more enlightened view of the accomplishment in setting aside the Yellowstone region "for the benefit and enjoyment of the people" came from an eastern magazine, which noted:

> It is the general principle which is chiefly commendable in the act of Congress setting aside the Yellowstone region as a national park. It will help confirm the national possession of the Yo Semite, and may in time lead us to rescue Niagara from its present degrading surroundings. That the park will not very soon be accessible to the public needs no demonstration.[65]

Those words foretold both the greatness of Yellowstone National Park, as the pilot model for a system of Federal parks, and the travail of its early years. At the moment, Americans were pleased with their new playground, and a few were also undismayed at its remoteness. Even as the organic act was being signed into law, the first visitors of that throng which swelled to more than 48 million persons in the first century were outfitting at the town of Bozeman for their park trip.[66] As a nation, we had come to realize a very important fact, which the New York *Herald* expressed this way:

> Why should we go to Switzerland to see mountains, or to Iceland for geysers? Thirty years ago the attraction of America to the foreign mind was Niagara Falls. Now we have attractions which diminish Niagara into an ordinary exhibition. The Yo Semite, which the nation has made a park, the Rocky mountains and their singular parks, the canyons of the Colorado, the Dalles of the Columbia, the giant trees, the lake country of Minnesota, the country of the Yellowstone, with their beauty, their splendor, their extraordinary and sometimes terrible manifestations of nature, form a series of attractions possessed by no other nation in the world.[67]

128

1. Charles W. Cook

2. Walter W. deLacy

3. Gustavus C. Doane

4. Truman C. Everts

5. *David E. Folsom*

6. *Warren C. Gillette*

7. *Samuel T. Hauser*

8. *Ferdinand V. Hayden*

9. Cornelius Hedges

10. Nathaniel P. Langford

11. William and Jessie Peterson

12. *Benjamin Stickney*

13. *Jacob Smith*

14. *Henry Dana Washburn*

Biographical Appendix

WILLIAM A. BAKER. Born in County Donegal, Ireland, in 1832; died Mar. 31, 1874, at Fort Ellis, Montana Territory. The sergeant of the military escort that accompanied the Washburn party through the Yellowstone region in 1870.

He was an itinerant peddler prior to his enlistment Nov. 6, 1854, in Company F, Second Dragoons (the Second U.S. Cavalry after 1861). The enlistment papers describe him as 5 feet 8½ inches in height, with blue eyes, brown hair, and a fair complexion.

Sergeant Baker earned his stripes in rough campaigning during the Civil War, and thus was a well-seasoned noncommissioned officer—experienced with all manner of men, as well as in formal and Indian warfare. He was quiet, efficient, and well-liked, and he should have retired from his beloved Company F as a senior NCO at the conclusion of a long and faithful service; instead, he was killed by Private James Murphy in the course of the latter's murderous attack upon a comrade in the barracks at Fort Ellis.

Sources: The National Archives, RG–94, AGO—Enlistment papers and register, and "Homocide at Fort Ellis," in the Bozeman, Mont. *Avant Courier*, Apr. 3, 1875, p. 3. Followup items appear in the issues of September 18 and 25.

JOHN WHITNEY BARLOW. Born in Wyoming County, N.Y., June 26, 1838; died Feb. 27, 1914, at Jerusalem, Palestine. The engineer officer in charge of the Army's 1871 party of Yellowstone explorers and co-author of the official report.

Entering West Point as a cadet in 1856, he graduated with the class of 1861 (2 months early because of the fall of Fort Sumter). He was commissioned a second lieutenant of artillery on May 6 and employed as an instructor of volunteer troops until May 15, when he received a commission as first lieutenant.

He took part in the Battle of Bull Run and served through the Peninsula Campaign with Battery M, Second U.S. Artillery. His gallant and meritorious service at the battle of Hanover Court House, Va., earned him the brevet rank of captain.

On June 13, 1863, Captain Barlow was given command of Company C, Battalion of Engineers, serving with the Army of the Potomac until Feb. 16, 1864, and gaining the permanent rank of captain of engineers on July 3, 1863. He was with General Sherman's army in the Atlanta Campaign, receiving the brevet ranks of major, July 22, 1864, and lieutenant colonel, March 13, 1865—both for "gallant and meritorious service."

After the war, Barlow superintended engineering work on coastal fortifications in Florida and New York, and harbor improvements on Lake Champlain. He reached the permanent rank of major of engineers Apr. 30, 1869, when he was assigned to General Sheridan's staff as Chief Engineer of the Military Division of the Missouri, serving in that capacity until July 1874. His field work during that period included several scientific expeditions, his reconnaissance of the Upper Yellowstone in 1871 being the most important. While with a Northern Pacific Railroad surveying party the following year, his escort fought off an attack by a thousand Sioux under Sitting Bull.

From 1874 to 1883 he had charge of fortification and harbor work on Long Island Sound; then on harbor improvement for Lakes Superior and Michigan until 1886, and on the improvement of the Tennessee and Cumberland Rivers, including the building of a ship canal at Muscle Shoals, which was completed Nov. 10, 1890.

From 1891 to 1896, Colonel Barlow (he received the permanent rank of colonel of engineers on May 10, 1895) was the senior commissioner of the International Boundary Commission charged with remarking the boundary with Mexico west of the Rio Grande River, which was followed by engineering work in the Southwest Division.

In 1898, Colonel Barlow was stationed in New York City with charge of improvement work on the Hudson River while serving on a number of important commissions. He was retired with the rank of Brigadier General and Chief of the Corps of Engineers on Apr. 30, 1901.

This tribute was paid him in the *Report of the Annual Reunion, June 11, 1915*, prepared by the Association of Graduates, USMA, p. 51:

"Modesty and courtesy were the characteristic features of his life. Wise and sincere, brave courteous and altogether loveable, he leaves a memory of Christian manhood which all who knew him will cherish."

Sources: The publication of the Association of Graduates, USMA, cited above, and data provided by Colonel Barlow's daughter in 1963.

COLLINS JACK [JOHN H.] BARONETT. Born in 1827 in Glencoe, Scotland; still living as late as 1901. The rescuer of Truman C. Everts, who was lost from the 1870 Washburn party of Yellowstone explorers and wandered alone for 37 days in the wilderness.

Many of the details of the colorful career of Jack Baronett (better known as "Yellowstone Jack") come from the biographical sketch that Hiram M. Chittenden included in his 1895 edition of *The Yellowstone National Park* (pp. 291–92). From it we know that he went to sea at an early age, but deserted his ship in China in 1850 in order to go to the gold fields of California. The lure of gold drew him to other strikes in Australia and Africa, and he made a voyage to the Arctic as the second mate on a whaling ship before returning to California in 1855. He served as a courier for Gen. Albert Sidney Johnston during the Mormon War and took part in the Colorado gold rush on the eve of the Civil War.

Baronett's sympathies were with the South, so he joined the First Texas Cavalry. Abandoning the "lost cause" in 1863, he took service briefly with the French under Maximilian in Mexico.

Baronett came to Montana Territory in September of 1864 and his movements afterwards are better known. He was a member of one of the prospecting parties that crossed the Yellowstone plateau that fall and was with the "Yellowstone Expedition" of 1866. He wintered at Fort C. F. Smith and was among those prospectors who made their way through the hostile Sioux to the Gallatin Valley to obtain relief for the nearly starved garrison of that northernmost outpost on the Bozeman road.

Service as a scout with General Custer's expedition to the Black Hills and another foray into the Yellowstone country in 1869 increased Baronett's familiarity with the region. Thus, when Truman C. Everts was lost from the Washburn party in 1870, Baronett was considered best qualified to search for him. As a result, the unfortunate explorer was found in time to save his life.

Immediately after the dramatic rescue of Everts, Baronett built a toll bridge over the Yellowstone River near its junction with the Lamar, and he operated it for many years as a vital link in the road to the mining region on the Clark Fork River. The care of his bridge was often left in other hands as Baronett guided hunting parties, scouted for the military, and continued his search for elusive mineral riches.

One of the men he guided in the park in 1875, Gen. William E. Strong, has left an excellent description of Baronett. He says:

" 'Jack Baronett,' as he is best known, is a celebrated character in this country, and, although famous as an Indian fighter and hunter, he is still more celebrated as a guide . . . he is highly esteemed by those who know him and his word is as good as gold. He is of medium stature, broad-shouldered, very straight and built like Longfellow's ship, for 'strength and speed.' Eyes black as a panther's and as keen and sharp; complexion quite dark with hair and whiskers almost black. He speaks well, using good English, and his manner is mild, gentle and modest; is proud of his knowledge of the mountains and of his skill with the rifle. I took to him at once . . . ." See "A Trip to the Yellowstone National Park in July, August, and September, 1875" (1876), 43.

While in the Black Hills during the winter of 1876–77, Baronett became involved in a dispute with W. H. Timblin over the recording of mining claims. Fired upon by Timblin, he returned the shots with mortal effect. This event led to the following comment: "As well might the eastern miners walk with shot guns into a gulch lair of Hogback Grizzlies, as to arouse Barronette, the Buchannons and other comrades from the upper Yellowstone." Letter, J. S. Farrar to P. W. Norris, Feb. 26, [1877], in P. W. Norris Collection, Henry E. Huntington Library, Pasadena, Calif.

Despite his service for the Confederacy, Baronett enjoyed the respect and confidence of his former enemies. He was the preferred guide of Gen. Philip H. Sheridan on several junkets through the park and also the only member of the original civilian police force to be retained when the Army took over management of the area in 1886. He thus became the first scout to serve the new administration (he had even been considered for the superintendency, upon the recommendation of the Governor of Montana Territory in 1884).

Baronett married Miss Marion A. Scott, of Emigrant Gulch, at Bozeman, Mont., on Mar. 14, 1884. His wife later held the position of postmistress at Mammoth Hot Springs in the park.

Baronett's 35-year association with the Yellowstone region has been justly recognized by coupling his name to an outstanding peak which flanks the road to the park's northeast entrance, but, otherwise, life did not treat him well. His toll bridge, in which he had invested $15,000, was taken from him in 1894, and he spent $6,000 in lawyer's fees to obtain from Congress a niggardly compensation of $5,000. That money was invested in an expedition to Nome, Alaska, during the last great "gold rush," but his schooner and his hopes were both crushed in the Arctic ice.

Thereafter, the old man's health failed rapidly and he was soon too feeble to earn a living at the rough work available to him. The trail ends at Tacoma, Wash., in late January or early February of 1901, when he was given a ticket by a charitable organization to get him to a friend at Redding, Calif., and it ends with a touch of irony: Six weeks after Baronett's disappearance, he was sought as the only heir of a titled brother killed in the Boer War.

Sources: Hiram M. Chittenden, *The Yellowstone National Park* (Cincinnati, 1895), pp. 291–2. "Capt. Baronette" in The Livingston (Mont.) *Enterprise*, Apr. 20. 1901, and the P. W. Norris Papers, Henry E. Huntington Library, San Marino, Calif.

CHARLES W. COOK. Born in Unity, Maine, in February 1839; died in White Sulphur Springs, Mont., Jan. 30, 1927. A member of the 1869 Folsom party of Yellowstone explorers, and co-author of the first magazine article describing the Yellowstone region.

Charley Cook attended the Quaker Academy at Vassalboro, Maine, with his boyhood friend, David E. Folsom. Together, they went on to the Moses Brown Quaker School at Providence, R.I., where Cook completed his education after David was forced to drop out because of ill-health. From there, the spirit of adventure swept him westward.

Drawn by reports of a rich gold strike near Pikes Peak, Cook made his way to Colorado—only to find there was no fortune awaiting him there. Early in 1864 he joined a band of drovers who were moving 125 head of cattle to Virginia City, a new mining town in what had just become Montana Territory. The eight men were stopped by Sioux and Cheyenne Indians near Green River—where they had to pay a steer for the privilege of passing on with their herd.

The remaining cattle were delivered safely on Sept. 22, 1864, just as the placer mining in Alder Gulch was at the peak of its frantic activity. There being no more ground available, Cook moved on to Last Chance Gulch (present Helena), and then to Confederate Gulch. There he found a job managing the Boulder Ditch Co., which supplied water to the placer mines around Diamond City. One of the men he employed soon after taking over in 1865 was William Peterson. His old chum, David Folsom, joined him there in the fall of 1868.

It was that summer when Cook first thought of visiting the Yellowstone region. An eastern mining man with business around Diamond City (which was then without a hotel) boarded for a time at the headquarters of the ditch company, where he heard some of the rumors then current concerning the wonders lying south of Montana's settlements. Immediately interested, this guest proposed an exploration of the region, but it was already too late to organize a trip there that season. However, the notion persisted with Cook.

When notice of the intention of a party of citizens from Virginia City, Helena, and

Bozeman to make just such an exploration appeared in the *Helena Weekly Herald* of July 29, 1869, Cook and Folsom sought permission to accompany the expedition, and they were greatly disappointed when the project collapsed at the last moment for lack of a military escort. Having already made their preparations for the trip, the two Quakers decided to go anyhow, a resolution in which they were joined by William Peterson.

The party left Diamond City on Sept. 6, 1869, well armed and outfitted, and their trip of 36 days introduced them to the principal features of wonderland. The considerable interest evidenced in the information they brought back induced these explorers to combine their notes in an account suitable for publication in magazine form. The modest, well-written article prepared by Folsom was sent to Cook's mining friend, who had offered to find a publisher; however, attempts to place it with prominent magazines, such as *Scribner's* and *Harper's*, were rebuffed. It was finally accepted by the Chicago *Western Monthly Magazine*, which used the account in a somewhat abbreviated form, and under Cook's name, in the issue of June 1870.

Cook left the Boulder Ditch Co. soon after his return from the Yellowstone adventure, serving briefly as the receiver for a Gallatin Valley flour mill before driving a band of sheep from Oregon to the Smith River Valley in 1871. He developed a large ranch called "Unity" on land he had claimed about 10 miles east of Brewer's Springs (now White Sulphur, Mont.), and it was there that he brought his bride—a Miss Kennicott, of New York—in 1880. They raised three children, one of whom has survived to this writing.

Charles W. Cook outlived his comrades, and he alone was still alive and present at the celebration of Yellowstone Park's 50th anniversary in 1922. The presence of that tall, spare old man with the craggy face and piercing eyes provided a direct link with the park's era of definitive exploration, and he was lionized. But even greater honor came to him before his death. It was in the form of a letter which arrived in February 1924, with this message:

"My Dear Mr. Cook:

Through the courtesy of Mr. Cornelius Hedges, Jr., and of Congressman Scott Leavitt, I have learned that you are within a few days to celebrate your 85th birthday anniversary. As one of the pioneers of the great intermountain West, the first explorer of what is now Yellowstone Park, and one of the men responsible for the founding of the national park system, you have rendered a series of national services of truly notable character. Upon these I wish to extend my felicitations, and my congratulations upon your approaching birthday. I hope you may live to enjoy many more celebrations of the same anniversary."

That kindly tribute was signed by Calvin Coolidge, President of the United States.

Sources: Lew L. Callaway, *Early Montana Masons* (Billings, Mont., 1951), pp. 29–33, and family records made available by Mrs. Oscar O. Mueller, Lewistown, Mont.

WALTER WASHINGTON DELACY. Born in Petersburg, Va., Feb. 22, 1819; died in Helena, Mont., May 13, 1892. Leader of a party of prospectors who passed through the southwest corner of the Yellowstone region in 1863, and compiler—with David E. Folsom—of the first map (deLacy's 1870 edition) to show most of the prominent features with reasonable accuracy.

He was the son of William and Eliza deLacy of Norfolk, Va. They came of a noble Irish family that had declined on these shores, and young Walter lost both parents while yet a boy. His upbringing was left to a pair of maiden aunts and a bachelor uncle, who did well by him. In fact, his uncle even moved to Emmetsburg, Md., to be nearby while the young man attended Mount Saint Mary's Catholic College (where he specialized in mathematics and languages—French, Portuguese, and Spanish).

Since civil engineering was the career he wished to follow, deLacy's uncle obtained for him an appointment to the U.S. Military Academy at West Point, but that schooling was denied him through official chicanery. The wrong was soon righted personally by Professor Dennis Hart Mahan, who felt a responsibility to the boy's family. He took Walter to West Point for tutoring by himself and other officers, thus providing him with what was undoubtedly the finest education in civil and military engineering available in that day.

In the year 1839, while deLacy was working as a railroad surveyor, he was called to Washington to take an examination for a commission in the regular army. With the rank of lieutenant, the young man became an assistant instructor in French at the Military Academy, but he soon resigned that position to take a similar one with the U.S. Navy. Future officers were then schooled at sea and deLacy taught languages to midshipmen aboard ships until 1846.

Returning to his true interest, engineering, deLacy was employed by a group of wealthy men to search for abandoned Spanish silver mines, and he was in the Southwest when war began with Mexico. He took a brave part in that conflict, gaining a captaincy, and during the years immediately following he was employed in the West on a number of Government projects—a survey for a railroad across the Isthmus of Tehuantepec, the survey of the 32d parallel from San Diego, Calif., to San Antonio, Tex., and hydrographic surveys on Puget Sound.

The latter work put deLacy in position to play a very important role in the Indian war of 1856 in the struggling new Territory of Washington. Governor Isaac I. Stevens made him engineer officer with responsibility for planning and constructing the blockhouses and forts that protected the settlements while the volunteer troops campaigned in the Indian country east of the Cascade Mountains.

Having proven himself as a military engineer, deLacy was given employment on a favorite project of Governor Stevens—the construction of the Mullan Road. He was the man who set the grade stakes for the crews, and, at the eastern terminus, he later laid out the town of Fort Benton at the head of navigation on the Missouri River.

Apparently deLacy's experience in Mexico gave him faith in the mineral possibilities of Idaho and Montana. He followed the succession of stampedes that opened up the northern Rocky Mountains, and it was a prospecting tour in 1863—with a party he called "the 40 thieves" that took him across the southwestern corner of the present Yellowstone Park. There he saw Shoshone Lake and the Lower Geyser Basin, but failure to publish his discoveries adequately prevented his getting the credit his exploration merited.

But there was a valuable result. In 1864 the first Territorial Legislature of Montana commissioned deLacy to prepare an official map to be used in establishing the counties, and his map, published in 1865, showed just enough of the Yellowstone region to whet the interest of Montanans (on it was the lake and the falls of the Yellowstone River, with a "hot spring valley" at the head of the Madison River). The map was periodically improved during the 24 years it was in print, and a copy of the 1870 edition—complete with the route of the Folsom party of the previous year, and extensively corrected to accord with their observations—was carried by the Washburn party of 1870.

In Montana's Sioux War of 1867, deLacy assumed a familiar role when he was appointed colonel of engineers for the Territorial Volunteers. In that conflict he displayed his usual quiet bravery by going to the relief of Federal troops beleaguered at Fort C. F. Smith on the Bozeman trail. Loading a wagon train with Gallatin Valley potatoes and flour for the famished garrison, he pushed through with a handful of volunteers—despite warnings that the Sioux would gobble them up.

The remaining years of deLacy's life were occupied with surveying and civil engineering. He fixed the initial point and laid out the base line for the public land surveys of Montana, prepared a map for the Northern Pacific Railroad that greatly influenced the choice of a route through the territory, and accomplished a perilous survey of the Salmon River. He was later city engineer for Helena, Mont., and an employee in the office of the Surveyor General there. He worked to within a few weeks of his death.

Source: "Walter Washington deLacy," *Contributions to the Historical Society of Montana* 2 (1896), pp. 241–251.

GUSTAVUS CHEENY DOANE. Born in Galesburg, Ill., May 29, 1840; died in Bozeman, Mont., May 5, 1892. The officer in command of the military escort that accompanied the Washburn party through the Yellowstone region in 1870. He was also the author of an official report that appeared as a congressional document, thus providing information recognized as reliable.

Doane's parents moved to Oregon Territory by ox-wagon when he was 5 years old, and in 1849 they were lured south to the gold fields of California, so that the lad grew to manhood in the exciting atmosphere of the mushroom camps and towns of the Argonauts. It was that environment, and the University of the Pacific at Santa Clara, that shaped the man.

In 1862, young Doane went east with the "California Hundred," determined to serve the Union cause. Enlisting in the Second Massachusetts Cavalry on Ocotber 30, he had advanced from private to sergeant by Mar. 23, 1864, when he was commissioned a first lieutenant of cavalry. He was honorably mustered out of service on Jan. 23, 1865.

For a time after the war, Doane was involved in the military government of Mississippi, holding offices that included that of mayor of Yazoo City. He married a southern girl, Amelia Link, on July 25, 1866, but it was an unhappy union that ended 12 years later when she divorced him at Virginia City, Mont.

Doane returned to military life July 5, 1868, being commissioned a second lieutenant in the Second U.S. Cavalry. His company arrived at Fort Ellis in May 1869 to become part of the garrison of that post established less than 2 years earlier for the protection of the Gallatin Valley in Montana Territory. And so, when a detail was needed to escort the Washburn party of 1870 into the Yellowstone wilderness, there was just the right officer available at the post that was the logical point of departure.

The assignment was routine—"proceed with one sergeant and four privates of Company F, Second Cavalry, to escort the surveyor general of Montana to the falls and lakes of the Yellowstone, and return"; but Lieutenant Doane made a better-than-routine report upon his visit. That remarkably thorough description was the first official information on the Yellowstone region and its unusual features, and it was characterized by Dr. F. V. Hayden, U.S. Geologist, in these words: "I venture to state, as my opinion, that for graphic description and thrilling interest it has not been surpassed by any official report made to our government since the times of Lewis and Clark."

Great interest was created by that report, and as a result, Doane was often referred to as "the man who invented wonderland." He was described as of splendid physique, standing 6 feet 2 inches, straight as an arrow, and swarthy, with black hair and a dark handlebar mustache. He was 200 pounds, "tall, dark and handsome," and endowed with a loud voice and an air of utter fearlessness. Add to that all the competence of a natural frontiersman, including superb horsemanship and deadly proficiency with a rifle, and there stands the man of whom a soldier once said, "We welcomed duty with the lieutenant." There is also praise of the finest type in the published memoir of Maj. Gen. Hugh L. Scott, one of Doane's shavetails who made it all the way to chief of staff; he looked back over the years and said of that adventurous officer he had served under, "I modeled myself on him as a soldier."

Being a restless, energetic, intelligent man with great powers of endurance, Doane was always busy. He was in demand to escort official parties through the Yellowstone region—as he did the Barlow-Heap and Hayden Survey parties in 1871, and the grand excursion of Secretary of War William W. Belknap in 1875—and when not so employed he volunteered to lead scouting parties and developed a force of Crow Indian auxiliaries of considerable value during the Nez Perce Campaign of 1877 (a war which was a disappointment to Doane because his orders kept him out of the real action).

Late in 1876, Lieutenant Doane was sent on one of the most unusual and bizarre expeditions ever fielded by our army in the West. It was nothing less than a winter exploration of the Snake River from its Yellowstone headwaters to the junction with the mighty Columbia—a task to be accomplished with a detail of six men and a homemade boat. It was his good fortune to lose the boat—but not his men—in the Grand Canyon of Snake River, thus ending in an early disappointment a venture which could only have matured into tragedy.

On Dec. 16, 1878, Doane married his second wife, Mary Hunter, daughter of the old pioneer who was the proprietor of Hunter's Hot Springs on the Yellowstone River at present Springdale, Mont. After a honeymoon in the "States," where Lieutenant Doane had a winter assignment, the couple returned to Montana and life at Fort Ellis.

In 1880, Doane was involved in what promised to be the grandest adventure of his life, one that might have taken his life had he not refused to go through with it. He was ordered East to be considered for duty in the Arctic—as the commander of a party which was to implement the "Howgate Plan" for the study of Arctic weather and living conditions. For its part, the U.S. Army was to establish and maintain a station at Lady Franklin Bay on Ellesmere Island, less than 500 miles from the North Pole. Doane sailed north on the *Proteus*, a leaky and inadequate vessel that was unable to reach its destination (and almost failed to get back). The experience was enough for Doane and he declined the duty, letting it go to a young Signal Corps officer named A. W. Greely.

A promotion to the rank of captain came to Doane Sept. 22, 1884, and his subsequent service was mainly on the Pacific Coast and in the Southwest. While doing monotonous duty at dusty outposts, he dreamed of explorations in Africa, and he made serious tries for the superintendency of Yellowstone National Park in 1889 and 1891.

But Doane's days were numbered. His health began to fail under the hard field duty required of him in Arizona, and he reluctantly asked for retirement. It was not allowed him because he had neither the age (64 years) or the service (40 years) required at that time, and all that could be done was to allow him 6 months leave. He returned to his home at Bozeman, Mont., but contracted pneumonia and died there.

Sources: Hiram M. Chittenden, *The Yellowstone National Park*, (Cincinnati, 1895), pp. 293–95; Francis B. Heitman, *Historical Register and Dictionary of the United States Army* 1 (Washington, 1903), p. 375, and various newspaper items from the Montana press.

TRUMAN C. EVERTS. Born in Burlington, Vt., in the year 1816, died in Hyattsville, Md., Feb. 16, 1901. A member of the 1870 Washburn party of Yellowstone explorers, whose loss in the wilderness and subsequent rescue after 37 days heightened public interest in the expedition; also, author of a timely article in *Scribner's Monthly* a year later, when the movement to create Yellowstone Park was taking form.

Helpful as that account was in creating an awareness of the Yellowstone region and what it contained, just as a group of determined men were opening that campaign which eventually led to creation of a Yellowstone National Park, it provided very little personal information about the man who survived such incredible hardships, and nearly his entire life before and after the Yellowstone adventure remained obscure until August 1961 when his son walked into park headquarters at Mammoth Hot Springs with some facts.

Thus, we now know that Truman C. Everts was one of a family of six boys. His father was a ship captain and the lad accompanied him as cabin boy during several voyages on the Great Lakes. It is unlikely that he received anything more than a public school education, though nothing is certainly known of his life before the age of 48 except that he had been married.

On July 15, 1864, President Abraham Lincoln appointed Truman Everts to be Assessor of Internal Revenue for Montana Territory, an indication he had been a staunch supporter of the Republican party. Yet he was unable to weather the political intrigues of the Grant administration and lost his patronage position on Feb. 16, 1870. Everts lingered in Montana for a time, in the hope of obtaining something else, but by midsummer he had decided to return to the East with his grown daughter, Elizabeth, or "Bessie," who was his housekeeper and also the belle of Helena society. An entry in the diary of Cornelius Hedges shows the purchase of household effects auctioned by Everts on July 6, in preparation for the move.

Everts' accompaniment of the Washburn party into the Yellowstone wilderness was in the nature of a between-jobs vacation—though it turned out somewhat differently. The details of his travail are available in his "Thirty-Seven Days of Peril" (in *Scribner's Monthly* for November 1871). He was rescued at the last possible moment by "Yellowstone Jack" Baronett and George A. Pritchett. While the one nourished the feeble spark of life remaining in a body wasted to a mere 50 pounds, the other went 75 miles for help, so that the lost man undoubtedly owed his life to those hardy frontiersmen who had set aside their usual pursuits to succor him.

It would seem that Everts' gratitude would know no limits; yet, it did not even extend to the payment of that reward his friends had offered for his rescue, he maintaining he could have made his own way out of the mountains. Unfortunately, there was more to his ingratitude than that. When Baronett called on Everts several years later in the course of a visit to New York, he was received so coldly that he afterward said "he wished he had let the son-of-a-gun roam."

Following the passage of the Yellowstone Park act, there was a strong sentiment for making Everts superintendent of the area. However, he was reluctant to accept the position without some provision for a salary, and, before that was resolved, he became a delegate to the Liberal Republican convention at Cincinnati. By thus joining Horace Greeley's attempt to split the party, he passed beyond the pale of orthodoxy and was given no further consideration.

The Bozeman, Mont., *Avant Courier* of May 9, 1873, indicated that Everts had just returned to that town after securing a part interest in the post trader's store at Fort Ellis; but he did not remain there, despite the statement that he "will be permanently located among us."

In 1880 or 1881, Truman C. Everts married a girl who was said to have been 14 years old at the time, and they settled on a small farm at Hyattsville, Md., which was then on the outskirts of Washington, D.C., but has since been absorbed in its urban sprawl. The couple had a child—Truman C. Everts, Jr.—born Sept. 10, 1891, when the father was 75 years old. This son understood that his father was a minor employee of the Post Office Department in his declining years, and that the family went through some very hard times during the Cleveland administration, when his politics were of the wrong persuasion.

Sources: Nathaniel P. Langford, *The Discovery of Yellowstone National Park* (St. Paul, Minn. 1905), p. xviii, and an interview with Truman C. Everts, Jr., in Yellowstone National Park, Aug. 11, 1961.

DAVID E. FOLSOM. Born in Epping, N.H., in May 1839; died in Palo Alto, Calif., May 18, 1918. A member of the 1869 Folsom party of Yellowstone explorers, coauthor of the first magazine article descriptive of the Yellowstone region, and proponent of a suggestion (the second such known to have been made) for reservation of the area and its wonders in the public interest.

Since his was a Quaker family, Dave Folsom was sent to the academy at Vassalboro, Maine, with his boyhood friend, Charles W. Cook, and they both went on to the Moses Brown Quaker School at Providence, R.I. It was there, while he was preparing for a career as a civil engineer, that Folsom's health broke down, so, following his physician's recommendation, he started for the West.

The gold mines of Idaho beckoned young men in 1862, and Folsom was proceeding in that direction when he heard that the Fisk party was organizing at Fort Abercrombie, on the Red River of the North, for the purpose of pioneering a northern route to the mines. Reaching the rendezvous with the same Minnesota contingent that included Nathaniel P. Langford, Folsom was accepted as a herder for the train of 52 wagons that departed with its escort of soldiers in midsummer.

The ineptness of the man detailed to supply wild meat for the 130 men, women, and children of the wagon train led Folsom to volunteer his services as hunter for the party. Earlier hunting in Maine had made him a good woodsman and an excellent shot, so he had no difficulty keeping the expeditioners well supplied as they journeyed across Minnesota and the Territory of Dakota to Fort Benton, and then along the Mullan Road toward Washington Territory (which then abutted on Dakota along the Continental Divide).

As the Fisk party was about to cross the Rocky Mountains, word was received that the diggings on Salmon River, which had been their objective, were "played out", so many of its members turned to a new strike on Grasshopper Creek, where a town called Bannock had already appeared. Folsom spent the winter of 1862–63 there, then moved on to Virginia City and a chancy altercation with outlaw George Ives. The latter's attempt to provoke Folsom into an unfair fight was met in a manner as unexpected as it was untypical of his Quaker background—he floored the bad man with a flung pool ball! It was a rash act, from which Folsom escaped with his life only because friends got him out of town until the work of the vigilantes was completed.

Soon becoming discouraged with placer mining, Folsom took employment on the ranch of Henry C. Harrison at Willow Creek, in Madison County, before settling on land in that vicinity. In addition to the ordinary vicissitudes of pioneer ranching, life there was an unending struggle against inroads of ferocious grizzly bears. Four years of that was enough to turn him briefly to surveying for a livelihood before he joined his old friend, Charley Cook, in the operation of the ditch company at Confederate Gulch in the winter of 1868–69. This employment led him into the Yellowstone wilderness with Cook and Peterson, in what was the first step in the definitive exploration of the area now included in Yellowstone National Park.

Following that adventurous trip, Folsom went to work in the office of the Surveyor General of Montana Territory, at Helena. As a result of this association, he was able to furnish Henry D. Washburn with much information about the Yellowstone region and its "wonders" (also advancing a suggestion that the area should be reserved for public use), and he collaborated with Walter W. deLacy in the revision of the latter's *Map of the Territory of Montana, With Portions of the Adjoining Territories*, so that the Yellowstone region was at last delineated with reasonable accuracy. A copy of this 1870 edition of deLacy's map was carried by the Washburn party of explorers.

Folsom formed a partnership with deLacy and they engaged in land surveying until 1875. Returning to New Hampshire in that year, Folsom remained there until his marriage to Miss Lucy Jones in 1880. The couple settled in Montana, developing a large sheep ranch on Smith River, near the Cook homestead.

Following his return to Montana, Folsom was also prominent in public life. He served as the treasurer of Meagher County from 1885 to 1890, and he was a State senator in the third and fourth sessions of the Legislative Assembly (actually president *pro tem* of the Senate during the fourth). He was an appointed member of the commission that supervised the construction of the State Capitol at Helena, and in 1900 he ran for the governorship of Montana but was defeated.

The Folsoms moved to California when their son, David, Jr., enrolled at Stanford University. The young man was assistant professor of mining engineering there at the time of his father's death.

Source: Lew L. Callaway, *Early Montana Masons* (Billings, Mont. 1951), pp. 29–33.

WARREN CALEB GILLETTE. Born in Orleans, N.Y., Mar. 10, 1832; died in Helena, Mont., Sept. 8, 1912. A member of the 1870 Washburn party of Yellowstone explorers, and the leader of the group that remained behind to make a last, desperate search for the lost Truman C. Everts.

Warren was the eldest of five children raised by parents of French Huguenot origin. Upon completing public school he entered Oberlin College, in Ohio, and studied there into his 18th year before succumbing to that restlessness that eventually took him to Montana.

After stopping for a time in Columbus, Ohio, Gillette returned to New York State where he worked as a clerk in Oneida County until 1855. He then removed to Chicago, working for E. R. King & Co., wholesale hatters and furriers, until 1859. On the basis of that experience he opened a retail store at Galena, Ill., but abandoned the business after 2 years. Returning once more to his home State, he worked at the manufacturing of furs in New York City until the spring of 1862, when word of the discovery of gold in Idaho reached the East.

Lured by the prospect of sudden wealth, Gillette made his way westward. At St. Louis he boarded the steamer *Shreveport*, intending to go by the Missouri River route to Fort Benton landing, and from there overland to the Salmon River mines. But low water stopped the vessel between Fort Buford and the mouth of Milk River, so that its passengers and freight were put ashore short of their Montana destination.

The emigrant party Gillette was with had brought wagons and teams with them, and their journey was continued overland toward Fort Benton. Two days later they met Indians, some of whom were inclined to turn them back. While the Indians were holding a council to decide the matter, the emigrants turned about with the intention of avoiding trouble by voluntarily returning to the Missouri River. But the Indians then informed them they could not go back, but must go on to Fort Benton, which they were glad to do.

By the time this party reached Montana City on Little Prickly Pear Creek it was rumored that gold had been discovered on Grasshopper Creek. While most of the party rested there in "Camp Indecision," a delegation was set to look over the new strike. However, Gillette went on to Deer Lodge (then "La Barge City") where he purchased a cabin with the intention of opening a store.

But the word that came back from Grasshopper Creek was so encouraging that Gillette moved there in December of 1862, becoming a pioneer merchant in the developing town of Bannack. He brought his goods—an assortment of miner's supplies—directly from Fort Benton by packhorse, gaining valuable experience in freighting and the ways of horsethieves while so employed.

The store was moved to the new town of Virginia City after gold was discovered in Alder Gulch in 1863. It was there that Gillette became associated with James King in a partnership that lasted until 1877. With the opening of Last Chance Gulch, King and Gillette moved their stock from Virginia City to Helena, remaining in the freighting and merchandising business there until 1869. After that time the partners engaged in mining operations, particularly in the development of the Diamond City placer mines.

A project undertaken very early by King and Gillette showed their foresight and ingenuity. All travel between Fort Benton and Helena avoided the impassable Little Prickly Pear Canyon by using a difficult road over Medicine Rock and Lion Mountains, but the partners decided it would be to their advantage to build a toll road through the

10-mile canyon. The equipment available for the work was two plows, which cost them $175 apiece, picks, shovels, and blasting powder, and with such means the road was completed in 1866 at a cost of $40,000. Tolls returned that amount within 2 years and the road remained a profitable enterprise to the expiration of the charter in 1875.

At the time of the Yellowstone expedition, Gillette was considered the best woodsman of the party, and his willingness to remain behind in the wilderness, with two soldiers, to continue the search for the lost Truman Everts was a generous act of a man whose humanity was expressed thus in his diary: "I hated to leave for home, while there was a chance of finding poor Everts . . . is he alive? is he dead? in the mountains wandering, he knows not whither?" It was an unsuccessful search, but not for lack of diligence.

After 1877, Gillette turned to State politics and to sheepraising. He served four times in the Legislative Assembly of Montana Territory, twice on its Legislative Council, and was a member of the convention that framed the constitution for statehood. His 12,000-acre ranch near Craig, in Deer Lodge County, carried 20,000 head of Merino sheep and he did much to popularize that breed.

Gillette never married: a spinster sister, Eliza, was his housekeeper and companion until her death in 1897.

Sources: A. W. Bowen & Co., *Progressive Men of the State of Montana* (Chicago, c.1902) pp. 177–78; M. A. Leeson, ed., *History of Montana, 1739–1885*, (Chicago, 1885), p. 1214, and the obituary file, Montana Historical Society, Helena.

SAMUEL THOMAS HAUSER. Born in Falmouth, Ky., Jan. 10, 1833; died in Helena, Mont., Nov. 10, 1914. A member of the 1870 Washburn party of Yellowstone explorers.

A basic education in the public schools of his native State was improved by the careful tutoring of his cousin, Henry Hill, who was a Yale graduate. In that manner, he gained the qualifications for his first employment.

In 1854, Hauser went to Missouri, where he progressed from a railroad surveyor to an assistant engineer on the construction of the Missouri Pacific Railroad. On the eve of the Civil War, though but 28 years old, he was chief engineer on the Lexington branch of that line.

There in Missouri, in that last year before hostilities, Hauser was involved in a local event that changed his life entirely. He heard that a man was to be tried for his life by a Justice of the Peace of a nearby settlement, and, being skeptical of the legality of such a procedure, he rode over with a friend to see what was going on. They found that a young man stood accused of poisoning a spring, a charge that the "court" sustained without a show of evidence. The trial had been held merely to condemn the man, and with that done a rope was instantly produced for his hanging. At that point Hauser, who was on horseback at the edge of the crowd, made an objection. The onlookers reacted so violently to that interference with their judicial proceedings that only the quick action of his friend saved Hauser from being shot off his horse. The condemned was hanged, and the obvious unfairness of the trial so angered Hauser that he commented on it in the Booneville newspaper (published by George Graham Vest, later U.S. Senator and defender of Yellowstone National Park). As a result, the meddling railroader was warned to leave those parts.

News of the finding of gold in Idaho reached the East at that time and Hauser decided to try his luck there. He boarded a Missouri River steamer which landed him at Fort Benton in June 1862. He went overland to the Salmon River placers, prospected for a time and then moved to Grasshopper Creek that fall. A season in the town of Bannack that developed there convinced Hauser he would have to look elsewhere for his fortune, so he joined James Stuart's "Yellowstone Expedition" of 1863. This exploration of the country along the lower Yellowstone River found no gold, but it did run into hostile Indians whose night attack on the party came near finishing Hauser. In the course of that melee he was struck in the chest by a ball that penetrated a thick notebook he was fortunately carrying, then came to rest on a rib over his heart.

In 1865, N. P. Langford assisted Hauser and William F. Sanders to establish a bank at Virginia City, Montana Territory, under the firm name of S. T. Hauser & Co. Hauser soon after organized a mining company and built the first smelter in the territory at Argenta, and the following year he organized the First National Bank of Helena and the St. Louis Mining Co. at Phillipsburg. His later activities included establishment of banks at Missoula, Butte, Fort Benton, and Bozeman, the building of six branch railways and interest in numerous mining and smelting enterprises.

142

While in the Yellowstone region with the Washburn party, Hauser used his engineering skill to good purpose on several occasions by measuring the heights of waterfalls and an eruption of the Beehive Geyser, and sketch-mapping Yellowstone Lake. He also kept a messy but revealing diary of much of the trip.

Hauser was always a Democrat in his politics. He was a delegate to the Democratic National Convention in 1884, and was appointed Governor of Montana Territory by President Grover Cleveland in June 1885. He was the first Montana resident to be named Governor, serving 18 months in that capacity.

Samuel Thomas Hauser married Miss Helen Farrar, the daughter of a St. Louis physician, in 1871, and they had two children.

Sources: A. W. Bowen & Co., *Progressive Men of the State of Montana* (Chicago, c. 1902), pp. 202–03, and the obituary file, Montana Historical Society, Helena.

FERDINAND VANDIVEER HAYDEN. Born in Westfield, Mass., Sept. 7, 1829; died in Philadelphia, Pa., Dec. 22, 1887. The U.S. Geologist and head of the Geological Survey of the Territories (Hayden Survey), which made the first official investigation of the Yellowstone region in 1871.

Hayden's boyhood was brief. His father died when he was 10 and he went to live with an uncle in Ohio. There, he began teaching in country schools at the age of 16 and entered Oberlin College 2 years later. Following graduation in 1850, he studied at the Albany Medical School in New York, where he also obtained a sound education in paleontology and geology while earning his medical degree. The diploma proved less important to Hayden than his introduction to the sciences.

Upon leaving medical school in 1853 he was induced to spend a summer collecting tertiary and cretaceous fossils in the White River Badlands near Fort Pierre, Dakota Territory. That adventuring turned Hayden's interest irrevocably toward geology. With financing supplied by individuals, organizations, and the Federal Government, he continued his field work which was his apprenticeship as a scientific explorer.

The Civil War years were passed as a surgeon in the Union Army, from which he was mustered out in 1865 with the rank of brevet lieutenant colonel. Immediately following that conflict Hayden was elected a professor of mineralogy and geology in the medical department of the University of Pennsylvania, but that wedding of his two fields of interest did not last.

Hayden was able to obtain $5,000 of unexpended Federal funds in 1867 for use in conducting a geological survey of the new State of Nebraska. That modest budget launched the Hayden Survey, which was thereafter financed by a combination of appropriated funds and contributions from private sources. When his fledgling organization came under the control of the Secretary of the Interior in 1869, it also received a formal title, becoming "The U.S. Geological Survey of the Territories."

The Washburn expedition of 1870 created a public interest in the Yellowstone region, and Hayden—who had come so close to penetrating its mysteries while a geologist with the Raynolds expedition in 1860—capitalized upon that interest by persuading the Congress to grant him $40,000 for a scientific investigation of its features. The work of the Hayden Survey during the summer of 1871 established a basis of facts that was undoubtedly of crucial importance in obtaining passage of the act that created Yellowstone National Park. But, as certainly, there would have been no legislation without Hayden's persistent efforts on its behalf during the winter of 1871–72.

The Hayden Survey accomplished important work in Yellowstone Park and the surrounding area in 1872 and 1878, before its merger with the surveys of King and Powell to form the U.S. Geological Survey (1879). It has been claimed that Hayden "worked so rapidly and published so quickly that shoddiness became the hallmark of his reports"; yet, overall, he was essentially correct in his geological interpretation of a staggering extent of the unknown West.

Dr. Hayden, who held LL.D. degrees from the Universities of Rochester and Pennsylvania, was a member of 17 scientific societies in this country and also a corresponding member of 70 foreign societies. His published titles exceeded 158 at the time of his retirement from the U.S. Geological Survey in 1886 because of failing health. He died the following year—a man described by historian Chittenden as "intensely nervous, frequently impulsive, but ever generous . . . his honesty and integrity undoubted." Time has proven him a man whose work for his Government, and for science, was a labor of love.

Sources: John Wesley Powell, "Ferdinand V. Hayden," in *Ninth Annual Report of the United States Geological Survey to the Secretary of the Interior, 1887–88* (Washington, 1889), pp. 31–38, and Charles A. White, "Memoir of Ferdinand Vandiveer Hayden, 1829–87," in *Biographical Memoirs* of the National Academy of Science 3 (Washington, 1893), pp. 395–413.

DAVID PORTER HEAP. Born in San Stefano, Turkey, in March 1843; died in Pasadena, Calif., Oct. 25, 1910. An army engineer officer attached to the 1871 Barlow party of Yellowstone explorers and co-author of the resulting official report.

The son of the U.S. Minister to Turkey, his basic education was obtained at the Germantown Academy, Pennsylvania, and Georgetown College. He entered the U.S. Military Academy in 1860 and graduated seventh in the class of 1864. He was immediately promoted to first lieutenant, Corps of Engineers, and assigned to the Engineer Battalion of the Army of the Potomac, with which he served for the remainder of the Civil War. He was breveted a captain on Apr. 2, 1865, for gallant and meritorious services during the siege of Petersburg, Va.

After the war he was employed in harbor improvement work on Lake Michigan, and in other engineering work, until February 1870, when he became chief engineer of the Department of Dakota. Thus, his immediate superior was Maj. John W. Barlow, whom he accompanied on a reconnaissance of the Upper Yellowstone in 1871.

Captain Heap returned to his headquarters at St. Paul with the topographic notes, which were thus saved from destruction in the great Chicago fire which consumed Barlow's specimens and photographs, and he was able to produce from them the first map of the Yellowstone region based on adequate instrumental observations.

From March 1875 to May 1877, Heap was in charge of preparations for the participation of the Corps of Engineers in the International Centennial Exhibition, and he represented the United States in 1881 at the International Electrical Exhibition held at Paris, France. He was later engineer of various lighthouse districts, secretary of the Lighthouse Board, and a member of several boards concerned with improvement of rivers and harbors. He retired with the rank of brigadier general on Feb. 16, 1905, after 40 years of service.

Source: *Report of the Annual Reunion, June 12th, 1911*, prepared by the Association of Graduates, USMA, pp. 89–90.

CORNELIUS HEDGES. Born in Westfield, Mass., Oct. 28, 1831; died in Helena, Mont., Apr. 29, 1907. A member of the 1870 Washburn party of Yellowstone explorers, proponent of the idea of reserving the Yellowstone region in the public interest (this was the third expression of the idea), and special correspondent for the Helena Herald.

Hedges received his elementary education in the village school and the academy in his hometown of Westfield, in the Woronoco Valley of Massachusetts. As was the custom of the time, he attended classes mainly in the winter and spent the growing seasons working on his father's acres. The family home was on Broad Street and it was the boy's daily chore to take the slow-moving oxen along "William's driving way" to the fields on the north side of Great River, where he labored with his father. The hard-working, thrifty conservatism of the land he came from is well illustrated in the manner of Hedges' going-away to college. The day before his departure to begin his schooling at Yale, he cradled a field of buckwheat.

Upon graduating in 1853, Hedges taught school at the academy at Euston, Conn., and also "read law" in a local office, as the prevailing practice of studying under an established lawyer was called. After a year of that double duty he entered the Harvard Law School and was graduated in 1855. That same year he was admitted to the practice of law in the courts of Massachusetts on the motion of Benjamin F. Butler.

On July 7, 1856, Hedges married Edna Layette Smith of Southington, Conn. After another period of schoolteaching, the young couple moved to Independence, Iowa, where he opened a law office and assisted in editing a newspaper. From the latter experience Hedges gained a liking for printer's ink that lasted a lifetime.

In 1864, Hedges moved his family back to Connecticut and struck out for the gold fields of Montana. He walked from Independence, Iowa, to Virginia City, Mont., hunting along the route of the slow-moving wagon train. He worked several claims with the usual miner's luck before moving on to a new camp where the town of Helena soon came into existence. There, he made the acquaintance of the local sheriff, who turned some legal business his way. That allowed him to establish a law office and bring his family out to Montana Territory in 1865.

Hedges was a peaceful man who managed to live in that turbulent environment without becoming involved in its violent happenings—except once. He was a staunch Union man, and though the Territory of Montana had been all but taken over by that Southern element that went West to escape the Civil War (known collectively as the "left wing of General Price's army"), he had decided, along with a few men of like sentiments, to show the colors. The town's loyal women sewed a flag, which was run up the day word of General Lee's surrender was received. The Secessionist element swore they would rip the flag down, so Hedges sat all that first night at his office window, rifle in hand, to prevent it. Fortunately, no attempt was made.

By 1870, Hedges was active in Masonic affairs, an elder in the Presbyterian Church, had established a public library, and was an editorial writer for the *Helena Herald*. He was coming along, but life was not yet easy. His diary indicates that the Yellowstone trip cost him $280, and that he was uneasy about the expense.

It has been stated that the national park idea was a direct outgrowth of a suggestion made by Cornelius Hedges beside a campfire at Madison Junction on the evening of Sept. 19, 1870. There is no reason to doubt that he advanced a proposal for the reservation of the area the Washburn party had just passed through, so that it would be held for the public good rather than for private aggrandizement. In that, however, he was only restating a proposal he had heard Acting Territorial Governor Thomas Francis Meagher make in October 1865. Undoubtedly, Hedges' comrades recognized his proposal as a restatement of an idea that had surfaced twice before (David E. Folsom of the 1869 expedition made a similar suggestion to Washburn prior to the departure of the 1870 party); thus, Hedges' contribution lay not in a novel suggestion, but in that series of fine articles, so descriptive of the Yellowstone region, which he contributed to the *Helena Herald* on his return. He was a reporter, and it speaks well for his basic honesty that he never personally claimed to have originated the idea—only that "I first suggested the uniting of all our efforts to get it made a National Park, little dreaming that such a thing were possible."

Following his return from the Yellowstone trip, Hedges continued in the quiet, constructive way of life so typical of him. President Grant commissioned him U.S. Attorney for Montana Territory on Mar. 3, 1871, and he became active in the Montana Historical Society in 1873 (serving as recording secretary from 1875 to 1885). He was Superintendent of Public Instruction for Montana from Jan. 27, 1872, to Jan. 15, 1878, and again from Feb. 22, 1883, to Mar. 17, 1885, most of that time having judicial duties also. Hedges was probate judge of the court at Helena from 1875 to 1880, and from 1880 to 1887 he was the Supreme Court reporter.

In 1884, Hedges was a member of the Constitutional Convention for statehood, and in 1889 he became the first Montanan elected to the State Senate from Lewis and Clark County. His late years were spent almost entirely in the service of the Masonic Order, in which he held high and influential offices.

Upon his death, the *Helena Daily Record* had this to say of him: "Thoughtful, kind, charitable, ever ready to heed the call of the unfortunate, without selfishness or guile, no better man has ever lived in Montana, nor to any is there a higher mead of praise for what he did and gave to Montana."

Sources: Lew L. Callaway *Early Montana Masons* (Billings, 1951), pp. 10–12; A. W. Bowen & Co., *Progressive Men of the State of Montana* (Chicago, c. 1902), pp. 1–2; and the obituary file, Montana State Historical Society, Helena.

NATHANIEL PITT LANGFORD. Born in Oneida County, N.Y., Aug. 9, 1832; died in St. Paul, Minn., Oct. 18, 1909. A member of the 1870 Washburn party of Yellowstone explorers, author of a book on the expedition and one of the group that worked for establishment of Yellowstone National Park.

As the 11th of 13 children born to George and Chloe (Sweeting) Langford, his formal education was limited to what was available at a rural district school, where the schooling was fitted into the slack season between fall harvesting and spring plowing. Though his youth included more farming than schooling, he developed into a well-informed young man—probably one of the advantages of having many older sisters.

Langford remained at home until after the death of his father in 1853, when he removed to St. Paul, Minn., and entered the banking business (he already had 2 years experience as a clerk in the Oneida Bank of Utica). He stayed in St. Paul until 1862, and in June of that year he joined an expedition bound for the Idaho gold fields under the guidance of James L. Fisk.

The overland trip, accomplished by following a route north of the Missouri River, required 3 months, during which the party had many adventures. Arriving first at Gold Creek in Deer Lodge County, they went next to Bannack after the discovery of gold there. In 1863, Langford moved to yet another strike—at Alder Gulch—and he was present when the first building was erected at Virginia City. He returned to the East that year and enroute his party had a narrow escape from the desperados of Plummer's gang.

Two months after the establishment of the Territory of Montana, Langford was commissioned Collector of Internal Revenue on July 15, 1864. He held the position until 1868, when he was removed by President Andrew Johnson, but reinstated by the Senate. Almost before the tumult had died down, Langford resigned his position of collector on the understanding that Johnson would appoint him to the governorship of Montana. However, the Senate, having fought to secure one position for him, refused to confirm another, so Langford was out of a job.

The year following his visit to the Yellowstone region Langford lectured in the East and worked for reservation of its wonders for the public benefit. After a national park was established, he became its first superintendent, holding that position from May 10, 1872, until Apr. 18, 1877, when he was replaced by Philetus W. Norris. The first superintendency was a sterile period during which the park was neither developed nor protected; indeed, one man, without appropriated funds and already fully employed as U.S. Bank Examiner for the Territories and Pacific Coast States, could hardly have been expected to do more than he did—make three brief visits to the area and prepare one report.

Langford married Emma Wheaton, the daughter of a St. Paul physician, Nov. 1, 1876, but his bride died soon after. Eight years later, he married again—to Clara Wheaton, sister of his first wife. After 1885, his life centered in St. Paul, where he engaged in the insurance business and, beginning in 1897, served as president of the Ramsey County Board of Control, handling city and county relief matters until his death from injuries received in a fall.

Sources: Olin D. Wheeler, "Nathaniel Pitt Langford," in *Collections of the Minnesota Historical Society 15* (1912), pp. 631–68; A. W. Orton, "Some Scattered Thoughts On The Early Life of N. P. Langford," an unpublished manuscript in the Yellowstone Park Reference Library (1966); and the Langford Papers in the manuscript collection of the Minnesota Historical Society, St. Paul.

WILLIAM LEIPLER. Born in Baden, Germany, in 1845. He was a private of the military escort that accompanied the Washburn party through the Yellowstone region in 1870, and the only casualty on that expedition (he was kicked by Stickney's horse on the return). He evidently was made a sergeant immediately upon the return to Fort Ellis, for that was his grade when he volunteered to go with the party that brought Truman C. Everts back to civilization after his rescue.

Leipler was a pianoforte maker before he enlisted in Company B, 20th Regiment of New York Cavalry, on Nov. 23, 1863. Following his discharge from active service at the end of the Civil War, he was unable to adjust to civilian life and enlisted in Company F, Second Cavalry, on Dec. 7, 1866, becoming the most typical of "old soldiers." Described then as being 5 feet, $8\frac{1}{2}$ inches in height, light-haired, and of a florid complexion, he served with the same cavalry outfit—fighting in the Piegan Campaign, the Sioux Campaign (at Lame Deer, Muddy Creek, and Baker's battle on the Yellowstone River), and in the Nez Perce Campaign—until Aug. 5, 1893, when his request for retirement was approved by Gen. Nelson A. Miles. His retirement address was Roos Alley, Buffalo, N.Y. See The National Archives, RG–94, AGO—Enlistment papers, and carded Service Record, Doc. File 13699 PRD–1893.

GEORGE W. McCONNELL. Born in Adams County, Ind., in 1848. He was a private of the military escort that accompanied the Washburn party through the Yellowstone region in 1870, serving as Lieutenant Doane's orderly on the expedition.

At the time of his enlistment he was 5 ft, 6 inches in height, with grey eyes, brown hair, and a fair complexion. He had been a farmer and evidently was satisfied with one hitch in the army. See The National Archives, RG–94, AGO—Enlistment papers.

CHARLES MOORE. Born in Canada in 1846; died Feb. 17, 1921. Though only a private of the military escort that accompanied the Washburn party through the Yellowstone region in 1870, he is noteworthy for having made the earliest pictorial representations of Yellowstone features—those pencil sketches at Tower Fall and at the great falls of the Yellowstone River of which historian Chittenden has said: "His quaint sketches of the falls forcibly remind one of the original picture of Niagara, made by Father Hennepin in 1697."

Moore's enlistment papers show him to have been 5 feet, 5½ inches in height, blue-eyed, dark-haired, and of a ruddy complexion when he enlisted at Cincinnati, Ohio, on November 7, 1868. He served only one hitch with the cavalry, his reenlistment in 1874 being with the Battalion of Engineers; and it was from Company B of that organization that he retired as a sergeant on May 11, 1891. See The National Archives, RG–94, AGO—Enlistment papers.

WILLIAM PETERSON. Born on one of the Bornholm Islands of Denmark, Dec. 3, 1834; died in Salmon, Idaho, Nov. 28, 1919. A member of the 1869 Folsom party of Yellowstone explorers.

Peterson was raised as a farm boy, yet he finished the schooling required under Danish law before he was 15—and also developed an adventurous turn of mind out of keeping with that environment. One day he met a sea captain in the town of Ruma and was bold enough to ask for a place as cabin boy on the man's ship. It was arranged, and that trading voyage to Iceland for tallow, wool, eiderdown, and furs was the beginning of a sea-faring life in which Peterson saw much of the world and advanced himself as far as second mate.

But a seaman's life was also a hard life, and, after 11 years, Peterson decided to try California instead. Being a sailor, he went to his promised land in typical sailor-fashion—by signing on at New York as a hand "before the mast" on the *Mary Robinson*, which was 120 days making San Francisco by way of the Horn. A gold strike in Idaho was the exciting news in California's great port at that time, so he continued up the coast to Portland, Oreg., then a small town with very muddy streets, from which he ascended the Columbia by river boat to The Dalles.

Peterson reached Elk City early in the summer of 1861 with a partner he had picked up on the boat. Leaving his partner to work their claim, he made a prospecting excursion nearly to the head of Clearwater River, only to find, on his return from that wild region, that the partner had "struck it rich" on their claim while he was away, had sold out for several thousand dollars, and had left the country without dividing with him. Though left destitute, Peterson stayed on, working for wages, running a pack train, and serving as watchman for idle mining properties.

Those years of following one "excitement" after another were long on experience but short on profit, and so, when Peterson moved across the Continental Divide into Montana in 1865, he looked for a less chancy occupation and found it with the Boulder Ditch Co. at Diamond City, in Confederate Gulch. Thus, at the time of his Yellowstone trip in 1869 he was an old employee of the concern managed by Charley Cook.

Each member of the party had particular skills to contribute, and Peterson's were a sailor's expertise with cloth and cordage, a packer's mastery of the diamond hitch, and the all-around caginess of a man who had survived most of a decade in the rough-and-tumble of the mining frontier. He was also an ideal companion, with just the right mixture of common sense and good humor.

Following the return of the best-managed expedition that ever passed through the Yellowstone wilderness, Peterson continued to work for the Boulder Ditch Co. to the end of the 1870 season, when he left Diamond City and went to Grasshopper Creek, near Montana's earliest mining town of Bannock. There he bought some cows and yearlings brought up from Utah and moved them to the Lemhi Valley, where he went into the cattle business. He developed a ranch on a stream which became known as Peterson Creek, but he later sold that place and moved, first to the Lost River country and then to the vicinity of the present town of Salmon, Idaho. Settling permanently there, William Peterson married Jesse Notewire late in 1888 or early in 1889, and they had two children—a boy, Harold, who lived to the age of 14, and a girl, Jesse, who died in infancy.

Peterson was twice mayor of Salmon and is remembered for bringing electricity to that community by building a powerplant there.

Source: "A Reminiscence of William Peterson," in the manuscript file, Yellowstone Park Reference Library.

JACOB WARD SMITH. Born in New York City, in the year 1830; died in San Francisco, Jan. 23, 1897. A member of the 1870 Washburn party of Yellowstone explorers.

When he was 2 years old, Jacob's father, a New York City baker, died of cholera, and his mother remarried—to Andrew Lang, a butcher. At his stepfather's stall in the Catherine Street Market Jacob learned the butcher's trade, and, whatever his schooling was, it was probably less of an influence than the give-and-take of the market place; anyhow, the man who matured in that environment was very much a hustler, resilient, an inveterate practical joker, and merciless with whatever he came to consider a stupidity.

It was also at the market stall that Jacob met Jeannette, the daughter of Capt. Joel N. Furman, who supplied fish and shellfish from the waters of Long Island Sound. The acquaintance ripened into an engagement upon the young lady's graduation from the Charlottesville Ladies' Seminary in 1858.

The following year, Jacob Smith removed to Virginia City, Nev., where he established the City Market. Jeannette followed him there and they were married in San Francisco on Oct. 26, 1861. During the following years, speculation and politics proved more enticing than the butcher business, and he rapidly accumulated a modest fortune as a stockbroker, speculating in silver. He was also elected an assemblyman for Storey County in Nevada's first legislature, but the decline of the silver mines eventually led to bankruptcy and "Jake," as he was familiarly known, moved to Montana Territory in the summer of 1866.

He immediately went into the tanning business with John Clough—the Montana Hide & Fur Co.—at the corner of Breckenridge and Ewing Streets; but it was a venture that ended in another failure. The Yellowstone adventure took place in the hiatus that followed.

In 1872, Jake returned to San Francisco at the insistence of his wife, and reestablished himself as a broker. Within a decade he was a millionaire, but lost his considerable fortune just as rapidly. His wife returned to the East with their four children in 1885 and divorced him 7 years later. Jake then married Ora C. Caldwell, by whom he had a son before his death by apoplexy in San Francisco.

Those are the principal facts in the life of a man who has been presented by Nathaniel P. Langford as "too inconsequent and easy-going to command our confidence or to be of much assistance;" yet, it is quite probable Jake's "good-natured nonsense" and keenly perceptive wit barbed the dignified Langford. Be that as it may be, the likeness we have of Jacob Ward Smith shows a large, good-looking man in a Prince Albert coat, a carnation in the buttonhole, cane and silk top hat in hand; a confident, even imperious man with shrewd eyes well-placed above a Guardsman's mustache. It is not the portrait of a shiftless, ne'er-do-well, but the very image of an American business tycoon of yesterday.

Source: letter from a grandson, Herbert F. Seversmith, on Sept. 13, 1963.

JAMES STEVENSON. Born in Maysville, Ky., Dec. 24, 1840; died in New York City, July 25, 1888. Managing director of the Geological Survey of the Territories (Hayden Survey), and Hayden's assistant during the fieldwork in the Yellowstone region.

"Jim" hailed from the same Kentucky town from whence the legendary John Colter was recruited into the service of the Lewis and Clark expedition in 1803. Like him, this slender, brownhaired 16 year old went forth to a life of adventure in the exploration of the West.

While employed on the surveys of Lt. G. K. Warren and Capt. W. F. Raynolds, he came to know the doctor-turned-geologist Ferdinand V. Hayden, and the old trapper-guide, Jim Bridger. From the one he gained a scientific curiosity, and from the other a taciturn competence. Intervening winters spent with the Sioux and Blackfoot Indians provided him with a knowledge of their language and customs that served him well during later expeditioning and laid the foundation for the ethnological studies of his last years.

The Civil War interrupted this training of a scientific explorer, but it, too, contributed to his development. Enlisting as a private in the 13th New York Regiment, he reached the rank of lieutenant during the war years, and was a seasoned leader of men by the end of that conflict.

In 1866, James Stevenson accompanied Hayden into the badlands of Dakota Territory in a search for fossils, and from that time on he was the assistant of the great geologist in every venture until the Hayden Survey was merged with those of King and Powell to form the U.S. Geological Survey in 1879. His skill in managing the so-often meager finances—supplementing inadequate means by wheedling passes from the railroad and stagecoach companies, borrowing arms, tentage, and wagons from frontier garrisons, and cadging rations from army stores—was genius enough; but he also organized, trained, and often led detachments that moved with dreamlike perfection through a vast expanse of western wilderness, always accomplishing the intended purpose without incident or serious injury.

Quiet and reserved, like the traditional frontiersman he had become, Stevenson spoke no more than he had to, but he meant every word. He might have bragged of his part in the first ascent of the mighty Grand Teton, but he said not a word, nor did he write anything of his strenuous life, for memorabilia were not his forte; yet, when his wild, young scientists hazed the pack mules with stones on the Snake River plain, he was vocal enough—and also gave the culprits extra camp chores as penance.

Upon the formation of the Geological Survey in 1879, James Stevenson became its executive officer, but his interest had turned increasingly to the study of the American Indian, and he was soon detailed to the Bureau of Ethnology to do research in the Southwest for the Smithsonian Institution. He explored cliff and cave dwellings and lived among the Zuni and Hopi Indians, where his rare tact made it possible for him to gather remarkable collections of pottery, costumes, and ceremonial objects. He was stricken with "mountain fever"—probably Rocky Mountain spotted fever—while so employed in 1885, and never really recovered from it.

A relapse in 1887 left Stevenson with a damaged heart, and he was returning to the city of Washington, D.C. with his wife, after an extended convalescence in New England, when he died suddenly at the Gilsey House in New York.

James Stevenson left few records behind, for he was too busy to write much; but he has appropriate memorials in the Indian collections he made for the Smithsonian, and in those place names (an island in Yellowstone Lake and a summit of the Absaroka Range) which Hayden said were given: "In honor of his great services not only during the past season, but for over twelve years of unremitting toil as my assistant, often times without pecuniary reward, and with but little of the scientific recognition that usually comes to the original explorer . . . ."

Sources: "James Stevenson," *Ninth Annual Report of the United States Geological Survey to the Secretary of the Interior, 1887–88* (Washington, 1889), pp. 42–44; and "James Stevenson," in *American Anthropologist*, N.S. 18 (1916), 552–59.

BENJAMIN F. STICKNEY. Born in Monroe County, N.Y., Oct. 23, 1838; died in Florida during February 1912. A member of the 1870 Washburn party of Yellowstone explorers, serving as the chief of commissary.

When he was 6 years old, Benjamin's parents moved to Ogle County, Ill., where his education was obtained by desultory attendance at a country school. Much of his time, until he left home at 19, was spent working on the farm, and after that he regularly sent part of his earnings to his parents.

Going to St. Joseph, Mo., Stickney found employment as a bridge carpenter with the Hannibal & St. Joseph Railroad Co., and, in 1860, he hired out as a teamster for the Lyons & Pullman Co., driving an outfit to Central City, Colo. He then engaged in prospecting and mining, with fair success, until the fall of 1863.

In that year Stickney decided to go to Montana Territory, so he bought a team and wagon and hauled a load of provisions to Virginia City. There he combined freighting with mining for a time. He was eventually able to purchase a claim in Bevin's Gulch, and it yielded him a good return; then he went back to freighting. In that manner he built up a considerable freighting business which he sold to John A. Largent and Joseph Hill in 1872. Thus, he was a freighter at the time of the visit to the Yellowstone region.

Following the sale of his freighting business, Stickney turned to ranching by pre-empting 160 acres of land near the Missouri River just east of Craig, Mont. Grasshoppers ate up his crops for six seasons, but he managed to get by raising cattle. Later he engaged in sheep raising, purchasing 2,498 acres of additional land and leasing some. In 1872,

Stickney obtained an interest in the Craig ferry, and after 1875 he operated it alone. He also opened a store in Craig in 1886 and ran it for 10 years.

Stickney married Rachel Wareham on Nov. 3, 1873, and they reared three children.

Sources: A. W. Bowen & Co., *Progressive Men of Montana* (Chicago, c. 1902), pp. 1823–24; and the obituary file, Montana Historical Society, Helena.

WALTER TRUMBULL. Born in Springfield, Ill., in 1846; died in Springfield, Oct. 25, 1891. A member of the 1870 Washburn party of Yellowstone explorers, writer (contributing to the *Helena Rocky Mountain Gazette* and *The Overland Monthly*) and amateur artist.

He was the eldest son of Senator Lyman Trumbull, and, upon completion of his public school education at Springfield, he entered the U.S. Naval Academy. However, he resigned his appointment at the conclusion of the Civil War and embarked on an extended voyage on the *Vandalia*, under Captain Lee, before taking up journalism as a reporter for the New York *Sun*.

Prior to his visit to Yellowstone with the Washburn party, Trumbull had been employed under Truman C. Everts as an assistant assessor of internal revenue for Montana Territory. He probably owed the position to the influence of his father, but even that veteran of 16 years in Congress could not protect his son from being displaced in the struggle for patronage that marked President Grant's administration.

Thus, Walter Trumbull was on a between-jobs vacation when he entered the Yellowstone region, and the closing sentence of the article he wrote for *The Overland Monthly* of May and June 1871 indicates he had some understanding of the area's potential. He said: "When, however, by means of the Northern Pacific Railroad, the falls of the Yellowstone and the geyser basin are rendered easy of access, probably no portion of America will be more popular as a watering-place or summer resort than that we had the pleasure of viewing, in all the glory and grandeur of its primeval solitude." Aside from his plug for railroad tourism, Trumbull's writing did not go beyond travelogue.

Though there was no mention of reservation in what he wrote, Trumbull had at least two other opportunities to assist in the creation of Yellowstone National Park. As a special correspondent of the *Helena Herald*, he accompanied William H. Clagett throughout that candidate's successful campaign for election as Montana's Delegate to Congress, which would have given him ample opportunity to interest Clagett in the Yellowstone region, and it is even more likely that Senator Lyman Trumbull's support of park legislation was influenced by his son's favorable opinion of the area.

Walter Trumbull married Miss Slater, a stepdaughter of James H. Roberts of Springfield, and their first son was born in 1879—the year in which Trumbull went to Zanzibar as assistant consul. It seems likely that it was there, in that center of East African trade— a cesspool of world commerce combining a murderous climate with pestilential conditions—that his constitution was undermined, leading to the appearance of the consumption which eventually claimed his life.

On the advice of his physician, Trumbull moved to Albuquerque, N. Mex., in the hope of improving his health. He was admitted to the bar there, but found the practice of law too strenuous and engaged instead in the mercantile business until 1889, when he had to abandon all business activities.

The remainder of Walter Trumbull's life was spent seeking relief from his affliction. He was a patient at the sanatorium at Dansville, N.Y., and at Battle Creek, Mich., but neither place was able to help him and he died at his father's house at Springfield, at the age of 45.

Sources: Louis C. Cramton, *Early History of Yellowstone National Park and Its Relationship to National Park Policy* (Washington, 1932), pp. 13, 23, 25, 59; and clipping file, Illinois Historical Society, Springfield.

HENRY DANA WASHBURN. Born in Windsor, Vt., Mar. 28, 1832; died in Clinton, Ind., Jan. 26, 1871. The leader of the 1870 Washburn party of Yellowstone explorers and author of the first account of its discoveries made available to the press of the nation.

Henry Washburn's parents moved to Wayne County, Ohio, in the year of his birth, and it was there that he lived until 1850. His public school education was interrupted at the age of 13, when he was apprenticed to a tanner, but that trade was not to his liking and he abandoned it to become a school teacher.

It was while he was teaching at Helt's Prairie, near Clinton, Ind., that he met Miss

Serena Nebeker of that town at a spelling bee. Serena went on to the Edgar Academy at Paris, Ill., for "finishing," then taught school for a time on the Grand Prairie while Henry took some preparatory work at Oberlin College and obtained a degree at the New York State and National Law School.

He was able to open a law office in Newport, Ind., in 1854, and he and Serena were married December 28 at the home of her parents. The young couple made their home at Newport where four children were born in the years before the Civil War. During that time Washburn supplemented his legal practice by serving as Vermillion County Auditor.

At the onset of war in 1861, he raised a company of volunteers at Terre Haute and was elected their captain. His unit became Company C, 18th Regiment of Indiana Volunteer Infantry. Before the regiment was mustered into Federal service on Aug. 16, 1861, Henry D. Washburn received the Governor's commission as its lieutenant colonel.

The 18th Indiana served in the Missouri campaigns under Generals Fremont and Hunter, receiving a battlefield commendation for recapturing the guns of a Peoria battery at the Battle of Pea Ridge. The regiment also campaigned in Arkansas, where Washburn became its colonel on July 15, 1862. Under his leadership, the 18th Indiana served at the siege of Vicksburg, where the exposure incident to trench life initiated that wasting consumption that contributed to his early death. Further campaigning under General Sheridan in the Shenandoah Valley led to a brevet rank of brigadier general on Dec. 15, 1864. He was mustered out of the Army at Savannah, Ga., July 26, 1865, with the brevet rank of major general, given in recognition of his "gallant and meritorious service during the war."

General Washburn's service papers describe him as 6 feet tall, with blue eyes, light complexion, and light hair, and it is evident from photographs taken of him after the war that he was sparely built, but of a very commanding appearance.

While yet in the army, General Washburn was pressed to run for the seat in the national House of Representatives held by Daniel W. Voorhees. He took leave to campaign in Indiana and was successful at the polls despite the election frauds charged to the opposition. Following the war he was able to occupy his seat in the House, to which he was reelected. But the labors of his office were so destructive of his war-ravaged health that he refused to run for a third term and applied to President Grant for the position of Surveyor General for Montana Territory in the hope that life in the West would restore his vigor. The other contender for that office was Col. Philetus W. Norris, of Michigan, but General Washburn received the appointment Apr. 17, 1869.

Surveyor General Washburn started for Montana in May with his wife, two children, and several relatives. They boarded the steamer *Submarine No. 14* at St. Louis, with household goods and a grand piano, arriving at Fort Buford, near the mouth of the Yellowstone, 1 month and 2 days later. Here they transferred to the light-draught steamer *Lacon* for the remainder of the voyage to Fort Benton, but the low stage of the water in the upper Missouri prevented the boat from reaching Cow Island. After 3 weeks of fruitless toil over numerous sandbars, they turned back. On the return trip they were "snagged" and had to defend a sunken boat from Indian attack while laboring on short rations to refloat it. Rescued by their own resources alone, crew and passengers brought the boat back to Omaha on August 6.

The Washburns had accomplished nothing except the loss of their household goods by their voyage of 70 days, so Henry decided to go on to Helena alone while the others returned to their Indiana homes. He completed the journey by way of the newly built Union Pacific Railroad to Corinne, Utah, and from thence by bone-jolting stagecoach northward into Montana. His arrival in the Territory in company with Governor Ashley and Senator Lyman Trumbull was noted by Thomas H. Canfield, who characterized them as "all good N.P.R.R. men."

In 1870, General Washburn was gradually involved in events that led to the Yellowstone expedition, for which he proved to be the ideal leader. As Cornelius Hedges later pointed out, he was able to unify and guide a potentially fractious party composed of men "each of whom considered himself a host; all unusually self sufficient and self reliant, and singularly disposed to individual judgment," and he did so "with no articles of war to aid in the enforcement of discipline, which was still so essential to the general success and individual safety." His natural ability as a leader, coupled with uniform and impartial consideration for others, and his constant willingness to take up a load, brought the party through with credit.

For General Washburn the strain was too great. A cold caught while searching for the lost Truman C. Everts in miserable weather south of Lake Yellowstone advanced his lingering consumption, so that he was forced by ill health to start for his home in Indiana early in January 1871. And yet, despite his illness, he was able to write an account of the Yellowstone adventure which the *New York Times* commended as distinguished by its "graphic directness and unpretending eloquence," noting that "rarely do descriptions of nature come to our hands so unaffectedly expressed."

Washburn arrived at the home of his father-in-law, Aquilla Nebeker, in Clinton, Ind., after what must have been a harrowing trip. There, he was put to bed and given all the care that could be had; yet he lived only a few days. He was buried in Clinton in a ceremony conducted by the Knights Templar. In time a letter arrived, signed by all the employees of his office at Helena, saying simply that he "fulfilled all the duties of his official position in a manner which has endeared him to us all." It was typical of the man.

Source: Washburn family papers in the Yellowstone Park Reference Library.

JOHN WILLIAMSON. Born in Frederick, Md., in 1843. He was a private of the military escort that accompanied the Washburn party through the Yellowstone region in 1870, and the fact that he was picked to accompany Warren C. Gillette and Private Moore on that final search, south of Lake Yellowstone, for the missing Truman C. Everts, hints that he was rugged and resourceful.

Williamson enlisted at Laramie, Wyo., on Jan. 19, 1869, being then a 6-footer with grey eyes, brown hair, and a sallow complexion. He evidently did not care enough about army life to reenlist. See The National Archives, RG–94, AGO—Enlistment papers.

Notes

INTRODUCTION

[1] Hiram M. Chittenden was first to call attention to the national park idea. In his book, *The Yellowstone National Park* (Cincinnati: The Robert Clarke Co., 1895), he devotes a chapter, pp. 87–97, to a discussion of its origin and realization.

[2] Ralph Waldo Emerson, "Nature" (1844), *The Selected Works of Ralph Waldo Emerson*, Brooks Atkinson, ed. (New York; Modern Library, 1950), p. 409.

[3] *The Standard History of the World* (Cincinnati: Standard Historical Society, 1931), pp. 251, 253, 268.

[4] Wilhelmina Jashemski, "Pompeii," *Natural History* 73, No. 10 (December 1964): p. 39.

[5] James Fisher, "The Idea of a Wilderness," *The Listener* (London) 68, No. 1726 (Apr. 26, 1962): 722.

[6] *The Encyclopaedia Britannica* 6 (1929), pp. 124–28.

[7] Hans Huth, "Yosemite: the Story of An Idea," *Sierra Club Bulletin* 33, No. 3 (March 1948): 61–62.

[8] Information on early conservation measures is contained in a series of articles by various authors in *American Forests* 41, No. 9 (September 1935): 416–539.

[9] Roderick Nash, "The American Wilderness in Historical Perspective," *Forest History* 6, No. 4 (winter 1963): p. 3.

[10] Donald Culross Peattie, *Green Laurels* (New York: The Literary Guild, 1936), p. 271.

[11] Huth, "Yosemite," pp. 48–59.

[12] Harold D. Hampton has provided a good analysis of the content of "'Transcendentalism," which he calls "a mixture of faith, philosophy, mysticism and religion. Its origins have been traced to the revolutionary thought of Rousseau, the idealism of Kant, the literary romanticism of Coleridge, Wordsworth, and Carlyle, and the mysticism of Oriental writers. Its theological base was that of Unitarianism; for its psychological base it drew from the various elements of Yankee shrewdness, self-reliance and conscience." From "Conservation and Cavalry: A Study of the Role of the United States Army in the Development of a National Park System, 1886–1917," Ph.D. dissertation, University of Colorado, 1965, p. 6.

[13] Henry David Thoreau, "Walking" (1862), in *Harvard Classics* 28 (New York: P. F. Collier & Son, 1910), p. 407.

[14] These excerpts have been drawn from the essays on "Walking" and "Nature," cited in notes 2 and 13.

[15] Walter J. Black, *The Best of Ralph Waldo Emerson* (New York: Walter J. Black, Pub., 1941), p. xvii.

[16] Suzanne T. Cooper, "Summertime Revisited," *American Heritage* No. 4 (June 1963): pp. 36–37.

[17] Huth, "Yosemite," p. 60.

[18] This suggestion is said to have appeared first in the New York *Daily Commercial Advertiser* in 1833, but the text quoted is from the book, *Letters and Notes on the Manners, Customs, and Conditions of the North American Indians* 1 (New York, 1842), p. 262.

[19] "Chesuncook," *Atlantic Monthly* 2 (August 1858): 317.

[20] Huth, "Yosemite," p. 62. In transcendentalist poems like "Thanatopsis" and "A Forest Hymn," Bryant expressed the sort of romantic reverence for nature that inspired the scenic cemetery movement.

[21] The Central Park project was not finished in accordance with the plan of Olmsted and Calvert Vaux until 1876. *The Encyclopedia of American Facts and Dates* (New York: Thomas Y. Crowell Co., 1959), p. 309.

[22] Act of June 30, 1864 (13 Stat. 325).

[23] Hampton, "Conservation and Cavalry," p. 27. The same thought is presented in his recent book, *How the U.S. Cavalry Saved Our National Parks* (Bloomington: Indiana University Press, 1971), p. 19.

PART I

[1] Published in full in Clarence E. Carter, ed., *The Territorial Papers of the United States*, 13 (Washington: Government Printing Office, 1948), p. 199.

[2] James Wilkinson (St. Louis) to Thomas Jefferson (Washington, D.C.), Oct. 12, 1805, "Jefferson Papers, Library of Congress." Printed in *The Territorial Papers of the United States* 13, p. 243. Wilkinson confuses the Big Horn River, which is here called "Lycorne"—properly, La Corne or The Horn—with the main Yellowstone, then known more generally by its French denominations as *Roche Jaune* and *Pierre Jaune*, both literal, translations of the Minnetaree Indian expression, *Mi tse a-da-zi*. The English equivalent Yellowstone, is attributed to David Thompson (1798). See Chittenden, *The Yellowstone National Park*, pp. 1–2.

[3] According to Curator James A. Bear of the Thomas Jefferson Memorial Foundation, Charlottesville, Va., an 1809 "Catalogue of Paintings etc. at Monticello" describes this map, under entry No. 17, as "an Indian map of the Southern waters of the Missouri, by a Ricara chief, on a buffalo pelt."

[4] *Life, Letters, and Journals of George Ticknor* 1 (Boston: James R. Osgood & Co., 1876), pp. 34–35.

[5] Julian Boyd (Princeton University Library) to Oliver W. Holmes (National Archives), Oct. 27, 1970.

[6] The *History of the Expedition under the Command of Captains Lewis and Clark*, as prepared by Paul Allen (Philadelphia: Bradford and Inskeep, 1814), vol. II, p. 396, states: "The Rockejaune, or Yellowstone River, according to Indian information, has its remote source in the Rocky Mountains, near the peaks of the Rio del Norde, on the confines of New Mexico, to which country there is a good road during the whole distance along the banks of the Yellowstone. Its western waters are probably connected with those of Lewis's river, while the eastern branches approach the heads of Clarke's river, the Bighorn, and the Platte; so that it waters the middle portion of the Rocky Mountains for several hundred miles from the northwest to southeast."

[7] Reuben Gold Thwaites, ed., *The Original Journals of the Lewis and Clark Expedition* 6 (New York: Dodd, Mead, 1905), pp. 266–67. This is the origin of a belief, which was widely held in later years, to the effect that Indians regarded the Yellowstone thermal features with superstitious dread. While that may have been true of those whose contact with whites had developed a conception of an underworld, no such theological fears troubled those Shoshonean "Sheep-eaters" who were the furtive residents of the Yellowstone Plateau. Archaeological evidence indicates that their predecessors lived among the hot springs and geysers for several millennia.

[8] "A Map of part of the Continent of North America . . . Compiled from the information of the best informed travelers through that quarter of the globe . . . by William Clark. Laid down by a scale of 50 miles to the inch," this map is Coe No. 303–IV, Beinecke Library, Yale.

[9] The airline distance from the northern extremity of Jackson Lake to the end of the south arm of Yellowstone Lake is approximately 26 miles (a distance shown as 22 miles on Clark's map), while the airline distance from the outlet of Yellowstone Lake to the Bannock ford is approximately 25 miles (just as on Clark's map). The scale for this part of the manuscript map was established by taking the distance from the southern shore of Lake Eustis to its outlet as 20 miles.

[10] *A Map of Lewis and Clark's Track Across the Western Portion of America, from the Mississippi to the Pacific Ocean, By Order of the Executive of the United States in 1804, 5 & 6.* Copied by Samuel Lewis from the original drawing of William Clark. Copy in RG77, Office of the Chief of Engineers, US 529, NA.

[11] Stallo Vinton, *John Colter, Discoverer of Yellowstone Park* (New York: E. Eberstadt, 1926), pp. 61–62.

[12] Dorothea G. Doubt (Chicago) to "The Secretary of the Museum" (Mammoth Hot Springs), Sept. 7, 1933. Perhaps Mr. Rollins' "X" marked the spot where J. C. took his swim!

[13] Alexander Ross, *The Fur Hunters of the Far West; A Narrative of Adventures in the Oregon and Rocky Mountains* 1 (London: Smith, Elder & Co., 1855), p. 267.

[14] Hiram M. Chittenden, who saw this inscription about 14 years after it was discovered, thought the date was August 19, but admits, "It is now practically illegible from overgrowth." *The Yellowstone National Park*, p. 35.

[15] Philetus W. Norris, *Fifth Annual Report of the Superintendent of the Yellowstone National Park* (Washington: Government Printing Office, 1881), pp. 40–41. The tree stood about one-quarter mile above the Upper Fall of Yellowstone River, in the shallow ravine spanned at its mouth by the concrete structure known as "Canyon Bridge."

[16] A. Decker (St. Paul, Minn.) to the "Manager, Yellowstone Park," June 20, 1931. It was delivered to the Yellowstone Park Co. and forwarded to Superintendent R. W. Toll on the 23d.

[17] Agnes Laut, *Conquest of the Great Northwest* (New York: G. H. Doran Co., 1908), pp. 255–57. Mrs. Laut had access to material in the archives of the Hudson's Bay Co., at London.

[18] Philetus W. Norris, *Report Upon the Yellowstone National Park to the Secretary of the Interior, for the Year 1878* (Washington: Government Printing Office, 1879), p. 989.

[19] Merrill J. Mattes, *Colter's Hell and Jackson's Hole* (Yellowstone Library and Museum Association, 1962), pp. 33–34.

[20] Daniel T. Potts ("Sweet Lake" [Bear Lake, Utah]) to Robert T. Potts (Philadelphia) July 8, 1827, published in the *Philadelphia Gazette and Daily Advertizer*, Sept. 27, 1827 (with some editorial changes intended to clarify the writer's defective spelling and punctuation); reprinted without further change by *Niles Register* (Philadelphia) Oct. 6, 1827. Neither publication named the author of this informative letter, and, as interest developed in the fur trade of the West, its authorship was attributed to various trappers known to have been literate. Such speculation continued until 1947, when two grandnieces of trapper Potts, Mrs. Kate Nixon and Miss Anne G. Rittenhouse, offered this letter, with others describing his western experiences, to the National Park Service. They were purchased by the Yellowstone Library and Museum Association and are held in the park reference library at Mammoth Hot Springs. The Potts letters, including this one, were published in full in *Yellowstone Nature Notes* 21, No. 5 (September–October 1947), pp. 49–56.

[21] Several biographies of fur-trade notables refer to such visits, particularly the following: J. Cecil Alter, *James Bridger, Trapper, Frontiersman, Scout and Guide* (Columbus, Ohio: Long's College Book Co., 1951); and LeRoy R. Hafen, *Broken Hand: The Life Story of Thomas Fitzpatrick, Chief of the Mountain Men* (Denver, Colo.: The Old West Publishing Co., 1931) These references are vague and must be taken on the authority of the authors, which is also the way that somewhat more specific account of Henri

Le Bleau must be taken. See Helen G. Sharman, *The Cave on the Yellowstone, or Early Life in the Rockies* (Chicago: Scroll Publishing Co., c 1902), pp. 77–80.

[22] Francis Fuller Victor, *The River of the West* (Hartford, Conn.: R. W. Bliss & Co., 1870), pp. 75–76.

[23] Chittenden, *The Yellowstone National Park*, p. 43.

[24] Hiram M. Chittenden, *The American Fur Trade of the Far West* 3 (New York: Francis P. Harper, 1902), pp. 941–45. Additional information on Johnson Gardner is available in the sketch "Johnson Gardner"—by the author—in *The Mountain Men and the Fur Trade of the Far West* 2, ed. by LeRoy R. Hafen (Glendale, Calif.: Arthur A. Clark Co., 1965), pp. 157–59.

[25] Warren Angus Ferris, *Life in the Rocky Mountains, 1830–1835*, ed. by P. C. Phillips (Denver: Old West Publishing Co., 1940), p. 192.

[26] Their route lay over the Madison Plateau, which is covered with lodgepole pine. This took them past Summit and Little Summit lakes and their associated ponds and marshes.

[27] The deposited "formation" is silicious sinter—of volcanic rather than sedimentary origin.

[28] It seems likely that Ferris observed eruptions of Splendid Geyser. There are no large geysers in the lower or middle basins approximating the description given by Ferris, and, of the six in the Upper Geyser Basin that erupt to heights above 100 feet, three—Old Faithful, the Giant, and the Beehive—can be eliminated because they are cone-type geysers (note Ferris' subsequent remark that the geyser had a basin 30 feet across). Of the fountain-type geysers, the Giantess is an infrequent performer whose eruptions last from 12 to 36 hours, while the Grand has a water column 6 feet in diameter, with 45-minute eruptions spaced 18 to 90 hours apart. Thus, the only major geyser in the Upper Geyser Basin that fits the description is the Splendid, which has a basin 22 by 25 feet from which it plays for 2 to 10 minutes, to heights between 100 and 165 feet. Its initial eruption is usually followed by as many as four others spaced from 1 to 3 hours apart, and also, before the turn of the century, it enjoyed a reputation for regularity second only to that of Old Faithful.

[29] Canadian traders had exposed these Indians to some theological concepts.

[30] The Mud Volcano and Sulphur Mountain areas in Hayden Valley.

[31] This feature cannot now be identified; however, there are many hot springs that discharge into the lake waters from submerged orifices, and also some pools in other parts of the park where the agitation is produced by the discharge of gases, rather than steam.

[32] The foregoing account was published under the title, "Rocky Mountain Geysers," in the Buffalo, N.Y., *Western Literary Messenger*, July 13, 1842; and that part describing the visit to the Upper Geyser Basin reappeared in the issue of Jan. 6, 1844, as part of a longer presentation of Ferris' experiences brought out serially as "Life in the Rocky Mountains." The original article was reprinted—without crediting the *Western Literary Messenger*—in the Nauvoo, Ill., *Wasp*, Aug. 13, 1842 (available in the historian's office, Church of Jesus Christ of Latter Day Saints, Salt Lake City, Utah), and this printing was republished by the Helena, Mont, *Weekly Independent*, May 1, 1874, under the title, "Visit to the Yellowstone Geysers 41 Years Ago." More recently, Ferris' account has appeared in two books, both published in 1940 under the title Ferris had used for his manuscript—*Life in the Rocky Mountains, 1830–1835*. One of these was edited by Paul C. Phillips (Denver: The Old West Publishing Co.), and the other by Herbert S. Auerbach and J. Cecil Alter (Salt Lake City: Rocky Mountain Book Shop).

[33] The diary carried by Russell while a trapper is lost, but an account prepared from it by him in 1846 is in the Beinecke Library, Yale (Coe Collection No. 411). This account, titled "Journal of a Trapper or Nine Years Residence among the Rocky Mountains Between the Years of 1834 and 1843 . . .," is written in ink on letter paper with a faintly bluish cast, the pages being bound in cardboard covers bearing a pasted-on legend. There are 156 text pages, followed by 34 separately numbered appendix pages and two unnumbered pages of verse. The orthography, spelling, and punctuation are peculiar and erratic, and the pages are crowded. Although intended for publication, the manuscript account was not printed until 1914, when a grand-nephew, L. A. York, put it out

in a heavily edited form as *Journal of a Trapper, or, Nine Years in the Rocky Mountains, 1834–1843* (Boise, Idaho: Sims-York Co., 1914), 105 pp. This was reprinted in 1921, with an introduction and letters, which increased the size to 167 pp., including everything. A new edition, edited from the original manuscript by Aubrey L. Haines, was published as *Osborne Russell's Journal of a Trapper* (Portland, Oreg.: Champoeg Press, 1955), 209 pp.; reprinted, by special arrangement with the Oregon Historical Society, in 1965 in a Bison Book edition by the University of Nebraska Press, 223 pp.

[34] Named for L.Q.C. Lamar, Secretary of the Interior from Mar. 6, 1885, to Jan. 16, 1888.

[35] Now called Lamar Valley, but known to Russell on subsequent visits as "Secluded Valley."

[36] These Yellowstone residents were "Sheepeaters"—mountain dwellers of Shoshonean linguistic stock. Lacking horses and guns, such impoverished bands eked out a miserable existence hunting mountain sheep in the ancient manner. Thus, their name indicated a status and a way of life within the Shoshone-Bannock culture, but not a distinct people.

[37] At the ford opposite Tower Fall, where the Bannock Indian trail crossed the river.

[38] Named for Johnson Gardner, who trapped there in 1831–32 (see note 24).

[39] This water connection between the Pacific and Atlantic drainages—Bridger's "Two-ocean river"—was considered a trapper's tale until verified by the Jones Expedition in 1873. See William A. Jones, *Report upon the Reconnaissance of Northwestern Wyoming, Including Yellowstone National Park, Made in the Summer of 1873* (Washington: Government Printing Office, 1875), pp. 39–40.

[40] The upper end, where Thorofare and Atlantic Creeks enter, is commonly known as "The Thorofare" in dim remembrance of the coming and going of the trappers and prospectors of an earlier time. Appropriately, that locality has a Bridger Lake.

[41] Near present Fishing Bridge.

[42] Yellowstone Lake is neither oblong nor crescent-shaped; rather, its deep indentations create an outline which has been best likened to the print of a maimed left hand. See Walter Trumbull, "The Washburn Yellowstone Expedition," *The Overland Monthly* 6, No. 6 (June 1871): 489–90. Russell was correct in giving the lake a 100-mile shoreline.

[43] It and Lewis Lake appeared for the first time, cartographically, on Walter W. de-Lacy's *Map of the Territory of Montana* (1865), where they were correctly related to the Snake River drainage. This beautiful body of water was known as "deLacy's Lake" until renamed by the Hayden Survey in 1872.

[44] The Shoshone Geyser Basin. Russell's estimate seems conservative for Allen and Day found 13 active geysers there in 1930—three of which erupted to heights over 50 feet. See E. T. Allen and Arthur L. Day, *Hot Springs of the Yellowstone National Park*, Publication No. 466, Carnegie Institution of Washington, 1935.

[45] None of the geysers now active in the Shoshone Geyser Basin fit Russell's description, so that the "hour spring" is now either dormant or very different in its eruptive cycle.

[46] Russell accurately described the effect visible in the steam above the Grand Prismatic Spring, the largest hot spring in the Midway Geyser Basin.

[47] W. A. Ferris, *Life in the Rocky Mountains* (Philips edition), pp. 85–86, explains the origin of the name: "The Burnt Hole is a district on the north side of the Piney Woods, which was observed to be wrapped in flames a few years since. The conflagration that occasioned this name must have been of great extent, and large forests of half-consumed pines still evidence the ravages. . . ." Thus, the name by which the trappers knew that great basin on the western border of the present park dates at least from 1832.

[48] The encampment was on the prominent bench east of Pelican Creek, where the present highway enters the forest.

[49] Baptiste Ducharme came to the northern Rocky Mountains with William Ashley's expedition in 1822, afterwards becoming a free trapper. He is said to have visited the Yellowstone region in 1824 and 1826. Eugene S. Topping, *The Chronicles of the Yellowstone; An Accurate and Comprehensive History* (St. Paul, Minn.: Pioneer Press, 1883), pp. 14–15.

[50] From the Crow Indian name, *Echeda-cahchi-ichi*. For more on this, see "The Name Yellowstone," *Livingston Enterprise* (Montana), Oct. 23, 1883.

[51] William T. Hamilton, *My Sixty Years on the Plains* (Columbus, Ohio: Long's College Book Co., 1951), pp. 94–95. This is a reprint of the same title published at New York by Forest & Stream Publishing Co., 1905. The Firehole branch of the Madison was known to the trappers at least as early as 1832, and possibly 8 years before that, but it did not receive its present name until 1850.

[52] This "Map of the Northwest Fur Country" is said to have lain in a family trunk for a century prior to its publication by Dr. Paul C. Phillips in his edition of "Life in the Rocky Mountains (1940)." (see note 32).

[53] Mattes, "Colter's Hell", p. 51.

[54] "Map exhibiting the practicable passes of the Rocky Mountains; together with the topographical features of the country adjacent to the headwaters of the Missouri, Yellowstone, Salmon, Lewis' and Colorado Rivers: by Wash: Hood Capt T. Engrs, 1839." The original is in RG–77, Office of the Chief of Engineers, US 110, NA.

[55] William Clark Kennerly, *Persimmon Hill: A Narrative of Old St. Louis* (Norman: University of Oklahoma Press, 1948), pp. 156–57.

[56] Olin D. Wheeler, "The Late James Gemmell," *Contributions to the Historical Society of Montana* 2 (Helena, Mont.: State Publishing Co., 1896), p. 331. The quotation is from an interview in July 1880. A tantalizing entry in the "Journal History" maintained in the church historian's office, Church of Jesus Christ of Latter-Day-Saints, Salt Lake City, Utah, hints that the Mormons may have gained some knowledge of the Yellowstone region at this time. Under the date of Nov. 24, 1846, this statement is made in connection with the visit of Justin Grosclaude, a trader for the American Fur Co.: "Mr. 'G' gave an interesting account of the sources of the Yellow Stone and sketched a map with a pencil of the country. . . ."

[57] Topping, *Chronicles of the Yellowstone*, p. 16.

[58] Russel, *Journal of a Trapper* (1955 ed.), pp. 45–46.

[59] William F. Raynolds, *The Report of Brevet Brigadier General W. F. Raynolds on the Exploration of the Yellowstone and the Country Drained by That River*, 40th Cong., 1st session, Sen. Ex. Doc. No. 77, July 17, 1868, p. 77.

[60] Eugene F. Ware, *The Indian War of 1864* (New York: St. Martin's Press, 1960), pp. 214, 204, 206, 250. This work was originally published under the same title at Topeka, Kans., by Crane & Co., in 1911.

[61] James Stevenson (U.S. Geological Survey, Washington, D.C.) to Prof. J. D. Butler, Feb. 28, 1886, 12 pp., RG 57, NA.

[62] Charles L. Camp, ed., *James Clyman, American Frontiersman, 1792–1881* (San Francisco: California Historical Society, 1928), p. 26.

[63] George F. Ruxton, *Life in the Far West*, ed. by LeRoy R. Hafen (Norman: University of Oklahoma Press, 1959), pp. 7–9. This is a reprint of the same title, published originally at New York by Harper & Bros. in 1849. Ruxton picked up his version of the petrified forest story in Colorado 2 years earlier.

[64] Raynolds, *Report on Exploration*, p. 77.

[65] Nelson A. Miles, *Personal Recollections and Observations of General Nelson A. Miles* (Chicago: The Werner Co., 1897), p. 137.

[66] Chittenden, *The Yellowstone National Park* (1895), p. 56. No authority is given for the version he offers (here quoted in part only), but, from its well-turned phrasing, it was undoubtedly his own work. In addition to his other talents, Chittenden was a recognized poet.

[67] This story, told by Capt. James L. Humfreville in *Twenty Years Among the Hostile Indians* (New York: Hunter, 1903), is repeated by Alter, *James Bridger*, p. 385.

[68] P. W. Norris, *Report* . . . (1878), p. 989. For a latterday version of this story, refer again to Chittenden's *The Yellowstone National Park* (1895), p. 54.

[69] Raynolds, *Report on Exploration*, p. 77.

[70] Ware, *Indian War*, pp. 205–06.

[71] "Chart of the Head of Yellow Stone," captioned by Fr. Pierre-Jean DeSmet; manuscript map at St. Louis University, Jesuits, Missouri Province, Archives, IX: DeSmetiana, C–B: Atlas, 2, No. 10.

[72] Hiram M. Chittenden and Alfred T. Richardson, ed., *Life, Letters and Travels of*

Father Pierre-Jean DeSmet, S.J., 1801–1873, (4 vols., New York: Francis P. Harper, 1905), pp. 181–82. The "fragmental journal in French of voyage of Father DeSmet in 1839, from Council Bluffs to the Sioux country" includes this comment which seems to apply to the Yellowstone River: "All the country as you ascend the river seems evidently to be of volcanic formation. In several places moreover you can see steam and sulphurous flames escaping from the bosom of the earth. I learned from a traveler who had been all over this region for a number of years, that subterranean noises are often heard, resembling those of volcanic districts."

[73] Untitled manuscript map drawn in pencil on linen; St. Louis University, Jesuits, Missouri Province. Archives, IX: DeSmetiana, C–B: Atlas, No 5.

[74] Mattes, *Colter's Hell*, p. 80. The quotation is from a letter written to officials of the Department of the Interior, July 1, 1857, in regard to their suggestion that the map should be printed. DeSmet's rebuttal, "In my humble opinion, therefore, it can be of very little service for your purposes, in which accuracy of instrumental measurements and observations seems to be absolutely necessary . . .," probably relegated his very useful map to the obscurity of the official files.

[75] Chittenden and Richardson, *De Smet 2*, pp. 660–62. This material is included in Letters IV and V, Second Series, Western Missions and Missionaries, covering the trip from Fort Union to Fort Laramie, July to September 1851.

[76] Indians with some knowledge of the white man's culture might have entertained such romantic notions, but the resident Shoshone-Bannocks accepted the thermal features as a natural enough part of their surroundings. DeSmet repeated this idea 13 years later, in a letter written on board the Missouri River steamer *Yellowstone*, June 4, 1864. Ibid. 4, pp. 1377–78.

[77] J. W. Gunnison, *The Mormons, or, Latter-Day Saints* (Philadelphia: Lippincott, Grambo & Co., 1852), p. 151.

[78] Joaquin Miller, *Illustrated History of the State of Montana* (Chicago: The Lewis Publishing Co., 1894), p. 426.

[79] John Mullan, *Report on the Construction of a Military Road from Walla-Walla to Fort Benton* (Washington: Government Printing Office, 1863), p. 53.

[80] Raynolds, *Report on Exploration*, p. 86.

[81] *Ibid.*, pp. 10–11.

[82] "U.S. War Department Map of the Yellowstone and Missouri Rivers and Their Tributaries explored by Capt. W. F. Raynolds Topl Engrs and 1st Lieut. H. E. Maynadier 10th Infy Assistant 1859–60 to accompany a report to the Bureau of Topographical Engineers Lt Col Bache in charge." Original in RG–77, Office of the Chief of Engineers, Q 106–1, NA.

[83] Raynolds, *Report on Exploration*, p. 98.

[84] W. W. deLacy, "Map of the Territory of Montana with Portions of the Adjoining Territories, Showing the Gulch or Placer diggings actually worked and Districts where Quartz (Gold & Silver) Lodes have been discovered up to January 1865." The original of this map in pencil, partly inked-over, is in the collection of the Montana Historical Society at Helena.

[85] Surveyor-General Meredith of Montana Territory had the larger of the two lakes shown as "DeLacy's Lake" on the map prepared in his office in 1867, and it was known by that name until changed to Shoshone Lake by Professor Frank H. Bradley, of the U.S. Geological and Geographical Survey of the Territories (Hayden Survey). In discussing the change in his report to Dr. Hayden, Bradley states: "The numerous and outrageous errors of the map [deLacy's, as cited in note 84] show that neither as discoverer nor as mapper of this lake has Mr. DeLacey any claim to a perpetuation of his name; and, since the lake occupies a position entirely different from that assigned to DeLacey's lake, we have decided to drop that title, and to call this, in our maps and reports, Shoshone Lake, as being the head of one of the principal forks of the Shoshone or Snake River." See F. V. Hayden, *Sixth Annual Report of the United States Geological Survey of the Territories* (Washington: Government Printing Office, 1873), p. 244. Bradley's unkind statement came to the attention of deLacy, who said: "When I saw this note in his report of 1873, I wrote a short narrative of the trip, and sent it, together with my original notebook and the original map, to Dr. Hayden, by the hands of Mr. Lang-

ford, with a request that he would do me justice. He stated to this gentleman that the note had been inserted by one of his assistants, without his knowledge, and that it should not occur again. He had a photographic copy of the map made, and said that he had some idea of writing to some prominent journal in the West on the subject—and there the matter rested. I still remain under a stigma in a published report, such as I never before received, in a long professional career, and, as I think, unjustly, and against which I now protest." See Walter W. deLacy, "A Trip Up the South Snake River in 1863," *Contributions to the Historical Society of Montana* 1 (Helena, Mont.: Rocky Mountain Publishing Co., 1867), p. 142.

[86] Published by Rossiter W. Raymond, *Mineral Resources of the States and Territories* (Washington: Government Printing Office, 1869), pp. 142–43. A further reference to the Yellowstone thermal features in Raymond's publication of the following year will be mentioned later.

[87] Their west course had taken them to Beula and Hering Lakes, which lie on the divide between Falls and Lewis Rivers.

[88] Shoshone Lake resembles a misshapen dumbbell, and what deLacy thought was the southern end was only the lower end of the eastern enlargement. The western reaches of the lake were not visible from the mouth of Moose Creek.

[89] P. W. Norris says of this place name: "The above narrative, the high character of its writer, his mainly correct description of the regions visited, and the traces which I have found of this party, proves alike its entire truthfulness, and the injustice of changing the name of DeLacy's Lake; and fearing it is now too late to restore the proper name to it, I have, as a small token of deserved justice, named the stream and park crossed by our trail above the Shoshone Lake after their discoverer." *Fifth Annual Report* (1881), p. 44.

[90] The precipitous flank of National Park Mountain, which forms the west wall of Firehole Canyon.

[91] From an interview in the Louisville, Ky., *Courier-Journal*, Apr. 13, 1884; see "Yellowstone Park," p. 12.

[92] Later established as 109 feet.

[93] This statement is difficult to reconcile with Davis' earlier remark that "I and two others left for the head waters of the Upper Yellowstone." Either there were more than three in the party that left Jackson's Hole, or they were joined by others prior to their arrival at the Yellowstone Falls.

[94] The development of this incident into the place name Pelican Creek is attested by F. V. Hayden, *Twelth Annual Report of the United States Geological and Geographical Survey of the Territories . . . for the Year 1878* (Washington: Government Printing Office, 1883), part II, p. 302.

[95] Topping, *Chronicles of the Yellowstone*, pp. 24–25.

[96] Norris, *Fifth Annual Report* (1881), pp. 44–45. Their idea that the cold, vapor-laden air of the geyser basins was noxious led to a persistent myth of the "death valley"— a fiction which continued to appear in later writings.

[97] "Notes Collected by Newell Joyner Concerning Various Explorers." c 1930; type-script in the Yellowstone Park Reference Library, unpaged (see under Bacon).

[98] P. W. Norris noted that near Bozeman, in the spring of 1870, he "found an old used up mountaineer named Dunn, who claimed to have gone with Jones and Bridger and another trapper who was soon after killed by the Indians in Arizona, via Yellowstone Lake to Green River, in 1865, and, from his statements made a rough map of their route." See "Meanderings of a Mountaineer, or, The Journals and Musings (or storys) of a Rambler over Prairie (or Mountain) and Plain," a manuscript prepared about 1885 from newspaper clippings of Norris' adventures, 1870–75, amplified with his handwritten notes, p. 16. Original in the Huntington Library, San Marino, Calif.

[99] Merrill G. Burlingame (Montana State College, Bozeman) to the Librarian, Yellowstone National Park, Feb. 15, 1957.

[100] From a reply written by Father Kuppens from St. Xavier's Church, Cincinnati, Ohio, on Sept. 3, 1897, to a correspondent identified only as "Rev. and Dear Father," who had sought information on Kuppen's visit. This letter was published under the title, "The Origin of the Yellowstone National Park," *The Woodstock Letters* 21, No. 3 (1897): pp. 400–02.

[101] Topping, *Chronicles of the Yellowstone*, pp. 44–45.

[102] Virginia City *Montana Post*, July 14, 1866.

[103] "Interesting from the Yellowstone," *Helena Weekly Herald*, Apr. 11, 1867. This informant adds: "We have a steamboat [Steamboat Springs] on the side of the big lake above here that shoots puffs of smoke out of a volcanic peak over the bosom of the waters. The top of another peak [Crater Hills] emits sulphurous odors and smoke, and occasionally showers of ashes. It may be that some of those suspicious places have renewed their old-time fury."

[104] Topping, *Chronicles of the Yellowstone*, pp. 62–63.

[105] Virginia City *Montana Post*, June 29, 1867.

[106] Discovery of some locally rich placers higher up Emigrant Gulch was immediately hailed as "A New Gulch—Stampede—The Gold Belt of the Yellowstone, etc.," in Virginia City *Montana Post*, Aug. 17, 1867.

[107] Topping, *Chronicles of the Yellowstone*, pp. 65–67.

[108] "The Upper Yellowstone," Virginia City *Montana Post*, Aug. 24, 1867.

[109] The distance is nearer 70 miles, for there is no indication the Curtis-Dunlevy party went beyond Mammoth Hot Springs.

[110] This, like most of the previous statement, is an exaggeration. F. V. Hayden's examination of the springs 4 years later showed nothing so extensive; in fact, the activity on the terraces was generally similar to today's.

[111] The principal mineral carried by these waters is lime, and there is not enough of any other solutes to effect the taste materially when cool.

[112] "The Upper Yellowstone" Virginia City *Montana Post*, Aug. 31, 1867. Reprinted by the *New York Times*, Sept. 14, 1867.

[113] Solfataras (vents discharging hot volcanic gases, rather than steam) can often be ignited in that manner, particularly those at the Calcite Springs, where the gases also contain some volatile bituminous products.

[114] This is the earliest description of that traffic in stolen horses and mules which was carried on between Idaho and Montana until the turn of the century. Several devious routes through the Yellowstone wilderness were utilized.

[115] A. B. Henderson, "Journal of the Yellowstone Expedition of 1866 Under Captain Jeff Standifer. . . . Also the Diaries Kept by Henderson During His Prospecting Journeys in the Snake, Wind River and Yellowstone Country During the Years 1866–72"; a copy made from the original journal by Granville Stuart prior to Mar. 31, 1894, is Coe Collection, No. 452, Beinecke Library, Yale. The excerpts presented here are from pp. 76–77, 79–80 of the Stuart transcript.

[116] Probably the 1866 edition of deLacy's "*Map of the Territory of Montana*" . . ., which became available at Virginia City early in November of that year (sold at the city book store for $2.50). This map portrayed Yellowstone Lake as a lanceolate body of water oriented on a northwest-southeast axis and separated from the Madison River drainage by a northward extension of the Wind River Mountains. Just below the lake's outlet was the notation "Falls", and below that, "Alum Cr." was shown entering Yellowstone River from the east, above a "Canon" which is identifiable as the third or Black Canyon of the Yellowstone. Below it, "Bear Cr." enters the river from the east and "coal" is noted on the west bank. This map is now known only in its manuscript form.

[117] They were on an aboriginal trailway which passed over the Washburn Range at Dunraven Pass, as the road does now. It served to connect the Bannock Indian trail (an east-west route) with the interior of the Yellowstone plateau.

[118] Legh Richmond Freeman was an ex-Confederate who came to Montana Territory by the Bozeman Trail in 1866. He was interested in a store about 20 miles below the present town of Livingston, and in Tomlinson's sawmill on Mill Creek, near Emigrant Gulch. It is said that he heard of the Yellowstone region from Lou Anderson and decided to explore it, making the trip on foot with his supplies packed on draught cattle. See M. A. Leeson (ed.), *History of Montana, 1739–1885* (Chicago: Warner, Beers & Co., 1885), p. 335. Freeman began publishing the *Frontier Index* at least as early as June 4, 1867, issuing it from a box car which advanced with the Union Pacific railhead.

[119] "The Headwaters of the Yellowstone," *Helena Weekly Herald*, Dec. 12, 1867. A

somewhat similar item appeared in the *Virginia Tri-Weekly Post* (Virginia City, Mont.), Feb. 4, 1868. under the heading, "Niagara Eclipsed." These cannot be compared with the original in the *Frontier Index* since the file of that newspaper is incomplete.

[120] "Good Story," *Helena Weekly Herald*, Dec. 26, 1867. It would appear that Mr. Parsons found the inspiration for his fanciful tale in an article reprinted by the "Frontier *Index* of July 26, 1867, from the *New Albany Commercial* (Indiana), the original being an exaggerated reporting of the discovery of "Mound-builder" relics.

[121] *The Frontier Index* published at (Fort Sanders, D.T.), Mar. 6, 1868. The article is signed "Legh."

[122] "California," in *The Frontier Index* 7 (published at Laramie City, D.T.), May 5, 1868.

[123] "Brevities Communicated from the Sanotum of the American Libertarian," ibid., June 16, 1868.

[124] "The Great Soshone Falls of Snake River," *The Frontier Index*, (Green River, D.T.), Aug. 21, 1868.

[125] Henderson, *Journal*, p. 87.

[126] They camped at the mouth of the unnamed fork which heads between Cache Mountain and The Needle.

[127] This thermal area, which was never as large as Henderson indicates, is no longer active and is not shown on the latest edition of the park map.

[128] Additional details of this incident are available in "A Remiscence of James A. Gourley, Prospector of 1870," recorded Mar. 28, 1929; typed transcript in the Yellowstone Park Reference Library, 4 pp.

[129] Named for Adam "Horn" Miller, a member of this party, who guided Superintendent Norris into the Hoodoo Basin in 1880. See P. W. Norris, *Annual Report of the Superintendent of the Yellowstone National Park, to the Secretary of the Interior, for the Year 1880* (Washington: Government Printing Office, 1881), p. 7.

[130] These men had more reason than their recent skirmish for the touchiness they exhibited. Two of their comrades—Jack Crandall and his partner, Daugherty—had been surprised and killed by Indians the previous fall at their camp on a headwater of the Clark Fork River.

[131] This account, which Charles R. Sunderlee contributed to the issue of May 18, 1870, as "A Thrilling Event on the Yellowstone," was taken directly from a Crow Indian legend. See Ella E. Clark, *Indian Legends from the Northern Rockies* (Norman: University of Oklahoma Press, 1966), pp. 323–24.

PART II

[1] Cornelius Hedges, "An Account of a Trip to Fort Benton in October 1865, with Acting Governor Thomas F. Meagher to Treat with the Blackfeet Indians," *Rocky Mountain Magazine 1*, No. 3 (November 1900): 155. Further details are available in Hedges' diary for 1865, original in the collection of the Montana Historical Society, Helena (see entries for Oct. 20 through 28), and in the account of Lyman E. Munson, "Pioneer Life in Montana," *Contributions to the Historical Society of Montana 5* (1904): pp. 214–16.

[2] Francis X. Kuppens, "The Origin of the Yellowstone National Park," *The Woodstock Letters* 26, No. 3 (1897): p. 401. This letter has been reprinted in *The Jesuit Bulletin* 41, No. 4 (October 1962): 6–7; and, under the heading "Former St. Charles Priest Helped Found Yellowstone," in *St. Louis Review* (Missouri), June 21, 1963. A brief statement regarding Meagher's advocacy of park status for the Yellowstone region appears in an article credited to Father Kuppens but published 15 years after his death, as "Thomas Francis Meagher, Montana Pioneer," *Mid-America, An Historical Review* 14 (N.S. III), No. 2 (October 1931): 128. Correspondence with Father Wilfred P. Schoenberg, archivist at Gonzaga University, Spokane, Washington, concerning the disposition of the records of St. Peter's Mission, elicited the following interesting comment in his

reply of Aug. 13, 1970: "You need not be anxious about Kuppen's memory. He was incredible for remembering detail."

[3] Francois "Crazy" Vielle, who is mentioned in the John Healy Papers, Montana State Historical Society, Helena. Capt. John Healy had, himself, prospected the Yellowstone region prior to 1865.

[4] Charles W. Cook, "Preliminary Statement to the Cook-Folsom Diary," *Haynes Bulletin* (December 1922): 7–8.

[5] "Expedition to the Yellowstone," *Helena Weekly Herald*, July 29, 1869.

[6] Cook, "Preliminary Statement."

[7] "A Reminiscence of William Peterson," ed. by Aubrey L. Haines, *The Yellowstone Interpreter* 2, No. 5 (September–October 1964): 59. The reminiscences, which appear to have been recorded prior to 1900, were furnished by Mrs. Ralph Irvin, of Salmon, Idaho, through the kindness of Librarian Eunis Robertson of that place.

[8] Charles W. Cook, "Reconstructed Diary of the Cook-Folsom Expedition in 1869 to the Yellowstone Region," *Haynes Bulletin* (January 1923): 1. Concerning the original diary carried through the Yellowstone region, Cook says in his preliminary statement to the 1922 reconstruction: "Sometime about the year 1903, I loaned the copy of the diary that I had, to Mr. V. K. Chestnut, then an instructor in agriculture at Bozeman, Mont. I understand from him that he made exact copies of this diary or portion secured, but lost the original, having left it at Bozeman, when he left there to take up his duties at Washington, D.C., where he is now located."

[9] David E. Folsom (White Sulphur Springs, Mont.) to Capt. George L. Anderson (Mammoth Hot Springs, Wy.), Apr. 28, 1894. Yellowstone Archives, Letters Received.

[10] Cook, "Preliminary Statement."

[11] Charles W. Cook, "The Valley of the Upper Yellowstone," *Western Monthly* (Chicago) 4 (July 1870): 60–67. Nathaniel P. Langford reprinted this article as *The Folsom-Cook Explorations of the Upper Yellowstone, 1869* (St. Paul, Minn.: H. L. Collins Co., 1894), 22 pp., attributing it to David E. Folsom; and he later presented it again, in the same form, in *Contributions to the Historical Society of Montana* 5 (1904): 355–94. The text presented here is from the original magazine article.

[12] Interesting descriptions of this meeting by Cook and Folsom, as well as many observations deleted from the original magazine article, are available in the reconstructed account published as *The Valley of the Upper Yellowstone*, edited by Aubrey L. Haines (Norman: University of Oklahoma Press, 1965), pp. 3–49.

[13] The "Third Canyon," now called the Black Canyon of the Yellowstone, which begins above the town of Gardiner, Mont., and extends nearly to the mouth of Lamar River.

[14] The "Fourth Canyon," which the Washburn party of the following year would call the Grand Canyon of the Yellowstone.

[15] Editorial revision of the original account has created a confusing impression at this point. The Folsom party reached the Yellowstone River 3 miles about the mouth of the Lamar, at the Bannock Ford, and they camped on the west bank at that Indian crossing-place while exploring in the vicinity of Tower Fall. This is explained in the reconstructed account (1965, p. 22) in these words: "*September 15*, Just below our present camping place is a canyon 3 miles long, and, while passing around it yesterday, we caught glimpses of scenery surpassing in grandeur anything we have before seen so we concluded to lay over 1 day and give it a more thorough examination than our limited time last evening would permit."

[16] This feature, though variously called "The Needle," "Cleopatra's Needle," and "Column Rock," has no official name.

[17] The Calcite Springs.

[18] It is probable that the tales of volcanism told by trappers and prospectors grew out of observations such as these.

[19] The mountains they saw from the summit were all part of the Absaroka Range, though the available map (deLacy's) erroneously coupled the northern end of that extended mountain chain to the Big Horn Mountains, and the southern end to the Wind River Range.

[20] Probably the hot springs known as the Basin Group on Shallow Creek.

[21] Josephs Coat Springs on Broad Creek. This group includes the Whistler Geyser.

[22] Cook's description of their arrival at the Grand Canyon is worth repeating. He says: "I was riding ahead, the two pack animals following, and then Mr. Folsom and Mr. Peterson on their saddle horses. I remember seeing what appeared to be an opening in the forest ahead, which I presumed to be a park, or open country. While my attention was attracted by the pack animals, which had stopped to eat grass, my saddle horse suddenly stopped. I turned and looked forward from the brink of the great canyon, at a point just across the canyon from what is now called Inspiration Point [they were in the notch between Artist and Sublime Points]. I sat there in amazement, while my companions came up, and after that, it seemed to me that it was 5 minutes before anyone spoke."

[23] On the east bank of Yellowstone River just above Chittenden Memorial Bridge.

[24] Later determined as 109 feet. Cook's son-in-law, Oscar O. Mueller, of Lewistown, Mont., has described the measuring of the Yellowstone Falls in his article, "Yellowstone Map Drawn in 1870 Shows Cook & Folsom Route of 1869," *Haynes Bulletin 3*, No. 1 (March 1924): 2–3. According to this recollection, "Mr. Cook and Folsom had no other way with which to measure the falls except by a ball of twine to which they tied a rock for a weight. In measuring the Lower Falls of the Yellowstone, Mr. Folsom used a forked pole on which he laid, extending the fork over the edge of the falls and with this he let the twine down through the forks so that it would clear the edge of the rock, and Mr. Peterson, a member of the party below, gave the signals to lower it. The strong air currents prevented accurate work here."

[25] Now considered to be 308 feet.

[26] This passage does not read as intended. The reconstructed account (1965, p. 34) gives it as, "This is the northern slope of a high plateau between the waters of the Yellowstone and Snake Rivers." The route followed above the falls was along the east bank of the Yellowstone River to a crossing opposite the Crater Hills (they had previously tried to ford the river between the falls but were unable to get their horses up the west bank).

[27] The Mud Volcano.

[28] The Dragon's Mouth Spring.

[29] They had crossed back to the east bank of the Yellowstone River near the Mud Volcano, reaching the lake about one-quarter mile southeast of Squaw Lake.

[30] For their progress around the north shore to the geyser basin at present West Thumb, it is necessary to refer to the reconstructed account (1965, pp. 36–38) because the *Western Monthly* editor deleted that portion from the magazine account.

[31] The Thumb Paintpots.

[32] This awareness of the impact visitation would ultimately have on the beauty of the Yellowstone region undoubtedly stimulated Folsom to make the suggestion for preservation of its wilderness values that he advanced during the winter of 1869–70.

[33] Shoshone Lake, which they reached at a point mid-way along its eastern shore. From there, they followed the shore to the mouth of deLacy Creek, ascended that stream to a crossing of the Continental Divide and descended White Creek to the Lower Geyser Basin.

[34] Shoshone Lake drains into Snake River, rather than the Madison, and had been correctly mapped by deLacy in 1865; however, the Folsom party was not alone in erroneously assigning it to an east-slope drainage. The Washburn party (1870) and Hayden Survey (1871) did the same.

[35] The Great Fountain Geyser. Of it, Cook says: "Soon this geyser was in full play. The setting sun shining into the spray and steam drifting towards the mountains, gave it the appearance of burnished gold, a wonderful sight. We could not contain our enthusiasm; with one accord we all took off our hats and yelled with all our might." Cook, "Preliminary Statement."

[36] This is the first notice of the eruptive nature of that greatest of all the geysers—the Excelsior.

[37] As previously mentioned, this designation was a product of the prospecting era. It was while encamped in the Lower Geyser Basin that the members of this party discussed the propriety of reserving the Yellowstone region for public use. As Charles W. Cook later recalled it, their conversation about the scenic beauty of the area and the wonders they had seen was given a reflective turn in this manner:

"Peterson remarked that probably it would not be long before settlers and prospectors began coming into the district and taking up land around the canyons and the geysers, and that it would soon be all in private hands.

"I said that I thought the place was too big to be all taken up, but that, anyway, something ought to be done to keep the settlers out, so that everyone who wanted to, in future years, could travel through as freely and enjoy the region as we had.

"Then Folsom said: 'The Government ought not to allow anyone to locate here at all.'

" 'That's right,' I said, 'It ought to be kept for the public some way.' "

The foregoing is taken from "Remarks of C. W. Cook, Last Survivor of the Original Explorers of the Yellowstone Park Region, on the Occasion of His Second Visit to the Park in 53 years, During the celebration of the Park's Golden Anniversary" (at Madison Junction, July 14, 1922). A copy of the official transcript is in the Yellowstone Park Reference Library.

[38] Preface to *The Folsom-Cook Explorations of the Upper Yellowstone, 1869*, by N. P. Langford, p. 8.

[39] Nathaniel P. Langford, *Diary of the Washburn Expedition to the Yellowstone and Firehole Rivers in the Year 1870* (St. Paul, Minn.: J. E. Haynes Co., 1905), p. xi.

[40] H. D. Washburn, "Map of the Public Land Surveys in Montana Territory to accompany the Annual Report of the Commissioner of the General Land Office 1869"; a manuscript map at the scale of 1 inch = 15 miles, in RG 49, GLO (OMF), Mont. 3, NA.

[41] It was necessary to specify the outlet as a point of reference because deLacy's portrayal of his lake is grotesque—being both misaligned and nearly twice too large. The Cook-Folsom view of Shoshone Lake as triangular is understandable, since they could not see its western enlargement beyond the narrow waist; something approximating their impression can be gained by ignoring the western lobe of the lake as presently mapped.

[42] "Map of the Territory of Montana to Accompany the Report of the Surveyor General—1869," in RG 49, GLO(OMF), Mont. 2, NA. While the endorsement of Nov. 1, 1869, indicates this map also accompanied the Commissioner's Annual Report for 1869, it is obviously of earlier origin—probably compiled by Surveyor-General Meredith from the first deLacy map.

[43] "Map of the Territory of Montana, with portions of the Adjoining Territories, compiled and drawn by W. W. DeLacy of the Surveyor General's Office, Helena, M.T., 1870," (engraved, printed and published by G. W. & C. B. Colton & Co., New York).

[44] Mueller, "Yellowstone Map."

[45] Langford, *Diary*, p. xx.

[46] The exact nature of this suggestion is unknown, though Langford describes it as encompassing the "grand cañon and falls of the Yellowstone," *Ibid*. However, the statement of C. W. Cook, cited in note 37, would indicate the explorers of 1869 were thinking in broader terms. Of particular interest is the passage, "It was probably from this suggestion that the recommendation for the creation of the national park later arose in the minds of the members of the Washburn-Langford Expedition."

[47] A "private and confidential" circular of the Philadelphia office of that concern notes under the date of Oct. 20, 1869: "The Financial Agency of the North Pacific Railroad Co. was confided to us in May last . . ." Minnesota Historical Society, NPRR Papers, Box 2, Secretary, Series 2, correspondence unregistered, 1865—May 1870.

[48] Thomas H. Canfield to "Dear Governor" [Smith], Oct. 25, 1869. *Ibid*. Six days later, in a fit of misgiving about the Northern Pacific's future, Canfield asked for the return of his letter.

[49] Eugene V. Smalley, *History of the Northern Pacific Railroad* (New York: Putnam's Sons, 1883), pp. 171, 185.

⁵⁰ "Inauguration of the Northern Pacific Railroad," St. Paul *Pioneer Press* (Minn.), Feb. 16, 1870.

⁵¹ Samuel Wilkeson to "Dear Governor" [Smith], Mar. 27, 1870. Minnesota Historical Society, NPRR Papers, Box 2, Secretary, Series 2, correspondence unregistered, 1865—May 1870. Ashley, who was Governor of Montana Territory until midsummer of that year, also received sizable fees from Jay Cooke for speaking on behalf of the railroad enterprise; thus, his opportunism was looked upon as particularly reprehensible. The "rich man" referred to could have been that former Ohioan, Philetus W. Norris, whose account of this period indicates he was doing just what the railroaders complained of. See "The Great West . . . Letter No. 4, Hell Gate, Montana Ty., Aug. 16th, 1870," published in the Norris *Suburban* (Michigan), date unknown. A clipping is preserved in Scrapbook No. 1, pp. 18–20, P. W. Norris Collection (HM506), Huntington Library.

⁵² Letter, Samuel Wilkeson to "Dear Governor" [Smith], Apr. 20, 1870, Minnesota Historical Society, NPRR Papers, Box 2, Secretary, Series 2, correspondence unregistered, 1865—May 1870.

⁵³ Letter, F. E. Woodbridge to Hon. J. Gregory Smith, July 8, 1870. *Ibid.* Correspondence unregistered, June 1870—July 1871.

⁵⁴ As early as Jan. 19, 1870, Jay Cooke wrote Marshall: "We hope to see you here as soon as you can make it . . . have important matters to talk over." On Feb. 7 the relationship was clarified by this statement: "I feel that our enterprise will be as much benefited by your connection with it, as you will be benefited . . . a good and liberal salary will be paid you for current services." See Private Letters of Jay Cooke—Northern Pacific Letters, No. 1, Jan. 10, 1870, to Sept. 27, 1871, pp. 41–42. Pennsylvania Historical Society, Philadelphia. The services performed by Marshall were, at first, such tasks as reviewing the laws of Minnesota with regard to statutes which might be favorable or unfavorable to the railroad, the selection of lands to be taken under the railroad's grant, and lobbying.

⁵⁵ Based on a letter, A. Ramsey to Smith, Sept. 17, 1870, seeking $75 per month salary for Taylor. See "James W. Taylor: A Biographical Sketch," *Minnesota History Bulletin* 1, No. 4 (Nov. 4, 1915).

⁵⁶ A. W. Orton, "Some Scattered Thoughts on the Early Life of N. P. Langford," unpublished MS., September 1966, p. 8. A copy is available in the Yellowstone Park Reference Library.

⁵⁷ President Andrew Johnson removed Langford from his position as collector in 1868, but the Senate came to his support and caused his reinstatement. Somewhat later, the President agreed to appoint Langford Governor of the territory and he resigned the collector's position in anticipation. However, the Senate refused to confirm the appointment, an outcome due as much to Langford's antagonism of Colonel Saunders' following in Montana as it was to Johnson's imbroglio with the Senate. See the confidential letter written by A. J. Simmons to S. T. Hauser, Nov. 2, 1868, in the Hauser Papers, Montana Historical Society, Helena.

⁵⁸ This personal diary covering the years 1869–71 is in the Langford Collection (box 1, vol. 2), Minnesota Historical Society, St. Paul. It is a 3 by 5-inch pocket book intended for the year 1870 but also containing earlier and later entries. There are notable gaps in the record, the most important being the period Aug. 14 to Sept. 30, 1870, when Langford was involved in the Yellowstone exploration.

⁵⁹ Samuel Wilkeson to "Dear Governor" [Smith], undated, but filed as Mar. 19, 1870. Minnesota Historical Society, NPRR Papers, Box 2, Secretary, Series 2, correspondence unregistered, 1865—May 1870. At the end of the passage quoted, someone long ago added, "For 'interest' read *bribe.*"

⁶⁰ This article, titled "The Northern Pacific Railway," ends thus: The deep political significance of the Northern Pacific Railway at the present moment—*It solves in our favor the problem of British American annexation.* That immense region lying to the north . . . will be filled with scores of millions . . . by the Northern Pacific Railroad."

⁶¹ G. S. Spaulding to Smith, May 15, 1870, and William R. Marshall to Smith, May 30, 1870. Minnesota Historical Society, NPRR Papers, Box 2, Secretary, Series 2, correspondence unregistered, 1865—May 1870.

⁶² In a letter to his brother Jay, Henry D. Cooke wrote on June 2: "Mr. Langdon [*sic*], the brother-in-law of Gov. Marshall and who accompanied him on his late expe-

dition to the Red River Country, was in today. I took him over to the President's but he was too busy getting ready to get off to see him." Jay Cooke Papers, correspondence, June 1 to July 6, 1870, Pennsylvania Historical Society.

[63] Jay Cooke's palatial estate in the suburbs of Philadelphia.

[64] Langford, *Diary*, p. xii.

[65] From "The Great West . . . Letter No. 4, Hell Gate, Montana Ty., Aug. 16, 1870," clipped from the Norris (Mich.) *Suburban*, n.d., Scrapbook No. 1, Norris Collection (HM506) Huntington Library. The editorial emendation supplied by Norris at a later date has been retained.

[66] When Norris departed for the Columbia River in August, he left this map and his notes with T. C. Everts, who lost both, with his own effects, in the Yellowstone wilderness. *Ibid.*, p. 96.

[67] Henry Henselbecker, a half-brother, called "Hank."

[68] Gardner River, which drains the southeastern flank of the Gallatin Range.

[69] Frederick Bottler, though a good mountaineer, was in poor condition for such a strenuous adventure as he was not fully recovered from a mauling suffered 6 months earlier when he attempted to rout a family of grizzly bears from a berry patch.

[70] Letter No. 4, cited in note 65.

[71] He narrowly missed Langford, whose diary indicates he left Corinne, bound for Helena, on July 25.

[72] His resolve to explore the Yellowstone region could have had no longer standing than a few months.

[73] This last statement indicates that Letter No. 4 was published subsequent to the 1875 expedition, despite its early date.

[74] Langford, *Diary*, p. xii.

[75] Camp to Gen. Alfred Sully, Superintendent of Indian Affairs for Montana, July 5, 1870. RG 393, U.S. Continental Command, Fort Ellis, Mont., Dispatches received, NA.

[76] Col. John Gibbon (Headquarters, District of Montana) to Maj. E. M. Baker (Fort Ellis), July 1, 1870. *Ibid.*

[77] Langford presented this letter, dated Aug. 9, 1870, in facsimile form in his *Diary*, pp. xiii–xv. However, it is not quite what one would expect as a reply. Instead, it seems to have been prompted by Stickney's letter, being more of an amendment to some previous understanding with Hauser and Langford. Perhaps the answer lies in those entries in Langford's personal diary recording a round trip to Deer Lodge (Stuart's home) on the 6th and 7th. It seems likely he went there with a letter of introduction from Sam Hauser—who was better acquainted with Stuart—to make the initial arrangements in person.

[78] In that attack on the "Big Horn Expedition" of 1863, Hauser's life was saved by a thick notebook he carried in a breast pocket.

[79] The desire to explore unknown places was one of the driving forces of Doane's life. In this case, it is probable that his interest was aroused by the Norris-Everts visit, and that Judge Hosmer heard of it from Everts.

[80] Doane (Fort Ellis) to Washburn (Helena), Aug. 12, 1870. The original is in the Hauser Papers, Montana State Historical Society.

[81] Langford, *Diary*, pp. xv–xvi.

[82] Hancock (Headquarters, Department of Dakota) to Gibbon (Headquarters, District of Montana), Aug. 15, 1870. RG393, U.S. Continental Commands, Fort Ellis, Mont., Letters Received, NA.

[83] John Gibbon (Fort Shaw), to Washburn (Helena), Aug. 15, 1870. *Ibid.*

[84] "The Yellowstone Expedition," in the issue of Aug. 13, 1870.

[85] *The Helena Daily Herald*, Apr. 20, 1870, stated: "This gentleman, who has held the office of Assessor of Internal Revenue ever since the organization of the Territory, retires today. . . . His removal, caused by a misapprehension, hardly pardonable, will deprive the Government of one of its ablest territorial officers. . . ."

[86] In his *Diary*, p. xvii, Langford says: "While we were disappointed in our expectation of having James Stuart for our commander and advisor, General Washburn was

chosen captain of the party. However, it is evident that Washburn was chosen *before* Stuart was called for that jury duty from which the Federal judge declined to excuse him.

[87] Cornelius Hedges served as correspondent for the *Herald*, while Walter Trumbull wrote for another Helena paper, the *Rocky Mountain Gazette*.

[88] "Departure of the Expedition," in the issue of Aug. 18, 1870.

[89] "Diary of Cornelius Hedges, June 24, 1870, to Oct. 16, 1871," p. 12. Original in the collection of the Montana State Historical Society, Helena (Acc. 2165, Drawer 15). Published as "Journal of Judge Cornelius Hedges," *Contributions to the Historical Society of Montana* 5 (1904): 370–94.

[90] "Diary of Samuel T. Hauser, Aug. 17 to Sept. 4, 1870," p. [2]. The original is Coe Collection Manuscript No. 249, Bienecke Library, Yale.

[91] "Diary of Warren Caleb Gillette, Aug. 7 to Sept. 27, 1870," pp. 4–5. Original in the Montana Historical Society, Helena.

[92] Langford, *Diary*, pp. 2–3.

[93] This incident is described in detail by Gillette: ". . . Jake Smith, with a pint of beans opened a game he called 'twenty-one' dealing out his beans at 10¢ each, and continually crying out, 'No limit Gentlemen.' Soon however, Hauser having to go off in a carriage with Mrs. Bromley [a widow], passed in the beans he had won (say $5.00) which called for more money than Smith had, so his unlimited game came to an inglorious end." See Gillette's "Diary," p. 8.

[94] "The Yellowstone Expedition," *Helena Daily Herald*, Aug. 24, 1870. (From dispatch dated Aug. 22).

[95] "Official Report of the Washburn-Langford-Doane Expedition into the Upper Yellowstone in 1870," as it appears in the handwritten copy made at Fort Ellis, M. T., Dec. 15, 1870. The original is in the Montana State University Library, Bozeman, 76 pp. This report was published, with considerable editorial revision, as *Report of Lieutenant Gustavus C. Doane Upon the So-called Yellowstone Expedition of 1870*, 41st Cong., 3d sess., Sen. Ex. Doc. No. 51 (Washington: Government Printing Office, 1871), 40 pp., and it has been reprinted by Louis C. Cramton (ed.), in *Early History of Yellowstone National Park and its Relationship to National Park Policy* (Washington: Government Printing Office, 1932), pp. 113–148.

[96] The packers were Elwyn Bean and Charles Reynolds, and the negro cooks are known only as "Nute" and "Johnny." Nute brought along a dog called Booby.

[97] Gillette adds this interesting note: "Here, Smith in order to raise money to start another game of '21,' allowed the party to shoot at his hat for 25¢ each shot. his hat was riddled, and with the money he opened another bank. Fortune however favored him not, for he soon arose from his blankets without a cent; he stood his loss & the jests of the party with the greatest good humor." ("Diary," p. 9). He also describes an embarrassing incident of the following morning, when the herders turned the horses loose about 5 o'clock to graze. The cavalry animals took advantage of this freedom by starting for Fort Ellis, and the soldiers had to borrow mounts to retrieve theirs. Thus, the outfit "Got a rather late start."

[98] This incident was variously reported. Gillette says: "About 4 O clock P. M. saw 3 Crow Indians on the other side of the Y. S. They did not come over to us." ("Diary," p. 11). According to Hedges there were "Many Indians on the river observing us with the eye of a horse thief." ("Diary," p. 14.) Langford wrote of "one hundred or more of them watching us from behind a high butte as our packtrain passed the valley," and speculated on their chances of surviving an attack. (*Diary*, pp. 9–10.)

[99] Hauser says they "Campt in the rain—near the house." ("Diary," p. 5), and Langford indicates they were comfortable enough lying "heads and tails" in the big tent that night (*Diary*, p. 12). Everts did not share that experience, for he had become ill during the afternoon from gorging on wild fruit along Trail Creek, and a place was found for him in the Bottler cabin. The camp was not moved until it was evident Everts was improving and would be able to follow them. (Hedges, "Diary," p. 14.)

[100] Their campsite, one-half mile above Tom Miner Creek, was called "Camp Euphemia." (Hauser, "Diary," p. 5.) It was a pleasant place where they could "spread out on the pricklypears" under the stars. (Hedges, "Diary," p. 15.) Several expeditioners

climbed a nearby glaciated knob and promptly dubbed it "Washburne's Peak." See Walter Trumbull, "Yellowstone Papers—No. 2," Helena *Rocky Mountain Daily Gazette* (Montana) Oct. 19, 1870. Everts came into camp—from Bottler's Ranch—at 10:30 A. M., just as the expedition was moving out, and Gillette stayed with him to the next encampment at Gardner River.

[101] Gillette says of this Indian trail: ". . . to an unexperienced eye it would seem impossible to go over it on a horse." ("Diary," p. 14.)

[102] The Washburn party named this unusual formation The Devil's Slide. It is an outcropping of iron oxide, rather than ore of mercury, but something of the original misidentification is retained in the name now applied to the entire ridge—Cinnabar Mountain.

[103] This stream had been called "Gardner's Fork," for a freetrapper named Johnson Gardner who plied his trade on its headwaters about 1831, but that designation had been replaced by "Warm Stream Creek" during the prospecting era. Resurrection of the earlier name by this party is undoubtedly due to Langford's contact with Jim Bridger in 1866 (*Diary*, p. viii), and the "i" in the name, as reestablished in 1870, appears to be a rendering of the old trapper's Virginia drawl. The local belief that the town of Gardiner, Mont., was named for two Gardiner brothers who were early settlers there has no basis in fact.

[104] Langford interpreted the smoke as being from the signal fires of Indians (*Diary*, p. 14). However, it is more likely, from their experience on the following day, that they were viewing vestiges of a forest fire that had recently burned over much of the height now called Mount Everts.

[105] Strangely, the other diarists did not mention these men, who could not have spent an evening by the expedition's campfire without providing some interesting information.

[106] This Black Canyon of the Yellowstone, through which the Yellowstone River flows above the mouth of Bear Creek, was then called the "Third Canyon" by the prospectors of the area. They considered it to extend to the great falls; however, the southward swing of this great trench, where it passes around the base of Mount Washburn, is now rightly recognized as a separate feature—the Grand Canyon of the Yellowstone.

[107] The name used by prospectors for Tower Creek.

[108] Known earlier as the "Little Falls," the present name was given by Hauser, who wrote: "Campt near the most beautiful falls—I ever saw—I named them "Tower Falls'—from the towers and pinnacles that [overhang] them height 115 feet". ("Diary," p. 6.) See also Walter Trumbull, "The Washburn Yellowstone Expedition," *The Overland Monthly* 6, No. 5 (May 1871): 433–34.

[109] General Washburn took advantage of the layover at "Camp Comfort," as Everts named this camp, to scout ahead. Hedges notes: "Washburn & Williamson have been out to find trail up west side to save crossing river returned near night, reporting having seen lake The route practicable. Scenery fine. resolved to go that way." ("Diary," p. 21.) The summit Washburn had reached was "spontaneously and by unanimous vote" given the name of Mount Washburn (Langford, *Diary*, p. 22), while Hedges gave the name of "Prospect Point" to an aerie he discovered atop the overhanging cliff. With the passage of time, the name has been shifted many miles westward to a summit of the Washburn Range—Prospect Peak. Here, as at most of the expedition's campsites, there was time for card playing, but it is unlikely that the game was as unfair as Langford indicated (*Diary*, pp. 18–19). In fact, Langford could have borrowed details from that game played at Fort Ellis, on the eve of departure, to support his growing animus toward Jake Smith (a feeling aroused by Jake's attitude toward the guard duty he thought unnecessary).

[110] There was another sufferer in that camp. "Booby," the dog, had become sore-footed and mocassins of deer skin had to be made for him. It was a kindness amply repaid at a later date.

[111] The route followed from Tower Fall was southward, up the open ridge between Antelope and Tower Creeks to the base of Mount Washburn, from whence a group (Hauser, Gillette, Stickney, Trumbull, and Langford) went to the summit, while the others shepherded the packtrain through "a gap in the ridge" (Dunraven Pass). Doane's

use of the term "Elephant's Back" to denote the Washburn Range is his interpretation of the proper location for that vagary which appeared first on Raynolds map (1860). It is undoubtedly better located as shown on modern maps.

[112] The single aneroid barometer carried to the top was made to render three other values: Hauser, 10,700 feet; Gillette, 10,579 feet; and Langford, 9,800 feet. Gillette came closest to the true elevation of 10,243 feet.

[113] Sulphur Creek.

[114] The Washburn Hot Springs. Cornelius Hedges described them in his article "Hell-Broth Springs," *Helena Daily Herald*, Oct. 19, 1870. The members of this expedition originated the satanic nomenclature so popular in the early days of Yellowstone Park, but now out of fashion. Of 31 place names that once flaunted the devil's proprietorship, only three remain—Devils Den, on Tower Creek, and, on the terraces at Mammoth Hot Springs, Devils Kitchen, and Devils Thumb. Hell has suffered in a lesser degree, being now represented by three place names out of an original 10.

[115] Cornelius Hedges made his way laboriously down the creek discovering the cascades—Crystal Falls—for which he named the stream (Langford, *Diary*, pp. 27–28).

[116] Of his work at the Lower Fall, Langford says: "Three times in its descent the cord was parted by abrasion, but at last, securing the weight with a leather band, I was enabled to ascertain by a measurement which I think quite exact, the height of the fall. It is a little more than three hundred and twenty feet; while the perpendicular wall down which I suspended the weight was five hundred and ten feet." (*Diary*, p. 36). Evidently, none of the expeditioners were confident enough of the work at the Lower Fall to use the new value, preferring, instead, Folsom's measurement.

[117] Hauser notes: "Ben & I went dow[n] river 3½ miles. descended cannon to river and took a drink. The *first* men that ever reach[ed] bottom of cannon below Lower falls." ("Diary," p. 9.) He also discovered a waterfall he named "Silverthread fall" (Silver Cord Cascade) which was estimated to plunge 1,500 feet from the South rim (an exaggeration as the canyon has a depth of only 1,200 feet at that point).

[118] This place name, which was a holdover from an earlier time, first appeared on the deLacy map (1865) to indicate a stream entering Yellowstone River from the east, below the great falls—probably present Broad Creek. But Doane saw fit to transfer the name to the stream it presently identifies. His decision was not immediately acceptable to all, for Washburn gave that name to Pelican Creek a few days later, and, the following year, the Hayden party applied it to two other streams (now called Sour Creek and Alluvium Creek).

[119] Present Sour Creek. Doane evidently misunderstood information obtained from prospectors.

[120] Doane did not have a consensus in his use of this name. The other members of the party called the place the Crater Hills (Hauser, "Diary," p. 12), to which has been added a name of less certain origin—Sulphur Mountain.

[121] Appropriately called "Mud Geyser" by Langford (*Diary*, p. 41), but his usage may be retrospective. Hauser called it "Mud Spring" ("Diary," p. 16).

[122] Cornelius Hedges had an unpleasant experience when he climbed upon the outer rim of this feature. Langford says he "endangered his life by his temerity, and was thrown violently down the exterior side of the crater by the force of the volume of steam emitted. . . ." (*Diary*, p. 45.)

[123] While the pack train was progressing toward Lake Yellowstone, Washburn and Langford rode back to the Crater Hills to search for additional features in that fascinating locality. In the course of examining an alum spring they had previously missed, Langford nearly fell in, which would have resulted in serious injury or death. He described his experience thus: "The border of this spring below the surface had been undermined in many places by the violent boiling of the water, to the distance of several feet from the margin, so that it was unsafe to stand near the edge of the spring. This, however, I did not at first perceive; and, as I was unconcernedly passing by the spring, my weight made the border suddenly slough off beneath my feet. General Washburn noticed the sudden cracking of the incrustation before I did, and I was aroused to a sense of my peril by his shout of alarm, and had sufficient presence of mind to fall suddenly backwards at full length upon the sound crust, whence, with my feet and legs extended over the spring, I rolled to a place of safety." (*Diary*, pp. 46–47).

[124] Pelican Creek, which Washburn tried to rename Alum Creek. See note 118.

[125] According to Langford, who was acting surgeon: "When Doane was told that we were ready, he asked, 'Where is the chloroform?' I replied that I had never administered it, and that after thinking the matter over I was afraid to assume the responsibility of giving it. He swallowed his disappointment, and turned his thumb over on the cartridge box, with the nail down. Hedges and Bean were on hand to steady the arm, and before one could say 'Jack Robinson,' I had inserted the point of my penknife, thrusting it down to the bone, and had ripped it out to the end of the thumb. Doane gave one shriek as the released corruption flew out in all directions upon surgeon and assistants, and then with a broad smile on his face he exclaimed, 'That was elegant!'" (*Diary*, p. 51.) Relief was immediate, but Doane's writing hand was permanently impaired (Dr. Merrill G. Burlingame of Montana State University was so informed by Mrs. Doane, and a comparison of Doane's handwriting before and after the operation supports that conclusion.)

[126] Langford and Hedges remained behind to measure distances to points around the lake, but their inability to establish a base line of sufficient length led to abandonment of the project "after some 2 hours of useless labor." (Langford, *Diary*, p. 53.)

[127] This area, drained by Alluvium Creek, is so known on present maps. Langford accompanied Doane in an examination of its thermal features.

[128] The decision to attempt this short-cut was made by Cornelius Hedges, who was in charge of the packtrain at that time. He notes: "Went out nicely for 2 miles & came to deep bayou. in thick tall willows. backed out & took side hill." ("Diary," p. 29.) They camped on the north side of Beaverdam Creek about where the trail crosses now; "Poorest camp we have had in tangled woods."

[129] Present Colter Peak, elevation 10,683. Langford's description of this ascent is more informative. He says: "We followed along the high bank adjacent to the bottom through which the river runs in a direction a little south of east for the distance of about three [2½] miles, when we entered a heavily timbered ravine [Cabin Creek], which we followed through the underbush for some three miles, being frequently obliged to dismount and lead our horses over the projecting rocks, or plunging through bushes and fallen timber. At the end of two hours we reached a point in the ascent where we could no longer ride in safety, nor could our horses climb the mountain side with the weight of our bodies on their backs. Dismounting, we took the bridle reins in our hands, and for the space of an hour we led our horses up the steep mountain side, when we again mounted and slowly climbed on our way, occasionally stopping to give our horses a chance to breathe. Arriving at the limit of timber and vegetation [a saddle at 9,920 feet], we tied our horses, and then commenced the ascent of the steepest part of the mountain, over the broken granite [dacite, a volcanic rock of similar appearance], great care being necessary to avoid sliding down the mountain with the loose granite. . . . At the point where we left our horses there was, on the east slope of the mountain, a body of snow, the surface of which was nearly horizontal, and the outer edge of which was thirty feet in perpendicular height. This body of snow is perpetual [during a retracement of this ascent on August 21, 1963, the cirque was found nearly empty of snow, and the scattered remnants were nowhere over two feet in depth]. At this point the elevation, as indicated by our aneroid barometer, was 9,476 feet, while at the summit it was 10,327 feet, a difference of 581 [763] feet, which was the broken granite summit." (*Diary*, pp. 58, 61.) It should be noted here that this peak, which General Washburn subsequently named "Mount Langford" in appreciation of the helpful information brought back from the summit, is not the peak so designated on present maps. Of the change, Langford later said: "Dr. Hayden, the geologist in charge of the U.S. geological survey, made his first visit to this region the following year (1871), and on the map which he issued in connection with his 1871 report, the name 'Mount Langford' was given to another mountain far to the northeast. Since that time my name has again been transferred to a mountain on the southeast [not so—Hayden's error stands]. I think that Dr. Hayden must have been aware at that time that this mountain bore my name." (*Diary*, p. 66.)

[130] Sam Hauser had prepared such a map—at the encampment at Park Point (Hedges, "Diary," p. 29), but it was neither as detailed nor as accurate as the one provided Washburn. A photographic copy of this map, as drawn in Washburn's diary, is available in the Langford Papers, Minnesota Historical Society, St. Paul.

[131] This tantalizing report was recorded by Hedges as "geysers spouting 500 feet of steam." ("Diary," p. 30.)

[132] Hedges later named the height he and Everts climbed "in honor of Everts." ("Diary," p. 30; see also "Mount Everts," *Helena Daily Herald*, Oct. 8, 1870).

[133] Langford has a fuller version of this ridiculous episode, in which a hunting party "decorated themselves as walking armories" and went in pursuit, only to have a change of heart when the bears made a stand in a dense thicket. (*Diary*, pp. 67–78.)

[134] Had they reached Heart Lake, they would probably have found Everts who was then sheltering in the geyser basin at the western end.

[135] They had made a 2-day reconnaissance of the back-track, searching for Everts, and were caught in a severe snow storm on the return. Of this, Langford says: "On their near approach to camp, when the trail was no longer discernible, their dog 'Booby' took the lead when they were at fault, and brought them into camp all right. They think they might have been forced to lie out all night but for the sagacity of 'Booby'." (*Diary*, p. 90.)

[136] Gillette, who was considered the best woodsman of the party, also seems to have been the most concerned over the loss of their comrade. His diary entry for the 14th (p. 52) notes: "Poor Everts I fear he has perished. What a shame that we did not stay at our camp of the 9th till all search was deemed useless." And on the following day he wrote: "This snow is a sad thing for Everts. How I pity him, hungry, wet and cold. I wonder if he killed his mare. I would do it, and dry the meat, so I could pack enough on my back to carry me to the settlements" (p. 53). Such thoughts were gnawing at Gillette on the morning of the 16th when General Washburn decided they must start for the settlements. Gillette asked if he deemed further search useless, and Washburn agreed to "take the sense of the party." As a result, Smith's proposal that they move immediately was put to a vote, of which Gillette says: "I being the only one voting in the negative" (p. 54). But Gillette was unable to accept such an admission of defeat and proposed to continue the search personally. On the 17th he wrote: "This morning I told Washburn that if anyone of the party would go with me I would return and make further search for Everts. Hauser remarked that, that was a pretty good bluff, as I knew that no one would be willing to stay back from the train. Washburn asked Lieut. Doane if he would give me two men and a pack animal to go back and look for Everts. He said he would & immediately ordered them to stay. I had my blankets gotten to-gether & borrowed a pair of boots of Mr. Hedges, who kindly offered them, mine being entirely used up. The Soldiers Moore & Williamson were ready as soon as I and we left what we called the Hot Spring Camp about the same time as the main party." ("Diary," pp. 55–56.)

[137] Langford's idea of the lake's situation was the correct one: "As we passed the large lake on our left today, I observed that there was no ridge of land between us and the lake; therefore I believe that it is in the Snake River Valley." (*Diary*, p. 102.)

[138] Kepler Cascades.

[139] Hedges caught the excitement of that arrival: "crossed creek little above in bad place. lost one of my gloves. my pack horse went in all over. many packs got wet. All rushed up side of geyser . . . forgot all my bad feelings of the morning." ("Diary," p. 37.)

[140] This place name made its appearance in 1851 on DeSmet's map (map 5), as "Fire Hole Riv." While the term implies a basin-like feature, Doane is the first to couple it to a particular locality.

[141] In regard to the naming of geysers by this party, Langford says: "We gave such names to those of the geysers which we saw in action as we think will best illustrate their peculiarities." (*Diary*, p. 108.) The names bestowed were particularly apt.

[142] Some idea of the propriety of this name can be had by a comparison of its erruptions (estimated at 250,000 gallons) with those of Old Faithful (10,000 gallons).

[143] Langford claims that Private Williamson crawled through its steamy labyrinth between eruptions (*Diary*, p. 110), but it could not have been since he had remained with Gillette to search for Everts.

[144] The Fan, also called "Fan Tail Geyser."

[145] Named the Beehive, for the resemblance of its cone to an old-fashioned, straw hive.

[146] This geyser was named Excelsior in 1881, when, for a brief period, it was probably the most powerful geyser in existence.

[147] References to Doane's "Map of the Route of the Yellowstone Expedition," prepared in September 1870, to accompany his official report (map 11), shows that his understanding of the Yellowstone region was based on deLacy's 1870 map (map 10) with its misconception of the Madison drainage. The original of Doane's map is in RG77, Office of the Chief of Engineers, Q. 329—No. 30, NA.

[148] It was at this encampment where the Firehole and Gibbon Rivers join to form the Madison that the subject of reserving the Yellowstone region and its wonders for public use was said to have been discussed. Cornelius Hedges is credited with advancing the suggestion—an idea that was not original with him, since he was present in the fall of 1865 when Thomas F. Meagher made a similar proposal. None of the extant diaries kept by members of the party mentions this discussion. In fact, Hedges seems to have been concerned with other things: "No fish in river. grub getting very thin. oposite a stream comes in on right side. mud bottom . . . Tues. 20. Didn't sleep well last night. got to thinking of home & business. seems as if we are almost there." ("Diary," p. 39.) The details of the discussion came mainly from Langford, who published them 35 years later, as follows:

"Last night, and also this morning in camp, the entire party had a rather unusual discussion. The proposition was made by some member that we utilize the result of our exploration by taking up quarter sections of land at the most prominent points of interest, and a general discussion followed. One member of our party suggested that if there could be secured by preemption a good title to two or three quarter sections of land opposite the lower fall of the Yellowstone and extending down the river along the cañon, they would eventually become a source of great profit to the owners. Another member of the party thought that it would be more desirable to take up a quarter section of land at the Upper Geyser Basin, for the reason that locality could be more easily reached by tourists and pleasure seekers. A third suggestion was that each member of the party preempt a claim, and in order that no one should have an advantage over the others, the whole should be thrown into a common pool for the benefit of the entire party [that such a division was at least contemplated, finds a confirmation in Hauser's diary, where the first page—originally blank—was used to list names of party members opposite prominent features].

Mr. Hedges [whose name was not included in the listing just mentioned] then said that he did not approve of any of these plans—that there ought to be no private ownership of any portion of that region, but that the whole of it ought to be set apart as a great National Park, and that each one of us ought to make an effort to have this accomplished. His suggestion met with an instantaneous and favorable response from all— except one—of the members of our party, and each hour since the matter was first broached, our enthusiasm has increased. It has been the main theme of our conversation to-day as we journey. I lay awake half of last night thinking about it;—and if my wakefulness deprived my bed-fellow (Hedges) of any sleep, he has only himself and his disturbing National Park proposition to answer for it.

Our purpose to create a park can only be accomplished by untiring work and concerted action in a warfare against the incredulity and unbelief of our National legislators when our proposal shall be presented for their approval. Nevertheless, I believe we can win the battle.

I do not know any portion of our country where a national park can be established furnishing to visitors more wonderful attractions than here. These wonders are so different from anything we have ever seen—they are so various, so extensive—that the feeling in my mind from the moment they began to appear until we left them has been one of intense surprise and of incredulity. Every day spent in surveying them has revealed to me some new beauty, and now that I have left them, I begin to feel a skepticism which clothes them in a memory clouded by doubt." (*Diary*, pp. 117–118.)

Langford's account of the discussion at the Madison Junction encampment will receive further attention in part III.

[149] Langford and Johnny left for Virginia City before the remainder of the party were up. (Hedges, "Diary," p. 42.)

[150] The expeditioners parted with the military escort in the afternoon, after Stickney's horse created a last-minute casualty by kicking Private Leipler. Hedges says "all the

animals showed signs of fatigue." ("Diary," p. 42.) Langford went from Virginia City to Helena, arriving by coach on the evening of the 25th. Washburn and Hauser came in the same way on the following day, while Hedges and Smith accompanied the pack train, reaching home on the 27th.

[151] Before Gillette and the soldiers had returned to civilization, the following appeared in a Montana newspaper: "Mr. F. [T] C. Evarts, who strayed and got lost from the Yellowstone party, is still missing. From circumstances recently brought to light, it is thought by some that he encountered the fugitive coach robbers, and has been killed by them. Detectives, who are in search of the road agents, were seeking them in that direction, and came upon the notices posted to guide the missing man to camp. Mr. Gillette and others still pursue the search." Deer Lodge *New North-West*, Sept. 30, 1870.

[152] They had passed down Outlet Creek to Heart Lake, of which Gillette made an unmistakable sketch on p. 110 of his diary. (The preceeding page is occupied by a sketch of Yellowstone Lake similar to those appearing in the diaries of Hauser and Washburn.) At that point the would-be rescuers were very near to the object of their search. Had they gone over to the geyser basin, at the northwest extremity of the lake, they would have seen the pitiful shelter occupied until that morning by Everts—who had left it in a fruitless attempt to reach the West Thumb Geyser Basin; and had they looked across the lake that evening, they would have seen the smoke from the fire he made with a lens from his opera glass upon his return to Heart Lake.

[153] "Yellowstone Party Heard From," in the issue of Sept. 23, 1870. The Deer Lodge *New North-West* of the same date carried the Virginia City dispatch (p. 3), adding this comment of its own: "While it scarcely seems possible that he could be lost . . . it must be recollected that Mr. Everts' vision is very bad, it being impossible for him to recognize persons a few feet distant without the aid of glasses." The Helena *Rocky Mountain Daily Gazette* of the 24th also noted the return of the Yellowstone expedition and the loss of Everts, but without providing anything new except some guesses about his fate.

[154] "The Yellowstone Expedition." This issue also noted the arrival of S. T. Hauser and Surveyor General Washburn, and expressed a hope that the latter's report would be available in time for publication on the 27th.

[155] "The Yellowstone Expedition," *Helena Daily Herald*, Sept. 27 and 28, 1870.

[156] They did not cross Bozeman Pass, but went over the divide between Meadow and Trail Creeks—a route quite as good as Bozeman's.

[157] Washburn says "recrossed" because they had forded the river on the previous day to see some hot springs on the east bank.

[158] September 13, 4 days after Everts was lost (on the 9th).

[159] "Exploring Expedition," Salt Lake City *Deseret Evening News* (Utah), Sept. 27, 1870.

[160] "A Montana Romance," Denver *Daily Rocky Mountain News* (Colorado), Oct. 8, 1870.

[161] "The Yellowstone Wonders," Deer Lodge *New North-West* (Montana), Oct. 21, 1870.

[162] "Montana Geysers," Oct. 9, 1870, and "The Yellowstone Expedition," Oct. 14, 1870.

[163] "The Yellowstone Expedition," *New York Times*, October 14, 1870.

[164] See "The Great Falls of the Yellowstone," Portland *Morning Oregonian*, Sept. 29, 1870. Only a few issues of the *Montana Pick and Plow* have survived, so there is no way of knowing how extensive its coverage of these events may have been.

[165] Original in the Jay Cooke Papers, Pennsylvania Historical Society. Letters Received.

[166] "Arrival of Warren C. Gillette, of the Yellowstone Expedition," *Helena Daily Herald* (Montana), Oct. 3, 1870.

[167] "The Lost Man.—$600 Reward Offered," *Helena Daily Herald*, Oct. 6, 1870.

[168] John H. Baronett—his real name—also called himself Collins Jack Baronett, which led to the nickname of "Yellowstone Jack."

[169] *Helena Daily Herald*, Oct. 8, 1870.

[170] This appeared Oct. 21, 1870, in a paper tentatively identified as the *Springfield Weekly Republican* (Massachusetts). A clipping is in the Hedges Papers, VIII (6), at the Montana Historical Society, Helena.

[171] A brief account of the exploration, as given in that letter, appeared in the Westfield, Mass., newspaper. See the clipping in the Hedges Papers, VIII (9), at the Montana Historical Society, Helena.

[172] The Hedges articles are reproduced by Cramton, pp. 97–112. It would appear that Hedges intended to write at least one more article, for the incomplete draft for a description of the "Great Geyser Basin" remains in the Hedges Papers, VIII (3), at the Montana Historical Society, Helena.

[173] Substitution of Absaroka Range will give the sense as intended.

[174] "The Cataracts and Geysers of the Upper Yellowstone—Why They Should be Given in Perpetuity to Montana," Bozeman *Avant Courier*, Dec. 7, 1871. In this, the editor asks that Congress donate the Yellowstone region to Montana Territory, "to be set apart and protected under appropriate local legislation," and he added that he understood Montana's delegate would introduce such a bill in Congress.

[175] The "Yellowstone Lake" article was published verbatim in the issue of Dec. 7, 1870. Hedges had assisted with editing that paper prior to 1864.

[176] These were: "Yellowstone Expedition," Oct. 3, 1870. and "Yellowstone Papers," appearing serially in the daily (only the issues of Oct. 18 and 19 are now available) with a condensed version published in the weekly issues of Oct. 24 and 31, 1870.

[177] "The Long-Lost Found."

[178] Official redtape prevented the commandant at Fort Ellis from rendering the assistance he was inclined to give, but help was obtained at the nearby town of Bozeman. Charles Wright, who ran the livery stable, hitched up a light spring wagon and started at once with Dr. O'Neil. At Fort Ellis they found three volunteers—Harry Horr, a civilian employee of the Post Sutler, and two soldiers, Sergeant Leipler (who had been Private William Leipler on the expedition) and Private Mallory. The story of this rescue mission was later told in a jocular manner by Horr in an article entitled "Harry Horr's Hot Spring Claim," Bozeman *Avant Courier* (Montana), Jan. 11, 1883. This trip was particularly important to the future Yellowstone Park because what Horr saw on it led him to return the following summer and establish a claim, with James C. McCartney, to the Mammoth Hot Springs (which he named).

[179] This refers to a letter from S. W. Langhorne, of Bozeman, from which the *Helena Herald* printed an excerpt mentioning the rescue of Everts, and also stated: "This is reliable news, but he may not live." See the issue of Oct. 21.

[180] Crescent Hill. As previously noted, he was found near the pass called The Cut, but confusion over which "Warm Spring Creek" Pritchett was referring to caused the Hayden party to place the event on the stream Hauser had called "Lost Trail Creek" (Langford's "Antelope Creek"); thus, they changed the name to Rescue Creek, and so it has remained.

[181] "More About Mr. Everts," *Helena Daily Herald*, Oct. 22, 1870.

[182] "The Finding of Hon. T. C. Everts," in the issue of Oct. 26, 1870.

[183] "The Lost and Found," *Helena Daily Herald*, Oct. 28, 1870.

[184] "Letter from Mr. Everts," *ibid.*, Oct. 22, 1870. His story of having thought his right leg was one man, his left another, his arms two more, and his stomach a fifth, and of having conversed with them, indicates the sort of hallucinatory state sought by young Indian men engaged in a vision quest, where deliberate exposure was the means used. Though Everts appears to have approved payment of the reward offered for his rescue, that resolution evidently flagged. When questioned on this point some years later, Baronett stated: "His friends refused to pay me because I found him alive, they saying that it was his place to pay the bills. He would not pay me because he said that if I had left him alone he would have found his own way out." See Theodore Gerrish, *Life in the World's Wonderland* (Biddleford, Maine: n.p., 1887), p. 240. Some further evidence of ingratitude is provided by R. C. Wallace, *A Few Memories of a Long Life* (p.p., n.p., 1900), pp. 57–61.

[185] "The Yellowstone Banquet," *Helena Daily Herald*, Nov. 14, 1870. (The invitation and acceptance were both published in the issue of Nov. 12.

[186] "Our Washington Letter," *ibid.*, Nov. 14, 1870.

[187] See telegram cited in note 82.

[188] Doane's "Map of the Route of the Yellowstone Expedition" is in RG–77, Office of the Chief of Engineers, Q. 329—No. 30, NA. Washburn's map is known only from a copy in the Yellowstone Park Reference Library marked, in the upper right corner, "Route of Washburn's party 1870, being a tracing of map made to accompany Washburn's report to Dept of Interior." It provided information incorporated in the Blaine map.

[189] In its issue of Sept. 26, 1870, the *Helena Daily Herald* noted: "It is the intention of Mr. Langford to prepare for publication, as soon as practicable, a detailed report of the journey to and from this most interesting region."

[190] The original, in the manuscript collection of the Yellowstone Park Reference Library, consists of 185 pages, with 9 pages of handwritten notes on folded legal paper.

[191] From the issue of Nov. 11, 1870. This item suggests that Langford and Ashley were involved in similar enterprises. The relationship of Ashley's lecturing to Jay Cooke and the Northern Pacific Railroad is clear. Cooke's influence obtained for him an assignment on a lyceum circuit to deliver 50 lectures on the resources of Montana. That was followed by temporary employment directly in the interest of the Northern Pacific. Langford's activity is presumed to have followed a similar pattern.

[192] "A Grand Lecture," *Helena Daily Herald*, Nov. 17, 1870.

[193] "Virginia City Correspondence," *ibid.*, Nov. 26, 1870.

[194] "Yellowstone River," Washington *Daily Morning Chronicle* (D.C.), Jan. 20, 1871. It is an interesting coincidence that this issue carries an item proposing "A National Park For Washington"—the beginning of a movement which eventuated as the National Zoological Park.

[195] Chittenden, *The Yellowstone National Park*, p. 95.

[196] *Ibid.*, p. 92.

[197] Albert Matthews, "The Word Park in the United States," in *Publications of the Colonial Society of Massachusetts 8* (April 1904): 378–81.

[198] *Ibid.*, p. 380.

[199] *Ibid.*, p. 379. The scrapbook referred to is not with the Langford Papers at the Minnesota Historical Society, St. Paul.

[200] "Wonders of Montana," in the issue of Jan. 23, 1871. The subtitle is, "The Geysers and Cañons of the Yellowstone Region—Important Discoveries—Lecture by the Hon. N. P. Langford."

[201] The articles were "Wonders of Montana," *New York Herald*, Jan. 22, 1871, and "Travels in Montana," *New York Times*, Jan. 22, 1871. The *World* had no coverage.

[202] The Washington letter to the *Corinne Reporter* (Utah) is quoted thus: "N. P. Langford, of Montana, is here working for various interests in that Territory. He is a delightfully courteous gentleman, and ought to be able to secure the modest favors which Montana asks, ditch bill and all."

[203] Henry James, who visited Niagara Falls in 1871, has left a vivid description of conditions there. See *Encyclopedia of American Facts and Dates*, p. 295.

[204] From the manuscript cited in note 190, pp. 183 and 185.

[205] Letter of Jan. 24, 1871, in the Jay Cooke Papers, Pennsylvania Historical Society, Philadelphia. A note of instruction on the reverse adds: "Write Langford that I want to see him here Phila & to have him give some lectures for N Pacific at once & to talk Etc JC."

[206] Letter of Jan. 29, 1871, in the Jay Cooke Papers, Pennsylvania Historical Society, Philadelphia.

[207] Langford to Jay Cooke, Mar. 4, 1871, Jay Cooke Papers, Pennsylvania Historical Society, Philadelphia.

[208] Langford to Jay Cooke, Mar. 16, 1871, in the Jay Cooke Papers, Pennsylvania Historical Society, Philadelphia. Also, letter written by Pitt Cooke to his brother, Jay, Mar. 17, 1871, in the same place.

²⁰⁹ Lamb to J. Gregory Smith, Feb. 14, 1871, Letterbook of the President, vol. 1, p. 156, N.P.R.R. Papers, Minnesota Historical Society, St. Paul.

²¹⁰ An entry in Langford's personal diary on Dec. 15, 1870, includes the notations "Julius Bien 16818 Park Place" [a lithographer], and "Thos Moran 61 Sherman Avenue Newark N.J." Moran was then a struggling artist who did woodcuts for *Scribner's* as a means of supplementing a meagre income.

²¹¹ "Wonders of the Yellowstone," *Scribner's Monthly* 2, No's 1 & 2 (May and June 1871): 1–17, 113–128, was Langford's most important contribution because of the many readers who were thus made aware of the Yellowstone region; however, like his lecture notes, Langford's article does not propose reservation of the area in the public interest, but ends with a plug for the Northern Pacific Railroad. In fact, the ending differs only slightly from that of the lecture.

²¹² Untitled notes for a lecture on Montana Territory, intended to be presented in the interest of the Northern Pacific Railway; dated from content as written in 1871, p. 43. The original, written in ink on 59 pages of a large notebook, is with the Langford manuscripts in the Yellowstone Park Reference Library.

²¹³ Quoted from Cramton, *Early History of Yellowstone National Park*, p. 18. There is also an entry in Langford's personal diary for May 14, noting: "Lectured at Chillain Hills."

²¹⁴ From a personal letter in the possession of James Taylor Dunn, former librarian of the Minnesota Historical Society. "Tan" was the pet name by which other members of the family referred to Langford.

²¹⁵ Vol. 6, Nos. 5 & 6, pp. 431–37, 489–96.

²¹⁶ Telegram dated Nov. 16, 1870, forwarded by the Adjutant, 7th Infantry, on Nov. 19. RG–393, Continental Commands, Fort Ellis, Mont., L.R., NA.

²¹⁷ As reported by D. Wolfe, phonographer, and published in pamphlet form, p. 19. A copy is in the James Hill Library, St. Paul, Minn.

²¹⁸ *Helena Daily Herald*, Nov. 14, 1870.

²¹⁹ Spencer Baird to Hayden, Oct. 29 and Nov. 10, 1870. RG–57, Records of the Geological and Geographical Survey of the Territories, L.R., NA.

²²⁰ Hayden's rise can be judged by the funds made available for his survey activities: $5,000 in 1867 and the same amount the following year; $10,000 in 1869, when his miniscule organization acquired its name and was taken from the supervision of the Commissioner of the General Land Office and made directly responsible to the Secretary of the Interior (this was the underlying cause of the feud with Commissioner Wilson), and $25,000 in 1870.

²²¹ Secretary of the Interior Columbus Delano to Hayden, May 1, 1871. RG 48, L.S., Patents & Misc. Division, vol. 6, pp. 176–177, NA.

²²² Secretary of War William W. Belknap to commanding officers of posts on the route of the geological explorations by Professor Hayden, Mar. 25, 1871. RG–57, "Records of the Geological Survey of the Territories," Letters Received from Government Agencies, NA. This was confirmed for the Department of Dakota by Gen. Winfield S. Hancock's letter of May 26 (RG–57, L.R.—vol. 1867–74—Military). It would appear that Hayden was not immediately aware of Hancock's action, for he wrote Gen. P. H. Sheridan, commanding the Military Division of the Missouri, on May 27, seeking a "suitable escort, if possible," and suggesting he would "be glad if Lieut. Doane could be ordered to accompany my party in command of the escort." The second endorsement, signed by General Hancock, indicated Doane was an indispensable witness before the General Court Martial then assembled at Fort Snelling and not available for field service. However, he was released in time to join the expedition at the geyser basins. Available on NA Microfilm 623, reel 14. This letter may have prompted General Sheridan to send Captain Barlow into the Yellowstone region (see note 224).

²²³ The list of technical personnel has been compiled from random sources, and does not include such facilitating personnel as guides, hunters, teamsters, packers, cooks, and laborers.

²²⁴ Barlow to Hayden, June 3, 1871. NA Microfilm 623, reel 2, frame 0117. A second letter sent that day says essentially the same thing (frame 0118).

²²⁵ A. B. Nettleton to Hayden, June 7, 1871. NA Microfilm 623, reel 2, frame 0120.

Evidently Hayden was unable to reply with sufficient dispatch, so Moran left for the West bearing a letter of introduction from Nettleton, dated June 16, which repeats most of the burden of his earlier missive, adding, however, that "He goes out under the patronage of Mssrs. Scribner & Co. Publishers N.Y. and our Mr. Cooke." (frame 0127).

[226] Baird to Hayden, June 16, 1871. NA Microfilm 623, reel 2, frame 0119.

[227] Hayden to Secretary of the Interior Columbus Delano, June 8, 1871. RG–57, Records of the Geological Survey of the Territories, Letters Received from Government Agencies, 1870–73, NA.

[228] This hint that the prospectus included more than was accomplished that season is amplified in the columns of the *Helena Daily Herald* of July 10, 1871 ("Around Montana"), where the latter part of the plan is discussed thus: "Thence to the Yellowstone, and up as far as the lake, in the vicinity of which the party will remain for two months, then, if possible, they are to cross from the head of the Yellowstone to that of Snake River, and down to Fort Hall, surveying the entire route accurately, at the instigation of J. Cooke & Co., who contemplate running a branch road through this Pass to connect with the Central Pacific, if practicable."

[229] Barlow to Hayden, June 17, 1871. NA Microfilm 623, reel 2, frame 0129. The unnamed assistants were W. H. Wood, draughtsman; H. G. Prout, assistant topographer and Thomas J. Hine, photographer.

[230] Hayden to Delano. RG–57, Records of the Geological Survey of the Territories, Letters Received from Government Agencies, 1870–73, NA.

[231] This, and Hayden's letters of Aug. 28 and Sept. 9, 1871, are with the preceeding item.

[232] The hydrographic survey was made with the assistance of a small sailboat. The framework for this 12-foot craft had been packed to the lakeshore where it was fitted with a skin of well-tarred canvas. Named "Annie" for Miss Anna L. Dawes, daughter of the congressman from Massachusetts to whom Hayden was beholden for his appropriation, the boat proved quite satisfactory. In case it had not, the explorers were equipped with a whipsaw for building another from green timber.

[233] This letter was quoted in the *Helena Daily Herald*, Sept. 23, 1871.

[234] J. E. Hildegarth to Hayden, Oct. 30, 1871. NA Microfilm 623, reel 2, frame 0160. Capt. D. P. Heap also offered assistance from his field notes. (See his letter of Nov. 7, 1871, frame 0167.)

[235] This map, compiled and drawn by E. Hergesheimer in 1871, appeared in Hayden's *Preliminary Report of the United States Geological Survey of Montana and Portions of Adjacent Territories, Being a Fifth Annual Report of Progress* (Washington: Government Printing Office, 1872), p. 162. The original is in RG–57, Hayden Survey, Yellowstone National Park, NA.

[236] J. W. Barlow to Hayden, Nov. 9, 1871. NA Microfilm 623, reel 2, frame 0170.

[237] Barlow to Hayden, Jan. 13, 1872. NA Microfilm 623, reel 2, frame 0293. The arrangement with Hayden is detailed in Jackson's letter of Aug. 1, 1870, also in The National Archives (RG–57, Records of the Geological and Geographical Survey of the Territories).

[238] John W. Barlow and D. P. Heap, *Report of a Reconnaissance of the Basin of the Upper Yellowstone in 1871*, 42d Cong., 2d Sess., Sen. Ex. Doc. 66 (Washington: Government Printing Office, 1872), 43 pp. The report is accompanied by a "Sketch of the Yellowstone Lake and the Valley of the Upper Yellowstone River," drawn by Emil Henback, Feb. 28, 1872, from notes obtained during the reconnaissance of the preceding summer. The original is in RG–77, Office of the Chief of Engineers, Q. 181, NA (see map 14).

[239] R. W. Gildess to Hayden, Sept. 11, 1871. NA Microfilm 623, reel 2, frame 0143. The article produced in response to this request was "Wonders of the West—II; More about the Yellowstone," *Scribner's Monthly 3*, No. 4 (Feb. 1872): 388–96. The title of this article is puzzling, in that it implies a previous installment. However, the prior article appears to have been Langford's, cited in note 211.

[240] Quoted from "The Yellowstone Country," Bozeman *Avant Courier* (Montana), Sept. 13, 1871.

[241] "The Yellowstone Expedition," in the issue of Sept. 18, 1871.

²⁴² In the issue of Oct. 23, 1871. The earliest known use of "Wonderland" as a sobriquet for the Yellowstone region is made in the manuscript diary of A. Bart Henderson on July 24, 1871 (p. 107). However, the area was not yet generally accepted as being among the unique features of our country, for a contemporary newspaper listing of the "Wonders of America" did not admit it to the company of such features as Niagara Falls, Mammoth Cave, the Mississippi River, Lake Superior, the Cedar Creek Natural Bridge in Virginia, and the Iron Mountain deposit in Missouri. Boise City *Idaho Democrat*, July 8, 1871.

²⁴³ "Great Soda Mountain and Jupiter's Baths, in the Yellowstone Region," pp. 44–45.

²⁴⁴ Everts' account of his experiences while lost in the Yellowstone wilderness appeared as "Thirty-seven Days of Peril," *Scribner's Monthly 3*, No. 1 (November 1871): 1–17. It has been reprinted under the same title by James Richardson (ed.), *Wonders of the Yellowstone* (New York: Scribner, Armstrong & Co., 1873), pp. 198–249; in *Contributions to the Historical Society of Montana 5* (1904): 395–427, and as *Thirty-seven Days of Peril; A Narrative of the Early Days of the Yellowstone* (San Francisco: Edwin & Robert Grabhorn, 1923), 56 pp.

²⁴⁵ See "Notes on the Way to Wonderland, or, A Ride to the Infernal Regions," by C. C. Clawson, which appeared serially in the fall and winter of 1871–72. The following installments, several under a variant title, have been identified: Sept. 9, 16, 23, and 30; Oct. 14; Nov. 4, 11, 18, and 25; Dec. 2 and 16; Jan. 13 and 27, and Feb. 10 and 24.

²⁴⁶ The beginnings of this settlement are recorded in "The Mineral Springs of the Yellowstone—Wonderful Health Restoring Qualities," Helena *Rocky Mountain Gazette* (Montana), July 24, 1871, while its subsequent history is traced by Aubrey L. Haines, "McGuirk's Medicinal Springs," *Yellowstone Nature Notes 2*, No. 21 (1947): 22–23.

²⁴⁷ H. R. Horr to Superintendent D. W. Wear, July 6, 1885. Yellowstone Archives, Document 1049.

²⁴⁸ For the story of this structure, see Aubrey L. Haines, "The Bridge That Jack Built," *Yellowstone Nature Notes 21*, No. 1 (1947): 1–4.

²⁴⁹ See "Journal of the Yellowstone Expedition of 1866 under Captain Jeff Standifer ... Also the Diaries Kept by Henderson During His Prospecting Journeys in the Snake, Wind River and Yellowstone Country During the Years 1866–72," Coe Collection, Beinecke Library, Yale. Henderson's firm became the "Bozeman Toll Road Company," which soon failed. However, a portion of the road passed into the hands of George James ("Yankee Jim"), who operated it for many years as a toll road through the canyon later named for him.

PART III

¹ A. B. Nettleton was Jay Cooke's office manager. As an engineer officer during the Civil War, he had been very successful in the organization and operation of the military railroads which served the Northern armies, and it was his knowledge of railroading that made him so valuable to Cooke that, when Secretary Wilkeson (of the old Northern Pacific organization) attempted to destroy Nettleton's usefulness by an undeserved calumny, Cooke came to his assistant's defense, stating: "I have faith & confidence in Gen. Nettleton. He is a hand of power in the Northern Pacific enterprise. ... My labors are already enormous and I must have him." Correspondence with Frederick Billings, Oct. 2, 1871, Letters, Sept. 27, 1871, to Jan. 18, 1872, in Jay Cooke Papers, Pennsylvania Historical Society, Philadelphia.

² Letter of Oct. 27, 1871. RG–57, Hayden Survey, General Letters Received, 1864, 1866–74, vol. III, NA.

³ In addition to the popular article he had agreed to do for Scribner's, he was obligated to contribute a Yellowstone article to *The American Journal of Science and Arts*. This appeared later as "On the Yellowstone Park" (April, 1872, pp. 294–97).

⁴ Cooke to Roberts, Oct. 30, 1871, Letters, Sept. 27, 1871, to Jan. 18, 1872, in Jay Cooke Papers, Pennsylvania Historical Society, Philadelphia. Hayden apparently realized his official report would not be publicized in time to assist the park movement,

so he made a more immediate use of Kelley's suggestion by concluding his article in *Scribner's Monthly* with that thought. See "The Wonders of the West—II," 2, No. 4 (Feb. 1872): 396.

[5] Letters Received, Jay Cooke Papers.

[6] Though credited to the *Helena Herald*, this note appeared in the Bozeman *Avant Courier* (Montana), Nov. 9, 1871. Langford's diary shows him to have left Helena on Nov. 2 (he had arrived at 2 a.m. on Oct. 29). See original diary, vol. 2, in the Langford Collection, Minnesota Historical Society, St. Paul. Langford went directly to Philadelphia and Washington, arriving at the latter place sometime after Nov. 12. On the 19th, he went to New York, returning to Washington on Dec. 2. Brother-in-law Marshall, whose term as Minnesota's chief executive ended in 1870, was employed by Jay Cooke at this time.

[7] This item was located by Robert Budd on p. 35 in a volume labled "Nettleton," among the old Northern Pacific Railroad records stored in the Como warehouse. These have since been transfered to the Minnesota Historical Society, but are yet (1970) unclassified.

[8] "The Cataracts and Geysers of the Upper Yellowstone—Why They Should Be Given in Perpetuity to Montana," Bozeman *Avant Courier* (Montana), Dec. 7, 1871.

[9] H. D. Hampton, "Conservation and Cavalry," p. 45. The idea of Federal management of wildlands for nonutilitarian purposes seems not to have been seriously considered prior to the framing of the Yellowstone legislation; however, it had been suggested. As early as 1841, George Catlin proposed "*A nation's Park*, containing man and beast in all the wild and freshness of their nature's beauty!" and Henry Thoreau asked, in 1858, "Why should not we . . . have our national preserves . . .?" (See Introduction to this volume.) The use of the term "National public park" by Josiah Whitney in *The Yosemite Book* published in 1868 came closer to the modern usage. Yet it was imprecise, because the area to which he referred was under the management of the State of California, not the Federal Government. The earliest known use of the term "national park" to identify an area of wild land devoted to recreational use under Federal management appeared in the Virginia City, Nev., *Daily Territorial Enterprise*, Jan. 1, 1872, in a mention of the "effort to have the Yellowstone region declared a National Park." The term entered into official parlance Jan. 29, 1872, when Secretary of the Interior Columbus Delano transmitted the report of U.S. Geologist F. V. Hayden to Representative Mark Dunnell. The new park received the title, "Yellowstone National Park" in a letter of May 10, 1872, by which Acting Secretary of the Interior R. B. Conway informed Nathaniel P. Langford of his appointment as first superintendent.

[10] Hampton, *ibid.*, pp. 46–47, and William H. Goetzmann, *Exploration and Empire* (New York: Alfred A. Knopf, 1966), p. 508. See also Hampton, *How the U.S. Cavalry Saved Our National Parks* (Bloomington and London: Indiana University Press, 1971), pp. 25–31 and note 26.

[11] Clagett's letter replying to an inquiry of July 9, 1894, by William R. Marshall, then Secretary of the Minnesota Historical Society, asking: "Who are entitled to the principal credit for the passage of the act of Congress establishing the Yellowstone Park?," published by N. P. Langford in *Diary*, pp. xx–xxiii. Clagett was a Republican who managed one term as Territorial Delegate by taking astute advantage of a bitter rift in the Democratic ranks. He was a frontier lawyer and an accomplished orator who could boast, "I have helped to bring more than one State into the Union." He also had a frontiersman's penchant for moving on.

[12] *Wonderland Illustrated; or, Horseback Rides Through the Yellowstone National Park* (Virginia City, Mont.: Harry J. Norton, 1873), 132 pp. This first of the area's many guidebooks was prepared after a trip into the new park in the fall of 1872—not 1870 (a visit duly reported in the Virginia City *Montanian* as well).

[13] The visit of H. J. Brown was made in the fall of 1871, in company with C. L. Weeks. According to the Deer Lodge *New North-West*, Oct. 14, 1871, they "have located a quarter section each, taking in the principal geysers on the Madison, have got a cabin up, and propose living there."

[14] The results of the election held Aug. 7 were contested, and not until Sept. 13 did Governor Potts issue a proclamation declaring Clagett the winner by 413 votes. See "Montana News," Bozeman *Avant Courier* (Montana), Sept. 13, 1871. The same issue

noted his intention to leave for the East with his family "on Saturday" (the 16th), and that was confirmed by the Deer Lodge *New North-West*, issues of Sept. 9, and Oct. 14. These indicate that Clagett left his family at Keokuk and went to Ohio, where he campaigned for Gen. Edward F. Noyes during October—helping him to win the governorship. He was there during Langford's very brief visit to Montana at the end of October, the latter's only appearance in the territory in 1871. Thus, although Clagett could have discussed the matter with Hedges, there could not have been a meeting in Helena involving Langford.

¹⁵ Cramton, *Early History of Yellowstone National Park* p. 30, offers this comment: "The bill does not seem to me the draft of an amateur who had only been a few weeks in Washington and had only served two weeks in Congress." Hampton, "Conservation and Cavalry" p. 47, believes that Clagett prepared the Yellowstone legislation under the guidance of Representative Henry L. Dawes, of Massachusetts, a view taken on the testimony of Senator George Graham Vest that Dawes "was the father of this park we may say, for he drew the law of designation" (*Congressional Record*, 47th Cong., 2d sess., vol. 14, pt. 3—No. 61, Feb. 17, 1883, pp. 2835–36; see also, vol. 17, pt. 8—No. 82, Aug. 2, 1886, p. 7843, and Aug. 3, 1886, p. 7915, for other statements to that effect). Evidently, Clagett felt some obligation to Dawes, for he said: "It has always been a pleasure to me to give to Professor Hayden and to Senator Pomeroy, and Mr. Dawes of Mass. all of the credit which they deserve in connection with the passage of that measure. . . ." In *How the U.S. Cavalry. . .*, pp. 27–28, Hampton states that Langford, Hedges, and Hauser "began to frame" the legislation with Clagett, under the "guidance" of Dawes.

¹⁶ The bill, which is definitely in Clagett's handwriting, contains no filled blank; in fact, it is an obvious "fair copy." The outside of the bill is marked, "Act to set apart a certain tract of land lying near the head waters of the Yellowstone River as a public park—H R 764 Dec 18, 1871, Read twice refered to the Committee on the Public Lands & ordered to be printed— x 575 Mr. Clagett, on leave 147 Clagett 1 R Pub Lands upon Introduced by Wm H. Clagett." See the bound volume of "Original House Bills, H.R. 745–H.R. 1091, 42d Cong., 2d Sess." The National Archives. Clagett's bill did not go to the Senate; it was the Senate version which became the Yellowstone Park Act, but with amendments.

¹⁷ Cramton, *Early History of Yellowstone National Park*, p. 29. See also, *The Congressional Globe*, 42nd Cong., 2nd Sess., Dec. 18, 1871, for Pomeroy's measure; it was the first new bill (S. No. 392), following two recommitted bills, while Clagett's measure (H.R. No. 764), on p. 199, was near the end of a long schedule of new bills.

¹⁸ These files, now in The National Archives, were examined by permission of the Clerk of the Senate.

¹⁹ Langford, "Diary," p. xxii.

²⁰ *Ibid.*

²¹ Hiram M. Chittenden, *The Yellowstone National Park*, reprinted from the first edition (Norman, Oklahoma: University of Oklahoma Press, 1964), p. 82.

²² Hayden's later statement, "So far as is now known, the idea of setting apart a large tract about the sources of the Yellowstone River as a national park originated with the writer," in *Twefth Annual Report of the United States Geological and Geographical Survey of the Territories . . . for the Year 1878* (Washington: Government Printing Office, 1883), pt. II, p. xvii, is not supportable, but the view of his assistant, Albert Charles Peale, merits serious consideration: "As has already been stated, the setting aside of the area now known as the Yellowstone National Park was one of the results of the survey of 1871, and it may be stated that the movement was started by Dr. F. V. Hayden, and its success was mainly due to his personal efforts." *Ibid.*, p. 69. This is a recognition of the fact that Hayden was a sparkplug of the park movement, though not its originator.

²³ Langford's previous experience as a lobbyist probably contributed to the success of that canvass Chittenden considered "the most thorough . . . of any bill that has ever passed Congress." Chittenden, *The Yellowstone National Park* (1964 ed.), p. 82.

²⁴ Dated Jan. 13, 1872, at Washington, D.C., Minnesota Historical Society NPRR Papers, Secretary, Series 2, Correspondence unregistered, Box 4, August 1871–May 1872.

²⁵ This characterization appears to have originated in a National Park Service press release of Dec. 22, 1936—"Art and Artists in the National Parks."

^{26} Letter written at Newark, N.J., Mar. 11, 1872. Moran received $10,000 from Congress for his completed oil painting, which hung in the Senate Lobby of the U.S. Capitol until 1950, when it and a companion picture—"The Chasm of the Colorado"— were turned over to the Secretary of the Interior. Both are now stored at the National Gallery of Art, but the Yellowstone picture should not be confused with the several copies made by Moran. One, "Grand Canyon of the Yellowstone 1893–1901" is a copy given to the National Gallery in 1928 by George D. Pratt (see the accession files). The Moran Papers held by the Gilcrease Museum, Tulsa, Okla., indicate Moran produced several copies, including the 40 by 60-inch oil on display there.

^{27} "Geyser Land," in the issue of Dec. 23, 1871.

^{28} The issue of Jan. 1, 1872. It is interesting that the *Helena Daily Herald*, the Montana newspaper that had provided the best coverage of Yellowstone matters during the period of definitive exploration, did not take notice of the park movement until Jan. 16, when the *Territorial Enterprise* item just quoted was belatedly reprinted. The only coverage yet found in Eastern newspapers, beyond the perfunctory listing of Senator Pomeroy's bill in the Washington *Evening Star* of Dec. 18, 1871 (Delegate Clagett's companion measure was not mentioned), was a brief item of unknown date reprinted from the *St. Joe Herald* (Missouri) by the Bozeman *Avant Courier* (Montana), Jan. 18, 1872. It would appear that the park movement attracted slight notice at the outset.

^{29} *The Congressional Globe*, 42d Cong., 2d sess., Jan. 22, 1872.

^{30} *Ibid.*, Jan. 23, 1872.

^{31} Within a decade, this prognosis proved entirely correct, so that the Secretary of the Interior had to prohibit hunting and limit fishing by amendment of the park rules and regulations, Jan. 15, 1883. See the Yellowstone Archives, documents No. 162 and 163. This remained one of the most difficult problems of the early years of the park.

^{32} Senator Cole's objection to the park legislation is hard to understand in view of his sponsorship, at that time, of legislation intended to convey a portion of the Presidio grounds at San Francisco to the city for park purposes, and his interest in the protection of the "buffalo, elk, antelope, and other useful animals running wild in the territories of the United States against indiscriminate slaughter and extermination." He certainly had conservation instincts, so that his objection probably came from his position as head of the Senate Committee on Appropriations, which was then adverse to any increase in the public expenditures. Hayden says: "I was myself compelled to give a distinct pledge that I would not apply for an appropriation for several years at least. . . ." See his letter to Secretary of the Interior Carl Schurz, Feb. 21, 1878, in 45th Cong., 2d sess. House. Ex. Doc. No. 75, Apr. 11, 1878.

^{33} Both Senators Samuel Clarke Pomeroy (Kansas) and Lyman Trumbull (Illinois) were members of the Congress that had enacted the Yosemite Grant legislation in 1864; also, the latter's son, Walter, had been a member of the 1870 Washburn Expedition and was then serving as the clerk of his father's Committee on the Public Lands.

^{34} Issue of Jan. 30, 1872.

^{35} "A National Park," *Helena Daily Herald*, Jan. 31, 1872.

^{36} The Memorial is printed under the title "The National Park—Memorial to Congress," *Helena Daily Herald*, Feb. 3, 1872. Hedges statement in 1905 (quoted in Matthews, p. 381) that the original copy of this memorial was given to the Montana Historical Society is incorrect, as the records of the Society reveal.

^{37} Item in the Bozeman *Avant Courier* (Montana), Feb. 1, 1872.

^{38} "The 'National Park' ", in the issue of Feb. 19, 1872.

^{39} "The New Wonderland," *Frank Leslie's Illustrated Newspaper*, Jan. 6, 1872, p. 263.

^{40} The newspaper account, titled "Natural Wonders," appeared as a full-page supplement to the issue of Jan. 13, 1872. Capt. John W. Barlow's report, co-authored with Capt. D. P. Heap, appeared as Sen. Ex. Doc. 66, 42d Cong., 2d sess., titled, *Report of a Reconnaissance of the Basin of the Upper Yellowstone in 1871*.

^{41} "The Wonders of the West—II. More About the Yellowstone," note the similarity of wording with Nettleton's letter to Hayden of Oct. 27, 1871. See note 4.

^{42} "On the Yellowstone Park," in *American Journal of Science and Arts* 103(April 1872): 294–97.

[43] See NA Microfilm No. 623, reel 2, frame 0379.

[44] The article in the *Enterprise* of Jan. 1, 1872. credits "The Hon. N. P. Langford of Montana, the leader of the famous Yellowstone Expedition of 1870, and several scientific and literary gentlemen" with the effort to have the Yellowstone region declared a national park, while the *Herald* (according to the Bozeman, Mont., *Avant Courier* of Jan. 18, 1872) stated: "The idea of declaring that marvelous tract of land in the canyon of the Yellowstone, and taking in the hot springs and geysers, a Government reservation, and hold it forever as a national park, is brought up again and being vigorously pressed by Hon. N. P. Langford, of Montana. Mr. Langford was the leader of the famous Yellowstone expedition of last year. . . ."

[45] RG–48, Records of the Department of Interior, Office of the Secretary, Lands and Railroads Division, Letters received, NA.

[46] *Ibid.*

[47] Barlow to Hayden, Jan. 17, 1871. NA Microfilm No. 623, reel 2, frame 0299.

[48] As recorded in *The Congressional Globe*, 42d Cong., 2d sess., pp. 1243–44, "Public Park on the Yellowstone River."

[49] The Delegate from Montana, William Horace Clagett, was in charge of the bill in the House, and he should have reported it out of committee. However, he was involved in the forwarding of several railroad bills of interest to Montanans, and in securing legislation for the removal of the Flathead Indians from their ancestral home in Montana's Bitterroot Valley (a locally popular measure). By his own statement, he was "at the other end of the Capitol" on this crucial day. See Langford, *Diary*, p. xxii.

[50] At this point Chairman Dunnell submitted Hayden's synopsis, which was "laid on the table and ordered to be printed" as of that date (Feb. 27, 1872). It appeared later as Report No. 26 (to accompany bill H.R. 764), House of Representatives, 42d Cong., 2d sess.

[51] The basis of the present "exclusive jurisdiction" held by the United States in Yellowstone National Park.

[52] Dawes did not go as far as Hayden had in his statement recommending reservation. The geologist had also drawn attention to the area's lack of mineral wealth, and to the preeminence of the Yellowstone geysers, worldwide, concluding with this statement: "The withdrawal of this tract, therefore, for sale or settlement takes nothing from the value of the public domain, and is of no pecuniary loss to the Government, but will be regarded by the entire civilized world as a step of progress and an honor to Congress and the nation." From the report cited in note 50.

[53] That the management of the Yosemite Grant by the State of California was less than satisfactory is evident in a comment that appeared in the *San Francisco Chronicle* of Feb. 29, 1870. "Perhaps it would have been as well, however, for the United States to keep these curiosities and take care of them."

[54] This was a perfectly logical argument, but evidently of no more concern to Dawes than it was to the ordinary frontiersman. Except for this remonstrance, there appears to have been no concern for Indian rights in the area. Probably, they were unaware that a portion of the proposed park overlapped the Crow Indian Reservation established May 7, 1868—an oversight which was not rectified by the Congress until Apr. 11, 1882.

[55] Despite the reference to the appendix, the remarks are not there. Perhaps they were considered unnecessary in view of the prompt passage of the bill.

[56] The Washington *Evening Star* (D.C.) noted this in its issue of Feb. 27, 1872.

[57] "Our National Park," in the issue of Feb. 28, 1872.

[58] While the *Herald* posed Clagett as more active than he was, it is true that his identification with the Republican Party brought the park movement essential support. His Democratic predecessor, James M. Cavanaugh, would not have had enough friends in Congress—nor his Democratic successor either—to carry it off.

[59] "The Yellowstone Park Bill," *The New York Times*, Feb. 29, 1872.

[60] *Original Statutes of the United States, 1871–1872, 2nd Session, 42nd Congress*, part I, ch. xxiv. AN ACT to set apart a certain tract of land lying near the headwaters of the Yellowstone River as a public park (c. 24, 17 STAT., 32 and 33).

[61] The text presented here is taken from the engrossed copy bearing the President's

signature. Most printed copies vary slightly from this due to the presence of typographical errors and changes in punctuation.

[62] This item, quoted in the *Helena Daily Herald* of Mar. 1, 1872, was probably taken from the *Gazette* of the previous day (the available file of that newspaper is incomplete).

[63] "Our National Park," in the issue of Mar. 7, 1872.

[64] "The Park Again," in the issue of Mar. 9, 1872.

[65] *The Nation* 14, No. 349 (Mar. 7, 1872): 153.

[66] "Bound for the Mammoth Hot Springs," Bozeman *Avant Courier*, Feb. 29, 1872.

[67] Quoted by the Deer Lodge *New North-West*, Mar. 16, 1872, in an article titled "The Splendors of the West."

1. *William Clark's manuscript map, 1806–11. Courtesy Yale University.*

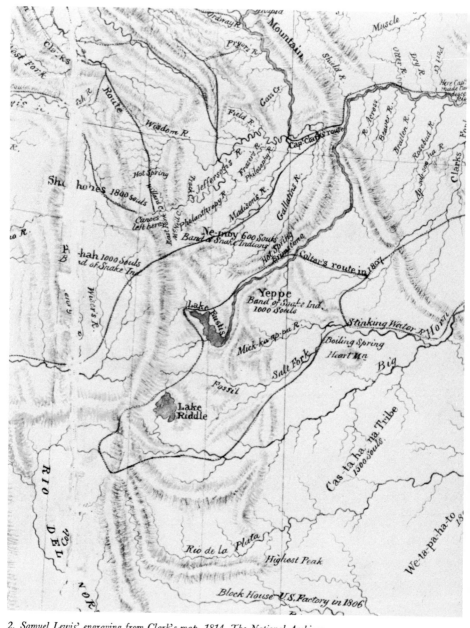

2. *Samuel Lewis' engraving from Clark's map, 1814. The National Archives.*

186

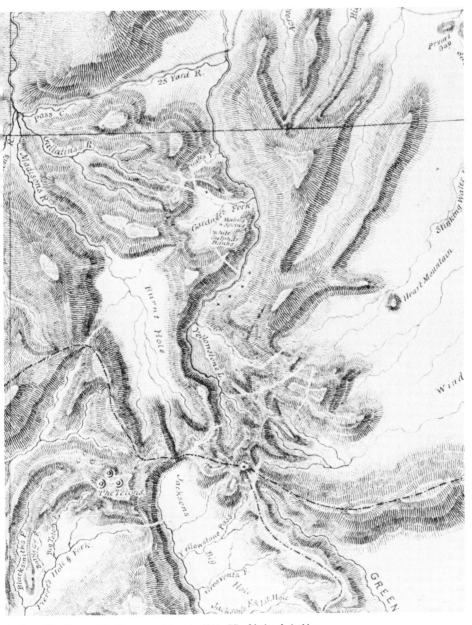

3. *Capt. Washington Hood's manuscript map, 1839. The National Archives.*

187

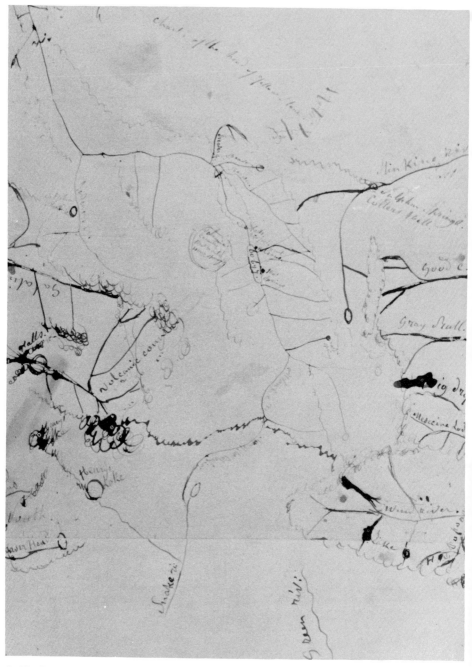

4. The Bridger-DeSmet manuscript map, 1851. Courtesy St. Louis University.

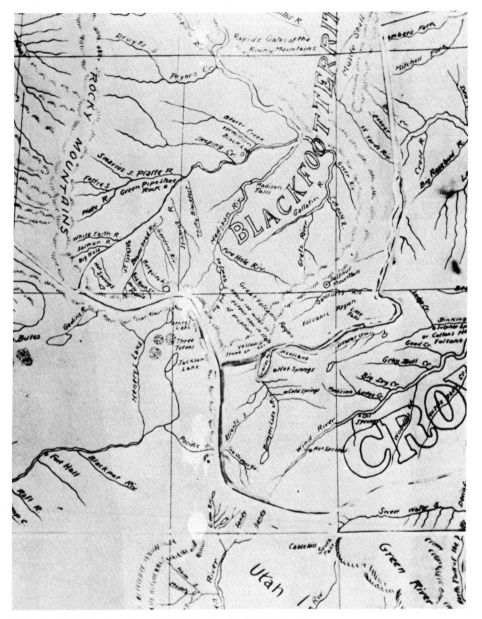

5. *Father DeSmet's manuscript map, 1851. Courtesy St. Louis University.*

6. Capt. William F. Raynold's manuscript map, 1860. The National Archives.

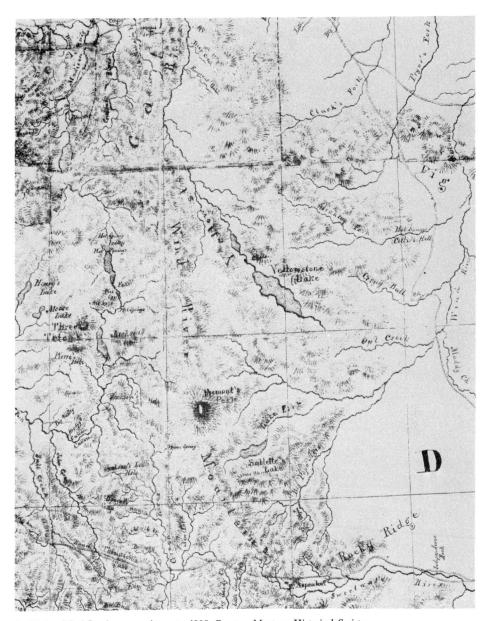

7. Walter W. deLacy's manuscript map, 1865. Courtesy Montana Historical Society.

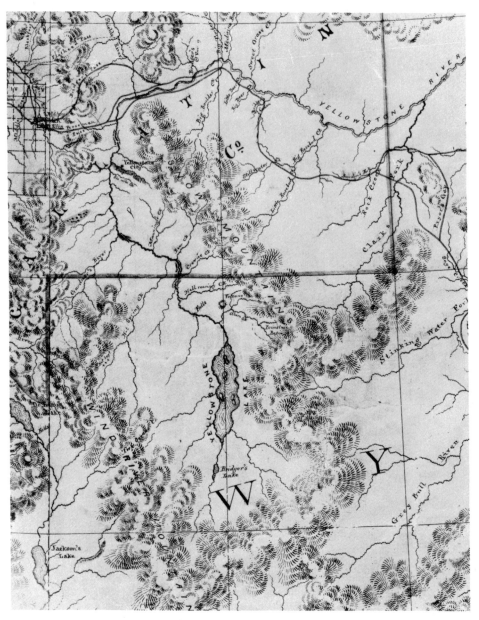

8. General Land Office manuscript map (Meredith's), 1869. The National Archives.

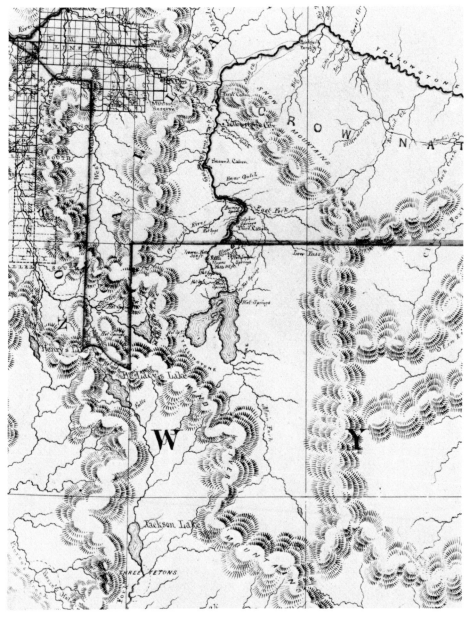

9. General Land Office manuscript map (Washburn), 1869. The National Archives.

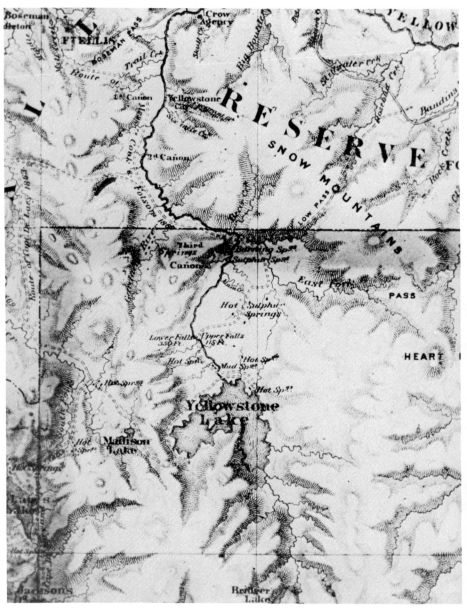

10. *The deLacy Map, ed. of 1870. The Library of Congress.*

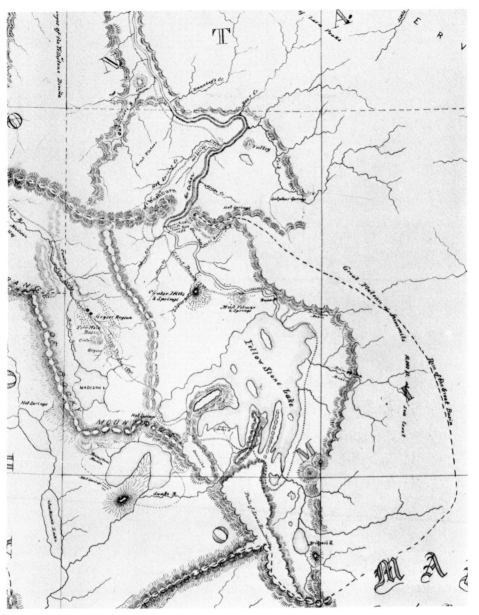

11. *Lt. Gustavus C. Doane's manuscript map, 1870. The National Archives.*

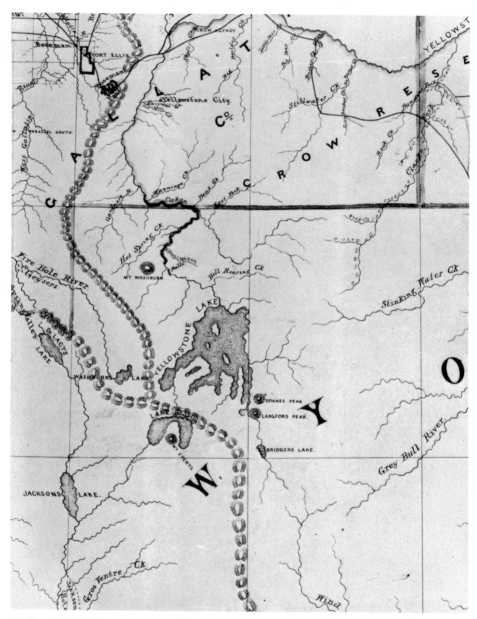

12. General Land Office manuscript map (Blaine), 1871. The National Archives.

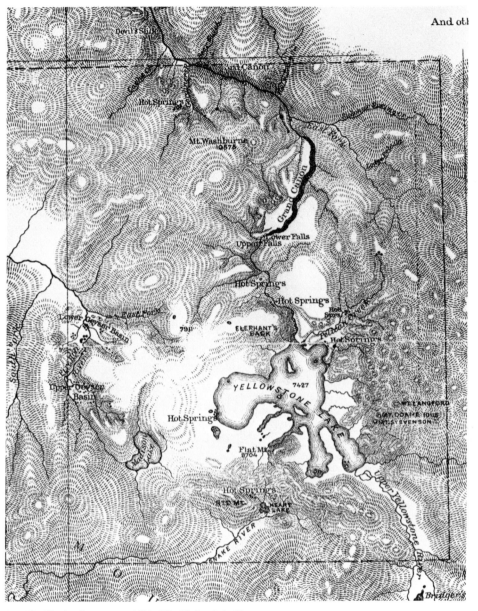

13. *The Hayden Survey map, 1871. The National Archives.*

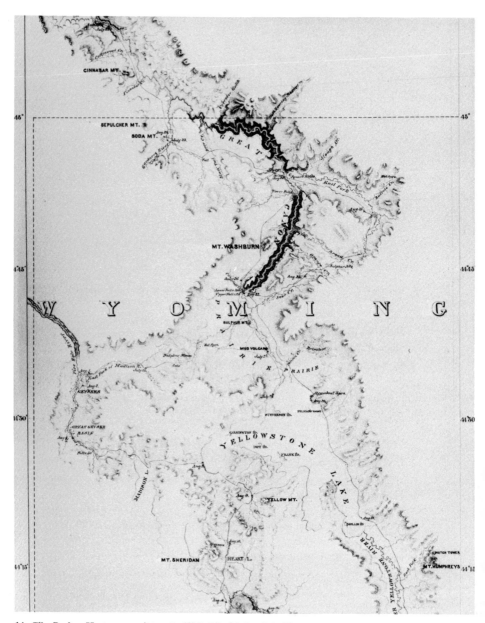

14. The Barlow-Heap manuscript map, 1871. The National Archives.

Bibliography

I. MANUSCRIPTS

A. National Archives, Washington, D.C.

1. Records of the Geological and Geographical Survey of the Territories ("Hayden Survey"), Record Group 57. Letters Received 1867–79. Reproduced as National Archives Microfilm Publication M623.

   Baird, Spencer, to F. V. Hayden. Oct. 29, Nov. 10, 1870; June 16, 1871 (M623, roll 2, frames 42, 47, 119).

   Barlow, John W., to F. V. Hayden. June 3, June 17, Nov. 9, 1871; Jan. 13, Jan. 17, 1872 (M623, roll 2, frames 117–8, 129–30, 170–1, 293–4, 299–300).

   Belknap, William H., to Commanding Officers of Posts on Route of the Geological Explorations by Professor Hayden. Mar. 25, 1871 (M623, roll 14, frame 319).

   Crofutt, George A., to F. V. Hayden. Feb. 19, 1872 (M623, roll 2, frame 379).

   Gildess, R. W., to F. V. Hayden. Sept. 11, 1871 (M623, roll 2, frames 143–4).

   Hancock, Winfield S., to F. V. Hayden. May 26, 1871 (M623, roll 14, frames 375–6).

   Hayden, F. V., to Lt. Gen. P. H. Sheridan. May 27, 1871 (M623, roll 14, frame 339); to Columbus Delano, June 8, July 18, Aug. 8, Aug. 28, Sept. 9, 1871 (not on microfilm).

   Heap, David P., to F. V. Hayden. Nov. 7, 1871 (M623, roll 2, frame 167).

   Hildegarth, J. E., to F. V. Hayden. Oct. 30, 1871 (M623, roll 2, frames 160–1).

   Jackson, William H., to F. V. Hayden. Aug. 1, 1870 (not on microfilm).

   Moran, Thomas, to F. V. Hayden. Mar. 11, 1872 (M623, roll 2, frames 468–70).

   Nettleton, A. B., to F. V. Hayden. June 7, June 16, Oct. 27, 1871 (M623, roll 2, frames 120–2, 127–8, 155).

   Stevenson, James, to Prof. J. D. Butler. Feb. 28, 1886 (not on microfilm).

2. Records of the U.S. Army Continental Commands, Record Group 393.
   a. Letters Received, Fort Ellis, Mont.
      Camp, E. M., to Gen. Alfred Sully. July 5, 1870.
      Gibbon, John, to Maj. B. M. Baker. July 1, 1870.
      Green, O. D., to Col. John Gibbon (telegram). Nov. 16, 1870.
      Hancock, Winfield S., to Col. John Gibbon (telegram). Aug. 15, 1870.

    b. Letters Received, District of Montana.
       Gibbon, John, to Gen. H. D. Washburn (telegram). Aug. 15, 1870.

3. Records of the Office of the Secretary of the Interior, Record Group 48.
    a. Letters Sent, Patents and Miscellaneous Division.
       Delano, Columbus, to F. V. Hayden. May, 1871. (vol. 6.)
    b. Letters Received, Lands and Railroads Division.
       Dunnell, Mark H., to the Secretary of the Interior. Jan. 27, 1872.

4. Records of the U.S. House of Representatives, Record Group 233.
    42d Congress, 2d session. Original House Bills. House Bill 764.
    "Original Statutes of the United States, 1871–72, 2d session, 42d Congress,"
    part I, ch. xxiv.

B. Library of Congress, Washington, D.C.

Wilkinson, James, to Thomas Jefferson. Oct. 12, 1805. Papers of Thomas Jefferson.

C. National Gallery of Art, Washington, D.C.

Accession files.

D. Yellowstone National Park.

1. Park Archives.
   Folsom, David E., to Capt. George L. Anderson. Apr. 28, 1894. Letters received.
   Horr, H. R., to Superintendent D. W. Wear. July 6, 1885. Document 1049.
   Documents 162–3.

2. Park Reference Library.
   Cook, Charles W. "Remarks of C. W. Cook, Last Survivor of the Original
   Explorers of the Yellowstone Park Region, on the Occasion of His Second
   Visit to the Park in 53 years, During the Celebration of the Park's Golden
   Anniversary." Official transcript, July 14, 1922.
   Gourley, James A. "A Reminiscence of James A. Gourley, Prospector of 1870."
   Recorded Mar. 28, 1929.
   Joyner, Newell. "Notes Collected by Newell Joyner Concerning Various
   Explorers." Compiled circa 1930.
   Langford, Nathaniel P. Text of a lecture given during the winter of 1870–71.
   Original MS.
   ———. Untitled text of a lecture on Montana Territory, to be presented in the
   interest of the Northern Pacific Railway, 1871. Original MS.
   Orton, A. W. "Some Scattered Thoughts on the Early Life of N. P. Langford."
   September 1966.
   Potts, Daniel T., to Robert Potts. July 8, 1827. Original MS.

3. Park Files.
   Burlingame, Merrill G., to Librarian. Feb. 15, 1970.
   Decker, A., to "Manager, Yellowstone Park." June 20, 1931.
   Doubt, Dorothea G., to "The Secretary of the Museum." Sept. 7, 1933.
   Press release. "Art and Artists in the National Parks." Dec. 22, 1936.

E. Montana Historical Society, Helena.

Doane, Gustavus C., to Gen. H. D. Washburn. Aug. 12, 1870. Hauser Papers.
Gillette, Warren C. "Diary . . . Aug. 7 to Sept. 27, 1870."
Healy, John. Papers.
Hedges, Cornelius. Diary, Oct. 20 to 29, 1865.
———. "Diary . . . June 24, 1870 to Oct. 16, 1871."
———. Papers.
Simmons, A. J., to S. T. Hauser. Nov. 2, 1868. Hauser Papers.

F. Montana State University Library, Bozeman.

   Doane, Gustavus C. "Official Report of the Washburn-Langford-Doane Expedition into the Upper Yellowstone in 1870." Original MS, Dec. 15, 1870.

G. Minnesota Historical Society, St. Paul.

   1. Northern Pacific Railroad Papers. Secretary, Series 2, Correspondence unregistered.
   Canfield, Thomas H., to "Dear Governor" [Smith]. Oct. 25, 1869. Box 2.
   Cooke, Jay & Co. Circular of Oct. 20, 1869. Box 2.
   Everts, Truman C., to J. Gregory Smith. Jan. 13, 1872. Box 4.
   Sexton, Jno. W., to Ja. G. Dudley (telegram). Nov. 14, 1871. Box 3.
   Spaulding, G. S., to William R. Marshall, May 30, 1870, and to J. Gregory Smith, May 30, 1870. Box 2.
   Wilkeson, Samuel to "Dear Governor" [Smith]. n.d. (filed as Mar. 19, 1870); Mar. 27, Apr. 20, 1870. Box 2.
   Woodbridge, F. E., to J. Gregory Smith. July 8, 1870. Box 3.

   2. ——. Letter Book of the President, vol. 1.
   Lamb, Henry L., to J. Gregory Smith. Feb. 14, 1871. p. 156.

   3. Langford Family Papers, 1702–1942.
   Langford, Nathaniel P. Diary, 1869–71. Box 1, vol. 2.

H. Pennsylvania Historical Society, Philadelphia. Jay Cooke Papers.

   Cooke, Henry D., to Jay Cooke. June 2, 1870.
   Cooke, Jay, to Frederick Billings. Oct. 2, 1871.
   ——. to William R. Marshall, Jan. 19, Feb. 7, 1870.
   ——. to W. Milner Roberts. Oct. 30, 1871.
   Langford, Nathaniel P., to Jay Cooke. Jan. 24, Jan. 29, Mar. 4, Mar. 16, 1871.
   Roberts, W. Milner, to Jay Cooke (telegram). Nov. 21, 1871.
   Wilkeson, Samuel, to Jay Cooke. Oct. 10, 1870.

I. Church Historian's Office, Salt Lake City.

   Church of Jesus Christ of Latter-Day Saints. "Journal History."

J. Beinecke Library, Yale University, New Haven. Coe Collection.

   Hauser, Samuel T. "Diary . . . Aug. 17 to Sept. 4, 1870." MS No. 249.
   Henderson, A. B. "Journal of the Yellowstone Expedition of 1866 Under Captain Jeff Standifer . . . Also the Diaries Kept by Henderson Durng his Prospecting Journeys in the Snake, Wind River and Yellowstone Country During the years 1866–72." MS No. 452.
   Russell, Osborne. "Journal of a Trapper or Nine Years Residence among the Rocky Mountains Between the Years of 1834 and 1843 . . ." MS No. 411.

K. Gilcrease Museum, Tulsa.

   Thomas Moran Papers.

L. Henry E. Huntington Library, San Marino. P. W. Norris Collection (HM 506).

   Norris, Philetus W. "The Great West . . . Letter No. 4, Hell Gate, Montana Ty., Aug. 16th, 1870." Clipped from the Norris, Mich., *Suburban*, n.d. Scrapbook No. 1.
   ——. Scrapbook No. 3.
   ——. "Meanderings of a Mountaineer, or, The Journals and Musings (or storys)

of a Rambler over Prairie (or Mountain) and Plain." MS prepared about 1885 from newspaper clippings of Norris' adventures, 1870–75.

M. Other.

Taylor, Chloe, to her daughter. May 3, 1871. Original in possession of James Taylor Dunn, former Librarian, Minnesota Historical Society, St. Paul.

II. MAPS

Barlow, John W., and David P. Heap. "Sketch of the Yellowstone Lake and the Valley of the Upper Yellowstone River." Drawn by Emil Heubach, Feb. 28, 1872. Headquarters map file, Q 181, records of the Office of the Chief of Engineers, Record Group 77, National Archives.

Blaine, John E. "Map of the Territory of Montana to Accompany the Report of the Surveyor General . . . 1871." Old map file, Mont. 5, Records of the Bureau of Land Management, Record Group 49, National Archives.

Clark, William. "A Map of Part of the Continent of North America . . . Compiled from the information of the best informed travellers through that quarter of the Globe . . ." MS no. 303–IV, Coe Collection, Beinecke Library, Yale University.

deLacy, Walter W. "Map of the Territory of Montana with Portions of the Adjoining Territories, Showing the Gulch or Placer diggings actually worked and districts where Quartz (Gold & Silver) Lodes have been discovered up to January 1865." Montana State Historical Society, Helena.

———. *Map of the Territory of Montana with Portions of the Adjoining Territories* . . . St. Louis: Hutawa; New York: Rae; and Baltimore: Fridenwald, 1865.

———. "Map of the Territory of Montana with Portions of the Adjoining Territories . . . 1866." Montana State Historical Society, Helena.

———. *Map of the Territory of Montana, with Portions of the Adjoining Territories.* New York: G. W. & C. B. Colton, 1870.

DeSmet, Pierre-Jean. "Chart of the Head of Yellow Stone." Drawn by James Bridger. Jesuit Archives, Missouri Province. IX: Desmetiana. C–B: Atlas, No. 10. St. Louis University.

———. [Untitled map]. Jesuit Archives, Missouri Province. IX: DeSmetiana. C–B: Atlas, No. 5, St. Louis University.

Doane, Gustavus C. "Map of the Route of the Yellowstone Expedition, Escort Commanded by Lieut. G. C. Doane, U.S.A., September 1870." Headquarters map file, Q 329–30, Records of the Office of the Chief of Engineers, Record Group 77, National Archives.

Hayden, Ferdinand V. "Yellowstone National Park." Compiled and drawn by E. Hergesheimer, 1871. Records of the Geological and Geographical Survey of the Territories, Record Group 57, National Archives.

Hood, Washington. "Map exhibiting the practicable passes of the Rocky Mountains; together with the Topographical features of the country adjacent to the headwaters of the Missouri, Yellowstone, Salmon, Lewis and Colorado Rivers . . . 1839." Headquarters map file, U.S. 110, Records of the Office of the Chief of Engineers, Record Group 77, National Archives.

Raynolds, William F. "U.S. War Department Map of the Yellowstone and Missouri Rivers and their Tributaries explored by Capt. W. F. Raynolds Topl. Engrs. and 1st Lt. H. E. Maynardier 10th Infy, Assistant, 1859–60, to accompany a report to the Bureau of Topographical Engineers, Lt. Col. Bache in Charge." Headquarters map file, Q 106–1, Records of the Office of the Chief of Engineers, Record Group 77, National Archives.

Surveyor General of Montana. "Map of the Territory of Montana to Accompany the Report of the Surveyor General . . . 1869." Old map file, Mont. 2, Records of the Bureau of Land Management, Record Group 49, National Archives.

Washburn, Henry D. "Route of Washburn's party 1870, being a tracing of map made to accompany Washburn's report to Dept. of Interior." Park Reference Library, Yellowstone National Park.

III. PRINTED DOCUMENTS

Allen, E. T., and Arthur L. Day. *Hot Springs of the Yellowstone National Park.* Carnegie Institution Pub. No. 466. Washington, 1935.

Barlow, John W., and David P. Heap. *Report of a Reconnaissance of the Basin of the Upper Yellowstone in 1871.* Senate Executive Documents, 42d Cong., 2d Sess., No. 66 (1872).

Carter, Clarence E., ed. *The Territorial Papers of the United States 13.* Washington, 1948.

Congressional Globe. 42d Cong., 2d Sess., 1871–72.

Congressional Record. 47th Cong., 2d Sess., 1882–83.

Cramton, Louis C. *Early History of Yellowstone National Park and Its Relation to National Park Policies.* Washington, 1932.

Doane, Gustavus C. *Report of Lieutenant Gustavus C. Doane upon the So-called Yellowstone Expedition of 1870.* Senate Executive Documents, 41st Cong., 3d Sess., No. 51 (1871).

Hayden, Ferdinand V. *Preliminary Report of the United States Geological Survey of Montana and Portions of Adjoining Territories, Being a Fifth Annual Report of Progress.* Washington, 1872.

——. *Sixth Annual Report of the United States Geological Survey of the Territories . . . for the Year 1872.* Washington, 1873.

——. *Twelfth Annual Report of the United States Geological and Geographical Survey of the Territories . . . for the Year 1878.* Washington, 1883.

Jones, William A. *Report upon the Reconnaissance of Northwestern Wyoming, including Yellowstone National Park, Made in the Summer of 1873.* Washington, 1875.

Mullan, John. *Report on the Construction of a Military Road from Walla Walla to Fort Benton.* Washington, 1863.

Norris, Philetus W. *Report upon the Yellowstone National Park to the Secretary of the Interior, for the Year 1878.* Washington, 1879.

——. *Annual Report of the Superintendent of the Yellowstone National Park, to the Secretary of the Interior, for the Year 1880.* Washington, 1881.

——. *Fifth Annual Report of the Superintendent of the Yellowstone National Park* [1881]. Washington, 1881.

Raymond, Rossiter W. *Mineral Resources of the States and Territories.* Washington, 1869.

Raynolds, William F. *The Report of Brevet Brigadier General W. F. Raynolds on the Exploration of the Yellowstone and the Country Drained by That River.* Senate Executive Documents, 40th Cong., 1st Sess., No. 77 (1868).

United States. Statutes at Large. 13 Stat. 325 (Act of June 30, 1864).

United States Congress. House of Representatives. Reports of Committees, 42d Cong., 2d Sess., No. 26 (1872).

——. House Executive Documents, 45th Cong., 2d Sess., No. 75 (1878).

IV. NEWSPAPER ARTICLES

Anonymous, by newspaper.

Avant Courier (Bozeman, Mont.)
"The Yellowstone Country." Sept. 13, 1871.
"Montana News." Sept. 13, 1871.
"Hon. N. P. Langford . . ." Nov. 9, 1871.
"The Cataracts and Geysers of the Upper Yellowstone—Why They Should be Given in Perpetuity to Montana." Dec. 7, 1871.
[Item from *St. Joe Herald*, Mo.]. Jan. 18, 1872.
"Harry B. Horr & James C. McCartney . . ." Feb. 1, 1872.
"Bound for the Mammoth Hot Springs." Feb. 29, 1872.
"Our National Park." Mar. 7, 1872.
"Harry Horr's Hot Spring Claim." Jan. 11, 1883.

Daily Morning Chronicle (Washington, D.C.)
"Yellowstone River." Jan. 20, 1871.
"A National Park for Washington." Jan. 20, 1871.

Daily Oregonian (Portland, Oreg.)
"The Great Falls of the Yellowstone." Sept. 29, 1870.

Daily Territorial Enterprise (Virginia City, Nev.)

"The Hon. N. P. Langford . . ." Jan. 1, 1872.

Deseret Evening News (Salt Lake City, Utah)

"Exploring Expedition." Sept. 27, 1870.

Evening Star (Washington, D.C.)

[Senator Pomeroy's bill—S. 392]. Dec. 18, 1871.

"Mr. Pomeroy Called up the bill . . ." Jan. 30, 1871.

"The following Senate bills . . ." Feb. 27, 1872.

Frank Leslie's Illustrated Newspaper

"The New Wonderland." Jan. 6, 1872.

Frontier Index (Fort Sanders, D. T.)

"The Greatest Bear Story Yet." Mar. 6, 1868.

Frontier Index (Green River, D. T.)

"The Great Shoshone Falls of Snake River." Aug. 21, 1868.

Frontier Index (Julesburg, Nebr.)

"Remarkable Discovery." July 26, 1867.

Frontier Index (Laramie, D. T.)

"California." May 5, 1868.

"Brevities Communicated from the Sanotum of the American Libertarian." June 16, 1868.

Helena Daily Herald (Montana)

"Truman C. Everts." Apr. 20, 1870.

"The Yellowstone Expedition." Aug. 13, 1870.

"Departure of the Expedition." Aug. 18, 1870.

"The Yellowstone Expedition." Aug. 24, 1870.

"The Yellowstone Expedition." Sept. 26, 1870.

"Interesting Data of the Trip, from Notes Furnished by Hon. N. P. Langford." Sept. 26, 1870.

"The Yellowstone Expedition." Sept. 27, 1870.

"Arrival of Warren C. Gillette, of the Yellowstone Expedition." Oct. 3, 1870.

"The Lost Man—$600 Reward Offered." Oct. 6, 1870.

"The Long-Lost Found." Oct. 21, 1870.

"More about Mr. Everts." Oct. 22, 1870.

"The Finding of Hon. T. C. Everts." Oct. 26, 1870.

"The Lost and Found." Oct. 28, 1870.

"Letter from Mr. Everts." Oct. 28, 1870.

"Lectures—Hon. N. P. Langford." Nov. 11, 1870.

"Our Washington Letter." Nov. 14, 1870.

"The Yellowstone Banquet." Nov. 14, 1870.

"A Grand Lecture." Nov. 17, 1870.

"Virginia City Correspondence." Nov. 26, 1870.

"N. P. Langford of Montana." Jan. 26, 1871.

"Around Montana." July 10, 1871.

"Exploration of the Yellowstone." Sept. 23, 1871.

"A National Park." Jan. 31, 1872.

"The National Park—Memorial to Congress." Feb. 3, 1872.

"Our National Park." Feb. 28, 1872.

"Our National Park." Mar. 1, 1872.

Helena Weekly Herald (Montana)

"Interesting from the Yellowstone." Apr. 11, 1867.

"The Headwaters of the Yellowstone." Dec. 12, 1867.

"Good Story." Dec. 26, 1867.

"Expedition to the Yellowstone." July 29, 1869.

Idaho Democrat (Boise City)

"Wonders of America." July 8, 1871.

Livingston Enterprise (Montana)
"The Name Yellowstone." Oct. 23, 1883.

Montana Post (Virginia City)
"The Scenery of the Yosemite . . ." July 14, 1866.
"Organized." June 29, 1867.
"From Emigrant Gulch." Aug. 17, 1867.
"The Upper Yellowstone." Aug. 24, 1867.
"The Upper Yellowstone." Aug. 31, 1867.

New North-West (Deer Lodge, Mont.)
"Yellowstone Party Heard From." Sept. 23, 1870.
"Mr. T. C. Everts . . ." Sept. 30, 1870.
"The Yellowstone Wonders." Oct. 21, 1870.
"Hon. Wm. H. Clagett, Delegate . . ." Sept. 9, 1871.
"Notes on the Way to Wonderland." Oct. 14, 1871.
"Ohio Papers State . . ." Oct. 14, 1871.
"Geyser Land." Dec. 23, 1871.
"The Park Again." Mar. 9, 1872.
"The Splendors of the West." Mar. 16, 1872.

New York Herald
"Wonders of Montana." Jan. 22, 1871.

New York Times
"The Yellowstone Expedition." Oct. 14, 1870.
"Travels in Montana." Jan. 22, 1871.
"The Yellowstone Expedition." Sept. 18, 1871.
"The New Wonderland." Oct. 23, 1871.
"The Yellowstone Park Bill." Feb. 29, 1872.

New York Tribune
"Wonders of Montana." Jan. 23, 1871.

Niles Register (Philadelphia, Pa.)
"From the West." Oct. 6, 1827.

Philadelphia Gazette and Daily Advertizer (Pennsylvania)
"Communicated for the . . ." Sept. 27, 1827.

Pioneer Press (St. Paul, Minn.)
"Inauguration of the Northern Pacific Railroad." Feb. 16, 1870.
"Montana Geysers." Oct. 9, 1870.
"The Yellowstone Expedition." Oct. 14, 1870.

Press (Philadelphia, Pa.)
"The Northern Pacific Railway." Mar. 19, 1870.

Rocky Mountain Daily Gazette (Helena, Mont.)
"Return of the . . . Party." Sept. 24, 1870.
"The Mineral Springs of the Yellowstone—Wonderful Health Restoring Qualities."
July 24, 1871.

Rocky Mountain News (Denver, Colo.)
"A Montana Romance." Oct. 8, 1870.

Rocky Mountain Weekly Gazette (Helena, Mont.)
"The National Park." Feb. 19, 1872.

St. Louis Review (Missouri)
"Former St. Charles Priest Helped Found Yellowstone." June 21, 1963.

San Francisco Chronicle
"Yosemite and the Big Trees." Feb. 29, 1872.

Virginia City Tri-Weekly Post (Montana)
"Niagara Eclipsed." Feb. 4, 1868.

Wasp (Nauvoo, Ill.)

"Rocky Mountain Geysers." Aug. 13, 1842.

Weekly Independent (Helena, Mont.)

"Visit to the Yellowstone Geysers 41 Years Ago." May 1, 1874.

Signed

Barlow, John W. "Natural Wonders." *Chicago Evening Journal*, Jan. 13, 1872.

Clawson, C. C. "Notes on the Way to Wonderland, or, a Ride to the Infernal Regions." *New North-West* (Deer Lodge, Mont.), Sept. 9, 1871, to Feb. 24, 1872.

Davis, John C. "Yellowstone Park." *Courier-Journal* (Louisville, Ky.), Apr. 13, 1884.

Elliott, Henry. "Great Soda Mountain and Jupiter's Baths, in the Yellowstone Region." *Frank Leslie's Illustrated Newspaper*, Sept. 31, 1871.

Fisher, James. "The Idea of a Wilderness." *Listener* (London), Apr. 26, 1962.

Hedges, Cornelius. "Mount Everts." *Helena Daily Herald* (Mont.), Oct. 8, 1870.

——. "The Great Falls of the Yellowstone, A Graphic Picture of Their Grandeur and Beauty." *Helena Daily Herald*, Oct. 15, 1870.

——. "Hell-Broth Springs." *Helena Daily Herald*, Oct. 19, 1870.

——. "From Montana." *Springfield Weekly Republican* (Mass.), Oct. 21, 1870.

——. "Pictures of the Yellowstone Country—Sulphur Mountain and Mud Volcano." *Helena Daily Herald*, Oct. 27, 1870.

——. "Yellowstone Lake." *Helena Daily Herald*, Nov. 9, 1870.

——. "Yellowstone Lake." *Independence Conservative* (Iowa), Dec. 7, 1870.

Sunderlee, Charles R. "A Thrilling Event on the Yellowstone." *Helena Daily Herald*, May 18, 1870.

Trumbull, Walter. "Yellowstone Expedition." *Rocky Mountain Weekly Gazette* (Helena, Mont.), Oct. 3, 1870.

——. "Yellowstone Papers—No. 1." *Rocky Mountain Daily Gazette* (Helena, Mont.), Oct. 18, 1870.

——. "Yellowstone Papers—No. 2." *Rocky Mountain Daily Gazette*, Oct. 19, 1870.

——. "Yellowstone Papers." *Rocky Mountain Weekly Gazette*, Oct. 24, 31, 1870.

V. PERIODICALS

American Forests 41 (Sept. 1935): 416–539 [Conservation series].

Cook, Charles W. "The Valley of the Upper Yellowstone." *Western Monthly* 4 (July 1870): 60–7.

——. "Preliminary Statement to the Cook-Folsom Diary." *Haynes Bulletin* (December 1922): 7–8.

——. "Reconstructed Diary of the Cook-Folsom Expedition in 1869 to the Yellowstone Region." *Haynes Bulletin* (January, February, May 1923): 1 & 9, 8, 7.

Cooper, Suzanne T. "Summertime Revisited." *American Heritage* 14 (June 1963): 35–49.

deLacy, Walter W. "A Trip up the South Snake River in 1863." *Contributions to the Historical Society of Montana* 1 (1876): 113–43.

Everts, Truman C. "Thirty-seven Days of Peril." *Scribner's Monthly* 3 (November 1871): 1–17.

——. "Thirty-seven Days of Peril." *Contributions to the Historical Society of Montana* 5 (1904): 395–427.

Ferris, Warren Angus. "Rocky Mountain Geysers." *Western Literary Messenger* 2 (July 13, 1842): 12–3.

——. "Life in the Rocky Mountains." *Western Literary Messenger* 3 (Jan. 6, 1844): 196.

Folsom, David E. "The Folsom-Cook Exploration of the Upper Yellowstone in the Year 1869." *Contributions to the Historical Society of Montana* 5 (1904): 349–94.

Haines, Aubrey L. "The Bridge That Jack Built." *Yellowstone Nature Notes* 21 (January–February 1947): 1–4.

——. "McGuirk's Medicinal Springs." *Yellowstone Nature Notes* 21 (March–April 1947): 22–3.

——, ed. "William Peterson's Reminiscences." *The Yellowstone Interpreter* 2 (September–October 1964): 55–61.

Hayden, Ferdinand V. "The Yellowstone National Park." *The American Journal of Science and Arts* 3 (April 1872): 294–7.

——. "Wonders of the West—II; More About the Yellowstone." *Scribner's Monthly* 3 (February 1872): 388–96.

Hedges, Cornelius. "An Account of a Trip to Fort Benton in October 1865, with Acting Governor Thomas F. Meagher to Treat with the Blackfeet Indians." *Rocky Mountain Magazine* 1 (November 1900): 155–8.

——. "Journal of Judge Cornelius Hedges." *Contributions to the Historical Society of Montana* 5 (1904): 370–94.

Huth, Hans. "Yosemite: the Story of an Idea." *Sierra Club Bulletin* 33 (March 1948): 47–78.

Jashemski, Wilhelmina. "Pompeii." *Natural History* 73 (December 1964): 30–41.

Kuppens, Francis Xavier. "The Origin of the Yellowstone National Park." *The Woodstock Letters* 26 (1897): 400–2.

——. "Thomas Francis Meagher, Montana Pioneer." *Mid-America, An Historical Review* 14 (October 1931): 127–40.

——. "On the Origin of the Yellowstone National Park." *The Jesuit Bulletin* 41 (October 1962): 6–7, 14.

Langford, Nathaniel P. "Wonders of the Yellowstone." *Scribner's Monthly* 2 (May–June 1871): 113–28.

Matthews, Albert. "The Word Park in the United States." *Publications of the Colonial Society of Massachusetts* 8 (April 1904): 373–99.

Mueller, Oscar O. "Yellowstone Map Drawn in 1870 Shows Cook & Folsom Route of 1869." *Haynes Bulletin* (March 1924): 2–3.

Munson, Lyman E. "Pioneer Life in Montana." *Contributions to the Historical Society of Montana* 5 (1904): 200–34.

Nash, Roderick. "The American Wilderness in Historical Perspective." *Forest History* 6 (winter 1963): 2–13.

"Notes." *The Nation* 14 (Mar. 7, 1872): 153.

[Potts, Daniel T.]. "Early Yellowstone and Western Experiences." *Yellowstone Nature Notes* 21 (September–October 1947): 49–56.

Trumbull, Walter. "The Washburn Yellowstone Expedition." *Overland Monthly* 6 (May–June 1871): 431–7, 489–96.

Thoreau, Henry David. "Chesuncook." *The Atlantic Monthly* 2 (August 1858): 305–17.

Wheeler, Olin D. "The Late James Gemmell." *Contributions to the Historical Society of Montana* 2 (1896): 331–6.

——. "James W. Taylor: A Biographical Sketch." *Minnesota Historical Bulletin* 1 (Nov. 4, 1915).

VI. BOOKS, PAMPHLETS, ESSAYS

Alter, J. Cecil. *James Bridger, Trapper, Frontiersman, Scout and Guide.* Columbus, Ohio, 1951.

Black, Walter J. *The Best of Ralph Waldo Emerson.* New York, 1941.

Camp, Charles L., ed. *James Clyman, American Frontiersman, 1792–1881.* San Francisco, 1928.

Carruth, Gordon, ed. *Encyclopedia of American Facts and Dates.* 2d ed. New York, 1959.

Catlin, George. *Letters and Notes on the Manners, Customs, and Conditions of the North American Indians* 1. New York, 1842.

Chittenden, Hiram M. *The American Fur Trade of the Far West* 3. New York, 1902.

——. *The Yellowstone National Park.* Cincinnati, 1895.

——. *The Yellowstone National Park.* Ed. by Richard Bartlett. Norman, Okla., 1964.

Chittenden, Hiram M., and Alfred T. Richards, eds. *Life, Letters and Travels of Father Pierre-Jean DeSmet, S. J., 1801–1873.*

Clark, Ella E. *Indian Legends from the Northern Rockies.* Norman, Okla., 1966.

Emerson, Ralph Waldo. "Nature" (1844). In *Harvard Classics* 5. New York, 1910.

Everts, Truman C. *Thirty-seven Days of Peril; A Narrative of the Early Days of the Yellowstone.* San Francisco, 1923.

Ferris, Warren Angus. *Life in the Rocky Mountains, 1830–1835.* Ed. by Auerback & Alter. Salt Lake City, 1940.

——. *Life in the Rocky Mountains, 1830–1835.* Ed. by P. C. Phillips. Denver, 1940.

Gerrish, Theodore. *Life in the World's Wonderland.* Biddeford, Maine, 1887.

Goetzmann, William H. *Exploration and Empire.* New York, 1966.

Gunnison, J. W. *The Mormons, or, Latter-Day Saints.* Philadelphia, 1852.

Haines, Aubrey L., ed. *The Valley of the Upper Yellowstone.* Norman, Okla., 1965.

Hafen, LeRoy R. *Broken Hand: The Life Story of Thomas Fitzpatrick, Chief of the Mountain Men.* Denver, 1931.

——, ed. *The Mountain Men and The Fur Trade of the Far West* 2. Glendale, Calif., 1965.

Hamilton, William T. *My Sixty Years on the Plains.* Columbus, Ohio, 1951.

Hampton, H. Duane. *How the U.S. Cavalry Saved Our National Parks.* Bloomington and London, 1971.

Humphreville, James L. *Twenty Years Among the Hostile Indians.* New York, 1903.

Kelley, William D. *The New Northwest.* An address presented to the American Academy of Music, Philadelphia, June 12, 1871. Published as a pamphlet by D. Wolfe. Copy in the James Hill Library, St. Paul, Minn.

Kennerly, William Clark. *Persimmon Hill: A Narrative of Old St. Louis.* Norman, Okla., 1948.

Langford, Nathaniel P. *Diary of the Washburn Expedition to the Yellowstone and Firehole Rivers in the Year 1870.* St. Paul, 1905.

———, ed. *The Folsom-Cook Explorations of the Upper Yellowstone, 1869.* St. Paul, 1894.

Laut, Agnes. *Conquest of the Great Northwest.* New York, 1908.

Leeson, M. A., ed. *History of Montana, 1739–1885.* Chicago, 1885.

Lewis, Meriwether, and William Clark. *History of the Expedition under the Command of Captains Lewis and Clark.* 2 vols. Prepared by Nicholas Biddle and Paul Allen. Philadelphia, 1814.

Mattes, Merrill J. *Colter's Hell and Jackson's Hole.* Yellowstone Park, Wyo., 1962.

Miles, Nelson A. *Personal Recollections and Observations of General Nelson A. Miles.* Chicago, 1897.

Miller, Joaquin. *Illustrated History of the State of Montana.* Chicago, 1894.

Norton, Harry J. *Wonderland Illustrated; or, Horseback Rides Through the Yellowstone National Park.* Virginia City, Mont., 1873.

Peattie, Donald Culross. *Green Laurels.* New York, 1936.

Richardson, James, ed. *Wonders of the Yellowstone.* New York, 1873.

Ross, Alexander. *The Fur Hunters of the Far West; A Narrative of Adventures in the Oregon and Rocky Mountains.* 1. London, 1855.

Russell, Osborne. *Journal of a Trapper, or, Nine Years in the Rocky Mountains, 1834–1843.* Ed. by L. A. York. Boise, Idaho, 1914, 1921.

———. *Osborne Russell's Journal of a Trapper.* Ed. by Aubrey L. Haines. Portland, Oreg., 1955, and Lincoln, Neb., 1965.

Ruxton, George F. *Life in the Far West.* Ed. by LeRoy Hafen. Norman, Okla., 1959.

Sharman, Helen G. *The Cave on the Yellowstone, or Early Life in the Rockies.* Chicago, c1902.

Smalley, Eugene V. *History of the Northern Pacific Railroad.* New York, 1883.

Standard Historical Society. *The Standard History of the World* 1. Cincinnati, 1931.

Thoreau, Henry David. "Walking." (1862). In *Harvard Classics* 28. New York, 1910.

Thwaites, Reuben Gold, ed. *The Original Journals of the Lewis and Clark Expedition* 4. New York, 1905.

Ticknor, George. *Life, Letters, and Journals of George Ticknor.* Boston, 1876.

Topping, Eugene Sayre. *The Chronicles of the Yellowstone; An Accurate and Comprehensive History.* St. Paul, 1883.

Victor, Francis Fuller. *The River of the West.* Hartford, Conn., 1870.

Vinton, Stallo. *John Colter, Discoverer of Yellowstone Park.* New York, 1926.

Wallace, R. C. *A Few Memories of a Long Life.* Privately printed, 1900.

Ware, Eugene F. *The Indian War of 1864.* New York, 1960.

VII. MISCELLANEOUS

Bear, James A., to Julian Boyd. Oct. 29, 1970. Copy to Aubrey Haines.

Boyd, Julian, to Dr. Oliver W. Holmes. Oct. 27, 1970. Copy to Aubrey Haines.

Hampton, Harold Duane. "Conservation and Cavalry: A Study of the Role of the United States Army in the Development of a National Park System, 1886–1917." Ph. D. dissertation, University of Colorado, 1965.

Schoenberg, Fr. Wilfred P., to Aubrey Haines. Aug. 13, 1970.

Index

Acres, Bob, 62
Absaroka Range, 15, 22
Adams, Robert, Jr., 100
Alder Gulch, 31
Allen, G. N., 100
Alum, 50, 82
Alum Creek, 55, 69
Alvarez, Manuel, 10
American Academy of Music, 98
American Falls, 39
Amethyst Mountain, 40
Anderson, Lou, 18, 34
"Antelope Creek," 68
Antelopes, 35
Anthony, Mr., 117, 118
Arapahos, 32, 41
Armstead, William, 31
Ashley, James M., 57, 58, 60, 61, 93
Atlantic Creek, 14
Atlantic and Pacific Creeks, 22
Avant Courier (Bozeman, Mont.), 128
Aztec Indians, 37

Bacon, George Harvey, 32
Baird, Spencer, 99, 101
Baker, E. M., 66, 98
Baker, William A., 63, 64, 67
  Biography, 135
Bannack City, 27, 28
Bannack tribes, 41
Bannock Indian camp, 18
Bannock Indian trail, 4, 5, 68
Barlow, John Whitney, 100, 102, 103, 122, 123
  Biography, 135
Barlow party (1871), xiii
Baronett, Collins Jack (John H.), 88, 91, 105
  Biography, 136
Basalt, columnar, 49
Basaltic mountains, 60
Beach Springs, 70
Beaman, J. W., 100

Bear Creek, 34
Bear Gulch, 36
Bear River, 24
Bears, 24, 40
  Grizzlies, 40, 72
Beaver and otter, 16
Beck, Mr., 111
Bee Hive, 83
Beecher, Henry Ward, 57
Beidler, X., 45
Bierstadt, Mr., 101
Big Horn Range, 50, 63, 81
Big Horn River, 23, 25, 30, 120
Big Trees, xxiii, 90
Bigelow, Jacob, xxi
Blackfoot Indians, 9, 16, 37, 45, 62
Blacktail Deer Plateau, 13, 68
Blaine, James G., 57, 93, 99
Boiling Fountains, 6, 8
Boiling Lake, 16
Boiling springs, 10–12, 15, 17, 26
"Boiling water volcanoes," 17
Boston Advertiser, 105
Boston Common, xviii
Bottler brothers, 60, 61
Bottler's ranch, 67, 102, 105
Boulder Valley, 64
Bozeman, John, 33
Bozeman City, 48, 60, 64, 66, 106, 127
Bozeman Pass, 80
Bozeman Trail, 45
Bradford, William, xix
Bridger, Jim, 14, 18, 19, 20, 24, 32, 60, 84
  Tales, 25, 26
Bridger Lake, 37, 71
Brimstone, 32, 71, 82
British trapping, 6, 8
Brown, "Uncle" Joe, 34
Bryant, William Cullen, xx, xxii
Bulbodacnitis scotti, 37
Buffalo, 29, 31, 33, 40
Buffalo Plateau, 39, 40
Bullock, Seth, 120

"Burning Spring," 55
"Burnt Hole," 16, 26, 53, 75, 83, 84

Cache Creek, 32, 40
Calaveras Big Trees, xxiii
Calcite Springs, 55
Cameron, Mr., 116, 117
Camp, E. M., 62, 65
Camp Baker, 62
Camp Comfort, 80
Camp Green Clay Smith, 34, 35
Camp Ida Thoroughman, 33, 34, 46
"Camp Stevenson," 101
Campbell, Major, 66
Cañon, 54, 80, 87
  Description, 48–51
Cascade Creek, 69, 78, 81
Castle Geyser, 74
Carrington, Campbell, 100
Carson, Kit, 18
Catlin, George, xxi, xxii
"Cave Spring," 70
Central Pacific Railroad, 100
Central Park project, xxii
Champagne, Baptiste, 32
Channel Mountain, 72
Chase, Salmon P., 58
"The Chemical Works," 50
"Chestnutville," 105
Chicago fire, 54, 103
Chicago Evening Journal, 122
Chicken Ridge, 72
Chief Big Lake, 32
Chief Washakie, 41
Chittenden, Hiram M., 9, 21, 94, 114
City park, xxii
Clagett, William Horace, 112, 113, 122, 126
Clark, William, xiv, 4
  Manuscript map, 5, 133
Clark Falls, 105
Clark Fork, 15, 32, 39, 40
Clawson, C. C., 105
Cleveland Herald, 105
Clyman, James, 20
Coal-oil spring, 25
Coffin, Carlton, 96
Cole, Mr., 118, 119
Colter, John, xiv, 4, 5
Colter's Hell, 23
Columbia headwaters, 23
Columbia River, 61
Columbia River Fishing & Trading Co., 12, 14
Committee on the Public Lands, 114–116, 122, 123
Committee on the Territories, 98, 114
"Commons," the, xviii
Conant Pass, 8
Conglomerate, pyramid of, 49
Congress, 114
Congressional Globe, 117

Conservation, colonial, xix
Continental Divide, 14–16, 25, 27
Cook, Charles W., 46, 48, 60, 129
  Biography, 137
Cook-Folsom article, 48, 54, 55
Cooke, Henry D., 57
Cooke, Jay, xiv, 59, 86, 96, 97, 110
Cooke, Pitt, 57
Cooper Union Hall, 94
Corps of Topographical Engineers, 17, 25
Coulter, John Merle, 5
Coulter Creek, 5, 6
Coulter's Hell, 46
Courier-Journal, 30, 31
Cramton, Mr., 113
Crandall, Mr., 41
Crater Hill, 36, 82
Craters, 79
Crevice Gulch, 34
Crofutt, George A., 122
Crow Agency, 40, 62, 67, 88
Crow Indians, 18, 31, 41, 62, 63, 80
Crystal Cascade, 81
"Curiosity Point," 37
"Curiosity Shop," 70
Curry, Thomas, 31
"Curry's Gulch," 31
Curtis, Charley, 35
Curtis-Dunlevy expedition, 35, 46

Daily Rocky Mountain News, 125
Daily Territorial Enterprise, 115
Daugherty, J. S., 41, 105
Davis, John C., 30, 31
Dawes, Chester M., 100
Dawes, Henry L., 99, 112, 123–125
"Death Valley," 53, 54
Deer, 24, 40
Deer Lodge City, 64, 65, 113
Deer Lodge Valley, 25
deLacy, Walter Washington, 27, 60, 129
  Biography, 138
  Map, 37, 55, 56
DeLacy Creek, 73
DeLacy Lake, 55
DeLacy Park, 29
Delano, Secretary, 122
Delusion Lake, 72
Department of the Interior, 99
DeSmet, Pierre-Jean, xv, 21
  Map, 3, 22, 23
"Devil's Den," 81
Devils Slide, 9
Dewing, John H., 5
Diamond City, 46, 55
Dixon, George B., 100
Doane, Gustavus C., xiv, 63–72, 75, 82, 98, 102, 104, 109, 120, 129
  Biography, 139–141
Dodge, Edward, 57
Downing, Andrew Jackson, xxii
Dragon's Mouth Spring, 70, 82

Drinking water, 70
Ducks, 52
Duncan, J. W., 100
Dunlevy, James, 35
Dunn, John, 32, 60
Dunnell, Mark H., 122, 123
Dunraven Pass, 68

Eagle Rock Bridge, 79
Edmunds, Mr., 118, 119
Electric Peak, 61
"Elephant's Back Mountain," 26
Elk, 14, 24, 30, 40, 76
Elliott, Henry W., 100, 104, 105, 122
Emigrant Gulch, 31, 32, 33, 35–37, 48
Emigration, promotion of, 96
Eustis Lake (Yellowstone), 4
Evening Star (Washington, D.C.), 119
Everts, Truman C., Jr., xv, 34, 60–62, 64, 67, 114, 120, *129*
    Article, 105
    Biography, 141, 142
    Found alive, 91
    Lost, 79
    Return, 92
    Reward offered, 88
    Search for, 72, 73, 75–77
Expedition notices, 34, 46
Explosions, underground, 51

Fahnstock, H. C., 57
Fallen timber, 71, 72, 78
Falls, 37–39, 46, 60, 69
Fan Tail, 84
Ferris, Warren Angus, 10, 12
    Manuscript map, 16
Finkelburg, Mr., 123
Firehole River, 15, 16, 19, 27–30, 32, 33, 55, 73, 74, 83, 84
Firehole River basins, 9, 102, 113
Fishing, 70, 83
Fiske, Robert, E., 58, 97
Flat Mountain, 72
Flint Creek, 40
Folsom, David, E., 46, 48, 54, 60, 109, *130*
    Biography, 142
Folsom party (1869), xiii, 31, 47–56, 69
Ford crossing, Yellowstone, 4, 5
Fort Benton, 32, 34, 45, 58, 95
Fort Bridger, 18, 103, 109
Fort D. A. Russell, 100
Fort Elizabeth Meagher, 33, 46
Fort Ellis, 60–64, 66, 67, 75, 102
Fort Hall, 16, 24, 103
Fort Laramie, 21, 25
Fort Parker, 40, 62
Fort Shaw, 64
Fox, 24
Frary, Leander W., 91
Freeman, Legh, 37, 38
Fremont, John Charles, xxii

Frontier Index (Green River, Wyo.), 38, 39
Fur traders, 6–21

Gallatin Valley, 48
Game, 24, 28, 29, 36, 40, 80
Game and fish protection, 117, 118
Game preserves, xviii, xix
Gardiner River, 24, 80
Gardner, Johnson, 10
"Gardner's Hole," 10, 13
"Gardner's Fork," 17
Gardner's River, 55, 67, 105
Geese, 52
Gemmell, James, 18, 32
Gemmell, Jeanette, 32
General Land Office, 55, 99
Geological Survey of the Territories, 94, 99, 109
Geysers, 27, 31, 32, 53, 55, 70, 77, 79, 82, 83, 102, 110
    Discovery of, 10
    Doane's description, 73, 74
    "Hour spring," 15
"Giant, The," 74, 83
"Giantess, The," 32, 74, 83, 84
Gibbon, John, 64, 65, 98
Gibbon River, 30, 75
Gildess, R. W., 104
Gillette, Warren Caleb, xiv, 64, 66, 67, 73, 75, 77, 79, 83, 86, *130*
    Biography, 143, 144
Glass mountain story, 21
Goetzmann, William, 112
Gold, 26, 31, 34, 39, 40, 58
Gold ornaments, 38
Gourley, James, 41
Grand Canyon, 22, 31, 33, 69, 80
    Painting, 115
Grand Prismatic Spring, 75
Grant, Ulysses S., 127
Grasshopper Creek, 27
Great Falls, 78, 81, 90, 95
Great Geyser Basin, 78, 109
Great Ponds Act, xix
Great Springs, 24
Green River, 8, 18, 38, 60
Greene, J. M., 64
Grizzlies, 40, 72
Gros Ventre fork, 25
Grotto, 84
Grouse Creek, 72
Gunnison, J. W., 24

Hamilton, "Wild Cat Bill," 16
Hamilton, William, 32
Hampton, H. D., xxiii, 111, 112
Hancock, Winfield S., 59, 64, 92, 98
Harris, Moses "Black," 19, 20
Hauser, Samuel Thomas, xiv, 54, 61, 62, 64–69, 72, 73, 79, 82, 87, 88, *130*
    Biography, 144, 145
Hawley, Mr., 123

Hayden, Ferdinand Vandiveer, 94, 99, 106, 109, 113, 114, 116, 120, 122, *130*, 140
  Biography, 145
Hayden & Barlow parties (1871), 99–106
Hayden party (1871), xiii, 99–106
Hayden Survey, 5, 72, 122
Hayden Valley, 16, 69, 70
Heap, David Porter, 102, 103
  Biography, 146
Heart Lake, 16, 73
Hedges, Cornelius, xiv, 45, 64, 65, 67, 69, 72, 79, 82, 88, 90, 109, 112, 113, 120, *131*
  Biography, 146, 147
Helena Daily Herald, 46, 57, 65, 85, 88–89, 90, 91, 92, 97
Hell Broth Springs, 78, 81, 90
Hell Roaring, 34, 39, 69
Henderson, A. Bart, xiv, 36, 39, 105
Henderson party, 37, 41
Henry's Fork, 28, 38
Henry's Lake, 26, 105
Hollow ground, 36
Holmes, Oliver Wendell, xxiii
Homie, Neil, 45
Hood, Washington, 17
Horr, Harry R., 105, 121
Horse thieves, 87
Hosmer, H. L., 34, 45, 61, 63
"Hot Spring Brimstone," 4
"Hot Spring Camp," 71
"Hot Spring Valley," 27
Hot springs, 14, 22, 23, 27–30, 40, 50, 51, 53, 55, 69, 77, 80, 81, 84
Hot Sulphur Spring, 49, 78
House of Representatives, 122–125
Hubbard, Elbert, 19
Hubble, A. H., 34, 36
Hudson Bay Co., 7, 8
Hudson River school of painting, xx
Humphreys, A. A., 102
Huse, F. J., 100
Huston, George A., 31–33
Huth, Hans, xix

Idaho, Territory of, 99
Idaho mines, 27
Idaho Statesman, 39
Independence (Iowa) *Conservative*, 91
Indian sources, 3
Indian catacomb, 38
Indian tribes, 100, 124
Indians, 11, 23, 25, 31–33, 37, 45, 48, 67, 88
  Hostile, 33, 40, 41, 62, 65
Instruments of observation, 99, 100
Islands (Stevenson, Frank and Dot), 70

J.O.R. Aug. 29, 1819, 6, 7
Jackson, William H., 100, 104
Jackson Lake, 15

Jackson's Hole, 8, 30
Jay Cooke & Co., 57, 96, 101, 109, 112
Jefferson, Thomas, 3
Jones, Jack ("John Bull"), 37
Judith River, 32

Kelley, William Darrah, 98, 109, 110, 112
Kuppens, Francis Xavier, 32, 45

Lake Abundance, 40
Lake Biddle (Jackson), 4
"Lake of Fire and Brimstone," 84
Lakeside Monthly, 54
Lamar River, 12, 15, 22, 31, 33, 40, 55, 68, 80
Lamar Valley, 14
Lamb, Henry L., 97
Landscape painters, xxi
Langford, Nathaniel Pitt, xiv, 54, 56, 58, 62, 64, 66, 67, 69–72, 75, 77–79, 87, 93–97, 104, 110, 112–115, 120, 122, *133*
  Biography, 147, 148
Langhorn, Samuel, 91, 92
Laut, Agnes, 7
Lava beds, 49, 72
Lava peaks, 40
Lawrence, Judge, 88, 92
Leipler, William, 67
  Biography, 148
Lectures, 93–97
Leslie's Illustrated, 105, 122
Lewis, Samuel, 5
Lewis and Clark, 3, 4
Lewis Lake, 15, 28
Lewis River, 27
Lignite coal beds, 26, 60
Lincoln, Abraham, 56, 141
Logan, William B., 100
Lone Star Geyser, 15
Longfellow, Henry Wadsworth, xx
"Lost Trail Creek," 68
Louisiana, purchase, 3
Lowell, James Russell, xx, xxiii
Lower Falls, 69, 78, 81
Lower Geyser Basin, 16, 29, 75
Lower Madison, 54
Lower Yellowstone, 81

McCartney, James C., 105, 121
McConnell, George W., 67, 69
  Biography, 148, 149
McGuire, H. H., 46
McGuirk, Matthew, 105
McGuirk's Medicinal Springs, 105
McKenzie, Donald, 6
Madison Lake, 55, 75
Madison River, 10, 17, 18, 26–28, 33, 53–55, 77, 84
Madison Valley, 16, 30
Mammoth Hot Springs, 17, 18, 22, 35, 36, 46, 61, 106
  Squatters, 121

Maps
  Barlow's, 103
  Bridger's, 22
  Buffalo pelt, 3, 4
  Clark's manuscript, 5
  deLacy's, 27, 37, 55, 56
  deLacy-Folsom, 92
  DeSmet's manuscript, 22
  Doane's, 92
  General Land Office, 55, 56
  Inadequate, 102
  Raynold's, 26
  Trapper's, 17
  Washburn's, 92
Marshall, William R., 58, 59, 110
Masonic Order, 66
Maynadier, H. E., 25
Meadow Creek, 48
Meagher, Thomas Francis, 33, 34, 45, 46, 109
Meek, Joseph L., 8, 9
Meldrum, Robert, 26
Miles, Nelson A., 20
Military Department of Dakota, 59
Military escort, 63, 98, 100
Military explorers, 21–26
Miller, Adam "Horn," 30
Miller, Joaquin, 24
Miller Creek, 40
Mineral springs, 126
Mirror Plateau, 33
Mission of St. Peter's, 32, 33, 45
Missionary explorers, 21
Missouri River, 22, 99
  Map, 3
Molly Islands, 72
Montana Pick and Plow, 86
Montana Territory, 33, 99, 111, 121
  Map, 27, 56
  Park's importance, 126
  Public use grant, 90
  Resources, 98
Montana volunteers, 46
Moore, Charles, 67, 76
  Biography, 149
Moorhead, William G., 57
Moose, 40
Moose Creek, 28
Moran, Thomas, xv, 101, 104, 115
Moran engravings, 97
Morgan, Mr., 124
Morton, Mr., 116
Mount Auburn, xxi
"Mount Everts," 67, 88, 89
"Mt. Gallatin," 26
Mount Holmes, 26
Mount Sheridan, 71, 73
Mount Washburn, 56, 68, 69, 78
Mud-cave, 51
Mud Geyser, 82
Mud springs, 50, 52, 53, 55, 78, 82

Mud Volcano, 33, 60, 82, 90
  Description, 70, 78
Mueller, Oscar O., 56
Mullan, John, 25
Munson, Lyman E., 45
Mysterious Mounds, 46

National park idea, 115
  Folsom suggestion, 56
  General Meagher, 45
  United forces, 112
National Park legislation
  Federal jurisdiction, 126
  Opposition, 121
Negley, D. Dev., 100
Nettleton, A. B., 57, 109, 112
New England philosophers, xx
New North-West, 105, 115, 128
New World Mining District, 40
New York Herald, 128
New York Times, 104, 126
  Washburn narrative, 85
New York Tribune, 48, 94, 95
New York World, 122
Newspaper reportage, 85, 86, 93, 122
Nez Perce Creek, 33
"Nez Perce ford," 70
Niagara Falls Reservation, 95
Norris, Philetus W., xv, 6, 7, 32, 60–62
Norris Geyser Basin, 9
Norris Suburban, 61
Northern Pacific Railroad, xiv, 7, 18, 57–61, 86, 95–98, 109, 110, 112, 114, 120
  Charter signed, 56
Norton, Harry, 113

Obsidian Cliff, 21
Ogden, Utah, 100, 102
Old Faithful Geyser, 83
  Doane's description, 73
Olmsted, Frederick Law, xxii
Omaha Herald, 105
Outdoor recreation, xxi
Outlet Lake, 76
The Overland Monthly, 98

Pacific Rail Road, 102
Paintings, xx, 101
Parasitic worms, 37
Park, origin of word, xviii
Park idea
  New England philosophers, xx
  Puritan attitude, xix
  State, xxii, xxiii
Park movement initiators, 112
Park Point, 71
Parsons, Edward, 38
Peale, A. C., 100
Pelican Creek, 14, 16, 31, 55
Pelicans, 52

215

Peterson, William, 46, 48
  Biography, 149
  William and Jessie, *131*
Petrified tree stories, 19, 20, 38, 39
Phelps, George, 48
Philadelphia
  American Academy of Music, 98
Philadelphia Public Ledger, 86
Photographs exhibited, 114
Pick and Plow (Bozeman, Mont.), 46, 86
Piegan Indians, 16, 32, 45, 62
Pilot and Index Peaks, 40
Pinnacles, 80
Pioneer Press, 85, 95
Pitchstone Plateau, 27, 28
Platte River, 23
Pomeroy, 113
  S. 392 proceedings, 115–118
Portland Oregonian, 86
Potts, Daniel T., xiv, 8, 61
Potts Hot Spring Basin, 8
Prickly Pear Cañon, 95
Pritchett, George A., 88, 91
Private enterprises, 121
Prospectors, 26–41
Puante (Stinking Water), 23
Public lands, unsurveyed, 128
Public park, xix, 94
Public use grant, 90

Quartz, veins of, 28

Railroads, 100
  Bonds, 96
  Grant, 57
  Publicity, 96
Raymond, R. W., 105
Raynolds, W. F., 19, 25
Raynolds Pass, 26
Ream, Charles, 27, 28
Red River, 97
Red River Valley, 59
Red Streak Mountain, 67
Reese, George W., 34
Rescue Creek, 68
Resorts, xxi
Roberts, W. Milner, 110
Roch, Mr., 7
Rocky Mountain Gazette, 91, 121, 127
Rocky Mountain News, 85
Rocky Mountains, 23
Rollins, Phillip A., 5
Romanticism, xix
Ross, Alexander, 6, 7
Rousseau, Jean Jacques, xix
Russell, Osborne, xiv, 12, 14, 15, 19

Sacramento Bee, 105
St. Joseph Herald, 122
St. Louis Times, 86, 125
Salt Lake City, 84, 99
San Francisco Chronicle, 86
Sawtell, Gilman, 105

Scenic cemetery, xxi
Schonbörn, Anton, 100, 103
Scientists' interest, 99
  Hayden party, 100
Scofield, Mr., 123, 124
Scoria, 82
Scribner's Monthly, 48, 98, 104, 105, 110,
  114, 115, 122
Sedge Creek, 37
Senate debates, 115–119
Settlers, 105, 121, 128
  Rights, 124
"Seven Hills," 69
Sexton, John W., 57, 110
"Sheep-Eaters," 41, 48
Shelton, Johnston, 31
Sheridan, Philip H., 101, 104, 137
Sherman, Mr., 117
Shield's River, 33
Shoshone Geyser Basin, 15, 28
Shoshone Lake, 15, 18, 27, 28, 55
Shoshone River, 15, 30
  North Fork, 40
Shoshon-Bannock, 41
Silver Cord Cascade, 82
Sioux Indians, 33, 62, 65
Sioux reservation, 124
Skepticism, 85, 104, 105
Slough Creek, 22, 34
Smith, A. J., 100
Smith, J. Gregory, 57, 114
Smith, Jacob Ward, 58, 59, 65–67, 72,
  79, *132*
  Biography, 150
Smith, Jedediah S., 8
Smithsonian Institution, 92, 99–101, 114,
  120
Snake Indians, 13
Snake River, 12, 15, 25, 37–39, 51, 75, 79
  Gold strikes, 26, 27
Snow Camp, 75
Snowy Range, 33
Soda Butte Creek, 31, 40
"Soda Mountain," 105
Solution Creek, 72
South Snake, 29
Southeast Arm, 72
Spa "Chestnutville," 105
Spanish Creek, 30
Specimen Ridge, 40
Speculators, 113
Spring Cañon, 60
Spring Creek, 73
Springs, 10, 11, 12, 50, 79
  Description, 52
Squatters, 57, 121
Squier, Major, 61
State of California, 90, 124
  Yosemite grant, xxiii
Statute of Merton, xviii
Steam, 50, 51, 53, 81, 82

Steam Boat Geyser, 17
Steamboat Point, 14, 55
Steamboat Springs, 16, 24, 29
Stevenson, James, 19, 100, 114, 124
  Biography, 150, 151
Stewart, (Sir) William Drummond, 17
Stickney, Benjamin, 63–65, 67, 69, 82, *132*
  Biography, 151, 152
Stinking River (Shoshone), 8, 22
Stoddard, Amos, 3
Stones, wave-formed, 37
Strong, William E., 136
Stuart, James, 30, 63, 64
Stuart expedition (1864), 48
Stuart party (1863), 65
Sublette, William, 9, 17
Subterranean noises, 23
Sulphur, 5, 49, 50, 78, 81
Sulphur Cauldron, 70
Sulphur Mountain, 22, 24, 60, 90
Sulphur springs, 52, 70, 82
  Colter's Hell, 22
Sulphurous waters, 23
Sun River, 45
Sundry Civil Act, 99, 100
Sunlight Creek, 40
Surprise Creek, 72, 76
Swans, 52

Taffee, Mr., 123, 124
Tall tales, 19–21, 38, 39
Taylor, Chloe, 97
Taylor, James Wicks, 58, 59
Terrace Spring, 30, 75
Territorial lines, 90
Territorial volunteers, 33
Tetons, 79, 81
Thomas, Cyrus, 100
Thomas, George C., 57
Thompson Falls, 57
Thoreau, Henry David, xx, xxii
Thoroughman, General, 34
Thrasher, A. F., 105
Three Forks rendezvous, 25
Thurman, Mr., 117
Ticknor, George, 4
Timblin, W. H., 136
Tipton, Mr., 118
Toll bridge, 105
Toll road, 106
Tonkeys, 48
Topographical work, 103
Topping, E. S., 18, 31, 34
Tourism, vanguard of, 105
Tourist, first (1833), 10
Tower Creek, 78, 80
Tower Fall, 4, 37, 56, 68, 81, 89
Trail Creek, 48, 67
Trappers, 6–21
  British, 6, 8
  Tales, 14, 17, 18, 19–21
Trout, 14, 37, 38, 52, 80, 83

Trout Creek, 55
Truett, M. F., 64
Trumbull, Walter, 46, 67, 72, 79, 91,
  117, 119, 120
  Biography, 152
"Turkey Pen Road," 67
Turnbull, Charles S., 100
Two Ocean Creek, 22
Two Ocean Pass, 14, 15, 17, 22, 37
Two Ocean Plateau, 72
Two Ocean River, 26

Union Pacific, 100
Union Pass, 25
U.S. Geologist, 99
Upper and Lower Falls, 18
  Measured, 69
Upper and Lower Geyser Basins, 18
Upper Geyser Basin, 32, 73, 75, 83, 85
Upper Falls, 30, 37, 78, 81
Upper Missouri, 23
Upper Yellowstone River, 55, 71, 95, 97,
  111
Upper Yellowstone Valley
  National Park, 126

Vibbard & Co., 58
Victor, Frances F., 8
Viell, Mr., 45
Vinegar Creek, 16
Virginia City, 28, 31, 32, 54, 58, 75, 77,
  93, 102, 127
Virginia Daily Territorial Enterprise, 122
Vitrified sandstone, 28
Vivion, Mr., 111
Volcanism, 21, 22

Ware, Eugene F., 19
Warm Spring Creek, 68, 91
"Warm-Stream Creek," 105
Washburn, Henry Dana, 55, 56, 60, 61,
  63–65, 67, 68, 70, 71, 74, 77, 79,
  88, *132*
  Biography, 152–154
  N.Y. Times comment, 85
  Report, 79
Washburn party (1870), xiii, 37, 54, 56,
  59–99, 120
  Civilians, provisions, 67
  Discoveries, 78, 79
  Military escort, 59, 63, 67
Washburn Range, 37, 68, 80
Water shed, 26, 71
Wayant, H. W., 32
Weaver, David, 36
West Gallatin River, 30
West Thumb, 55, 72, 73
Western Monthly, 48, 49, 54
Wheeler, Olin D., 7, 18
White Cloud-Pembina line, 59
White Creek, 27, 29
White Sulphur Banks, 17

Whitney, Asa, 109
Whittier, John Greenleaf, xx
Wilderness park idea, xxii
Wilkeson, Samuel, 57, 58, 86, 96
Wilkinson, James, xiv, 3
Williamson, John, 67, 76, 79
  Biography, 154
Willson & Rich, 66
Wilson, Joseph S., 55, 99
Wind River, 25, 38, 81, 120
Wind River Mountains, 50
Wind River Range, 90
Wind River Reservation, 41
Wolves, 24, 40
"Wonderland," 104
Woody, Tazewell, 5
Wyoming Basin, 25
Wyoming Territory, 56, 110, 120–122

Yankee Jim Canyon, 67, 80, 105
Yellow Stone, 37, 101
  Basin Survey, 103
  Boiling Springs, 10–12
  Expedition, 1805–1807, 3
  Features, 12, 13
  Headwaters, 24
  Lake, 8
Yellowstone Agency, 65
Yellowstone Canyon, 56
Yellowstone City, 36
Yellowstone Expedition, 64, 77
  Publicity, 92
  Roll call, 64
  Washburn Report, 79–84
Yellowstone Falls, 16, 39, 56, 60, 64
"Yellowstone Hell," 39
"Yellowstone Jack," 136

Yellowstone Lake, 16, 22, 36, 37, 39, 52,
    55, 60, 62, 70, 78, 81, 88, 90, 102
  Description 14, 53, 83
  Islands 70, 71
Yellowstone National Park
  Congressional suggestion, 98
  Documentary sources, xiii–xvii
  Establishment, 107, 112
  Federal management, xxiii
  Idea, 94, 104
  News coverage, 126
  Pilot model, 128
Yellowstone National Park Act, 127
Yellowstone Park legislation, 114, 122
  Clagett's account, 113
  House bill, yeas and nays, 125
  Paucity of editorials, 115
  Senate debates, 115–119
  Senate bill passed, 119
Yellowstone Pass, 17
Yellowstone region, 8, 9
  Lectures, 93, 94
  Newspaper reportage, 93
  Public use, 90, 109
  Thermal features, 4, 23, 27, 74
Yellowstone River, 9, 25, 30, 33, 37, 48,
    51, 60, 99, 102
  Crossing, 70
  Description, 81
  East Fork, 31, 40
  First bridge, 105
  Headwaters, 46
Yosemite Grant, xxiii, 111
Yosemite Valley, 33, 90
  Preemption claims, 119
  State jurisdiction, 123, 126
Yosemite/Yellowstone parallelism, 112

☆ U.S. GOVERNMENT PRINTING OFFICE: 1974 O—495-339